China Rising

China Rising

Power and Motivation in Chinese Foreign Policy

Edited by Yong Deng
and Fei-Ling Wang

ROWMAN & LITTLEFIELD PUBLISHERS, INC.
Lanham • Boulder • New York • Toronto • Oxford

ROWMAN & LITTLEFIELD PUBLISHERS, INC.

Published in the United States of America
by Rowman & Littlefield Publishers, Inc.
A wholly owned subsidary of The Rowman & Littlefield Publishing Group, Inc.
4501 Forbes Boulevard, Suite 200, Lanham, Maryland 20706
www.rowmanlittlefield.com

PO Box 317
Oxford
OX2 9RU, UK

British Library Cataloguing in Publication Information Available

Library of Congress Cataloging-in-Publication Data

China rising : power and motivation in Chinese foreign policy / edited by
    Yong Deng and Fei-Ling Wang.
       p.   cm. — (Asia in world politics)
    Includes bibliographical references and index.
    ISBN 0-7425-2891-X (cloth: alk. paper) — ISBN 0-7425-2892-8
(pbk.: alk. paper)
    1. China—Foreign relations—1976– I. Title: Power and motivation in Chinese
foreign policy. II. Deng, Yong, 1966– III. Wang, Fei-Ling. IV. Series.
DS779.27.C526 2005
327.51'009'0511—dc22

                                                                    2004013906

Printed in the United States of America

⊗™ The paper used in this publication meets the minimum requirements of American
National Standard for Information Sciences—Permanence of Paper for Printed Library
Materials, ANSI/NISO Z39.48-1992.

Contents

Preface

Chinese foreign policy is undergoing a metamorphosis never seen in the history of the People's Republic (PRC). The country has enjoyed a more secure place in the world than before, yet it has remained dissatisfied with its international status. China's quest for international legitimacy and a positive image is tested by its pursuit of security interests and the power politics logic of its own and other states. The emerging nontraditional threats have given rise at times to opportunities and at others to perils for China's foreign relations. Reformist China also creates a set of incentives and priorities representing a foreign policy nexus to a greatly restructured domestic front. Most striking, its new cooperative diplomacy has cultivated significant goodwill from the international community, yet suspicion and anxiety persist regarding China's rising power—and Beijing continues to threaten the use of force against Taiwan independence. Military planners in Beijing, Taipei, and Washington take pains in preparing for the eventuality of war across the strait. While embracing ideas of multilateralism, win–win cooperative approach, and peaceful ascent, China's foreign policy strategy has equally stressed the need to protect its national interests in a threatening world and the *struggle* to remold the international environment in line with its preferences. Clearly more than ever, PRC foreign policy is complicated, dynamic, and consequential.

The book seeks to account for the complex patterns in Chinese foreign policy. What animates us is an abiding interest in how Chinese foreign policy fits with traditional modes of international relations, particularly in terms of great power politics. We decided to illuminate the multifarious aspects of the China challenge by delving into the motivational structure behind Beijing's foreign policy choices. Such a focus allows us to discern the broad trajectory as well as the key driving forces in Chinese foreign relations. It also helps to illuminate how domestic and international factors interact to shape the foreign policy agenda of this rising great power. Collectively, we hope the book offers a comprehensive, albeit incomplete, diagnosis of the emerging paradigmatic thinking and strategic choices in Chinese foreign policy.

Our findings suggest that Beijing clearly seeks to distinguish its foreign relations from traditional international politics by emphasizing legitimacy building, responsible image making, and a restrained nonconfrontational mode of competition. These preferences are well grounded as they are tied to China's domestic agenda and the perceived constraints and incentives that the international society has to offer; yet, certain parameters of the Communist Party–state interests, China's status dissatisfaction under U.S. hegemony, Taiwan, and conventional international politics impose significant limits and uncertainties on Chinese foreign policy change. By focusing on how China struggles to manage its rise, our study offers some insights into how peaceful alternatives can come about in China's international futures.

We are most grateful for the contributors, whose fine work and enthusiasm toward the project made its expeditious completion possible. Despite their busy schedule, they endured the revisions and met the deadlines. We also thank the publisher's anonymous reviewer for encouragement and for specific suggestions for revisions. Susan McEachern, our editor at Rowman & Littlefield, was instrumental in bringing about our earlier volume *In the Eyes of the Dragon: China Views the World*. Her vision was equally critical for the genesis of this book. The editor of the Asia in World Politics series, Professor Samuel Kim of Columbia University, offered his sage advice. Reflective of the collaborative spirit that guides through the project, the final book title resulted from close consultations among four of us.

1

Introduction

Yong Deng and Fei-Ling Wang

Mainstream theories of great power politics posit that under international anarchy, states are motivated by securing relative power advantage and are thus locked in the security dilemma from which they cannot escape. Thus, as Robert Jervis bemoans, "The central theme of international relations is not evil but tragedy";[1] John Mearsheimer simply names his latest book *The Tragedy of Great Power Politics*;[2] and Dale Copeland contends, "Even good security-seeking states will be inclined to hostile acts in the face of deep and inevitable decline" of relative power.[3] With the growing power of the People's Republic of China (PRC), will the same "tragic" pattern of great power politics repeat itself? This book seeks to answer this question by focusing on the Chinese debates and struggles over how to manage its foreign relations. We do not share the generalization that all great power politics are exclusively an unmitigated power struggle. Nor do we agree with the realist claim, particularly that of the structural variants, that the state's motivation is identical, uninteresting, and can be safely assumed and that ultimately intentions are too uncertain to matter. Rather, our premise is that China's motivations are complex and dynamic and that they matter critically in determining Chinese foreign relations and the great power politics surrounding China's rise.

THE RISING POWER IN THE NEW WORLD

One of the most important realities in international relations today is the fast-growing power of China. Admittedly, gauging Chinese power is not easy, much less projecting its future growth. But the fact that China has been experiencing

1

a massive growth in economic power and other material capabilities for the past two and a half decades is beyond doubt.

From 1979 to 2003, the Chinese economy grew at an annual rate of 8 to 9 percent,[4] three to four times faster than the economies in the West and double the average growth rate of the developing nations. During the same period, China's foreign trade volume exploded twenty-four times exceeding the $1 trillion mark in 2004. As a symbol of its trading power, China now accumulates a massive foreign currency reserve, nearly $300 billion by 2003 (was only $10 billion in 1990), second only to Japan. China is now the world's largest or second-largest recipient of foreign direct investment (after the United States), receiving over $446 billion in foreign capital from 1979 to 2002.[5] It has also been actively investing abroad in recent years, becoming the largest foreign purchaser of the U.S. Treasury bonds since the mid-1990s. Goods made in China, increasingly capital- and technology-intensive, are sold in virtually every corner of the world. That China has more citizens traveling abroad than does Japan has resulted in millions of Chinese now joining the world's international tourist army as big spenders, in places such as Southeast Asia, Korea, Oceania, Europe, and even North America. While China has become presumably the second engine (after the United States) propelling the world's economic growth, its newfound wealth has also fueled the fear of China's economic threat, incurring (most recently) mounting international pressure for the Chinese currency to significantly appreciate against the U.S. dollar. Some have even started to view China as a mercantilist juggernaut, another Japan in the making.[6]

With a cheap labor force of over eight hundred million, a high national savings rate (reaching 42 percent in the late 1990s, second only to Singapore's 51 percent),[7] and a steady marketization of the economy, China's potential for growth is yet to be exhausted. A leading Chinese economist believes that the PRC economy will continue to grow rapidly, at a high speed of 7.3 to 8.3 percent annually during the 2001–2010 period and then at a slightly lower annual rate of 6.3 to 7.3 percent during the 2010–2020 period.[8] Barring any catastrophic international crisis or sociopolitical meltdown at home, China is expected to continue its ascendance in the great power ranks of the world, at least economically and technologically.

Since the 1990s, gauging the rate and level of China's rise has become a cottage industry in the academic circles and policy communities in Beijing. For one group of Chinese scholars, the world ranking of China's "comprehensive national power" (a concept that includes economic and military capabilities, governance, diplomatic influence, human and natural resources, and ecological health) advanced from eighth to seventh from 1990 to 2000. In terms of economic and military power, China is ranked much higher: third and fourth, respectively, in 2000 (see table 1.1). The overall conservative ranking of China's comprehensive power largely conforms to other major Chinese studies on this topic, reflecting the mainstream assessment among the political and intellectual élite.

Academic and policy communities in international relations outside China adopt different indexes in measuring Chinese power from those of the notion of "comprehensive national power," with almost exclusive focus on military and economic capabilities. While many studies tend to overstate China's military power, America's prominent China scholars on the People's Liberation Army (PLA) recently rejected the alarmist notion that China was quickly becoming a military rival to the United States. However, they also recognized Beijing's attempts to modernize its military through professionalization, foreign arms acquisitions, and technological advancement.[9] Still, most of the international concern and fear about China has originated from the sheer scale of its economic growth, the rate of its technological advancement (as dramatically demonstrated in its first successful manned space flight in October 2003, a part of an overall aggressive space program), the potential of its military modernization, and the ongoing PLA threat to Taiwan.

The varying estimations of the Chinese power notwithstanding, China's rise is beyond doubt, and its growing international impact is already being felt. History and mainstream international relations theory suggest a destabilizing effect of power change of such a magnitude and speed. For conventional

Table 1.1.   China's Self-Ranking of Its Comprehensive National Power

			Ranking of National Comprehensive Power		
	1990	*2000*	*2000 Scores*	*Economic Ranking*	*Military Ranking*
United States	1	1	2,740	1	1
Japan	2	2	1,851	2	2
Canada	4	3	1,608	5	7
Germany	3	4	1,570	4	9
France	5	5	1,525	6	6
United Kingdom	6	6	1,465	7	3
China	8	7	1,462	3	4
Russia	7	8	1,297	8	5
Australia	10	9	1,282	9	10
Italy	9	10	1,243	10	11
India	11	11	945	11	8
Brazil	12	12	919	12	13
South Africa	13	13	782	13	12

Source: Project Group of the Chinese Academy of Sciences, *2003 Zhongguo ke chixu fazhan zhanlue baogao* [Report on China's Sustainable Development Strategy, 2003] (Beijing: Kexue Press, 2003), 115–23.

realist theory, the material and normative international order is determined by the distribution of power. At its creation, the world order reflects the interests and preferences of the most powerful country, the hegemonic state. As relative power inevitably shifts, the interests of the rising power would inevitably clash with those of the hegemon and the international status quo that the reigning great power seeks to defend.[10]

But the record of Chinese behavior during its great growth period has heretofore defied the simplistic inference of revisionist Chinese intentions toward the existing world order.[11] In fact, while concerned about Beijing's Taiwan policy and uncertainties in its future strategic choice, many analysts have noticed contemporary China's cooperative and constructive foreign policy that reflects an increasingly positive and confident evaluation of not only the regional and international orders but also its own role within them.[12] The new leadership under president Hu Jintao and premier Wen Jiabao openly endorsed a "strategy of peaceful ascent," even though since the second half of 2004 the talk of cooperative diplomacy has been balanced with an equal emphasis on China's difficult struggle to deter Taiwan independence and protect its vital national interests.[13] To fully comprehend the complex dynamics of Chinese foreign policy, one has to consider how the "new world," in which China is a part, has determined its domestic priorities and shaped its international agenda.

We use the term *new world* deliberately to refer to three distinguishing features in the world politics that greatly bear on contemporary Chinese foreign policy. The first is the restructured political economy of China as an international actor. China's reforms and integration into the world have greatly transformed the domestic politics and internal mechanisms of its foreign policy making. Furthermore, the Chinese political élite understand that meeting the dominant and most pressing needs of the society, particularly in the economic arena, are critical for the security of the communist regime and their nation's own great power aspiration. The result is a domestically oriented foreign policy with multifaceted, complex linkage to the restructured and changing domestic front.

The second feature that defines the contemporary world concerns the United States–led international hierarchy. The U.S. hegemonic position has proven remarkably stable and secure. Neither confrontation toward the world order nor balancing against the United States has proven attractive to other major powers.[14] Indeed Chinese political élite have come to accept the durability of the United States–led international arrangement. As radical change to that order is prohibitively costly, they have adopted a more realist approach that puts a great premium on how China can positively engage the world to maximize the benefits while minimizing the costs (*quli bihai*). The events after the September 11 terrorist attacks have underscored the unrivaled power of the United States, but they have also infused cooperative dynamics in the Sino-American relationship and have induced international changes that animate the Beijing leadership to proactively mold the strategic environment conducive to China's rise.

The third feature of the new world has to do with the greatly institutionalized and globalized nature of world politics. Economic globalization has made China's growth possible. While sharing the benefits and economic values of the world market, Chinese élite have gradually come to appreciate how the political framework underpinning economic globalization also serves its interests. Moreover they have realized that interdependence, multilateralism, international institutions, and even nontraditional threats in the globalized world are reconfiguring the great power politics surrounding the rise of China. While exerting a complex impact on China's domestic governance and security environment, the globalized world offers the opportunity for China's economic success and peaceful advancement in international status.

Chinese foreign policy must contend with all these issues. Beijing's own white paper on China's national defense released in 2002 defines China's national interests as "primarily consisting of defending the state sovereignty, national unity, territorial integrity and security; steadily enhancing comprehensive national power through persisting in the central task of economic development; upholding and improving the socialist system; maintaining and promoting social stability and solidarity; striving for a long-term peaceful international environment and favorable periphery (*zoubian*) environment."[15] Such a conception of national interests clearly reflects the PRC élite's focus on the domestic front, preoccupation with China's sociopolitical stability, aspiration for China's great power status, and heightened concern over the myriad traditional and nontraditional threats in the complex and increasingly globalized world. Precisely how these factors bear on the motivational structure of China's foreign policy is the subject of this book.

GREATER UNDERSTANDING, GREATER DEBATE: WHAT REALLY MOTIVATES CHINESE FOREIGN POLICY?

Since the end of the Cold War, the studies of Chinese international behavior have witnessed a proliferation of foci, methodologies, and perspectives. The evermore pluralistic theoretical enterprise in international relations has also provided a wide range of analytical tools to facilitate the ever more vibrant scholarly inquiries into Chinese foreign policy. Not only does extant literature focus on traditional power politics and Chinese concern over territorial integrity, but it also deals with domestic linkage, elite discourse and beliefs, economic underpinnings, globalization and interdependence, international pressures, external restraints, and image interest that shape how Beijing interacts with the outside world. New variables are introduced; seemingly traditional variables are reconceptualized.[16]

The pluralist, vibrant field has greatly enhanced our understanding of the complex dynamics of Chinese foreign policy after the Cold War; yet, paradoxically, the field also demonstrates a tendency to resort to traditional great power theories and historical analogies to conjecture China's foreign orientations. For example, John Mearsheimer contends that, concerned about relative position, great powers are locked in a fierce zero-sum power struggle. Accordingly, "China and the United States are destined to be adversaries as China's power grows."[17] Others have attributed China's malign intentions to "its thoroughly anti-liberal institutions and ideology."[18] Threat perceptions vis-à-vis China are thus based on static judgment of the "character" of the Chinese state. While these approaches have their validities, we nevertheless need to guard against a simplistic and stereotypical approach to China's multifaceted interactions with the outside world in a state of flux.

In light of the gap in the literature, there is clearly a need for a comprehensive examination of the key variables that motivate Chinese international behavior. With that in mind, we decided to assemble this edited volume. The book takes advantage of and builds on the new scholarship and takes into account the latest developments in Chinese foreign policy.

To ascertain a nation's motives is inherently no easy task. The difficulty is compounded by the fact that China is still less than transparent, even though it has become more forthcoming on its foreign intentions than in the past. We believe, however, that an interpretation of the Chinese motivations is attainable, even without utilizing well-guarded, classified information on the inner workings of Beijing's decision making. There has been considerable scholarship on Chinese foreign policy inside, as well as outside, China. Most notably, the study of international relations is a thriving academic industry in China. Establishing a respectable, mainstream academic field in international relations has become something of a status marker for China's institutions of higher education and aspiring world-class universities. The subfield of Chinese foreign policy studies has also been undergoing a boom. Encouraged by the central leadership to "expand thinking space" (*tuozhan siweikongjian*), sophisticated and well-trained Chinese scholars are offering increasingly candid and diverse analyses of their country's foreign policy. New technology (e.g., the Internet), a pluralizing Chinese society, and fast-growing exchanges between Chinese scholars and their foreign counterparts have facilitated the flow of information into and out of China.

While drawing on the scholarship inside and outside China, we also rely on field research in mainland China, where most of us have visited frequently and have conducted formal and informal interviews with Chinese decision makers and policy analysts. All of us can, and indeed have, read and analyzed extensive Chinese literature, including governmental documents, academic publications, news reports, and even popular readings. Having considered the official views, we have identified patterns in Chinese foreign policy, to test the validity of our findings on motivations. What would reinforce our findings are behavioral manifestations closely correlated with the motivational patterns found in the official statements and academic discourse.

In terms of analytical framework, we are not constrained by any theoretical construct, be it realism, liberalism, or constructivism. Jack Snyder has wisely advised that studying international relations "requires thinking in terms of mutual feedbacks among material, institutional, and cultural elements."[19] We believe the same is true with the study of Chinese foreign policy. In other words, we need to consider the material logic of interstate competition; formal and informal institutional contexts for the domestic linkage and foreign policy choices; and factors concerning self-identification, social identity, and international image. We should not consider these forces in isolation but rather examine their interactions in discerning Chinese motivations.

We know that a single volume such as this one cannot cover every aspect of this topic—and issues covered are by no means dealt with exhaustively. We do hope, however, that our study is comprehensive and thorough enough to portray a basic picture on Chinese international aspirations. Other than agreeing on the book's main theme and its significance, the authors did their analyses and drew their conclusions independently. However, we are pleasantly surprised that, despite some disagreement and differed opinions, our basic conclusions are highly in sync and mutually supportive. While fully aware of the uncertainty in Chinese foreign motivations, we believe that uncertainty is reduced insofar as we have identified patterns that are deeply rooted in the new world of domestic politics and international system.

DOMESTIC ORIGINS OF CHINA'S FOREIGN POLICY AGENDA

Since PRC's inception in 1949, domestic politics has always played a decisive role in its foreign policy. For example, domestic political considerations figured prominently in Mao's military decisions.[20] The domestic agenda shaped the grand strategy and fateful policy choices toward the two superpowers during the Cold War.[21] The ideological impulse of communism contended with the imperative of national interests to influence Maoist Chinese foreign policy.[22]

The domestic politics of reformist China has undergone drastic changes and has in turn played a different role in shaping Chinese foreign policy. To survive, as Joanne Gowa points out, authoritarian regimes must be subject to domestic restraints, albeit more informally than democracies.[23] In other words, regardless of regime type, domestic politics may play an equally decisive role in the state's foreign policy making. Even though Chinese politics may not suit for a stylized "two-level game" analysis,[24] Beijing's illiberal regime, which seeks to co-opt and manage an increasingly pluralistic and unwieldy society, must be responsive to changes in the domestic front—even more so, with the bankruptcy of the communist totalitarian ideology. For example, Peter Cheung and James Tang have shown that on economic issues, provincial authorities are highly assertive in taking initiatives in foreign policy making, a domain traditionally monopolized by the center. Margaret Pearson shows that during the last stage of China's bid for its membership in the World Trade Organization (WTO), the central government's bargaining with its domestic constituents was so fierce that "trade politics [in China] seems to have been nearly as porous and subject to competing interests . . . as U.S. and European trade policymaking."[25]

To be sure, one should not draw too close a parallel between changes in economic area and political-security issues. But one should expect that China's domestic political reconfiguration must also have reconfigured its foreign policy paradigm in the international arena.[26] That is the case even with the sensitive issue of human rights. As Ming Wan argues in chapter 10, official policy and serious public discourse were absent under Maoist totalitarianism. During the reform era, China's human rights policy has evolved in tandem with the ups and downs of domestic political changes and a steady deepening of integration into the world. The Chinese Communist Party (CCP) leadership now must defend its record of human rights, including in the socioeconomic arena, to secure popular support at home and to mitigate the politically motivated fear of China threat abroad. But the predominant concern in maintaining one-party rule and social stability continues to dictate China's human rights policy.

The same domestic concern also underpins China's foreign policy in other areas. As Andrew Scobell argues in chapter 11, China's concern about terrorism originated from violent acts perpetrated by organized ethnic minority groups and disgruntled social elements who have borne the brunt of the pains in China's transition, as these acts could threaten the national unity and social stability of the CCP regime. Furthermore, the dimension of domestic security continues to influence Beijing's antiterrorism policy after the United States launched its global antiterror campaign following September 11, 2001.

The CCP's concerns about maintaining its one-party political monopoly, sustained economic growth, and domestic stability are the critical source of PRC foreign orientations. The CCP regime's interests explain Beijing's conservative, economically oriented, largely risk-averse foreign policy. Meanwhile, the central concern about fending off threats to the CCP rule has fueled nationalism and determination to stop Taiwan's de jure independence.[27] In chapter 2, Fei-Ling Wang underscores the domestic determinants of Chinese policy by focusing on the CCP's goals of regime preservation, economic prosperity, and pursuit of China's great power status. The dynamic interactions of the three goals generate varying foreign policy orientations and outputs. Such a peculiar incentive structure may help to explain why the rapidly rising dragon has yet to follow the great power expansion trajectory traditionally predicted by realist theories.

The CCP government seeks to buoy its legitimacy through controlled nationalism and the delivery of economic growth to the populace. The domestic drive for economic modernization dictated the abandonment of the Maoist radical and revolutionary foreign policy in the 1980s. As China integrates itself into the world, the task of "promoting self-interests while avoiding harms" in international interdependence has become even more complex with the stakes even higher in Chinese foreign relations. As Peter Gries points out in chapter 5, nationalism has proven difficult to control. Enflamed nationalism, economic successes, and frustrated power aspirations can lead to more aggressive foreign ambitions. But a confident China, secure at home and responsible abroad, will more actively contribute to global governance and regional stability.

The reform measures taken to shore up support for CCP may inadvertently lead to democratization and erosion of CCP power. With regard to foreign policy implications, Fei-Ling Wang cautions in chapter 2 that a democratic China would be less restrained by acute domestic concerns and could therefore be more assertive and even aggressive in its foreign policy. This plausible conjecture certainly complicates the task of speculating about the impact of political reforms on China's foreign policy.[28] It raises the question: With changed political calculations at home and after the probably turbulent process of democratization, would a democratic China's nationalism eventually take a more liberal, more cooperative form? This question underscores the contingent nature of the foreign policy implications of China's domestic liberalization. Much of the answer also depends in part on whether the United States and other leading democracies will treat a democratic, or even just a democratizing, China qualitatively differently from how they do now, thereby fundamentally reshaping China's foreign relations.

NOT ALL ROADS LEAD TO ROME: STATUS POLITICS UNDER
THE EMERGING INTERNATIONAL HIERARCHY

Apart from its domestic linkage, China's route to great power status is also determined by the international arrangements. Contrary to Beijing's wish for a multipolar world, post–Cold War international politics has witnessed increasing consolidation of the U.S. preeminence. The U.S. hegemony enjoys such a high level of security that a radically restructured, alternative world order is simply unrealistic, at least in the next quarter of a century. This has transformed the great power politics. As Stephen Brooks and William Wohlforth observe, "The result—balancing that is rhetorically grand but substantially weak—is politics as usual in a unipolar world" of unrivaled U.S. dominance.[29]

The U.S. hegemony certainly dominates China's foreign policy thinking. By far more than any other country, the United States impinges on vital CCP regime interests and Chinese national interests. Thus much of PRC foreign policy is centered on managing its relationship with the United States. With the loss of the common goal in containing the Soviet threat, as John Garver argues in chapter 8, U.S. support for strategic cooperation and China's domestic reforms has significantly eroded. Instead, conflict at the strategic, economic, and political levels has gained prominence to destabilize the U.S.–China relationship. Hardliners among the Chinese political and intellectual élite focus on the irreconcilable conflicts, calling for a more confrontational policy toward the United States. Their views gain grounds when Sino-American relations are strained. But mainstream analysts emphasize the cooperative and the conflictual aspects of the bilateral relations and see a stable relationship with the United States as not only possible but also in China's fundamental interest.

From the Chinese perspective, the post–Cold War world order is restructured into an international hierarchy dominated by the United States and its democratic allies. Under such an international arrangement, traditional power politics is no longer adequate to enhance national security. Rather, security and advancement in international status depends on tackling the origins of threat perceptions—namely, China's outlier status vis-à-vis the U.S.-centered great power group. In this sense, the turning point was the Tiananmen incident in June 1989, which (as Ming Wan points out) precipitated a drastic downfall of China's political standing in the international community. The ensuing human rights stigma and international isolation soon evolved into an unprecedented crisis of China's international status. As Yong Deng writes in chapter 3, Chinese foreign policy discourse has since shown a particular sensitivity to its "international status." China's status interest is characterized by concerns to simultaneously enhance its comprehensive national power and cultivate international legitimacy as a peacefully rising power, designed to create opportunities of upward mobility in the emerging international hierarchy.

Beijing's emphasis on social recognition in the international community and externally based political legitimacy has led to an evermore cooperative foreign policy in PRC history. This is evidenced in Beijing's views on multilateral institutions. As Jianwei Wang argues in chapter 7, China's unprecedented activism toward international institutions stems from the idea that multilateralism can help create a sense of security, community, and win–win growth as apposed to the security dilemma and neomercantilism that would fuel the fear of China threat. Hongying Wang's research presented in chapter 4 also finds that there were important cases—such as Chinese reactions to the Comprehensive Test Ban Treaty (CTBT) and to the Asian financial crisis in the 1990s—in which Beijing clearly sought to match its behavior with the image of the responsible power it attempted to project. However, she notes that Beijing's cooperative image has not made much inroad into the American public's perception of China—and the perceptual gap will likely continue unless consistent and effective measures are taken to reverse the ambivalent, partially adversarial nature of the bilateral relations between China and the United States.

Such will not be an easy task. As Yong Deng notes, the unresolved problems of managing China's growing power, its reunification goal over Taiwan, and its discontent in the international hierarchy could derail China's peaceful quest for great power status. Should China develop unrealistic power expectations or suffer mounting frustrations with its perceived unfair immobility, or even reversal in status, Beijing could likely resort to traditional great power politics or radicalism, forcefully pressing for desired systemic changes. Overall, the Chinese political elite seems to understand that the costs–benefits balance clearly favors the path of responsible power over a confrontational strategy. Even on the Taiwan issue, as Yun-han Chu argues in chapter 9, Beijing has to tread carefully lest a mishandling of it sabotage China's primary goal of building a well-off society in the next two decades.

NATIONAL INTERESTS IN THE WORLD OF INTERDEPENDENCE AND GLOBALIZATION

Liberal theorists have long argued how greater interdependence and the institutionalization of interstate relations increase shared interests while reducing uncertainty and mistrust pervasive under international anarchy. Cooperative foreign relations generally flow from strong economic ties and interconnect-edness.[30] Realist theorists dispute the liberal theses, questioning in particular the liberal claim that interdependence leads to complete aversion to the use of violence.[31] Regardless of its impact on the final outcome of war and peace, what we can posit with certainty is that interdependence and globalization significantly affect the cost–benefit balance of the state's various strategic choices. Such balance tends to favor a cooperative, restrained diplomatic approach. Indeed, even at the height of the Cold War, as Stephen G. Brooks and William C. Wohlforth have shown, the rising tide of economic globalization imposed stark material cost on the old Soviet-style economic autarky at home and its comprehensive confrontation toward the West. The futility of hostile balancing strategy ultimately persuaded the Soviet élite to shift course, leading to the end of the Cold War.[32]

China's domestic reforms and economic growth have proceeded in tandem with its deepening integration into the world. As others have also demonstrated, the dominant interests in the Chinese society are increasingly tied to the world market, to international institutions, to the advanced economies, and to neighboring regions in Asia;[33] consequently, China's foreign interests have been reconfigured. Most important, to fuel its continued growth in comprehensive power critical for Beijing's other goals, China must secure a peaceful environment and expand external sources of markets, investment, technology, management skills, and energy.

Interdependence engineers China's rise, but it also creates a vulnerability in its foreign relations. As Garver states in chapter 8, the greatly asymmetrical interdependence in favor of the United States has generated Chinese resentment and frustration as well as cooperative preferences. Furthermore, nationalist Chinese analysts have maintained that the United States and its allies have used globalization to secure its power position and leverage over China. Some have even warned that the United States is launching an anticommunist ideological warfare against China in the name of globalization.[34] However, as Dale Copeland reasons, states with confidence of sustained economic exchange will be committed to mutually cooperative ties. So long as Beijing can be reassured of the prospect of continued trade, Washington can take measures, even tough ones, to liberalize China's own markets and cultivate the good will arising from interdependence.[35]

Regardless of the dangers and pitfalls of interdependence, Chinese élite and the Chinese public hold a predominantly favorable view of globalization.[36] But the Chinese conception of globalization has undergone significant changes since the mid-1990s. Compared with that of the 1990s, when globalization was uncritically embraced as an economic opportunity, as Thomas Moore writes in chapter 6, Chinese discourse now shows a more realistic appreciation of the harms and defects of globalization. Likewise, there is a new emphasis on the linkage of globalization to China's political and security goals of "democratizing" the U.S. hegemonic order.[37]

Globalization and Beijing's drive for prosperity have recently led China to make a strategic decision to anchor its relations with great powers and Asian neighbors in strong economic ties. For many in Beijing, economic globalization can replace traditional great power rivalry with win–win competition, thereby reducing foreign fear of the rising Chinese power. It can also pluralize and democratize world politics while restraining the U.S. unilateralism and coercive use of power that may be aimed at China. So long as the U.S. power is constrained and as long as China's core interests (including Taiwan) are protected, as Moore argues, Beijing is likely to embrace globalization (even if globalization restrains China and strengthens U.S. preeminence).

Since the terrorist attacks on September 11, 2001, Chinese analysts have highlighted another, dark side of globalization that calls for enhanced multilateral cooperation—namely, the nontraditional and transnational threats such as terrorism, epidemics, and financial crises. The antiterror campaign has stabilized Sino-American relations, but as Scobell argues in chapter 11, Beijing is deeply concerned about the negative fallouts of what many Chinese analysts view as a U.S. unilateralist campaign to simultaneously fight terror and increase its own primacy. In response, China's latest white paper on national defense specifically refers to these "diversifying and globalizing" security threats as evidence in support of the notion of "cooperative security" that supposedly enhances security for all through joint efforts.[38] As Jianwei Wang shows in chapter 7, restraining U.S. power is a major explanation for Beijing's unprecedented embrace of multilateralism. For Beijing, the U.S. focus on global terrorism has also diminished "China threat theory," thereby significantly improving China's relations with the United States and the overall security environment.

Regardless of its intentions, growing Chinese enthusiasm for globalization does indicate a positive and optimistic evaluation of the world order and of China's own international role. To the extent that Chinese leadership and strategic analysts understand that globalization is the distinguishing feature of the U.S. hegemony and that its interests are best served by win–win competition and cooperative security, China's active participation in the globalized world pays security as well as economic dividends for itself and the world at large. Yet, insofar as China's threat of force persists against a democratic Taiwan with an increasingly independent identity, the Taiwan issue constitutes a hurdle most difficult for Beijing to surmount in becoming a fully peaceful, responsible great power. The Chinese leaders and policy analysts understand well the predicament of its Taiwan conundrum. While attaching supreme nationalist and strategic importance to Taiwan, as Yun-han Chu shows in chapter

9, they are nonetheless fully cognizant of the futility and prohibitive cost of forcing a military solution. Beijing is apparently unwilling to risk everything over Taiwan, yet it cannot afford the political cost of "losing" this "sacred Chinese territory." To keep the hope of reunification alive while maintaining a military threat to Taiwan, the Chinese leadership has become more flexible than before with its pursuit of the "one China" principle; it has sought U.S. cooperation to rein in the independence elements in Taiwan; and it has capitalized on the multifaceted cross-straits ties to dissuade Taiwan from pursuing de jure independence. As just about any of China's international motives is linked in one way or another to Taiwan, successfully managing the issue remains the pivotal task for Taiwan's destiny and China's international future.

CONCLUSION

The CCP regime's security, economic development, and quest for great power status are the central concern driving China's foreign policy. China has made important strides in fulfilling its aspirations within the United States–led, globalized world thereby facilitating its positive evaluation of the international status quo. However, Chinese élite clearly are not satisfied with their nation's international status and find the international arrangement sometimes disadvantageous to its interests. Despite its protestations of peaceful intent, the fear persists in the outside world regarding China as a threat. Furthermore, Beijing has not secured a stable international framework that fundamentally respects its sovereignty interest on Taiwan. While discontented with its power, status, and security, Beijing realizes that a lasting benign international environment is essential for China's "national rejuvenation." On the one hand, China's domestic politics and the world order are structured such that an ultranationalist, confrontational foreign policy serves none of the vital Chinese interests. The U.S.-dominated world order, characterized by a highly stable international hierarchy and globalization, extracts prohibitive costs on violent antagonism in China's foreign policy. On the other hand, such an international structure has offered strong incentives for China's nonviolent pursuit of legitimate great power status.

China's foreign policy discourse and behavior reflect a concerted effort to overcome the security dilemma intensified by its fast-growing power. The emerging awareness of the importance of China's own choice in improving its international environment is manifest in China's unprecedented efforts to align its interests closely with the United States, to promote a responsible image, to be proactive in cultivating great power diplomacy, and to evoke enthusiasm toward global and regional multilateralism. Beijing has also publicly embraced a new security concept that ostensibly rejects the self-help approach, downplays the role of coercive diplomacy and military force, and emphasizes win–win economic cooperation.

To be sure, motivations can change, and history shows how motivational change of a rising great power can wreak havoc in world politics. Ultimately, much of the international confidence in China's intentions depends on its firm embrace of international responsibility and domestic liberalization such that its peaceful aspirations are firmly embedded in its conception of great power status and at home. Our study suggests that although a great deal of uncertainties exists regarding China's future, the international community is uniquely equipped to influence and shape the foreign orientations of the rising dragon in the East. To do that, we need first to understand precisely what motivates Chinese foreign policy.

NOTES

1. Robert Jervis, *Perception and Misperception in International Politics* (Princeton, N.J.: Princeton University Press, 1976), 66.

2. John Mearsheimer, *The Tragedy of Great Power Politics* (New York: W. W. Norton, 2001).

3. Dale Copeland, *The Origins of Major Power* (Ithaca, N.Y.: Cornell University Press, 2000), 245.

4. There are different estimates of China's annual growth rate, but most agree that the Chinese economy grew at an average of above 8 percent every year for the past two decades. Nicholas R. Lardy, *Integrating China into the Global Economy* (Washington, D.C.: Brookings, 2002), 11–13.

5. Yasheng Huang, *FDI in China,* Case Study Series (Cambridge, Mass.: Harvard Business School, 2003), 8.

6. "What to Do about the Yuan," *Wall Street Journal*, July 17, 2003. Alan Beattie and Christopher Swann, "Greenspan Warns China on Currency Peg," *Financial Times,* July 16, 2003.

7. Yasheng Huang, *FDI in China*, 8. PRC scholars estimate that the Chinese saving rate was as high as 76.7 percent of China's GDP in 2001. Hu Angang, "Xiaokan shehui" [Little comfort society], in *2003 nian zhongguo shehui xingshi fenxi yu yuche* [Analysis and Forecast of China's Social Conditions in 2003], ed. Ru Xin et al. (Beijing: Shehui Kexue Wenxian Press, 2003), 218.

8. Hu Angang, "Xiaokan shehui" [Little comfort society], 217–18.

9. See, for example, David Shambaugh, *Modernizing China's Military: Progress, Problems, and Prospects* (Berkeley: University of California Press, 2002); Independent Task Force Report, *China's Military Power PLA Task Force* (New York: Council for Foreign Relations, 2003).

10. The classic statements of these realist propositions can be found in A. F. K. Organski and Jacek Kugler, *The War Ledger* (Chicago: University of Chicago Press,

1980); Robert Gilpin, *War and Change in World Politics* (Cambridge: Cambridge University Press, 1981). Robert Jervis argues that the post–September 11 U.S. strategy has abandoned the status quo bias as posited by traditional theories. Clearly the analytical notion of "status quo" is more complex than what many theorists have suggested. See Jervis, "Understanding the Bush Doctrine," *Political Science Quarterly* 118, no. 3 (Fall 2003): 365–88.

11. Alastair Iain Johnston, "Is China a Status Quo Power?" *International Security* 27, no. 4 (Spring 2003): 5–56.

12. See, for example, M. Taylor Fravel and Evan S. Medeiros, "China's New Diplomacy," *Foreign Affairs* 82, no. 6 (November/December 2003); Robert Sutter, "Why Does China Matter?" *Washington Quarterly* 27, no. 1 (Winter 2003–2004): 75–89; David Shambaugh, "China's New Engagement with the Region," *Asian Wall Street Journal*, February 19, 2004.

13. For a comprehensive collection of the major propositions of the peaceful rise strategy, see the Institute of International Strategy, the CCP Central Party School, *Zhongguo heping jueqi xingdaolu* [The New Route of China's Peaceful Ascent] (Beijing: Zhonggong zhongyang dangxiao chubanshe, 2004).

14. See G. John Ikenberry, ed., *America Unrivaled: The Future of the Balance of Power* (Ithaca, N.Y.: Cornell University Press, 2002).

15. Information Office of the State Council, "2002 nian zhongguo de guofang" [China's national defense, 2002], *Renmin Ribao*, overseas edition, December 10, 2002, 1.

16. For comprehensive book-length studies on Chinese foreign policy, see David M. Lampton, ed., *The Making of Chinese Security and Foreign Policy* (Stanford, Calif.: Stanford University Press, 2001); Yongjin Zhang and Greg Austin, eds., *Power and Responsibility in Chinese Foreign Policy* (Canberra, Australia: Asia Pacific Press, 2001); Michael D. Swaine and Ashley J. Tellis, *Interpreting China's Grand Strategy: Past, Present, and Future* (Santa Monica, Calif.: Rand, 2000); Michael Brown et al., eds., *The Rise of China* (Cambridge, Mass.: MIT Press, 2000); Yong Deng and Fei-Ling Wang, eds., *In the Eyes of the Dragon: China Views the World* (Boulder, Colo.: Rowman & Littlefield, 1999); Michael Pillsbury, *China Debates the Future Security Environment* (Washington, D.C.: National Defense University Press, 2000); Elizabeth Economy and Michel Oksenberg, eds., *China Joins the World: Progress and Prospects* (New York: Council on Foreign Relations Press, 1999); Alastair I. Johnston and Robert Ross, eds., *Engaging China: The Management of an Emerging Power* (New York: Routledge, 1999); Samuel S. Kim, ed., *China and the World: Chinese Foreign Policy Faces the New Millennium* (Boulder, Colo.: Westview Press, 1998); Andrew Nathan and Robert Ross, *The Great Wall and the Empty Fortress: China's Search for Securty* (New York: W. W. Norton, 1997); Michael E. Brown, Sean Lynn-Jones, and Steven Miller, eds., *East Asian Security* (Cambridge, Mass.: MIT Press, 1996).

17. Mearsheimer, *The Tragedy of Great Power Politics*, 4.

18. See, for example, John M. Owen IV, "Transnational Liberalism and U.S. Primacy," *International Security* 26, no. 3 (Winter 2001–2002): 117–52, quote on 138.

19. Jack Snyder, "Anarchy and Culture: Insights from the Anthropology of War," *International Organization* 56, no. 1 (Winter 2002): 7–45, quote on 37.

20. Allen S. Whiting, *China Crosses the Yalu: The Decision to Enter the Korea War* (New York: McMillan Company, 1960); *The Chinese Calculus of Deterrence: India and Indochina* (Ann Arbor: University of Michigan Press, 1975); "China's Use of Force, 1950–1996, and Taiwan," *International Security* 26, no. 2 (Fall 2001): 103–31.

21. Thomas J. Christensen, *Useful Adversaries: Grand Strategy, Domestic Mobilization, and Sino-American Conflict, 1947–1958* (Princeton, N.J.: Princeton University Press, 1996); Chen Jian, *Mao's China and the Cold War* (Chapel Hill: University of North Carolina Press, 2001).

22. See Samuel S. Kim, *China, the United Nations, and World Order* (Princeton, N.J.: Princeton University Press, 1979); Peter Van Ness, *Revolution and Chinese Foreign Policy: Peking's Support for Wars of National Liberation* (Berkeley: University of California Press, 1970).

23. Joanne Gowa, "Democratic States and International Disputes," *International Organization* 49, no. 3 (Summer 1995): 511–22.

24. Peter B. Evans, Harold Jacobson, and Robert Putnam, eds., *Double-Edged Diplomacy: International Bargaining and Domestic Politics* (Berkeley: University of California Press, 1993).

25. Peter T. Y. Cheung and James T. H. Tang, "The External Relations of China's Provinces," and Margaret Pearson, "The Case of China's Accession to GATT/WTO," in Lampton, *The Making of Chinese Foreign and Security Policy,* Peterson quote on 352.

26. For a discussion of domestic sources of the state's foreign preferences in light of the liberal traditions, see Andrew Moravcsik, "Taking Preferences Seriously: A Liberal Theory of International Politics," *International Organization* 51, no. 4 (Autumn 1997): 513–53.

27. See Thomas J. Christensen, "China," in *Strategic Asia: Power and Purpose 2001–2002*, ed. Richard J. Ellings and Aaron L. Friedberg (Seattle, Wash.: National Bureau of Asian Research, 2001), 27–69.

28. See Edward Friedman and Barrett L. McCormick, eds., *What If China Doesn't Democratize? Implications for War and Peace* (Armond, N.Y.: M. E. Sharpe, 2000). The broader debate over democratic peace can be found in Michael E. Brown, Sean Lynn-Jones, and Steven Miller, eds., *Debating the Democratic Peace* (Cambridge, Mass.: MIT Press, 1996).

29. Stephen G. Brooks and William C. Wohlforth, "American Primacy in Perspective," *Foreign Affairs* 81, no. 4 (July/August 2002): 29.

30. For a discussion of the interdependence–peace proposition literature and its relevance to Asia, see Ming Wan, "Economic Interdependence and Economic Cooperation: Mitigating Conflict and Transforming Security Order in Asia," in *Asian Security Order: Instrumental and Normative Feature,* ed. Muthiah Alagappa (Stanford, Calif.: Stanford University Press, 2003), 280–310.

31. See, Kenneth Waltz, "Structural Realism after the Cold War," *International Security* 25, no. 1 (Summer 2000): 5–41.

32. Stephen G. Brooks and William C. Wohlforth, "Power, Globalization, the End of the Cold War," *International Security* 25, no. 3 (Winter 2000–2001): 5–53.

33. David Zweig, *Internationalizing China: Domestic Interests and Global Linkages* (Ithaca, N.Y.: Cornell University Press, 2002). For a most recent overview, see

Thomas G. Moore, "China's International Relations: The Economic Dimension," in *The International Relations of Northeast Asia*, ed. Samuel Kim (Boulder, Colo.: Rowman & Littlefield, 2004), 101–34.

34. Liu Jianfei, *Meiguo yu fangong zhuyi: Lun meiguo dui shehui zhuyi guojia d yishixingtai waijiao* [The U.S. and Anticommunism: On the American Ideological Diplomacy against Socialist Countries] (Beijing: Chinese Social Science Press, 2001).

35. Dale Copeland, "Economic Interdependence and the Future of U.S.–Chinese Relations," in *International Relations Theory and the Asia–Pacific*, ed. G. John Ikenberry and Michael Mastanduno (New York: Columbia University Press, 2003), 323–52.

36. See Pang Zhongying, ed., *Quanqiuhua, fanquanqiuhua yu zhongguo: Lijie quanqiuhua de fuzhaxin yu duoyangxin* [Globalization, Antiglobalization, and China: Understanding the Complexity and Diversity of Globalization] (Shanghai: Renmin Press, 2002).

37. See also Yong Deng, "Globalization and Multipolarization in Chinese Foreign Policy," *Harvard China Review* 4, no. 1 (Fall 2003): 18–21; Yong Deng and Thomas G. Moore, "China Views Globalization: Towards a New Great Power Politics?" *Washington Quarterly* 27, no. 3 (Summer 2004): 117–36.

38. Jiang Zemin, "Quanmian jianshe xiaokang shehui, kaichuang zhonggguo teshe shehuihuizhuyi shiye xinjubian" [Building a well-off society in an all-out effort, creating a new situation for the cause of Chinese-style Socialism], report at the Sixteenth Chinese Communist Party Congress, November 8, 2002, *Renmin Ribao*, overseas edition, November 18, 2002, 1–3; Information Office of the State Council, "2002 nian zhongguo de guofang" [China's national defense, 2002], 1–4.

2

Beijing's Incentive Structure: The Pursuit of Preservation, Prosperity, and Power

Fei-Ling Wang

Few other things motivate a nation's foreign policy more than maintaining its domestic political order. China is no exception. In the early part of the first decade of the twenty-first century, Beijing's top concern in its making of foreign policy remains the preservation of the political system of the Chinese Communist Party (CCP). The new effort of political reform in the PRC (People's Republic of China), aiming for a more adaptive CCP and for better governance, has yet to change the preservational necessity for Beijing. Tangible and continued economic prosperity has become *the* avenue to reach that goal; international acceptance and approval have become major sources of legitimacy for the CCP at home, whereas nationalistic demands for more Chinese power and prestige have presented Beijing with an additional opportunity for, and a new challenge to, its political preservation. Together, a peculiar incentive structure of preservation, prosperity, and power/prestige fundamentally motivates China's foreign policy.

Ever since the 1980s, a deeply rooted sense of political insecurity as well as a burning desire for economic growth have colored decision making in the PRC. Both considerations led to Beijing's declared top objective of stability, at home and abroad. Consequently, China's foreign policy remains basically pragmatic, pro–status quo, and reactive. External respect has become a leading source of the CCP's political legitimacy, so Beijing cultivates carefully its peaceful and cooperative posture in international relations. Yet China's conservative foreign policy for political preservation and its drive for economic prosperity have combined to generate fuel for a rising sense of Chinese nationalism. On the one hand, rapid economic growth and technological advances have powered nationalistic sentiments and demands; on the other hand, Beijing's preservation-oriented and conservative foreign policy has frustrated many Chinese nationalists. To seek for more power, defined as influence and prestige, in international relations is a growing Chinese sentiment and one to be reckoned with.

This chapter describes those concerns, after a brief examination of China's strategic views of the world. A complex hierarchy among political preservation, economic prosperity, and national power has formed to constitute the foundation of the Chinese domestic incentive structure that guides China's foreign policy. This hierarchy, though predictable and fairly stable, can be dynamic and is subject to the influence of domestic and external developments and crises. Table 2.1 illustrates five versions of a three-P incentive structure. Beijing now believes that the post–September 11 "war on terrorism" and the U.S. invasion and occupation of Iraq have provided a "period of strategic opportunity" for the CCP to concentrate on its strategy for stability and development in the first two decades of this century.[1] So scenario 1 of the status quo may continue and, ideally, evolve into the desired scenario 4, without much political turbulence. However, how long that period will last is a function of many other factors, which may lead to alterations of this Chinese incentive structure that will in turn create new directions and efforts in the formulation and implementation of China's foreign policy in the years ahead.

CHINA'S STRATEGIC VIEW: A PECULIAR SENSE OF INSECURITY IN A SECURE WORLD

A new strategic view of the world emerged in the PRC in the mid-1990s, after two decades of phenomenal growth and change. Overall, China felt secure and confident as a nation: there was now no foreign invasion directly threatening China's sovereignty, territorial integrity, and independence; this was the best national security status China had had "since the Opium War" of 1840 to 1842.[2] More important, China was now in its "greatest era of reform and most prosperous era of construction" in history and, after the United States and Japan, China was granted "the third rare historical opportunity in 100 years" to make an economic takeoff to become a world-class economic power.[3] Given the massive population (a huge domestic market), the still very cheap labor force of nearly eight hundred million, one of the largest natural endowments in the world, and steadily advancing market institutions, the rapid economic growth of the PRC is expected to continue for some time to come.[4] External forces could make a major difference, especially if applied as a cohesive and effective effort like the containment policies led by the United States during the Cold War. Yet containment aimed at curbing Chinese growth

Table 2.1. Scenarios of Beijing's Incentive Structure (via the three-*P* method)

Scenarios	Three Incentives			Implication	
	Political Preservation	*Economic Prosperity*	*Nationalist Power Pursuit*	*China's Foreign Policy*	*Uncertainties*
1. Status quo	Threatened but manageable	Top priority	Increasing but controlled	Risk averse and conservative	For how long?
2. Democratization	Acute threats and challenges	Top priority, less political	Strong surge	More active and risk taking	Leads to scenario 3 or 5?
3. Democratized successfully	No longer a concern	No more urgency	Strong	More assertive and demanding	Ally of U.S.?
4. CCP-led world power	Not much of a concern	No more urgency	Strong	More assertive and demanding	Challenger to U.S.?
5. Regime collapse	Failed and chaos	Ignored and sacrificed	Desperately strong	Aggressive and militant	Worst-case scenario?

or limiting Chinese power appears to be unfeasible and undesirable at the moment. Beijing generally dismissed the possibility of a new Cold War against China, especially after the terrorist attacks on September 11, 2001.[5] Chinese analysts now believe that the United States needs engagement rather than containment as a way of "Westernizing" and "transforming" (*xihua* and *fenghua*) China and eventually incorporating China into an international system dominated by the West.[6]

Beijing appears to be betting its future on its efforts within the current international political and economic system. Two facts of today's international relations appear to be now widely accepted in China. First, the world is organized as an anarchic nation-state political system and as an international market economy, quite unlike the "Chinese world order" of the Middle Kingdom or the promised utopian land of world communism.[7] Second, China needs the Western capital, technology, and markets to pursue its dream of being equal to the West. Economic development is viewed as the key national objective; and conforming to, rather than challenging, the existing international order becomes the strategic choice. Indeed, after more than two decades of opening to the outside world (mainly the West), and as new Chinese élite who have great vested interest in the opening proliferate, China is now increasingly and genuinely developing shared values, interests, and even perspectives with the reigning Western powers.

At the same time, an increasingly strong sense of China's "vulnerability" and even "insecurity" is clearly present in Beijing. This contradictory and seemingly false view is driven by two real factors. First, the CCP has had a peculiar and persisting sense of political insecurity ever since 1989 and the end of the Cold War. A profound concern for the regime's survival, bordering on a sense of being under siege, has been present in Beijing for much of the past decade. There is a constant fear of being singled out and targeted by the leading powers, especially the United States, and an increasing realization of the growing problems of political legitimacy and governance in a rapidly developing and diversifying market economy. The debilitating impact of this beleaguered mentality has effectively constrained the foreign policy of rising Chinese power, leading to a conservative foreign policy for the PRC featuring the sometimes exclusive pursuit of the CCP's political preservation.[8]

Second, many Chinese élite, within and outside the CCP, are feeling the anxiety of unsatisfied nationalistic aspirations that is almost predetermined for a rising power. A deeply rooted longing for more Chinese power is perhaps only natural, as the nation still faces the historic "mission" of national unification while being organized significantly different from the reigning powers in politics, culture, and ideology. Some more ideology-oriented analysts believe that China is carrying not only the mission of rejuvenating Chinese civilization and restoring its past glory but also the grand task of safe-guarding and promoting global socialism.[9] Seeing that "a rapidly growing Chinese economy will inevitably become the locomotive of the world's economy in the 21st century," many in Beijing believe that

> a rising China will never be a nation that is satisfied with only food and shelter. Her development and progress will definitely make increasing contributions to the peace and prosperity of the world. China was such a [nation] in the past for thousands of years, so it will definitely become such a nation again in the new millennium. Our nation was a crucial player on the playground of international politics. [Its] enhancing economic capabilities, and its status of being a major nuclear power and a permanent member of the UN Security Council, will give our nation a larger and larger role in world affairs. Our nation enjoys a position as an irreplaceable major world power.[10]

CCP's politically motivated conservative foreign policy has created additional frustrations for the new generation of Chinese nationalists. Hence, the objectively secure nation of China is, interestingly, displaying a strong sense of insecurity and desire. An expanding power base and the "natural" aspiration for more power have paradoxically led many in Beijing to feel less powerful and secure, as many of China's aspirations are increasingly scrutinized by the reigning powers. This pessimistic strategic view reached its peak right before September 11, 2001. One article, on China's "international attitude, diplomatic philosophy, and basic strategic thinking," published in the influential journal *Strategy and Management*, describes it well. It argues that China currently lacks a sufficient sense of security for that "there is such a basic fact: As a rapidly developing non-Western power, China has considerably extensive and deep differences, conflicts, and mutual suspicion in the areas of current interests, future interest, ideology, and national culture and psychology with the superpower of the United States, which possesses enormous superiority in the world system for the next century." The article further warns that recent developments have worsened China's peculiar sense of insecurity and created a "palpable sense of being under siege that has been rarely seen in the last decade and thus raising obvious concerns about China's mid- to long-term security."[11]

Another article in the same journal argues similarly that "the fundamental cause for the deterioration of China's security situation since the latter part of the 1990s has been the radicalization of Sino-American structural and strategic conflicts: the United States is determined to contain China's rise." Therefore, China now faces thirteen major threats to China's national security, including the Taiwanese drive for full independence, with the support of the United States and Japan; the Korean problem; the nuclearization of South

Asia; and "ideological threat" and "Cold War thinking," such as "Western attacks on the grounds of human rights."[12] A senior foreign policy analyst has asserted that, due to the structural conflicts between a rising power (China) and the reigning power (United States), Beijing should expect to see "more, not less, confrontations and collisions with the United States."[13]

Therefore, despite a conservative and conformist foreign policy, Beijing's quest for regime preservation and political stability has transformed the CCP's political predicament to a peculiar but national sense of insecurity and frustration in China, at a time when the nation is rapidly developing while becoming secure and unprecedentedly open. Such a peculiar sense of frustration has clearly penetrated into the general public in China, as demonstrated by the outbursts of public feeling, from the numerous best-selling anti-American tabloids published since the mid-1990s, to the stoning of the American embassy in Beijing in 1999 by college students avenging the U.S. bombing of the Chinese embassy in Belgrade, to the almost one-sided anti-American Internet postings and rallies protesting the U.S. war against Iraq in 2003.

The horrific attacks of September 11, 2001, and the subsequent "war on terrorism" changed international relations and also affected Chinese views. Without a fundamental change of its domestic incentive structure, China's strategic assessment in the post–September 11 era has remained unchanged. However, there is noticeable relief in Beijing that the United States is less a direct challenge, since Washington is heavily preoccupied with the task of fighting international terrorism and is expected to do so for some time to come.[14]

Speaking in early 2003, some Chinese security analysts argued that in the aftermath of 9/11, Beijing now "enjoys the best international and neighboring environment since the establishment of the PRC." The main objectives of Chinese foreign policy remain "to seek a long-term peaceful environment for our nation's economic construction; and to promote our economic development through opening to the outside world." More specifically, China "no longer stresses establishing a new international order; rather, it is joining the existing international order" as it "realizes more and more the importance of participating in international affairs, including international organizations. However, China "is careful not to 'take the lead or carry the banner'" in world affairs. These analysts contend, "As long as our foreign policy benefits the stability of our international environment, our economic construction, and world peace and development, and we are not losing our sovereignty and territorial integrity, our diplomacy is mature." On the Taiwan issue, they maintain that "Taiwan is where China's core interest lies, . . . and there is no room for compromise on that issue. . . . Our nation's long-term diplomatic goal is clear, i.e., to realize national rejuvenation."[15]

With such strategic thinking, Deng Xiaoping's famous twenty-eight-word guideline of "keeping a low profile," proposed first in late 1989, still seems to be guiding China's foreign policy. The same goes for Jiang Zemin's sixteen-word guideline for China's U.S. policy—*Zeng jia xin ren, jian shao ma fan, fa zhan he zuo, bu gao dui kang,* "Enhance trust, reduce trouble, develop cooperation, and avoid confrontation"—which was first proposed in 1993.[16] In May–June 2003, in his first state visit to Russia and France amidst the crisis of the SARS (severe acute respiratory syndrome) epidemic, the new PRC president Hu Jintao basically reiterated Beijing's pro–status quo, conformist, and stability-seeking foreign policy line.[17]

However, the pre–September 11 nationalist aspirations, concerns, and anxieties remain in Beijing. "Right now, our national interest has already grown beyond our territory," argued prominent Chinese analysts in 2003. For them, "we must see not only that the United States needs cooperation from the major powers in its war against terrorism, but also the fact that the U.S. strategic objective is world hegemony. . . . The United States still treats China as a 'potential threat' and has never given up on the policy of containing China."[18] Hence, China must "unequivocally oppose hegemonism while upholding the banner of anti-terrorism" since terrorism "threatens China's security . . . through causing social panic and damaging the reputation and authority of the Party and the government"; while "hegemonism endangers world peace and stability" as well. They caution that "for a long time to come, it will be difficult to ascertain which is more threatening: terrorism or hegemonism." China must "watch out for the United States, which may take advantage of the war on terrorism and increase strategic pressure on China while seizing the opportunity presented by the war on terrorism to promote Sino-American relations" since "the United States is the main executioner of hegemonism but also is irreplaceable in the international community."[19]

With such a complicated view of the new world that makes Beijing feel insecure in a secure time, political preservation remains the top concern in the making of China's foreign policy.

STABILITY, ONE-PARTY RULE, AND GOVERNANCE: THE PRESERVATION CHALLENGE

Beijing has viewed its political preservation as the top priority of foreign policy since Mao's era. Partially due to its revolutionary ideology of class struggle and partially due to the history of the first three decades of the PRC, when the CCP almost always had open or covert foreign threats to its political survival, Beijing has a tradition of distrust and fear of foreign powers and influence.

Barely ten years into the reform and opening that showed a relaxation of CCP's beleaguered mentality, the June 4 uprising and its bloody ending in 1989 left a deep wound in the political memory of the CCP leadership. A combination of foreign forces with domestic adversaries, especially dissenting CCP insiders, is seen by many as fully capable of toppling China's political system and threatening the physical survival of the CCP and its leaders. The peaceful ending of the Cold War and the quick though sometimes bloody disappearance of the ruling Communist Party in many countries further convinced the CCP leaders that they cannot trust the democracy-promoting Western powers with their lives and their hope for a great Chinese rise.

Despite its ambitious plan and stated confidence of leading China into the promised land of "long lost" greatness, respect, and glory, the CCP regime has been contested in its legitimacy at home; its authority and official ideology are under constant challenges from within and without. Those internal and external pressures have forced Beijing to search for sanctuary in economic prosperity and nationalistic feelings, or "patriotism." Not surprisingly, given the authoritarian nature of the PRC political system, the CCP's insecurity has been translated, through its organizations and propaganda, to be the "national interests" of rising Chinese power. The leading arguments offered by the CCP to combine its political interests with China's national interests have been that "only the CCP can save China"; "China can only develop well under CCP leadership"; and "no CCP, no New China." The catchphrase of such strategic thinking has been "comprehensive security" or "new security," promoted by none other than Jiang Zemin himself in the past few years. A foreign ministry–backed journal published an article asserting straightforwardly that "any grand strategy" of China must be based on "comprehensive security" or "domestic and external security" and "not only military security but also political, economic, and cultural security."[20]

To be sure, such a line of argument has been rather convincing to many Chinese since it describes the nature and course of state-led Chinese modernization. Moreover, to value one's political system as a vital part of national interest is not exclusively a Chinese logic. The difference in the Chinese case is the striking predominance of the political preservation of a one-party political regime that is self-conscious about its persistent lack of legitimacy. While its legitimacy, through participation and expression, is still highly limited, and while its leaders' personal charisma and ideological callings are fading, Beijing's task of political self-preservation through force and through job performance is not easy even at the best of times. In an era of globalization and activism by the reigning hegemon, in addition to the inevitable development of social diversification and mobility in China, the task of political preservation has forced Beijing into a near-permanent status of crisis that consumes extraordinary energy and resources. Anything can become political or, worse, politically threatening.

Three aspects predominate the daunting task of the CCP's political preservation. First, overall sociopolitical stability and the status quo must be preserved. Revolutions, social uprisings, radical political changes, and social disturbances and chaos must not happen. This objective clearly favors the ruling CCP leadership and its supporters, who benefit disproportionately from China's economic development; however, it is evidently a still very popular wish in China, since the majority of the Chinese are gaining from current economic growth and from China's peaceful interactions with other nations. Few in China are currently envisioning an overhaul of the state's social and political system. To keep China stable, orderly, and peaceful appears to be in the interest of most nations around the world, hence the idea's international appeal. Therefore, it has been relatively easy for the CCP to argue that its top mission is to keep China stable, even at some expense to political democratization, free speech, and individual rights.

Second, political preservation in the PRC means the CCP's continuous monopoly of political power. Judging by the latest developments, the CCP has no intention of sharing its power with other parties. At the Sixteenth National Congress in 2002, the CCP redefined its new mission to strive to be "the ruling party of long governance and permanent tranquility" (*chang-zhi-jiu-an de zhi-zheng-dang*). This mission statement has little popularity outside of China in the post–Cold War world, but it is not questioned much inside the PRC for two simple reasons: many believe that the CCP has no viable replacement, and its demise would inevitably lead to political disorder and social chaos. Perhaps even more think that today's CCP is a fully committed developmentalist party, which is not inherently bad to the Chinese nation and Chinese civilization. There are plenty of anti-CCP Chinese in and outside the PRC, but few of them pose any serious organizational potential to topple, replace, or compete with the CCP for political power or for the rule of China. Unpopular, undesirable, and internationally challenged as it may be, the one-party rule by the CCP in the PRC appears strong, at least now and in the near future.

Third, how to provide effective and rational governance in a country that is growing and changing so rapidly remains the biggest challenge to the CCP's mission of political preservation. As some Chinese scholars have revealed, the CCP and its supporters have formed a ruling elite class in China that is founded on the compromise between economic development and sociopolitical stability. The decay of the CCP's one-party rule is likely to take place inside the party when it can no longer provide the governance to keep that compromise. Rampant corruption, bureaucratic inefficiency and unaccountability, and the enlarging gulf between the rich minority and the poor majority are breeding irrationality, lawlessness, violence, and the political crises that will ultimately threaten the CCP's political preservation. The one-party nondemocratic political system necessarily channels almost every kind of grievance toward the CCP. The dynamic and uneven nature of China's development forces the CCP to constantly react to the endless hot issues and new problems to prevent *the* crisis from emerging. The highly centralized one-party decision-making system lacks flexibility and room to maneuver, thus little cushion to ease strains at a time when development and diversification are daily countrywide occurrences. It makes the leadership look fragile and almost hysterical in dealing with dissention and diversity. Beijing thus has a chronic but realistic sense of being under siege, and the whole political system faces potentially annihilating threats that can result from even the smallest acts of bad governance and mismanagement. This is where the biggest challenge to Beijing's political preservation lies.

Driven by such a mentality, Beijing has repeatedly acted irrationally in its dealings with foreign actors, influence, and events. A clear mixture of insecurity and secrecy, always prevalent in China's domestic affairs, has deeply politicized China's foreign policy. Foreign events and actions are often judged by the CCP's political consideration rather than by China's national interest. Foreign criticism is often met with defensive and ultrasensitive counterattacks. Even the simple bad news of natural disasters, criminal cases, and epidemics are frequently suppressed and controlled in the name of sociopolitical stability, often at the expense of not only the welfare of the people but also the rationality and efficiency of governance. Yet the Internet age has rendered a centralized, tight control of information flow a largely futile effort. At the same time, foreign reports and actions on such suppressed bad news are often perceived with extraordinary attentiveness by the Chinese government and the increasing number of Chinese people who have access. Sometimes, only foreign pressure can force Beijing to relent in its obsession with control in the name of stability. In a dialectic way, such delayed or forced relaxation and reaction tends to lead to mass panic and the widespread loss of CCP's authority and credibility, a bigger blow to the CCP's goal of political preservation.

The worldwide scare of SARS (also known as "atypical pneumonia" in China) in the spring and summer of 2003 illustrates this dilemma for the CCP well. While initially identified in the province of Guangdong, the flu-like contagious pneumonia was almost automatically treated by the Chinese bureaucracy as bad news to be carefully controlled to minimize its impact on overall sociopolitical stability and economic activity. Haphazard actions and reassuring news releases took place only when citizens in Guangdong started to panic at the rumors. Only when "outside" areas such as Hong

Kong, Singapore, and Canada became affected by the epidemic, and especially when the World Health Organization and various national governments hurried to issue travel warnings against China, did Beijing realize how costly its "standard policy" had become.[21] With a rarely seen speed and transparency, but still in a centralized CCP style, Beijing quickly made an 180-degree turn and launched a "people's war on SARS." The new people's war quickly evolved into a familiar political campaign in the whole country, with the usual draping of mass mobilization, single-mindedness, hysteria, manipulation, overreaction, and local distortions. Thus, the SARS crisis damaged the Chinese economy, its international image, and Beijing's political authority immeasurably.[22]

With a wounded credibility to repair and a virus that may not be erasable by political campaigns, the new leadership of Hu Jintao and Wen Jiabao is now under pressure and has an opportunity to reconfigure for a better governance in the new world and a therefore better chance for political preservation.[23] The quick control of the SARS epidemic in places such as Beijing may have actually given the CCP a reason to claim credit. Beijing appears to have taken the lesson that nonpolitical, even local, issues can quickly become political and international if handled as in the old way. A transparent and free flow of *some* information may benefit the CCP's one-party rule. The challenge, however, remains: what information should be allowed to flow freely, and when should the mighty political machine of the CCP authoritarian regime apply? That is, how can the CCP stay in power and govern effectively in a new era and in a changed society? Presenting challenges and new perimeters for Beijing in its eternal struggle for political preservation are the powerful presence of foreign media and international organizations, as exemplified by the role of the World Health Organization (WHO) in the SARS epidemic, and the changed society inside the PRC, as exemplified by the whistleblowers such as Dr. Jiang Yanyong.[24]

As it has been for more than two decades, external comments and criticism are now the leading sources of CCP's political legitimacy and destabilization. Consequently, the CCP now tries to pin its legitimacy and ruling ability on a wholesale effort of "connecting to the standards of the world" (*yu shijie jiegui*). In the first three decades of PRC's history, Beijing was continually preparing for an "inevitable" world war, until 1983 when Deng Xiaoping assessed that a new world war was unlikely within ten years. Jiang Zemin in 1995 estimated that "it is possible to earn an international peace for the next fifteen years," until 2010, when China and, in the leadership's calculation, the CCP regime as well, would be strong enough to rid itself of the danger of annihilation. After September 11, the CCP believed that it had been granted a new "window of strategic opportunity" for the next one or two decades, relatively free from direct challenges and threats from the United States. A military invasion by foreign powers might be remote, but this fact does not appear to be able to ease CCP's sense of insecurity.

Indeed, in the post–September 11 world, the CCP regime still has good reason to feel internationally insecure. The dominant world powers, led by the United States, have appeared to be at odds with this last "communist" government. The democracy-promoting and human rights–advocating Washington is now also trying out its "preemptive and preventive" strategy by force in the Middle East and beyond. A PRC military officer wrote in 2002 that "the anti-China forces in the United States simply oppose and hate our socialist political system by instinct" and aim at "transforming China, destroying communism and realizing a monopoly of capitalism in the world.[25] A senior Chinese diplomat concluded in 2003 that

> the United States continued to relentlessly pressure us politically, even after 9/11 on human rights and other political issues . . . especially the Taiwan issue. Its basic assessment and hatred of China remains unchanged. . . . Washington does not trust us at all and is still demonizing China and trying to contain China.[26]

There are ways out. Political reform in the general direction of democratization is a major way for Beijing to relieve its sense of political insecurity, as a mass democracy will greatly enhance the PRC's political legitimacy and political stability (scenario 3 in table 2.1). In a new, more open democratic system, a decoupling of CCP's political interests from China's national interests may conceivably take place; political preservation of the CCP regime may subside as a major factor motivating China's foreign policy.[27]

In the past few years, Beijing has moved to politically reform China in some important ways. First, as personally led by Jiang Zemin since 2001, the CCP has adopted a "three represents" doctrine to revise its official ideology and mission statement.[28] "Communism with Chinese characters" appears to be philosophically (and strikingly) similar to the typical social democratic agenda of many European countries. The controversial policy of allowing business owners and capitalists to join the CCP simply accepted the new political landscape in China and formally opened the door to transform the party from a Communist Party for the proletariat to a Social Democratic Party just "for the people." The new "nontraditional" elements of the CCP's rank and file now are estimated to be at least in the millions—and growing.[29] One Chinese scholar penetratingly pointed out that the three-represents doctrine "simply is the political declaration of the formation of a newly institutionalized alliance among the [Chinese] political, economic, and intellectual élites."[30]

Substantial efforts have been made to institutionalize and routinize the CCP itself, from the now semitransparent succession process, as demonstrated by the Sixteenth CCP National Congress in 2002 and the Tenth National People's Congress in 2003; to the timely and open reports of the CCP politburo meetings; to the unprecedented speed and openness regarding some "bad news."[31] Discussions and debates about how to further democratize with Chinese characters have appeared often in the Chinese media, including some of the leading official newspapers and journals, especially on the Internet.[32] A leading view has been to launch a "gradual political reform based on China's political stability."[33] Building on years of discussion and experimentation, Beijing launched a national reform of its *hukou* (household registration) system, which now legally gives millions of Chinese greatly increased internal mobility and personal freedom.[34] In early 2003, political reform became the top issue among the senior cadres being trained at the CCP's Central Party School.[35] Hu Jintao in the spring of 2003 very noticeably emphasized that everyone in the PRC, including CCP members, must "respect and obey" the constitution.[36] Finally, in the summer of 2003, reports from Beijing leaked Hu Jintao's bold plans for democratizing the CCP from the inside out.

The CCP is perhaps making a historic effort to transform itself from "workers' pioneers" to "the pioneers of the Chinese people and nation." So the rising sense of nationalism, as "the most watched political asset in today's China," may be successfully tapped "to become a powerful spiritual force to resist Western pressures abroad and to solidify the nation at home."[37] Practically, such major changes of tradition and policy are to allow the CCP to expand its power base, to adapt to the new era and the changed society to become a successful, permanent ruling party.[38]

So far, however, China's political reform appears to be limited. A peaceful reform of the CCP political system that can rid Beijing of its sense of political insecurity requires a great amount of vision, courage, wisdom, skill, and time; none of which appears to be ensured within and for the central leadership. Furthermore, the decline and even disappearance of the CCP's besieged mentality as a major motivational factor, owing to a democratizing Chinese politics, may not be necessarily all good news for status-quo-loving countries. The democratization process usually creates incentives and driving forces for the rise of nationalism during instability and transition. In a country as diverse and unbalanced as China, democratization may turn out to be a factor that will completely alter the nature of Chinese foreign policy, making it much less conservative and more demanding than it currently is (scenario 2 in table 2.1). Naturally, an explosive and revolutionary collapse or change of the CCP regime may also fundamentally alleviate Beijing's need of political preservation (scenario 5 in table 2.1); but that is an entirely different game with consequences many of us would hate to imagine.

GLOBALIZATION AND GROWTH—MOTIVES OF PROSPERITY

Economic growth has been on the top of the CCP's policy agenda ever since the 1980s. Prosperity has become not only the objective that the CCP champions but perhaps also the avenue on which Beijing can seek political preservation through performance. Deng Xiaoping pinned economic development down as the "central task" for the CCP in the next one hundred years. For the Chinese, making money has become not only a politics in and of itself but also a new, quasi religion. For large segments of the Chinese people, who are increasingly more nationalist than communist, the search for prosperity is viewed as a key to realizing the century-old dream of rejuvenating the Chinese nation and Chinese civilization, to achieve the ideals of *fu-guo-qian-bin* (rich country and strong military) or its current version *fu-min-qiang-guo* (rich people and strong nation). Therefore, economic prosperity is not only the pathway for Beijing to strive for political preservation; it is also the foundation for China's rising nationalistic aspirations. In the triangular incentive structure of China's foreign policy, economic prosperity is the anchor of the other two objectives, political preservation and national power.

Tangible development and sustained growth have indeed taken place in China in the past quarter century. China's GDP (gross domestic product) has grown at a speed of 8 to 9 percent every year and is already one of the largest in the world.[39] China's per capita GDP also increased significantly. Only a small player in the international market not so long ago, China now commands a significant share of world trade and is the second-largest holder of foreign currency reserves (over \$400 billion by 2004). Comparatively speaking, China's search for prosperity in recent years has been quite impressive. By almost all indicators of socioeconomic development, China has clearly outperformed its neighbor, India, and the developing world at large (table 2.2).

With such an impressive report card, Beijing has successfully justified its political system to millions of Chinese, especially the élite. A new ruling class and a new developmentalist political consensus have emerged and strongly taken hold in China to stabilize the CCP's authoritarian one-party regime. "Under the neo-authoritarianism banner" of the CCP, China's "political, economic and intellectual élites have all reached a consensus and joined in an alliance" to rule China as a new ruling class that monopolizes political power.[40] Many CCP officials and leaders are so pro-business and so devoted to economic growth that they are almost identical to their counterparts in places such as Seoul, Taipei, and Singapore. Opinion polls and anecdotal evidence have widely suggested that the CCP's political monopoly is secure as long as the economy grows and the income of the people

Table 2.2.   China's Prosperity in a Comparative Perspective

	India	China	Developing Nations
Population (millions, in 1975)	620.7	927.8	2,898.3
Annual growth rate (1975–1999)	2.0%	1.3%	1.9%
GDP (billions US$, via the PPP method)[a]	2,242	4,534.9	16,201.9
Annual growth rate (1975–1999)	3.2%	8.1%	2.3%
Annual growth rate (1990–1999)	4.2%	9.5%	3.2%
Per capita GDP (by PPP, 2002)	$2,540	$4,400	$3,530 (1999)
Export (1999, million US$)	37,598	194,931	—
Import (1999, million US$)	47,212	165,699	—
Trade balance (1999, million US$)	−9,614	29,232	—
Export/GDP in 1990	7%	18%	26%
Export/GDP in 1999	12%	22%	29%
Hi-tech export/export (1999)[b]	16.6%	39%	—
Foreign direct investment/GDP (1999)	0.5%	3.9%	2.9%
Foreign exchange reserve (1999–2000)[c]	$35.1 billion	$161.4 billion	—
Annual inflation rate (1999–2000)	4.7%	−3%	—
Human development index (rank) (2001)	0.571 (115)	0.718 (87)	0.647 (49–162)
Human development index (rank) (1990)	0.439 (93)	0.716 (64)	— (46–130)
Technology achievement index (rank)	0.201 (63)	0.299 (45)	—

(continued)

Table 2.2. China's Prosperity in a Comparative Perspective (continued)

	India	China	Developing Nations
Gender development index rank (1999)	105	76	—
K–9th grade school enrollment	56%	73%	61%
People under poverty line	35.0–44.2%	4.6–18.5%	—
Life expectancy (years)	62.9	70.2	64.5
Infant mortality rate (per 1,000 births)	70	33	61
Underweight children at age 5	53%	10%	—
Undernourished people	21%	11%	18%
Adult literacy rate	56.5%	83.5%	72.9%

Sources: PRC State Statistics Bureau, *Zhongguo Tongji Nianjan* [China Statistical Yearbook, 2001] (Beijing: China Tongji Press, 2001), 4. Economist Intelligence Unit, *Country Profile 2000: China and Mongolia* (London: Author, 2001), 65–74. World Bank, *Country Data*, November 2001, at www.worldbank.com/data/countrydata/countrydata.html. United Nations Development and Planning, *Human Development Report* (New York: Oxford University Press, 1990), 128–43; *Human Development Report 2001* (New York: Oxford University Press, 2001), 48–54, 142–212. Reserve Bank of India, *Handbook of Statistics on Indian Economy 1999–2000* (New Delhi: Author, 2001), tables 113 and 140. Central Intelligence Agency, *World Factbook 2003*.

Note: Dashes (—) indicate where data were not available.

[a] PPP stands for purchasing power parity.
[b] China was ranked tenth of the world's top-thirty high-tech goods exporters in 1999. India was not on the list.
[c] China has been the second-largest foreign exchange reserve holder (after Japan) and second-largest foreign direct investment (FDI) recipient (after the United States) since 1997.

(mainly the politically potent urban population) increases. It seems that political legitimacy can be effectively purchased in China as well, at least for the time being.

Whether and when Beijing will follow or be forced to repeat the same path of postprosperity political democratization of Korea or Taiwan is quite uncertain. Economic development may not necessarily bring about political democracy in China any time soon. Unlike Korea and Taiwan, which are relatively small and under unique external influences, China is large and unevenly developed. The new rich, some of whom apparently have already accumulated world-class wealth, are likely to be much more interested in protecting their gains from the hundreds of millions of rural poor than in sharing political power with their fellow citizens. This is especially the case now, as the CCP openly recolors itself to be the party ruling for the rich few rather than for the masses of workers. When Japan was growing and modernizing rapidly from the 1870s to 1930s, its political development was anything but ensured democratization.

Prosperity in an era of globalization has motivated much of China's foreign policy, especially its foreign economic policy. Institutionally and practically, China has made major strides to merge itself into the existing international economic order, culminated by Beijing's last-minute decision, with surprisingly large concessions, to join the World Trade Organization (WTO) in 2001. *Interdependence* and *economic globalization* have become some of the hottest phrases in China. Indeed, China has acquired an unprecedented dependence on the world market. In 2003, 20 to 25 percent of China's GDP was directly related to foreign trade; China imports an increasing amount of oil from the troubled region of the Middle East.

Now not only a full member of all the world's economic institutions, China is also actively flexing its economic muscles. A leading example is the idea of constructing a free-trade zone that includes basically all of East and Southeast Asia, the so-called ten-plus-one or ten-plus-three scheme. In June 2003, at the invitation of the French, the Chinese for the first time attended the highly symbolic G-8 summit in Evian, France. It seems to the Chinese that selectively embracing globalization pays and that international political legitimacy can be purchased as well.

Problems and uncertainties that may delay and even derail the Chinese pursuit for prosperity are of course abundant. They range from banking crises, capital flight, institutional incompetence, income and regional inequality, and environmental degradation to widespread corruption. None of them is easy to fix, and many of them imply hellish consequences. For one thing, Beijing has yet to find enough jobs for the estimated 150 to 200 million unemployed or underemployed Chinese laborers.[41] The increased mobility of this many people, one-to-two times that of the existing urban population, can be unstable and precarious economically and especially politically. Political democratization can do little to alleviate this problem. The unemployed floaters may cause the urban-based élite to be even less inclined to support a genuine democratization in the foreseeable future.

Economic globalization, however, still appears to Beijing as a worthwhile gamble. A senior CCP official argued that, as long as China seizes the currently available "development opportunity that presents itself only once in a thousand years" to ride the tide and "catch the express train of economic globalization, we will realize our ideals of leap-frog development and having a powerful nation and rich people."[42] For that, China clearly needs to be part of the existing international economic institutions, trade aggressively with everyone, and especially maintain a good relationship with the developed nations.

Political preservation is the top priority of the CCP leadership, but it is economic prosperity that allows the CCP regime to survive while keeping the élite and the common people inspired in today's China. As a result, China's foreign policy often appears to be more directly and comprehensively motivated by the simple and concrete desire for money rather than by the dry and tedious doctrine of political stability itself. It is a godsend when Beijing's political agenda synchronizes with the nation's justifiable obsession with money. But when the two goals are somehow in conflict, one may start to see inevitable choices that tend to sacrifice economic interest for political needs. The hurried membership of the WTO,[43] largely motivated by political needs, has already been seen by many in China as having the potential to cause profound economic and social problems, with ultimately explosive and horrific implications to China's political stability.[44]

UNFULFILLMENT AND FRUSTRATION: THE POWER CRAVINGS

Despite the fact that China, as a nation, is now secure and enjoying at least the nominal status of a great power in the world, a persistent sense of frustration, insecurity, and even victimization still seems to color the Chinese national self-identity and its relations with Western powers. On the one hand, China's economic growth has given the Chinese unprecedented confidence and know-how to interact "equally" with other nations. There are also unprecedented resources and chances for the Chinese to pursue their interests in the world, including resolution of those lingering and often "humiliating" historical issues such as Taiwan. As discussed earlier, an increasingly strong sense of nationalist aspiration and even ambition is clearly growing in China. Chinese analysts, fully aware of China's overall position in the world, have "modestly" ranked China as sixth in the world in a comparison of "comprehensive national powers" but nonetheless ranked its economic power and military power as third (after the United States and Japan) and fourth (after the United States, Japan, and the United Kingdom) in the world, respectively.[45] The successful mission of the *Shenzhou-V* space flight and the image of the first Chinese astronaut, Lieutenant Colonel Yang Liwei, in mid-October 2003, serve as a great symbol of rising Chinese power, especially to the Chinese youth.

However, Beijing's preservation-driven conservative, reactive, and risk-averse foreign policy, sold to the Chinese people under the cover of China's weakness and poverty, has increasingly frustrated many Chinese nationalists and even ordinary citizens. Many events, external and internal, have led to a widespread feeling of powerlessness and humiliation. The agitating events are many: the U.S. Navy's search of China's cargo ship *Yinghe* on the high seas; the tragic bombing of the Chinese embassy in Belgrade by American planes; the U.S. spy plane's collision with a Chinese Air Force fighter; China's less-than-transparent dealings with neighbors on territorial settlements and Beijing's rushed concessions made for the consequential WTO membership; Taipei's creeping success in its drive for full independence; and Tokyo's stubborn refusal to offer contrition over its past atrocities against China, just to name a few.

All of these frustrations are officially explained away by Beijing either in terms of "evil" anti-Chinese international forces who want to suppress China or in terms of China's still-lingering weakness and powerlessness. Hence the people are told that China must lie low and bide its time. Basically, Beijing asserts that China lacks adequate power, either because of limitations imposed by its still-developing economy or because of political decisions that are deliberately putting every penny into nonmilitary projects to boost the economy. Consequently, China's international capabilities have shown a fairly limited growth, especially in the areas of military capability. Starting in the mid-1980s, the CCP leadership decided to hold military spending to a minimum to concentrate on economic development. China's military budget has remained fairly small and has grown at a speed significantly slower than that of the Chinese economy. As a result, recent studies have concluded that China's military power is falling increasingly behind that of the West. David Shambaugh argues that China's much-watched military modernization effort can hardly close the widening gap in military technology and capability between the PLA (People's Liberation Army) and Western militaries, perhaps with the exception of nuclear-capable land- and sea-based ballistic missiles.[46]

Many Chinese analysts themselves are now increasingly candid about the inadequacy of Chinese military capabilities. While the PLA may be capable of safeguarding the PRC's political system and the stability of the CCP regime against foreseeable domestic threats, it is clearly underequipped and poorly trained to carry out other missions that may be crucial to China's core national interest. The PLA obviously has little capability to unify the motherland by directly invading Taiwan. Beijing's minimal deterrence against Taiwan's push for independence, based on its ability to inflict mass destruction on the island with its land-based missiles, is likely to be costly and uncertain in a real showdown. Beijing clearly lacks the means to compel or control Taipei's actions or to influence the events in China's immediate neighborhood. Furthermore, the PLA's navy and air force can hardly offer any bluewater protection to the huge and indispensable Chinese shipping industry, leaving China's increasing dependence on imported oil from the Middle East in the hands of the U.S. Navy or pirates. The PLA is incapable of using force to solve the ongoing disputes over the South China Sea islets. A possible collision course between Pyongyang and Washington over the North Korean nuclear issue may force Beijing to fight the U.S. forces in a second Korean War, with a much slimmer chance for another stalemate.

China's military inadequacy, and its resultant sense of powerlessness and lack of international prestige, has been felt quite acutely in recent years. From the first Gulf War, in the early 1990s, to the second Gulf War, in 2003, the demonstration of modern weaponry by the United States in Iraq has highlighted the gap between the PLA and its American counterpart with a frightening and depressing clarity.[47] While the PLA commentators wishfully talk on Chinese television about an Iraqi "people's war" against U.S. forces, Beijing cannot help but acknowledge that the military power of the United States and its allies is a generation ahead of that of the Chinese. Despite an overwhelming desire to avoid direct confrontation with the lone superpower, some Chinese have nonetheless predicted a clash between the United States and China in the future over primarily the Taiwan issue. To foresee an "inevitable collision course" between China and the United States, while clearly appreciating the lack of capability to deal with American supremacy, must be a painful experience that adds great impetus to the drive for more Chinese power, especially military power. Some Chinese analysts have wished, "Had we had a strong enough fleet to appear in the Taiwan Strait first, who would have dared to try to interfere with Chinese domestic politics with force?"[48]

Consequently, increasingly many in the PRC are now calling for the quiet but steady building up and exercising of China's national power, especially in terms of military forces (space, missile, and blue-water naval capabilities in particular), to safeguard its political system and national sovereignty, fulfill its historical mission, protect its interests, seek the appropriate Chinese "sphere of influence," earn equality for the Chinese people in the world, and regain China's rightful great power status and influence.[49] This strong desire is based on a combination of an indoctrinated sense of national insecurity under the CCP's monopoly of the media and education, a genuine rise of national pride and of aspirations powered by China's economic growth, and the frustration and humiliation caused by China's conservative and unassertive foreign policy. Some Chinese economists have started to apply what they learned from the United States and have argued for the "economic benefits" of a larger and more powerful military.

PLA analysts now openly write that China "must increase" its military spending and keep its military spending growing at the same pace as the economy.[50] Leading Chinese economists also argue for a "massive increase of military spending," by as much as 50 percent, in the near future as key to a new grand strategy to make China a world-class power by the mid-twenty-first century.[51] Senior PLA officers interviewed in the spring of 2003 repeatedly asserted that, due to the widening gap between them and Western military powers, they will have to develop a few "killer-weapon" (*sha-shou-jian*) systems to provide some minimal counterbalance to the overwhelming military power of the United States and its allies. Professional military officers and soldiers are also building up pressure for an "appropriate" budget. With a fairly complete industrial system, reasonably sophisticated technology, millions of soldiers, and a booming economy, the PLA indeed could indulge a militarization to make the alleged "weapons of mass destruction" in the so-called axis of evil (Iraq, Iran, and North Korea) look like nothing. A fully mobilized military–industry complex in China would likely render futile any American effort for absolute security.

Beyond military power and other tangible pursuits of influence and prestige, a rather broad-based nationalist sentiment longing for a greater China or a greater PRC is also on the rise. The Chinese are eagerly seeking stature, acceptance, honor, and respect everywhere on the world stage. Serious scholars have openly argued for a more assertive and more demanding Chinese foreign policy.[52] The strong interest of Chinese readers has sustained the publication of hundreds of books filled with nationalistic rhetoric and even xenophobic writings. Some, like the popular reading cleverly titled *China's Grand Strategy*, even outlined the future of China's destined "re-integration of Asia" and "new leadership" of the world in the next fifteen to thirty years.[53]

Sounding like a realist strategist in the 1980s, Deng Xiaoping prescribed the following for the PRC:

> How much of a role we can play in international affairs depends on how much achievement of our economic construction. If our country develops and becames

more prosperous, we will play a larger role in international affairs. Our current role in international affairs is not small; but if our material basis and material capabilities are enhanced, [our] role will be even larger.[54]

More active Chinese participation in the management of international affairs and a more evenly constructed multipolar world seem to be highly appealing to Beijing. Many PRC analysts want to be first given a "great power" (*daguo*) responsibility in the Asian–Pacific region to ensure a "just and rational" new security order in the region. A quadrangular arrangement among the United States, Japan, China, and Russia should replace the unfavorable bilateral United States–Japan alliance. China can then "rightfully" play its role of "balancer" to "share" the major powers' responsibility for the region's security.[55] Beyond that, China could take advantage of the differences between the United States and its allies in Europe with the so-called strategy of "utilizing the West–West conflicts" by forging more ties between the "rising Asia" and the European Union. American–European–Asian tripolarity may thus replace American–European–Japanese dominance, and a five-power structure (United States, Russia, China, Japan, and European Union) may replace the current "one superpower plus multiple major powers" situation.[56] One analyst put the economic reasons for more Chinese power very bluntly:

China's sustained development in the future cannot be sufficiently supported by [its] domestic resources: we must have the right to share the world's resources and use them to support China's development.[57]

Fortunately for China's potential rivals, the rising nationalist aspirations for more Chinese power and influence is still under the conscientious control of the CCP. Ironically perhaps, the very CCP regime that is criticized and pressured by the West to change may actually do a better job in controlling the potentially dangerous nationalist pursuit of power with the modest goal of just seeking "appropriate" international status and acceptance. In a more open, richer, and confident China, the popular aspirations for power may inevitably push Beijing to demand more influence and presence and seek more gains in the international community than what it is demanding and seeking at present. At the least, any government in Beijing must address the explosive issue of Taiwan. A noncommunist Chinese government is by no means more likely to compromise on the issues of Tibet or the South China Sea islets. On the contrary, a "democratic" regime in Beijing, free of the debilitating concerns for its own survival but more likely to be driven by popular emotions, could make the rising Chinese power a much more assertive and even aggressive force, at least during the unstable period of fast ascendance to the ranks of world-class power. A democratizing China with many, and perhaps justifiable, strategic demands may actually be much more likely to become a systemic challenger.[58]

CONCLUSION: CHINA'S INCENTIVE STRUCTURE

In the early twenty-first century, Beijing's incentive structure has a three-*P* triangular shape (figure 2.1). Together, these three leading objectives motivate the formulation and implementation of China's foreign policy.

The three motives are not equal. First and foremost is Beijing's political preservation, which often overarches the interest of economic prosperity and national power. The three closely entangle and overlap. Some of the major foreign policy issues are mainly linked to one of the motives whereas others may fall into one area or into the overlapping areas of two or three. Those issues located in the overlapped areas tend to be some of the most essential issues in China's foreign policy. Currently, there are two examples of such key issues: the issue of Taiwan and the multifaceted relationship with the United States. The Taiwan issue directly affects the CCP's political preservation, China's economic prosperity, and its national power and prestige. For Beijing, there is indeed very little room for flexibility on the Taiwan issue. Concerning the future of Taiwan, one detects very little differences in attitudes among the Chinese élite, officials, youth, street people, and even political exiles.

The United States is the other external factor that has a deep and extensive impact on all three Chinese objectives. The Taiwan issue has been the key

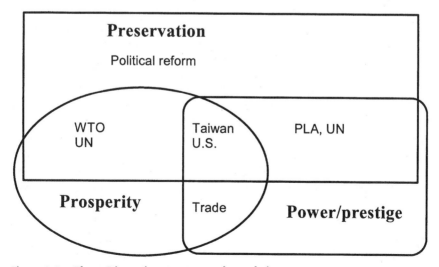

Figure 2.1. Three-*P* incentive structure and sample issues

problem between the United States and China as "the most important and most sensitive core issue of the Sino-American relationship."[59] The United States is the leading external player that can realistically undermine or accept, and hence legitimize, Beijing's political system. The United States is clearly indispensable to China's pursuit of prosperity. Furthermore, the world-dominating United States is likely to continue to reign for a long time. A senior "American hand" in Chinese government wrote in 2002 that "even if the U.S. economy and the Chinese economy maintain their 3 percent and 8 percent growth rates respectively, it will take 46 more years for China's GDP to reach the size of that of America's."[60] A Chinese scholar estimated that China's GDP, about 10.9 percent of the U.S. GDP in 2000, will only increase to about 18.6 percent of the U.S. GDP by 2015.[61] As a result of the disparity of power, multifaceted differences, and conflicts of interest, the United States is viewed as "influencing China's security everywhere. In the foreseeable future, the United States is the largest external factor affecting China's national reunification and national security."[62]

Fortunately, the current de facto antiterrorism alliance has offered the CCP leadership a breathing room. One official assessment indicates that although the United States has not changed its policy of concurrently engaging and containing China after September 11,

> right now, the tip of the U.S. spear is not fully pointed at China. This brings a rare opportunity for us to concentrate on economic construction and create a beneficial international environment. We must seize upon this rare opportunity after the ten years since the end of the Cold War. [We] should not stand out diplomatically so as to avoid drawing fire to ourselves; instead, [we] should concentrate on doing a good job internally, speeding up economic construction, and accelerating development to strive for a great elevation of China's comprehensive national power in the first ten to twenty years of the new century.[63]

The three *P* motives are different goals, and they may conflict with each other. How many differences and conflicts evolve and what kind of impact they may have on China's foreign policy naturally requires more issue-specific studies. However, it appears that while most Chinese would agree that China's national interest, reputation, and economic gains are of utmost importance to them, it is the CCP's goal of political preservation that may ultimately carry the day in the making and implementation of Chinese foreign policy. For that top concern, Beijing has shown a willingness to make compromises. Recent examples include Beijing's less-than-transparent moves in which a much poorer PRC "supported" Hong Kong financially after 1997, thereby allowing Taiwan to carry on its discriminatory trade policies against the mainland. China's voting record in the UN Security Council has been a show of caution and risk avoidance, especially on issues where Beijing disagrees with Washington. Reputation, money, and power are great pursuits that excite Beijing immensely, as they do elsewhere; but when the CCP's political preservation—code-named *sociopolitical stability*—is at stake, all bets are off.

With "a system in which an élite alliance rules and the public has been deprived of almost all political rights," observed one Chinese scholar in 2002, "the room for (political) rationality [in China] is very limited. Political corruption, crony capitalism, serious inequality and poverty, and major economic risks are inevitable consequences of such a system. . . . Injustice, especially corruption, inequality and poverty are the basic causes for instability. The triggers for a national crisis could be a severe economic recession, financial crisis, conflicts across the Taiwan Strait, the sudden death or grave ill of the leaders, and religious suppression."[64] Political preservation may be the sanctioned top concern, but it is also clear that bad handling of the pursuits of prosperity and power would be detrimental to the CCP, too. This great balancing act requires tremendous skill, energy, and luck; and it powerfully constrains the rising China.

As a government-reform measure, starting in early 2002, Beijing requires every new PRC civil servant and official to take the following oath on the first day of the job:

> I pledge to resolutely support the leadership of the Chinese Communist Party and be loyal to the Constitution, the government, and the people; to govern by the law, strictly obey disciplines, and keep secrets; to love my job and respect my duty, be honest and keep my word, and be free from corruption; to serve the people with heart and soul and to struggle for the prosperity and empowerment of the motherland![65]

Few other official statements convey more concisely and vividly the triangular incentive structure that is motivating Beijing in its current policy making, at home and abroad: the CCP's political preservation, China's economic prosperity, and more Chinese power and prestige.

NOTES

A different version of this chapter will be published as "Preservation, Prosperity and Power: The Motives behind the Chinese Foreign Policy," *Journal of Contemporary China* (forthcoming). The author thanks Tai Ling-Juan of the Renmin University of China for research assistance and Yvonne Y. Wang for editorial assistance. Yong Deng of the U.S. Naval Academy and the anonymous reviewer offered very helpful comments.

1. Jiang Zemin, political report to the Sixteenth CCP National Congress, Beijing, November 2002.

2. This assessment was first established by the Fourteenth CCP National Congress in 1992. For an analysis of Beijing's general assessment of its security environment, see Yong Deng and Fei-Ling Wang, eds., *In the Eyes of the Dragon: China Views the World* (Boulder, Colo.: Rowman & Littlefield, 1999). For the latest Chinese views of international relations, see Li Shengming and Wang Yizhou, eds., *2003 Nian quanqiu zhengzhi yu anquan baogao* [2003 Yellow Book of International Politics and Security] (Beijing: Shehui Kexue Wenxian Press, 2003), especially 1–15, 84–105.

3. Hu Angang, *Zhongguo xiayibu* [The Next Step of China] (Chengdu, China: Sichuan Renmin Press, 1996), 1, 20–22, 221.

4. Some have argued that China is facing a "coming collapse," as its internal problems will derail its economic development. For example, see Gordon Chang, *Coming Collapse of China* (New York: Random House, 2001). So far, however, this view has been a dissenting, fringe voice.

5. Author's interviews in Beijing and Shanghai, 2001–2003.

6. Liu Jiang, "Shixi Zhongmei jianshixin zhanlue huoban guanxi" [Preliminary analysis of the Sino-American strategic partnership relations], *Shijie xinshi yanjou* [Studies of World's Situations] (Beijing), no. 47 (1997): 2; "Zhongmei guanxi de xianzhuan he fazhan qushi" [The state and prospects of Sino-American relations], *Shijia xinshi yanjou* [Studies of World's Situations] (Beijing), no. 26 (1997): 3.

7. For a trace of the tumultuous alteration in China's worldview since the nineteenth century, see Wang Hui, "Diguo de haiyang shiye jiqi zai haiyang shidai de zhuanbian" [Imperial worldviews and its changes in the sea era], in *Zhongguo shehui kexue pinglun* [Chinese Social Science Review] (Beijing) 1, no. 2 (2002): 402–35.

8. Fei-Ling Wang, "To Incorporate China: A New Policy for a New Era," *Washington Quarterly*, 21, no. 1 (Winter 1998): 67–81. Also, Yong Deng and Fei-Ling Wang, *In the Eyes of the Dragon*, 21–45.

9. Zhang Tuosheng, ed., *Huanqio tongci liangre: Yidai lingxoumen de guoji zhanlue sixiang* [Same to the Whole Globe: The International Strategic Thoughts of a Generation of Leaders] (Beijing: Zhongyang Wenxian Press, 1993), 312.

10. Wen Jieming et al., eds., *Yu zongshuji tanxin* [Chat with the General Secretary] (Beijing: Zhongguo Shihui Kexue Press, 1997), 70, 232–33.

11. Shi Yinhong and Song Deji, "21 shiji qianqi zhongguo guoji taidu, waijiao zhixue he genben zhanlue sikao" [China's international attitude, diplomatic philosophy, and basic strategic thingking in the first part of the 21st century], *Zhanlue yu guanli* [Strategy and Management] (Beijing), no. 1 (2001): 10–11.

12. Qing Wenhui and Sun Hui, "Hou lengzhan shidai de zhongguo guojia anquan" [China's National Security in the Post–Cold War Era], *Zhanlue yu guanli* [Strategy and Management] (Beijing), no. 1 (2001): 3–9.

13. Ruan Zongze, "Dui 21 shiji zhongmeio xin sanjiao guanxi de jidian kanfa" [A few views on the new Sino-American–Russian triangular relationship in the 21st century], *Guoji wenti yanjiu* [Studies of International Affairs] (Beijing), no. 5 (2001): 17.

14. Author's interviews in Beijing and Shanghai, 2003. Su Ge, "Lun zhongmeie guanxi" [On the Sino-U.S.–Russian relationship], *Guoji wenti yanjiu* [International Affairs] (Beijing), no. 4 (2002).

15. "Qinghua-shizhi luntan: Zhongguo waijiao zouxiang chengshou" [Qinghhua-shizhi forum: Chinese diplomacy matures], *Shijie zhishi* [World Affairs] (Beijing), no. 3 (2003): 30–35.

16. Zhongguo Tongxun News Agency, "PRC: A Review of Developments in Sino-U.S. Relations," November 18, 1996, Foreign Broadcast Information Service–China (FBIS-CHI), FBIS-CHI-96-224. Also, in Xinhua News Agency, "China: Qian Qichen Discusses World and Foreign Affairs," December 30, 1996, FBIS-CHI-96-251. Wang Jisi, "Ezhi haishi jiaowang?" [Containment or engagement?], *Guoji wenti yanjiu* [International Affairs] (Beijing), no. 1 (1996): 6. A slightly different version of this article appeared in the *Beijing Review*, no. 43 (October 21–27, 1996): 6–9. "Qinghua-shizhi luntan: Zhongguo waijiao zouxiang chengshou" [Qinghhua-shizhi forum: Chinese diplomacy matures], 33.

17. Hu Jintao's speech at the summit meeting of the Shanghai Cooperation Organization, Moscow, May 30, 2003.

18. "Qinghua-shizhi luntan: zhongguo waijiao zouxiang chengshou" [Qinghhua-shizhi forum: Chinese diplomacy matures], 34.

19. Liu Jianfei, "Renqing fankong yu fanba de guanxi" [Understanding the relationship between anti-terrorism and anti-hegeminism], *Liaowang zhoukan* [Outlook Weekly] (Beijing), no. 8 (February 24, 2003): 54–56.

20. Tang Yongsheng, "Zonghe anquan yu zongti zhanlue" [Comprehensive security and grand strategy], *Shijie Zhishi* [World Affairs] (Beijing), no. 20 (October 16, 1996): 16–17.

21. Foreign media quickly started to criticize China's lack of action and transparency only a couple of days after the Hong Kong outbreak of SARS caught the attention of the world health community. Dan Mangan, "China's Fatal Secret," *New York Post*, March 17, 2003. Some leading foreign media soon started to suggest "quarantine China" as a way to punish Beijing for its action, or lack of action, regarding SARS. "Quarantine China," editorials in *Asian Wall Street Journal* (Hong Kong) and *Wall Street Journal* (New York), March 31, 2003. Chinese web-based media also carried numerous reports in April–May 2003. Finally, Chinese government openly acknowledged and even semidirectly apologized by April 20, 2003. *Xinhua Daily Telegraph*, Beijing, April 21, 2003.

22. All of China's media suddenly started to carry voluminous articles on the anti-SARS campaign after April 20, 2003. Major cities such as Beijing quickly had a chaotic panic, which was obviously not justified by either the contagiousness or the fatality of the epidemic. A political power struggle broke out; financial loses were estimated to be in the billions; and hundreds of millions of people were shaken and scared. The true impact of Beijing's inaction and of the sudden panicky action on SARS is clearly significant, although its full scope still remains to be seen.

23. For more on the Chinese reaction to the 2003 SARS epidemic, see Fei-Ling Wang, ed., *Chinese Law and Government*, special issues on SARS, 36, no. 4 (July–August 2003); 36, no. 6 (November–December 2003); 37, no. 1 (January–February 2004).

24. For the retired military doctor and his revelation of the SARS epidemic in Beijing, see *Time*, April 9, 2003.

25. Lou Yaoliang, *Diyuan zhengzhi yu zhongguo guofang zhanlue* [Geopolitics and China's national defense strategy] (Tianjin, China: Tianjin Remin Press, 2002), 190–91.

26. Author's interview with a top official at the PRC Ministry of Foreign Affairs, Beijing, March 2003.

27. To openly discuss the "fundamental relationship" between political stability and democratization in the PRC is no longer taboo. Recent examples include Wu Kechang, "Zhengzhi fazhan yu zhengzhi wending" [Political development and political stability], *Qiusuo* [Explore] (Changchun, China), no. 2 (2002); Wang Jianguo "Zhongguo zhaunxing shiqi zhengzhi minzhuhua yu zhengzhi wending de guanxi" [The relationship between political democratization and political stability in China's transitional period], *Shehui zhuyi yanjiu* [Studies of socialism] (Wuhan, China), no. 3 (2002).

28. Speech at the memorial meeting of the CCP's eightieth anniversary, Beijing, July 1, 2001. Jiang Zemin, *Lun sange daibiao* [On "Three Represents"] (Beijing: Zhongyang Wenxian Press, 2001). Three represents refer to the revisionist mission statement that the CCP "should represent the development requirements of China's advanced social productive forces, the progressive course of China's advanced culture, and the fundamental interests of the overwhelming majority of the Chinese people." *Communiqué of the 6th Plenum of the 15th CCP Central Committee*, Xinhua, Beijing, September 26, 2001.

29. One official survey in 2003 reported that as many as 29.9 percent of all private business owners in the PRC (up from 13.1 percent in 1993) were CCP members. *Beijing qingnian bao* [Beijing youth daily] (Beijing), November 15, 2003, A7. Other than trying to incorporate the business élites ever since the mid-1980s, the CCP has recruited heavily among educated youth. As a result, the majority of graduate students, many undergraduate students, as well as most of college faculty in China's top universities are now often CCP members. Author's interviews in China, 2001–2003.

30. Kang Xiaoguang, "Weilai 3–5 nian zhongguo dalu zhengzhi wendingxing fengxi" [Analysis of the political stability issue in Chinese Mainland in the next 3–5 years], *Zhanlue yu guanli* [Strategy and management] (Beijing), no. 3, (2003): 10.

31. In May 2003, amidst China's war on SARS, Beijing announced a submarine disaster with unprecedented speed and candidness. Xinhua and the China Central Television reports and photographs, May 25, 2003.

32. For example, see the substantial collection of such articles and essays at Chinese websites such as www.univillage.org/citizen/aduo.htm and www.wiapp.org/iappnew .html. Also see the articles on this subject in *Zhanlue yu guanli* [Strategy and Management] (Beijing), no. 6 (2002).

33. Xu Xianglin, "Yi zhengzhi wending wei jichu de zhongguo jianjin zhengzhi gaige" [China's gradual political reform based on political stability], *Zhanlue yu guanli* [Strategy and management] (Beijing), no. 5 (2000).

34. For a very concise summary of the *hukou* reforms, by a leading Chinese expert on the subject, see Wang Taiyuan, "Hukou qianyi zhidu de guoqu, xianzai he weilai"

[The past, present, and future of the *hukou* migration system], at www.ccrs.org.cn/big/ hkqyzddgqx.htm, accessed June 5, 2003.

35. China Central Television News, February 19, 2003.

36. Hu Jintao, "Xianfa wei jianshe xiaokang shehui tigong fali baozhang" [The Constitution provides the legal protection for the construction of *xiaokang* society], public speech in Beijing, February 4, 2003.

37. Fang Ning, "Zhiduhua chuangxin zhudao zhongguo zhengzhi dongxiang" [Institutional innovations leads China's political trends], *Zhonghua gongshang shibao* [Chinese Industrial and Commerce Times] (Beijing), January 9, 2003.

38. Li Junru (vice president of the CCP Central Party School), "Zhengque lijie he jianchi dang de jiajixing" [Correctly understand and uphold the party's class nature], in Lin Rong's *Xinshiji de sikao* [Thinking in the New Century], vol. 1 (Beijing: Central Party School Press, 2002), 163–72.

39. Estimates of China's economic growth vary, but most agree that the Chinese economy grows at an average of above 8 percent annually. Nicholas R. Lardy, *Integrating China into the Global Economy* (Washington, D.C.: Brookings, 2002), 11–13. *Financial Times* (October 13, 2003, 6) reports that China's GDP growth is perhaps underreported and could have been as high as 11 percent in 2003, despite the SARS epidemic.

40. Kang Xiaoguang, "Weilai 3–5 nian zhongguo dalu zhengzhi wendingxing fengxi" [Analysis of the political stability issue in Chinese Mainland in the next 3–5 years], *Zhanlue yu guanli* [Strategy and management] (Beijing), no. 3 (2003): 1–2.

41. Lin Rong, *Xinshiji de sikao* [Thinking in the New Century], vol. 1 (Beijing: Central Party School Press, 2002), 238.

42. Qiu Yuanping, "Mianxiang shijie de xuanyan" [Declaration to the world], *Qiushi* (Beijing), no. 3 (2003): 27–28.

43. The Chinese chief negotiator Long Yongtu recalled in 2003 how the top CCP leadership politically decided that they "must join the WTO" in late 1999. Cheng Yehui, "Nanwang shimao tanpan de zuihou guankou" [Can't forget the last hurdle of WTO negotiations], *Zhongguo jingji shibao* [Chinese economic times] (Beijing), September 19, 2003.

44. Zhang Wenmu, "Quanqiuhua jincheng zhong de zhongguo guojia liye" [China's national interest in the process of globalization], *Zhanlue yu guanli* [Strategy and Management] (Beijing), no. 1 (2002): 55–57.

45. Project Group of the Chinese Science Academy, *2003 Zhongguo ke chixu fazhan zhanlue baogao* [Report on China's Sustainable Development Strategy, 2003] (Beijing: Kexue Press, 2003), 115–23.

46. David Shambaugh, *Modernizing China's Military: Progress, Problems, and Prospects* (Berkeley: University of California Press, 2003), 10, 330–32.

47. Author's interviews with PLA officers in Beijing and Shanghai, 2002–2003.

48. Wen Jieming et al., eds., *Yu zongshuji tanxin* [Chat with the General Secretary] (Beijing: Zhongguo Shihui Kexue Press, 1997), 232–38.

49. Tang Shiping "Zailun zhongguo de da zhanlue" [Another treatise on China's grand strategy], *Zhanlue yu guanli* [Strategy and Management] (Beijing), no. 4 (2001): 29–37. Zhang Wenmu, "Quanqiuhua jincheng zhong de zhongguo guojia

liye" [China's national interest in the process of globalization], *Zhanlue yu guanli* [Strategy and Management] (Beijing), no. 1 (2002): 52–64.

50. Lou Yaoliang, *Diyuan zhengzhi yu zhongguo guofang zhanlue* [Geopolitics and China's National Defense Strategy] (Tianjin: Tianjin Remin Press, 2002), 255.

51. Hu Angang and Meng Honghua, "Zhongmeirieying youxing zhanlue ziyuan bijiao" [A comparison of tangible strategic resources among China, the U.S., Japan, Russia, and India], *Zhanlue yu guanli* [Strategy and Management] (Beijing), no. 2 (2002): 26–41.

52. Luo Weilong, "Zhongguoren yao shuo bu" [Chinese want to say no], *Taipingyang Xuebao* [Pacific Journal] (Beijing), no. 2 (1995).

53. Cai Xianwei, *Zhongguo da zhanlue: lingdao shijie de lantu* [China's Grand Strategy: A Blueprint for Leading the World] (Haikou, China: Hainan Press, 1996). For a critical review of this book, see John W. Garver, "China as Number One," *China Journal*, 1998.

54. Deng Xiaoping, *Deng Xiaoping Wenxuan* (1975–1982) [Selected Works of Deng Xiaoping] (Beijing: Renmin Press, 1986), 204.

55. Zhao Gancheng, "Yatai diqu xinzhixu yu zhongguo de zeren" [The new order in Asia-Pacific and the responsibility of China], *Guoji Wenti Luntan* [Forum on International Issues] (Beijing), no. 2 (1996): 49–51. Also see Shi Yongming, "Yatai anquan huanjing yu diqu duobian zhuyi" [Security environment in Asia-Pacific and regional multilateralism], *Guoji wenti yanjiu* [International Affairs] (Beijing), no. 1 (1996): 41–47.

56. For an extensive discussion on those ideas by Chinese scholars and analysts, see Xiao Ding, "Ya o hezuo yu fazhan wenti yantaohui jiyao" [Summary of the Symposium on Asian-European cooperation and development]," *Xiandai guoji guanxi* [Contemporary international relations] (Beijing) no. 7 (1996): 42–53.

57. Zhang Wenmu, "Quanqiuhua jincheng zhong de zhongguo guojia liye" [China's national interest in the process of globalization], *Zhanlue yu guanli* [Strategy and management] (Beijing) no. 1 (2002): 63.

58. For an analysis on the relationship between war proneness and political democratization, see Edward D. Mansfield and Jack Snyder, "Democratization and the Danger of War," *International Security* 20, no. 1 (Summer 1995).

59. During Hu Jintao's first formal meeting with George W. Bush in May 2003 and Wen Jiabao's visit to Washington in late 2003, the Taiwan issue was once again the major issue that required President Bush to reaffirm Washington's "one China" policy.

60. Wang Jisi, "Gailun zhongmeiri sanbian guanxi" [On the triangular relationship among China, the U.S. and Japan], in Lin Rong's *Xinshiji de sikao* [Thinking in the New Century], vol. 1 (Beijing: Central Party School Press, 2002), 3.

61. Tang Shiping, "2010–2015 nian de zhongguo zhoubian angquan huangjin" [China's neighboring security environment in 2010–2015], *Zhanlue yu guanli* [Strategy and management] (Beijing) no. 5 (2002): 40.

62. Zhu Tingchang et al., eds., *Zhongguo zhoubian anquan huanjin yu anquan zhanlue* [China's security environment and strategy in the neighboring areas] (Beijing: Shishi Press, 2002), 5.

63. He Dalong, "9.11 hou guoji xingshi d zhongda bianhua" [Major changes in international situations after 9/11], *Shishi ziliao shouce* (Beijing), no. 4 (October 20, 2002): 12, 15.

64. Kang Xiaoguang, "Weilai 3–5 nian zhongguo dalu zhengzhi wendingxing fengxi" [Analysis of the political stability issue in Chinese Mainland in the next 3–5 years], *Zhanlue yu guanli* [Strategy and management] (Beijing) no. 5 (2002): 15.

65. Decree of the PRC Ministry of Personnel, January 2002, *Shishi ziliao shouce* (Beijing), no. 4 (October 20, 2002): 67.

3

Better Than Power: "International Status" in Chinese Foreign Policy

Yong Deng

In the mainstream realist theory of international relations, power—understood primarily as material capabilities and their use for coercive purposes, including force—is the asset that makes the state's survival and other goals possible under the uncertainty and self-help anarchy of international relations. The state logically would want to maximize its own power while attempting to undermine other states' relative power. According to realism, that is the overriding motivation of the state in international relations. John Mearsheimer puts it succinctly, "What money is to economics, power is to international relations."[1] But in Chinese foreign policy discourse, "international status" seems to be the most desirable value, particularly since the mid-1990s. How does China conceptualize international status? What is the politics of status quest in Chinese foreign policy? Does China's status struggle differ from traditional power politics? This chapter seeks to address these questions.

Just as China's self-identity in world politics has undergone radical changes,[2] so too has its international status and status conception. The end of the Cold War brought about a peculiar status crisis never experienced in Chinese foreign relations. The result is a new national consciousness and reassessment of international status. What distinguishes China's present status conception is its emphasis on both material power and international legitimacy. To be sure, China is determined to strengthen its comprehensive power, including military capabilities, and it continues to resort to coercive measures and more traditional measures of power politics to defend its core interests and enhance influence abroad; but it also attempts to improve its social standing in the international community through cooperative and responsible means.

While recognizing the centrality of power, Chinese political élite understand the imperative of cultivating an image of a responsible player. The dualistic nature of China's status quest creates complex dynamics of its great power ambitions that require balancing the power logic with the need for international identification. The status gap has firmed up Beijing's determination to seek international legitimacy as a nonthreatening, rising power. Yet frustrations from perceived discriminatory denial of its rightful place at the great power table fuels discontent with the international hierarchy. China's reconfigured status conception underscores the challenge and the possibility of turning its great power aspiration into deepening commitment to a peacefully contested mode of status quest.

In Chinese writings and in English-language literature, there is significant confusion surrounding China's status motivations. China's nagging status concern is palpable, but the belief in its steady enhancement is beyond question. For the Chinese, status seems to be the magical solution to China's foreign policy problems—and China is entitled to a great power status, and such a pursuit should threaten no one. But for some observers outside China, Beijing's status drive is but the latest episode of the traditional zero-sum great-power game, in which hostile powers battle over higher position in the international pecking order—often through violent means. It thus represents evidence of the threat China poses to other great powers and the very foundation of the existing international arrangement. To clear away the confusion, this chapter starts with a discussion of precisely what is lacking in China's international status that worries the contemporary Chinese élite. The next section traces the historical evolution of China's status change, focusing on its reconfigured conception and assessment after the Cold War. The chapter then delineates and explores some broad patterns of China's policy calculations and manifestations stemming from its status concern. The brief conclusion summarizes the findings and briefly draws their policy implications.

BETTER THAN POWER: CHINA'S STATUS CONCERN
IN THE POST–COLD WAR WORLD

The prominence of Chinese concern about its "international status" is striking. A national survey on how the Chinese youth view the 1978–1998 reform era shows that 67 percent of the over twenty-five thousand respondents ranked China's international status among their three greatest concerns above economic development.[3] Public interest mirrors the top leadership's positions. Worried about the adverse effect of what Deng Xiaoping perceived as denigration of China's international status on Sino-American relations, Deng warned in 1981 that "those who misjudge China's status in world politics would at least be unable to adopt a proper international strategy."[4] For him, correct assessment of China's international status determines not only how other countries deal with China but also how China relates to the outside world. Even though his notion of status differs from contemporary leadership's conception, Deng's remarks do reflect the pivotal importance he and his successors attach to "international status."

Chinese writings on Beijing's foreign relations after the Cold War show a particularly heightened sensitivity to status. There is a nagging discontent with China's current status and a strong expectation of China's continued rise. Chinese analysts tend to assess status not just in terms of China's ranking in the power hierarchy but also in its ability to protect its interests and project influence in the international arena.[5] A key measure is whether China's great power aspiration is internationally accepted as legitimate and whether its core interests are respected by other great powers and neighboring states. Indeed, for Chinese analysts, status advancement is always associated with greater international support for its stand on Taiwan and with lesser fear of China threat. For them, what is lacking in China's international status lies not only in traditional power measures but also in its outlier social standing vis-à-vis the great power group circled around the United States. Compared to the power factor, the problem of social denigration may be more decisive and yet more difficult to overcome.

The power factor clearly plays a critical role in China's status conception, which is to be expected, as material power is an essential determinant of international status for any country, China included. As Samuel Crafton observed, "Even after you give a squirrel a certificate which says he is quite as big as any elephant, he is still going to be smaller, and all the squirrels will know it and all the elephants will know it."[6] But China's emphasis is on increasing "comprehensive national power" (*zhonghe guoli*). The Chinese definitions of the term have been vastly expansive to include national cohesion and government effectiveness or even history and culture—even though it is primarily about China's economic, technological, and military strengths.[7] More important, the Chinese leadership is keenly aware that China must secure a favorable international environment essential for its "national rejuvenation." Such would ultimately entail much reduced mistrust and uncertainties in the United States and the international community at large over China's international futures.

The Chinese public and élite are acutely aware of China's material weakness. After all, it was the painful realization of China's economic backwardness and the embrace of the developmental idea of "opening up to the outside world" that prompted the pragmatic turn in post-Mao Chinese foreign policy.

The public awareness of China's relative backwardness is evident in a nationwide survey by the popular newspaper *China Youth Daily* in 1995 on the worldviews of its young readers. When asked about their three-dimensional appraisals of China's standing in the world, the respondents gave the highest mark to China's political status, ranked the military status in the middle, and considered economic status as significantly lagging behind. But they were optimistic about the all-round advancement in the decades to come.[8]

Government-affiliated researchers have attempted more scientific measures to gauge China's national power in a comparative context. Leading think tanks, such as the Academy of Military Science, the Chinese Academy of Social Sciences (CASS), and the China Institute of Contemporary International Relations (CICIR), have all conducted such studies. Their assessments of China's present and projected ranking vary, even though all conclude that China's power is on the rise.[9] A CICIR research team reported in 2002 that China ranked seventh in comprehensive national power, below Japan, Russia, Germany, France, and England, and only constituting a quarter of the U.S. power.[10] This assessment likely fits with the mainstream view, as China's modest ranking helps defuse the "China threat theory."[11]

While realistic about their country's material weakness, Chinese élite are nonetheless optimistic about the steady growth in China's national power. Their optimism is probably well founded given the phenomenal growth rate of the Chinese economy in the past quarter of a century. But the rise of China threat theory in the United States, Japan, India, and elsewhere since the early 1990s underscores that its security and status advancement cannot simply rely on a single-minded pursuit of material power. In fact, growing power could adversely affect its security environment and foreign relations. Worse still, a vicious pattern of interaction could occur between material power and social status, exacting loss to both. Conversely, a virtuous interaction of power growth and legitimization would be mutually reinforcing, thereby steadily advancing China's international status.

China is as yet not fully accepted as a legitimate member of the U.S.-centered great power club, defined by shared in-group collective identity and a strong sense of security community. Reflecting the U.S. assessment of China's ambiguous international status, the strategic report released by the Bush administration in September 2002 states, "We welcome the emergence of a strong, peaceful, and prosperous China. . . . Yet, a quarter century after beginning the process of shedding the worst features of the Communist legacy, China's leaders have not yet made the next series of fundamental choices about the character of their state."[12] Applying the social identity measures, American scholars have assigned China to an outlier status from the peaceful great power group.[13] Dissatisfied with their nation's status, Chinese analysts tend to blame Western discrimination, ideological hostilities, and fear of rising Chinese power.

Beijing's sense of insecurity has been fueled by a heightened sensitivity to its inadequate social standing and by a lingering suspicion from the United States, other great powers, and neighboring states, notwithstanding having accomplished its fastest growth in key aspects of material power. As director of the Institute of International Studies of Tsinghua University, Yan Xuetong argues, "China still has a sense of being isolated, primarily by the United States–led club of Western countries. It's not that China does not want to join certain organizations, but is excluded by them."[14] Similarly, vice chairman of the Foreign Affairs Committee of the Chinese People's Political Consultative Conference (CPPCC), Zhang Yijun observes, "China's troubles stem from the fact that it feels it has already made an enormous effort to participate in the international system and abide by international rules, but it is still subject to discrimination and attacks because its political system and cultural background are different, its normal development is seen as posing a threat, its legitimate rights are not respected, and the most conspicuous problem is that the United States is blocking it from unifying the internationally-recognized Chinese territory of Taiwan."[15]

The global war on terrorism since September 11, 2001, has brought about some changes in great power relations and China's status politics. Most important, the antiterror campaign has in important ways directed the United States' attention away from China as a threat and toward untraditional, transnational, and subnational threats. While encouraged by subsequent improvement of United States–China relations, Beijing is nonetheless skeptical that the United States has embraced China as a strategic partner rather than as a potential rival. The international realignments have opened up opportunities while at the same time creating new challenges for China's great power diplomacy. China's status conundrum persists in the post–September 11 world—and so does its lack of a sustained, benign strategic environment.

A state's social standing and level of identification with other states decidedly shape its foreign relations. And under the U.S-dominated international hierarchy, to be cast inside or outside the link-minded great power group will determine how image is formed, whether malign intentions are attributed, and ultimately to what extent power is viewed as zero-sum. Literature in social psychology has conclusively shown that out-group would be subject to various forms of negative stereotyping, by which its members' character and capability is judged in ways to justify separate, disadvantageous treatment. Creative applications of this insight in international relations theory demonstrate that when dealing with out-group members, states tend to infer malign intentions and become ultrasensitive to relative power gains.[16] To be relegated to an out-group status would fundamentally disadvantage that country in terms of its overall security interests. For these reasons, the status locus becomes the pivotal concern for an aspiring great power such as China.

CHINA'S INTERNATIONAL STATUS: CHANGING CONCEPTUALIZATIONS AND ASSESSMENTS

In Chinese historical discourse, China was at the center of the harmonious premodern East Asian order. The Sinocentric international hierarchy was based less on Chinese coercive power and more on benign Confucian cultural principles. Outside China, this characterization of the *pax sinica* has been subject to intense debate, as scholars argue about the political–cultural, commercial, and military nature of the Chinese regional preeminence.[17] However, there is no doubt that China reigned supreme in East Asia before the mid-nineteenth century, and the Chinese dynastic rulers certainly considered China as possessing the highest material and normative power and enjoying unquestionable superiority in dealing with other societies. For the Chinese official historiography, modern China started with the decline and collapse of the Confucian regional order institutionalized through the tributary system. The Opium War (1839–1842) marked the beginning of the onslaught of Western powers and Japan, which led not only to the immediate collapse of the Chinese empire but also to a century of foreign victimization and humiliation suffered by the Chinese nation. Chinese analysts view the one hundred years as the "nadir" of China's international status.[18]

The official remembrance of China's victimization history as a semicolony has heavily defined Chinese foreign policy since the People's Republic of China (PRC) was established in 1949. Hence it is no surprise that the first and foremost component of Maoist China's definition of international status was independence. The imperative to secure the newly established regime and the drive to promote communist ideology meant that Beijing had to balance traditional power politics with revolutionary impulse in its foreign policy. While domestic radicalism often imperiled China's interests as a state actor in the international arena, the costs also compelled Mao Zedong to rein in his anti-systemic approach to international relations.[19] In fact, even at the most radical phase of its foreign policy, the Maoist PRC government conditioned its support for revolutions abroad with considerations of national interests as an independent state.[20] According to Kenneth Waltz's classical realist work, all states value autonomy under the self-help international anarchy but consider security and survival as the highest value.[21] While Mao had to pursue more conventional diplomacy, he often equated security with self-reliance and independence and even placed his notion of independence above China's national security. His determination not to play second fiddle to the Soviet Union or any other great power drastically worsened China's security during the 1960s. As Iain Johnston observes, "Mao was even willing to behave in ways that *jeopardized* China's security in order to preserve or expand China's autonomy and independence as a major player."[22]

Independence based on a rigid definition of sovereignty continued to be a central concern in the post-Mao Chinese conception of international status. In the early 1980s, Deng Xiaoping and other Chinese leaders were disappointed by the United States' support to Taiwan and by the West's less-than-enthusiastic support to China's economic reforms. They also reassessed the benefits and costs of China's strategic alignment with the United States, factoring in the changing Soviet threat as well. The result was an explicit "independence and autonomy" foreign policy line proclaimed in General Secretary Hu Yaobang's report to the Twelfth Chinese Communist Party (CCP) Congress in 1982.[23] When Deng Xiaoping warned against misjudging China's international status, he was concerned about the danger of the increasingly popular view that exaggerated China's dependence on the United States. For him, the proper understanding of China's international status must entail the realization that China is "not afraid of evil spirits" (*bu xinxie*) and that it "acts according to its own views" (*genju zhiji de jianjie xingshi*).[24]

The international isolation caused by the Tiananmen killings in 1989 and the ensuing collapse of communist regimes in Eastern Europe precipitated an unprecedented crisis in China's foreign relations. China became an international pariah, albeit temporarily. The experience heightened the awareness and spurred a rethinking of China's international status. In the immediate aftermath of the events, many Chinese observers contended that China was being confronted with the worst international environment in the PRC's history. However, less-pessimistic assessment soon began in 1991 and 1992, leading to an official declaration of "diplomatic breakthrough" in 1993. The view about the inevitable rise of multipolarity began to resurface, even gaining important grounds within the Chinese policy community. But the reality of growing U.S. power soon led to the adjusted characterization of the world as one of "one superpower, many great powers" (*yichao duoqiang*). Furthermore, since the mid-1990s, the prevailing Chinese view has been that the United States' unipolarity is fairly stable and is being constantly consolidated.[25]

The United States' preeminence is secured not just because of its vast power supremacy but also because of the lack of traditional balancing by other great powers. The United States' ties with the European Union and Japan are buttressed by a strong sense of security community and by a special bond between advanced democracies separating their mutual relationships from how they individually and collectively treat other major powers. Regarding their respective policies toward China, European powers and Japan may differ with, and have exerted their influence on, the United States. However, Europe and Japan ultimately tend to react to U.S. leadership, and their policy adjustments on Taiwan, human rights, and overall strategy have generally aligned with, rather than undercut, fundamental U.S. objectives.[26] To be sure, one must be careful not to overstate the unity and coherence of the foreign policy outlook of the United States and of other democratic powers, particularly in light of the Franco-German interest in lifting the post-Tiananmen arms embargo on China at variance with the U.S. policy and, more importantly, the transatlantic disputes over the second Iraq War in 2003–2004. There is nonetheless a shared sense of group mentality among the advanced democracies that separate ingroup members from other powers. Certainly from the Chinese perspectives, the democratic great powers' ambiguous treatment of China and possibly Russia indicates a boundary that assigns less-than-advantageous positions to the two "other" powers.

The understanding of world politics in terms of a fairly stable hierarchy has intensified China's concern about its status and has formed the basis for its status assessment after the Cold War. China considers status advancement as pivotal to its national security interests—and status can only be advanced on materialist and sociopolitical fronts. China's national rejuvenation cannot materialize on solely its material power; it must also entail carefully cultivating international confidence over its role in the Asia–Pacific region and within world politics at large.

How a state conceptualizes international status is illustrated by what it values as the most important "status cues." According to prominent sociologists Joseph Berger and Morris Zelditch Jr., "Status cues are indicators, markers, or identifiers which give information about the different statuses and task abilities people possess."[27] China's self-evaluation of the key status cues would provide a window to its conception of international status.

Chinese views after the Cold War have undergone some reconfigurations but have demonstrated significant consistencies. Both popular view and professional analyses have attached great importance to China's permanent membership in the United Nations (UN) Security Council and full membership in the nuclear powers club. That's why the respondents of the *China Youth Daily* survey in 1995 ranked China's political and military status much higher than its economic status. But since the mid-1990s, the significance of the two traditional status markers has diminished, with the seemingly decreased UN role and the failures of the nuclear nonproliferation regime. In particular, the nuclear proliferations in 1998 in South Asia reduced the status value of China's nuclear arsenals.

China's permanent seat in the UN Security Council still confers it a great deal of prestige. China would therefore prefer a central UN role in world politics. Yet neither the NATO war on Yugoslavia in 1999 nor the war on Iraq in 2003 was launched with UN official sanctions. These events have contributed to the steady decline of UN credibility and relevance. The utilities of the UN have been depreciated, but it remains an invaluable and irreplaceable status marker for China. The highlight of China's UN politics was the Millennium Summit of the permanent UN Security Council members, which was proposed by Beijing and held in New York City in September 2000.[28] Beijing will no doubt continue to push for the United Nations' playing a greater role in world politics so to preserve China's prerogative as a permanent member of the UN Security Council. Similarly, as demonstrated by its high profile and constructive role in 2003 and 2004 in finding the diplomatic means to create a nuclear arms–free Korean peninsula, China is more committed than ever before to the control of the weapons of mass destruction (WMD) proliferation, particularly to nuclear nonproliferation.

Besides the United Nations, China has sought to demonstrate its commitment to other international institutions, particularly the World Trade Organization (WTO), the Asia–Pacific Economic Cooperation forum (APEC), and the Shanghai Cooperation Organization (SCO). For Chinese commentators, their country's accession to WTO in November 2001 was clearly a major status booster. Its prominent role as the host of the first post–September 11 APEC summit in Shanghai also indicated China's rising status.[29]

Particularly noteworthy is China's leadership role in SCO's creation and continued growth. The organization evolved from the "Shanghai Five," the annual meeting for leaders of China, Russia, Kazakhstan, Kyrgyzstan, and Tajikistan, which was started in 1996 to enhance border security and confidence building among the member states. The meeting's addition of Uzbekistan, the formation of SCO in Shanghai in June 2001, and the 2003 decision to create a secretariat based in Beijing marked a steady institutionalization and formalization of the cooperative mechanism. SCO takes on special significance as it is "the first international organization named after a Chinese city."[30] For Beijing, it consolidates Sino-Russian cooperation and represents the model of China's new idea of "cooperative security," based on comprehensive, open, and voluntary cooperation that enhances security for all, but threatens none.[31]

Since the mid-1990s, China has attached great importance to cultivating an international image of a responsible cooperative power. The PRC government is under unprecedented pressure in its history, stemming from an international expectation that China must do more constructively to deal with regional and global problems. The challenge to play a confident leadership role in global affairs has led to the questioning of the traditional Chinese worldview. Most notably, one CASS scholar contends that China should move beyond the victim mentality cultivated through the nationalist remembrance of the China's experience of a semicolony under Western imperialism.[32] To fulfill its international responsibilities, argues another prominent scholar, China needs a "normal mentality" with a reconfigured dynamic notion of national interest. The scholar even questions the wisdom of China's 1998 use of veto power to block a UN-sponsored peaceful operation in Macedonia, in retaliation of that country's diplomatic recognition of Taiwan.[33] While it is hard to pinpoint the influence of these emerging ideas, what is clear is that China is under mounting pressure to wrestle with the idea of international responsibility in its foreign policy.

Chinese analysts have explicitly emphasized the factor of great power acceptance in China's status politics. Yan Xuetong forcefully argues that ascension of China's international status will decisively depend on "international acceptance," which is measured by the nature of China's relationships with the United States and other great powers. The key lies in the "compatibility of strategic interests with" the United States. "In case its strategic interest is incongruent with that of the hegemonic power," Yan argues, the rising power's "compatibility of strategic interests with the majority of other great powers [Japan, Russia, and Germany] might somewhat enhance, but rarely change its international acceptance qualitatively."[34] While Yan emphasizes interests compatibility as the measure of acceptance, his discussions show that much of the confrontation or congruence in "interest" is in fact a function of the psychological process of security dilemma and the social–constructive process of "self–other" identification.[35] Other Chinese analysts agree about the vital importance of China's America policy, although they contend that improved ties with Russia, European powers, and Japan might be essential to help strengthen Sino-American relations.[36]

The selection of the landmark diplomatic events by Xinhua depicted in table 3.1 shows that sovereignty and international institutions figured prominently in China's status conception. But its central concern was clearly focused on a relationship with the United States. The UN and APEC were important only insofar as these institutions served as a platform for positive engagement with the United States. Chinese analysts tend to assess China's status fluctuations largely based on the state of Sino-American relations. The period of 1997 to 1998 witnessed the most optimist Chinese evaluations, as the United States and China jointly declared to build a strategic partnership.[37] More sober analyses followed since, as Sino-American relationship returned to its "normal" state of ambivalence, characterized by mutual suspicion and a high degree of uncertainty.

Table 3.1.   Key Markers in China's International Status Advancement (1989–2002)

	Event	Significance
November 1993	President Jiang Zemin's presence at the APEC[a] unofficial summit in Seattle	Jiang had the "first formal meeting" with President Bill Clinton, which marked the end of China's post-Tiananmen diplomatic isolation and a new chapter in Sino-U.S. relations.
July 1, 1997	The reclaim of Chinese sovereignty over Hong Kong	With the return of Macao two years later, this represents "a major step forward in the grand cause of the reunification of the motherland."
September 2000	Millennium Summit of the permanent members of the UN Security Council in New York City	"On the initiative of China, the five permanent members of the UN security Council held their first summit in 55 years."
October 2001	APEC annual meeting in Shanghai	The meeting was hosted by China, held in the aftermath of September 11, and was attended by President George W. Bush.
October 2002	President Jiang's visit to President Bush's Crawford Ranch, in Texas	The meeting was the third between the two leaders in a year. It "served to maintain the sound momentum of high-level strategic dialogues and contacts between China and the United States."

Source: Yang Guoqiang and Qian Tong, "Pushing Forward the Lofty Cause of Peace and Development—Reviewing the Magnificent Path of China's Cross-Century Diplomatic Work" [in Chinese], Xinhua Domestic Service, November 13, 2002, FBIS: CPP20021113000096.
[a] APEC: Asia–Pacific Economic Cooperation

While Chinese analysts differ in their evaluations of the balance between cooperative and conflictual dynamics in the Sino-American relationship, the consensus tends to discern a mixed, "ambiguous" pattern that could conceivably turn more antagonistic or cooperative.[38] The United States–led global antiterror campaign since September 11, 2001, has somewhat reconfigured great power relations in general and Sino-American relations in particular, infusing in them a greater cooperative spirit. The transatlantic division over the war on Iraq has no doubt reduced the collective pressures from the established great powers on China, but mainstream Chinese analysts tend not to overstate the damage to the transatlantic alliance; they believe that the ties among leading democratic powers remain strong. However, they are also concerned about the uncertainties in

United States' unilateral attempt to remold the world and its impact on the Sino-American relationship.

While Chinese observers took particular notice of president George W. Bush's reference to president Jiang Zemin as "the leader of a great nation" at the APEC forum in Shanghai, they doubt that the United States has unambiguously accepted China as a legitimate rising great power. They complain that China's core security interests in Taiwan are not fundamentally respected by the United States. The China threat theory, based on the fear and hostility toward the Chinese power and intentions, still lingers in U.S. policy communities. As the prominent America watcher Zi Zhongyun observes, "During China's transitional period, the delicate state of [Sino-American relations] won't change for a while. In addition, as long as the Taiwan issue remains unresolved, the fundamental suspicion and hedging (*yilü he fangfan*) will not dissipate simply because of the anti-terror campaign."[39]

Since the end of the Cold War, Chinese political and intellectual elite have come to realize that material power alone cannot catapult China to its great power status. Only with greater international legitimacy as a rising great power can China enjoy a lasting benign strategic environment wherein it is no longer suspected as the most likely revisionist power bent on violently restructuring the international arrangement. And China's rise is embraced as an opportunity rather than a threat, with its core national interests in domestic stability, economic development, territorial integrity, and legitimate international demands being protected and respected.

INSPIRATION AND FRUSTRATION IN CHINA'S STATUS QUEST

Reflecting a realistic assessment of, and dissatisfaction with, their nation's international status, Chinese analysts are maintaining that China is a regional power with limited global significance while expressing strong expectation about its successful rise.[40] China is still relatively weak in comprehensive national power, but the lack of social standing as a legitimate great power candidate may be more difficult to overcome than the materialist obstacles. A negative social status that evokes Chinese threat to the world order could derail PRCs quest for national rejuvenation. Thus, it is the disadvantaged social standing that has been the main concern in China's status politics.

Indeed what is striking about Chinese assessment of international status is the prominence of the notion of responsibility, the commitment to institutional involvement, and the desire for international legitimacy. These features are eminently manifested in China's international strategy, which puts a premium on generally status-quo-oriented constructive activism in foreign affairs.[41] Although the content of responsibility remains somewhat contested, the recent, well-documented Chinese cooperative diplomacy indicates its motivation to project a favorable image, contribute to global governance, and align its interests closer to the United States and other great powers. Capitalizing on the power of the new idea, the United States has called on China to live up to its projected responsible image on issues ranging from environmental protection, human rights, and weapon proliferations to the international crisis over a North Korean nuclear standoff. Depending on the issue, China has demonstrated varying levels of compliance, in part to fulfill the image obligations.[42]

Influential analysts in Beijing are now openly advocating increasing Chinese "identification" (*rentong*) with, and "fusing into" (*rongru*), the regional and global community. To engineer China's status ascent, contends Chu Shulong, director of Institute of Strategic Studies at Qinghua University, China must proactively pursue a strategy of "common development and security."[43] And greater involvement in international institutions is part and parcel of that strategy. Apart from activism toward the UN, WTO, and APEC, Chinese leaders have sought to strengthen regional institutions such as the Shanghai Cooperation Organization and other multilateral cooperative efforts centered on the Association for Southeast Asian Nations (ASEAN) that would explicitly put in practice comprehensive, "cooperative security," the concept they have embraced since 1996.[44]

To the extent that the international arrangement disadvantages China's interests and status, Beijing however sees no alternative but to make changes within the United States–led hegemony. It has tried to influence the great power politics to facilitate a strategic understanding with the United States and ultimately to ease China's full acceptance into the great power club. In this connection, the attendance of Chinese president Hu Jintao at the 2003 Group of 8 (G-8) meetings hosted by France was an important step in China's great power diplomacy. Beijing had explicitly stated that China was not eager to join the group and had turned down earlier invitations by German and Japanese hosts to attend similar G-8 related meetings. Hu attended a G-8 ad hoc meeting on North–South issues and met separately with other leaders, including U.S. president George Bush and French president Jacques Chirac. Commenting on China's debut at G-8, Chinese analysts were already saying that the group was no longer the world's "rich men's club" formed exclusively of Western powers but a "great power forum" with a growing role in global governance. Furthermore, China's participation would help represent the interests of the developing countries. Analysts attributed much of the group's new identity to the admission of Russia in 1997 and the endangered role of the United Nations since the late 1990s. Despite positive reassessments of G-8, Chinese analysts continue to express reservations about the "discriminatory" nature of the Western-dominated, link-minded great power group. Beijing's official denial of any change to its policy notwithstanding, Hu's visit clearly represented somewhat of a breakthrough in its view on G-8.[45] Just as attempts at enlarging the UN Security Council permanent group have made little progress, so too will the formal G-8 membership expansion be a very difficult process. Realizing this, Beijing has instead focused on persuading the European Union (EU) to lift the arms embargo imposed on China in the aftermath of the Tiananmen Incident, not in the least for the EU act's symbolic gains for its great power diplomacy.

In tandem with its great power diplomacy, China has emphasized its identity as a regional constructive power,[46] which does not suggest that China has secured its hegemonic role in East Asia, as claimed by some observers.[47] Rather, it indicates a focus on consolidating its regional role in a nonthreatening fashion as a critical step toward global power status. To that end, Beijing's good-neighbor policy entails attempts to play a constructive role in regional affairs, project a responsible image, adopt confidence-building measures, strengthen economic ties, and advocate regional institution building. Similar spirit has led to Beijing's latest effort to create a sense of economic and security community with Southeast Asian nations.[48] Most noticeably, Beijing has openly accepted that "the American presence in the region is a product of history and an objective reality."[49] These steps have somewhat reduced regional suspicion toward Chinese intentions, but ambivalence and uncertainties remain over Beijing's behaviors and will likely increase as China grows stronger.

Seeking international identification evidences China's acceptance of the "established 'patterns' or 'international orders' to international interactions," which Jacek Kugler and Douglas Lemke call the international "status quo."[50] Both reformist China's record of cooperative behavior and its complex foreign policy dynamics suggest that simply categorizing China as a "revisionist power" is misplaced.[51] Zhang Yunling, director of the CASS Institute of Asia–Pacific Studies, maintains that, given how much contemporary China has benefited from the open international economic system, "accepting the existing order and safeguarding its basic stability are in China's fundamental interests."[52] But this does not mean that China's discontent with the international status quo can be overlooked or that Chinese confrontation or revisionism is out of the question, nor should China's international cooperation be taken for granted.

As discussed earlier, while seeking international identification, China considers the power factor as critical for its status advancement. The focused pursuit of comprehensive national power evidences this concern, and traditional power practices are by no means deemed anachronistic. Beijing heavily relies on coercive measures, including the threat of force, to stop Taiwan's de jure independence. The perceived damage to its status quest, by failure to stop Taiwan's independence, explains Beijing's ultrasensitivity to Taipei's diplomatic moves and any sign of international support to Taiwan. Ultimately China's status conception simply cannot imagine the "loss" of Taiwan.[53]

Chinese political élite and strategists believe that tight, unrestrained U.S. unipolar dominance is not conducive to China's status advancement, which is why China has consistently advocated multipolarization as its official policy. Since the late 1990s, China's multipolar vision of the world has been less concerned about a more dispersed, balanced power configuration, as the United States' unipolarity has been strengthened rather than reduced. Instead, China's policy of multipolarization has been geared toward restraining U.S. unilateralism and power politics in the name of promoting "democratization" and "pluralization" of international relations.[54] Beijing has advocated a "multicolored" world vision, wherein state sovereignty is respected and diverse political systems, economic models, and culturally beliefs can coexist. From the Chinese perspective, such a pluralistic world would relax or help redraw the intergroup boundaries in great power relations to facilitate China's status rise. At the regional level, China has sought to consolidate its good-neighbor ties under the name of promoting "cooperative security," a new security idea often presented as an antithesis of, and counterweight to, traditional military alliances and other forms of the "Cold War mentality."

The dualistic nature of China's status conception creates inherent tensions in Chinese international aspirations. More traditional power calculations may, and often do, conflict with the need to seek international acceptance and reassurance. The growth of material power is critical in its status quest, but China's rise may also fuel the fear of a "China threat." In some cases, such as certain arms control issues and the 1997–1998 Asian financial crisis, China managed to reconcile power with responsibility, with limited sacrifice to its materialist interests. But in other cases, such as the Taiwan issue, balancing traditional power considerations and broad status interest has proven difficult. At the heart of China's foreign policy struggle is the tension and sometimes incompatibility in the two streams of status advancement. But, fudamentally, defining its place under U.S. hegemony and securing the external environment conducive to China's rise require its legitimization as a rising responsible power, lest its ambiguous international role become a source of the China threat theory.

China's discontent with its international status is a source of inspiration and frustration. It has inspired Chinese policy élite and analysts to identify what China can do to earn the respect and recognition in the international society. Evidently dissatisfied with Chinese effort, Wang Jisi, director of the CASS

Institute of American Studies, has even criticized his government of lacking "a systematic approach to [constructively and proactively] dealing with the existing world order seen by the Chinese as 'United States–led.'"[55] Most remarkably, one Chinese scholar from the CCP Central Party School recently attributed China's inferior international status to its undemocratic polity. Framed this way, democratic change at home becomes national strategic interest in fulfilling China's great power aspiration.[56]

Conversely, frustration over perceived status immobility has fueled virulent nationalism and has strengthened traditional power politics thinking. For Maoist China, heightened status frustration tended to express itself in greater propensity to use force. For the reformist China, a widening status gap tended to fuel grievances over perceived mistreatment by foreign powers and facilitate an antiliberal turn in Chinese nationalism.[57] The uncertain domestic change and regime transition, combined with the intractable Taiwan issue, underscore the difficulties in managing China's status politics.

However, the Chinese political élite seems to understand that the costs–benefits balance clearly favors the path of responsible power over a confrontational strategy. China's foreign policy thinking since the mid-1990s suggests that its status discontent *can* be managed peacefully. First, as we've argued, China's conception of status now entails seeking international legitimacy as a rising great power. The need for acceptance and reassurance by the great powers has reined in the traditional logic of power politics in its status quest. Second, China has not set its expectation dangerously high. In fact assessments by Chinese officials and policy analysts of their country's comprehensive national power have been conservative. They define China as primarily a regional power and have not set a timetable regarding when it will achieve its aspired great power status. Finally, the daunting domestic agenda it faces adds further pressure to the Chinese leadership to adopt a more restrained foreign policy. Even on the Taiwan issue, prominent Chinese analysts are openly warning against obsessive, paranoid reactions, lest it derail China's "national rejuvenation," which requires sustained domestic reforms and economic development.[58] While acknowledging the encouraging signs, no realistic analyst can afford to underestimate the enormous challenge that the Taiwan question poses to China's status politics.

CONCLUSION

Historically, China's international status and its status conception have undergone significant changes. With the end of the Cold War and the diplomatic isolation following the Tiananmen killings, the PRC regime was confronted with an unprecedented setback to its international status. The Chinese political élite believed that the party-state was beleaguered, marginalized, and threatened in the emerging world order. The status crisis was intensified in light of the increasingly consolidated international hierarchy dominated by the United States and by other powerful democratic states.

Keenly aware of its material weakness and ultrasensitive to its outlier treatment in terms of other great powers, China has sought status advancement by enhancing its power and identification with the international society. The fear of a potential hardening of its out-group treatment constitutes both a source of Chinese discontent and a leverage with which to facilitate the peaceful rise of China. Perceived discriminatory denial of its great power aspiration engenders China's nationalist backlash against the international social structure. But status politics does not have to be a zero-sum game of "positional conflict," as claimed by some realist theorists.[59] Even the pioneers of the power transition model have contended that despite its growing power, China's revisionist impulse can be diminished through cultivation of its positive "evaluation of the status quo."[60] China's reconfigured status conception, which puts a premium on positive social reputation and foreign acceptance, suggests that China's status aspiration *can* be molded and fulfilled in ways that do not irreconcilably threaten the interests of the United States and other great powers. To that end, for China, maintaining peace across the Taiwan Strait and continued liberalization at home and in foreign policy are virtual prerequisites. Meanwhile, China's status conception will require corresponding international reactions that are much less dictated by the structural logic of the balance of power than that demostrated in traditional great power politics.

NOTES

1. John Mearsheimer, *The Tragedy of Great Power Politics* (New York: W. W. Norton, 2001), 12.

2. Lowell Dittmer and Samuel S. Kim, eds., *China's Quest for National Identity* (Ithaca, N.Y.: Cornell University Press, 1993).

3. "Major Investigative Report—1978–1998: 20 Years in the Eyes of Chinese Young People," *Zhongguo Qingnian Bao,* December 17, 1998, 8, in Foreign Broadcast Information Service (hereafter cited as FBIS): FTS19990112001848.

4. Deng Xiaoping, *Deng Xiaoping Wenxuan* [The Selected Works of Deng Xiaoping], vol. 2 (Beijing: People's Press, 1983), 376. Quoted in Chen Yue, *Zhongguo Guoji Diwei Fenxi* [Analysis of China's International Status] (Beijing: Contemporary World Press, 2002), 2.

5. See, for example, Chen Yue, *Zhongguo Guoji Diwei Fenxi* [Analysis of China's International Status].

6. Quoted in William Zimmerman, *Soviet Perspectives on International Relations, 1956–1967* (Princeton, N.J.: Princeton University Press, 1969), 123. Zimmerman in turn borrows this quote from William T. R. Fox, *The Super-Powers* (New York: Harcourt, Brace, 1944), 3.

7. See Chen Yue, *Zhongguo Guoji Diwei Fenxi* [Analysis of China's International Status], 43–65; Michael Pillsbury, *China Debates the Future Security Environment* (Washington, D.C.: National Defense University Press, 2000), chap. 5.

8. Guan Fu, "Analytical Report of the Chinese Youth Look at the World Survey," *Zhongguo Qingnian* (Chinese Youth), July 24, 1995, 1, FBIS: FTS19950724000041.

9. See Chen Yue, *Zhongguo Guoji Diwei Fenxi* [Analysis of China's International Status], 43–65; Pillsbury, *China Debates the Future Security Environment*, chap. 5.

10. *Zhongguo Shibao* (China Times), July 15, 2002.

11. According to Randall Schweller, a pole must have at least half of the military strength of the strongest power in the international system. See Schweller, *Deadly Imbalances: Tripolarity and Hitler's Strategy of World Conquest* (New York: Columbia University Press, 1997).

12. The Bush administration, "The National Security Strategy of the United States," released in September 2002.

13. See, for example, Robert Jervis, "Theories of War in an Era of Leading-Power Peace," *American Political Science Review* 96, no. 1 (March 2002): 1–14; Henry R. Nau, *At Home Abroad: Identity and Power in American Foreign Policy* (Ithaca, N.Y.: Cornell University Press, 2002).

14. "Yu fazhan de zhongguo xiangchu" [Getting along with a growing China], *Huanqiu Shibao* [Global Times], August 8, 2002, 3.

15. Zhang Yijun, "PRC-U.S.-Japanese Relations at the Turn of Century," *Shanghai Guoji Zhanwang*, no. 14 (July 15, 2000): 7, FBIS: CPP20000726000070.

16. Henri Tajfel, *Human Groups and Social Categories: Studies in Social Psychology* (Cambridge: Cambridge University Press, 1981); Michael A. Hogg and Dominic Abrams, *Social Identifications: A Social Psychology of Intergroup Relations and Group Process* (New York: Routledge, 1988); Roger Brown, *Social Psychology*, 2nd ed. (New York: Free Press, 1986); Alexander Wendt, "Collective Identity Formation and the International State," *American Political Science Review* 88, no. 2 (June 1994): 384–96; Jonathan Mercer, *Reputation in International Relations* (Ithaca, N.Y.: Cornell University Press, 1996).

17. For conventional cultural understandings of the sinocentric system, see Mark Mancall, *China at the Center: 300 Years of Foreign Relations* (New York: Free Press, 1984); John K. Fairbank, ed., *The Chinese World Order: Traditional Chinese Foreign Relations* (Cambridge, Mass.: Harvard University Press, 1968). Alastair Iain Johnston highlights the military nature of the system, *Cultural Realism: Strategic Culture and Grand Strategy in Chinese History* (Princeton, N.J.: Princeton University Press, 1995). For a Japanese perspective that focuses on the unequal economic ties of the tributary system, see Takashi Hamashita, "The Intra-regional System in East Asia in Modern Times," *Network Power: Japan and Asia,* ed. Peter Katzenstein and Takashi Shiraishi (Ithaca, N.Y.: Cornell University Press, 1997), chap. 3.

18. Zhang Yijun, "PRC-U.S.-Japanese Relations at the Turn of Century," 8–11.

19. See Robert A. Madsen, "The Struggle for Sovereignty between China and Taiwan," in *Problematic Sovereignty: Contested Rules and Political Possibilities*, ed. Stephen D. Krasner (New York: Columbia University Press, 2001), 150–58.

20. Peter Van Ness, *Revolution and Chinese Foreign Policy: Peking's Support for Wars of National Liberation* (Berkeley: University of California Press, 1970).

21. Kenneth Waltz, *Theory of International Politics* (New York: McGraw-Hill, 1979).

22. Alastair Johnston, "International Structures and Foreign Policy," in *China and the World* (4th ed.), ed. Samuel Kim (Boulder, Colo.: Westvew Press, 1998), 66 (emphasis in original). For further evidence, see Thomas J. Christensen, *Useful Adversaries: Grand Strategy, Domestic Mobilization, and Sino-American Conflict, 1947–1958* (Princeton, N.J.: Princeton University Press, 1997); Jian Chen, *Mao's China and the Cold War* (Chapel Hill: University of North Carolina Press, 2001).

23. Lu Ning, *The Dynamics of Foreign-Policy Decisionmaking in China*, 2nd ed. (Boulder, Colo.: Westview Press, 2000), 168–69.

24. Deng Xiaoping, *Deng Xiaoping Wenxuan* [The Selected Works of Deng Xiaoping], 376. See also Huan Xiang, *Zhongheng Shijie* [Overview of the World] (Beijing: World Affairs Press, 1985), 321–24.

25. Song Xinning, *Guoki Zhengzhi Jingji yu Zhongguo Duiwai Guan Xi* [International Political Economy and Chinese Foreign Relations] (Hong Kong: Social Sciences Press, 1997), 337; Yong Deng, "Hegemon on the Offensive: Chinese Perspectives on US Global Strategy," *Political Science Quarterly* 116, no. 3 (Fall 2001): 343–65.

26. On Sino-European relations, see David Shambaugh, "European and American Approaches to China: Different Beds, Same Dreams" (Asia paper, Sigur Center for Asian Studies, George Washington University, Washington, D.C., March 2002); and the special issue devoted to the subject in *China Quarterly*, no. 169 (March 2002), particularly Kay Moller, "Diplomatic Relations and Mutual Strategic Perceptions: China and the European Union," 10–32; Eberhard Sandschneider, "China's Diplomatic Relations with the States of Europe," 33–44. On Sino-Japanese relations, see Morton Abramowitz, Funabashi Yoichi, and Wang Jisi, *China-Japan-U.S.: Managing the Trilateral Relations* (Tokyo: Japan Center for International Exchange, 1998); James Przystup, "China, Japan, and the United States," in *The U.S.–Japan Alliance*, ed. Michael J. Green and Patrick Cronin (New York: Council on Foreign Relations Press, 1999), chap. 2.

27. Joseph Berger and Morris Zelditch Jr., *Status, Power, and Legitimacy: Strategies and Theories* (New Brunswick, N.J.: Transaction Publishers, 1998), 104.

28. "Major Power in International Arena," *Xinhua* [in English], December 17, 2000, FBIS: CPP20001217000053.

29. Geng Jianrong and Li Rong, "Jiefang Ribao Reporters Interview Minister Tang Jiaxuan on the Eve of the APEC Meeting," *Shanghai Jiefang Ribao* (Internet version), October 17, 2001, FBIS: CPP 20011018000294.

30. Wu Yingchun, "China's International Status Has Markedly Risen," *Renmin Ribao* (Internet version), September 30, 2002, FBIS: CPP 20021004000066.

31. "Summit Meeting Launches Shanghai Cooperation Organization," *People's Daily*, at http://english.peopledaily.com.cn/200106/15/eng20010615-72740.html; Xie Rong, "Shanghai hezuo zhuzhi—quyu hezuo de dianfan" [The Shanghai Cooperation

Organization—model for regional cooperation], *Renmin Wang*, www.people.com.cn, May 28, 2003.

32. Jin Dexi, "Zhongguo xuyao daguo xintai" [China needs great power mentality], *Global Times*, September 12, 2002, at www.people.com.cn/GB/paper68/7239/698878.html.

33. Pang Zhongying, "China's International Status and Foreign Strategy after the Cold War," *Renmin Wang WWW*, May 5, 2002, in FBIS: CPP20020506000022.

34. Yan Xuetong et al., *Zhongguo Jueqi—Guoji Huanjin Pinggu* [International Environment for China's Rise] (Tianjin: People's Press, 1998), chap. 3, quotes on 170, 173–74.

35. Robert Jervis, *Perception and Misperception in International Relations* (Princeton, N.J.: Princeton University Press, 1976), chap. 3; Wendt, "Collective Identity Formation and the International State."

36. "The Choice of China's Diplomatic Strategy," *People's Daily* [English] online, http://english.peopledaily.com.cn/200303/19.

37. Commentator, "Making Efforts to Establish Sino-U.S. Constructive Strategic Partnership," *Renmin Ribao* (Internet version), June 18, 1998, 1, FBIS: FTS 19980618000362; He Chong, "Yearender: China's Diplomatic Activities This Year Attract World Attention," *Hong Kong Zhongguo Tongxun She*, December 30, 1998, in FBIS: FTS19990114001801; Wang Jisi, "Achievements, Effects of Clinton's China Visit," *Hong Kong Wenwei Po*, September 14, A7, FBIS: FTS19980922000344.

38. Zhang Yijun, "PRC–U.S.–Japanese Relations at Turn of Century." Jianwei Wang, *Limited Adversaries: Post–Cold War Sino-American Mutual Images* (New York: Oxford University Press, 2000); Philip C. saunders, "China's American Watchers: Changing Attitudes towards the United States," *China Quarterly*, no. 161 (March 2001): 41–65.

39. Quoted in Guo Xuetang, "Zhuazhu zhanlue jiyu, bizhanlue fengxian" [Seize strategic opportunities, avoid strategic risks], *Global Times*, February 21, 2003, 2 at www.people.com.cn/GB/paper68/8525/800379.html. See also Chen Peiyao, "Changes in the US Security Strategy and Adjustments of its China Policy," *Zhongguo Pinglun*, no. 51 (March 1, 2002): 6–9, FBIS: CPP20020307000097; Jin Canrong, "An Assessment of Two Types of New Factors in China's International Environment," *Xiandai Guoji Guanxi*, no. 2 (November 20, 2002): 7–9, FBIS: CPP20021206000159; Xiong Guangkai, "The Global Challenge of International Terrorism," speech at the Munich International Security Policy Conference, February 8, 2003, at www.securityconference.de/konferenzen/rede.php?menu_20.

40. Chen Yue, *Zhongguo Guoji Diwei Fenxi* [Analysis of China's International Status], chaps. 5, 6; Xinnning, *Guoki Zhengzhi Jingji yu Zhongguo Duiwai Guan Xi* [International Political Economy and Chinese Foreign Relations]; Mao Xiaojun, "Transforming Concepts and Proactively Responding to Factors," *Xiandai Guoji Guanxi*, no. 11 (November 20, 2002): 22–24, FBIS: CPP20021209000250.

41. See Avery Goldstein, "The Diplomatic Face of China's Grand Strategy: A Rising Power's Emerging Choice," *China Quarterly*, no. 168 (December 2001): 935–64; Michael D. Swaine and Ashley J. Tellis, *Interpreting China's Grand Strategy: Past, Present, and Future* (Santa Monica, Calif.: Rand, 2000).

42. See Elizabeth Economy and Michel Oksenberg, eds., *China Joins the World: Progress and Prospects* (New York: Council on Foreign Relations Press, 1999); David M. Lampton, ed., *The Making of Chinese Foreign and Security Policy in the Era of Reform* (Stanford, Calif.: Stanford University Press, 2001).

43. Chu Shulong, "Quanmian jianshe xiaokang shehui shiqi de zhongguo waijiao zhanlue" [China's diplomatic strategy during the period of comprehensively building a well-off society], *Shijie Jingji yu Zhengzhi* [World Economics and Politics], no. 8 (August 2003). Accessed from the website of the Institute of World Economics and Politics (IWEP), Chinese Academy of Social Sciences (CASS). Chu emphasizes the importance of *rongru*.

44. Qin Yaqing, "Guojia shengfen, zhanlue wenhua he anquan liyi" [State identity, strategic culture, and security interests], *World Economics and Politics*, no. 1 (2003): 10–15. Accessed from the IWEP/CASS website. Qin underscores the importance of *rentong*.

45. Wang Fang, "Zhongguo nanbei fenghui xian fengliang" [China shows its weight at the South–North summit], *Global Times*, June 4, 2003 at www.snweb.com.cn/gb/gnd/2003/0604/a0604001.htm; "Hu's Trip Represents China's Global Diplomatic Perspective," *People's Daily* [English] online, July 6, 2003 at http://english.peopledaily.com.cn/200306/06/eng20030606_117795.shtml; Zheng Yu, "Zhongguo keyi jiaru baguo jituan" [China can join the Group-8], *Global Times*, May 30, 2003, at www.snweb.com.cn/gb/gnd/2003/0530/o0530001.htm; Antoaneta Bezlova, "China Enters the G8 Big League," *Asia Times*, May 23, 2003, at www.atimes.com/atimes/China/EE23Ad01.html; Shen Jiru, "Zhongguo bu keyi zhuiqiu jiaru baguo jituo" [China won't assiduously seek G-8 membership], at www.iwep.org.cn/fangtan/baguojituan.htm, accessed from the IWEP/CASS website, August 15, 2003.

46. For the regional focus in Chinese foreign policy during the reform era, see Michael Yahuda, *The International Politics of Asia-Pacific, 1945–1995* (New York: Routledge, 1996), chap. 6; Mark Selden, "China, Japan, and the Regional Political Economy of East Asia, 1945–1995," in Katzenstein and Takashi Shiraishi, *Network Power*, chap. 9; Bin Yu, "China and Its Asian Neighbors," in *In the Eyes of the Dragon: China Views the World,* ed. Yong Deng and Fei-ling Wang (Boulder, Colo.: Rowman & Littlefield, 1999).

47. Dave Kang proposes the resurrection of *pax sinica* as both the reality and future of international relations in Asia. See Kang, "Hierarchy and Stability in Asian International Relations," in *International Relations Theory and the Asia-Pacific,* ed. G. John Ikenberry and Michael Mastanduno (New York: Columbia University Press, 2003), 163–89.

48. See Wang Jisi, "China's Changing Role in Asia," Atlantic Council of the United States, January 2004, at www.acus.org/Publications/occasionalpapers/Asia/WangJisi-Jan-04.pdf; Fu Ying, "China and Asia in a New Era," *China: An International Journal* 1, no. 2 (September 2003): 304–12; "ASEAN, China Forge Strategic Partnership," http://english.peopledaily.com.cn/200310/09; "China, ASEAN Sign Nonaggression Pact," *Hong Kong AFP* [in English], October 8, 2003, FBIS: CPP20031008000023.

49. Fu Ying, "China and Asia in a New Era," 311.

50. Jacek Kugler and Douglas Lemke, "The Power Transition Research Program: Assessing Theoretical and Empirical Advances," in *Handbook of War Studies II*, ed. Manus I. Midlarsky (Ann Arbor: University of Michigan Press, 2000), 131.

51. See Alastair Iain Johnston, "Is China a Status Quo Power?" *International Security* 27, no. 4 (Spring 2003): 5–56.

52. Zhang Yunling, "How to Understand the International Environment China Faces in the Asia-Pacific Region," *Dangdai Yatai*, June 15, 2003, 3–14, FBIS: CPP20030717000218, 3.

53. See Thomas J. Christensen, "Posing Problems without Catching Up: China's Rise and Challenges for U.S. Security Policy," *International Security* 25, no. 4 (Winter/Spring, 2000–2001): 5–40; Suisheng Zhao, ed., *Across the Taiwan Strait: Mainland China, Taiwan, and the 1995–1996 Crisis* (New York: Routledge, 1999).

54. Chen Yue, *Zhongguo Guoji Diwei Fenxi* [Analysis of China's International Status], chap. 4; Tang Shiping, "China's Periphery Security Environment in 2010–2015," *Zhanglu Yu Guanli*, no. 5 (October 2002): 34–45, FBIS: CPP20021017000169.

55. Wang Jisi, "China's Changing Role in Asia," 5.

56. Liu Jianfei, "The Building of Democratic Politics in China and Sino-U.S. Relations," *Zhanlue Yu Guanli*, no. 2 (March 1, 2003): 76–82, FBIS: CPP20030506000226.

57. Alastair Iain Johnston, "China's Militarized Interstate Dispute Behavior, 1949–1992," *China Quarterly*, no. 153 (March 1998): 1–30; Joseph Fewsmith and Stanley Rosen, "The Domestic Context of Chinese Foreign Policy: Does 'Public Opinion' Matter?" in Lampton, *The Making of Chinese Foreign and Security Policy in the Era of Reform*, chap. 6; Peter H. Gries, "Tears of Rage: Chinese Nationalism and the Belgrade Embassy Bombing," *China Journal*, no. 45 (July 2001): 25–43.

58. Zhang Nianchi, "The 16th CPC National Congress and Cross-Strait Relations," *Hong Kong Zhongguo Pinglun*, no. 60 (December 1, 2002): 6–8, FBIS: CPP20021204000033.

59. Randall L. Schweller, "Realism and the Present Great Power System: Growth and Positional Conflict over Scarce Resources," in *Unipolar Politics: Realism and State Strategies after the Cold War*, ed. Ethan K. Kapstein and Michael Mastanduno (New York: Columbia University Press, 1999), chap. 2.

60. Kugler and Lemke, "The Power Transition Research Program," 158.

4

National Image Building and Chinese Foreign Policy

Hongying Wang

This chapter examines national image building as part of Chinese foreign policy. First, it traces the various images that the People's Republic of China (PRC) government has tried to project of China, revealing changes and continuities from the Maoist period to the present time. It then compares China's projected national images with others' perceptions of China, explaining the convergence and the divergence of images and perceptions. Finally, this chapter explores whether the projected national images affect Chinese foreign policy behavior and, if so, how they do? This examination draws on neoliberal institutionalism and constructivism in international relations theory to provide an answer.

> Some [foreign countries] have prejudices or have wrongly believed rumours, therefore what they think about China is not the true image of China. We will try every means to present a comprehensive and real picture of China to the outside world so that you can see the true image of China.
>
> —Zhu Muzhi, director, State Council Information Office[1]

> We will do our very best to educate the public and the Congress about the role China actually plays in working with the United States to maintain stability in the Asia-Pacific region. At the very least, these efforts will improve the international image of China and stop the negative tone of public opinion.
>
> —Hill and Knowlton, public relations firm hired by the PRC government[2]

> While carrying out the overseas publicity work, we should . . . make
> greater efforts to comprehensively brief the world about China . . . improve
> and safeguard socialist China's international images.
>
> —Jiang Zemin, Chinese president[3]

Since time immemorial, political leaders have recognized that images matter. They have tried to promote favorable characterizations and ameliorate unfavorable stereotypes of themselves and the polities they represent. In today's world, where democratization and the telecommunication revolution have greatly expanded the flow of information, governments everywhere have become especially attentive to their national images.[4] China is no exception. But so far, there has been little research on China's national image building.[5] In this chapter, I make a modest attempt to fill this void by exploring the following questions: What sorts of images has the Chinese government tried to project of China? Are the perceptions of China by others consistent with China's projected images? Do the projected national images have any impact on Chinese foreign policy behavior?

CHINA'S NATIONAL IMAGE BUILDING

As indicated by the remarks in the epigraphs, the Chinese government has become quite attentive to China's national image in recent years.[6] Chinese leaders have repeatedly called for the improvement of the country's image abroad.[7] To coordinate its image-building efforts, the Chinese Communist Party (CCP) established an Overseas Propaganda Department under the Party Central Committee in 1990, and the Chinese government established a new Information Office under the State Council in 1991.[8]

As part of its intensified image-building activities, the Chinese government has frequently issued white papers since the beginning of the 1990s on such subjects as human rights, the situation in Tibet, China's national defense, and the environment (see table 4.1). Such papers are designed to publicize and explain to the international community China's positions on these sensitive questions, representing a step forward from the days when the Chinese government brushed aside international criticisms of Chinese policies without engaging the arguments. In addition, the Chinese government has begun to hire international media expertise to polish its image.[9] For instance, in 1991 it employed the American firm Hill and Knowlton to lobby the U.S. Congress for the unconditional renewal of China's most-favored-nation trade status. In its bid for the 2008 Olympic Games, the Chinese government hired another American firm, Weber Shanwick Worldwide, to run its public relations campaign. Finally, the Chinese government has sponsored or organized cultural events in other countries to help improve its own image. For instance, in the summer of 2000 China spent millions of dollars and sent cultural groups on a road show in the United States. The director of the State Council Information Office explains the motive behind this undertaking: "I hope some day an American president will say something good about China."[10] In 2001 China reached an agreement with AOL Time Warner to begin broadcasting English-language programs in the United States around the clock, hoping to present Americans with an image of a softer, gentler China.

While the Chinese government has shown increasing enthusiasm and sophistication about public relations work abroad in recent years, national image building is by no means a new enterprise for the Chinese. In fact, projecting favorable images has been an important part of Chinese statecraft since ancient times. Just as the imperial rulers cultivated the images of China as the center of the universe and as a benign hegemon, the government of the PRC has sought from its outset to project a variety of images of the country.[11]

Exactly what sorts of images have the PRC government tried to establish of China? More specifically, what kind of an actor has the Chinese government portrayed China to be in international affairs? To answer this question, I conducted a quantitative content analysis of two official series—the *Peking*

Table 4.1.   Samples of White Papers Issued by China

Year	Title
1991	*Human Rights in China*
1992	*Criminal Reform in China*
1992	*Tibet: Its Ownership and Human Rights Situation*
1993	*The Taiwan Question and Reunification of China*
1994	*The Situation of Chinese Women*
1994	*Intellectual Property Protection in China*
1995	*Family Planning in China*
1996	*The Situation of Children in China*
1996	*Environmental Protection in China*
1996	*The Grain Issue in China*
1997	*On Sino-U.S. Trade Balance*
1997	*Freedom of Religious Belief in China*
1998	*China's National Defence*
1999	*National Minorities Policy and Its Practice in China*
2000	*China's Population and Development in the 21st Century*
2000	*China's Space Activities*
2001	*Tibet's March Toward Modernisation*
2001	*The Development-Oriented Poverty Reduction Programme for Rural China*
2002	*National Economy and Social Development of China*

Source: Official website of the Ministry of Foreign Affairs of China, www.fmprc.gov.cn.

Review (later renamed *Beijing Review*) and the government work reports (*zhengfu gongzuo baogao*).[12] The *Peking Review* was launched on March 5, 1958, by the Chinese government. It was the first and, for many years, the main weekly newsmagazine directed at foreign readers. Its purpose is for "foreigners to know about China's policies and study China's political situation and development trends."[13] In addition to being published in English, it is also published in French, Japanese, German, and Spanish. With regard to the other official source under review, the premier delivers the government work reports to the National People's Congress. Beginning with the first one in 1954, such reports have come out from time to time, in intervals ranging from one to eleven years. They are directed at domestic and international audiences. Given how limited foreign access to China was until the past twenty years, it is safe to assume that these work reports constituted a major window for China watching and that the Chinese government probably viewed them as such.[14]

Between 1958 and 2002, more than two thousand issues of the *Peking Review* were published. I randomly selected one issue from each year for analysis. Since my focus is on the images of China in international affairs as portrayed by the Chinese government, I coded only articles that have at least one paragraph relating to China's foreign relations. Between 1954 and 2000, nineteen government work reports were delivered and published. I included all of them for analysis and coded sections in each report dealing with China's foreign relations.[15]

Figures 4.1 and 4.2 summarize the results of the content analysis of the *Peking Review* and of the government work reports given to the National People's Congress. As these graphs show, they projected similar images of China as an international actor. According to these two documents, in the last forty-over years the PRC government has tried to build the following images of China in international affairs: peace-loving country, victim of foreign aggression, socialist country, bastion of revolution, antihegemonic force, developing country, major power, international cooperator, and autonomous actor. These data indicate that over time the images projected of China by the Chinese government have demonstrated changes as well as continuities. On the side of continuity, the government has consistently—though with different levels of vigor—pursued the images of China as a peace-loving nation, a victim of foreign aggression, an opponent of hegemony, and a developing country. On the side of discontinuity, the Maoist era saw the government emphasizing the images of China as a socialist country and supporter of revolution. During the reform period, the government has deemphasized those images. Instead it has highlighted the images of China as an international cooperator and a major power.

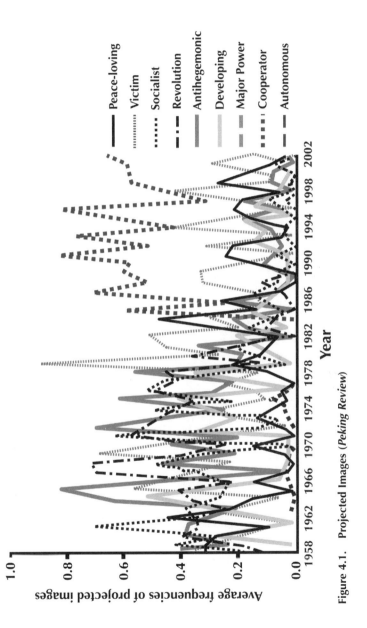

Figure 4.1. Projected Images *(Peking Review)*

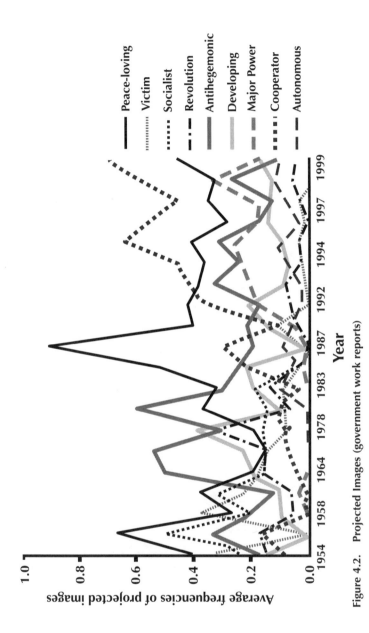

Figure 4.2. Projected Images (government work reports)

Now that we have determined what sorts of national images the PRC government tried to pursue, we can move on to address the remaining questions. Do others' perceptions of China correspond with China's projected images? Does image building provide feedback to, and as a consequence have any impact on, Chinese foreign policy behavior? While the first question is primarily the concern of the Chinese government, the second should be of great interest to countries interacting with China. The rest of this chapter examines each question in turn.

IMAGE BUILDING AND PERCEPTIONS

To find out if others' perceptions of China correspond with China's projected images, we should compare China's projected images with perceptions of China by the public of numerous countries. However, that task is too ambitious for this work. Instead, I provide only a limited answer to this question by examining how China's projected images fared in one country, the United States.

My assessment of the evolution of the American public opinion about China relies on data from the Roper Center for Public Opinion Research.[16] From the center's online data bank, I found more than five hundred survey questions about China, ranging from 1954 to 2002. My original intention was to detect American views of China from the answers to those survey questions, but I discovered that because the pollsters framed their China-related questions differently from year to year, it was difficult to aggregate the data embodied in the answers. Instead, I analyzed the survey questions themselves, treating their explicit or implicit assertions about China as data on American perceptions.[17] Figures 4.3 through 4.12 show the results of the analysis alongside earlier analysis of China's projected images.

As one can see from these graphs, American perception of China corresponds with some of the images projected by the Chinese government but contradicts others. First, Americans share the view that China is a socialist country (figure 4.5). Likewise, Americans generally agree with China's projected images of itself as a developing country and major power (figures 4.8 and 4.9). Second, Americans sometimes view China as exhibiting opposing hegemonic behaviors, but more often they see China as engaging in hegemonic behaviors (figure 4.7). They sometimes view China as a victim of foreign aggression but more often see China as victimizing its own neighbors (figure 4.4). Third, while China portrays itself as a peace-loving nation, international cooperator, and autonomous actor, Americans think exactly the opposite. According to the data here, they have never seen China

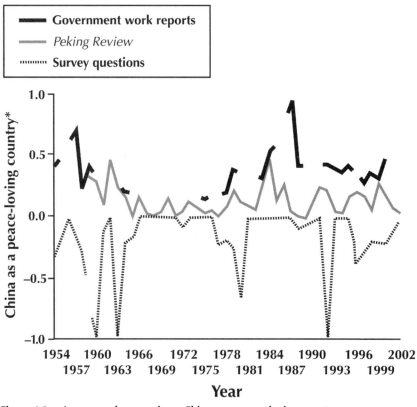

Figure 4.3.   Images and perceptions: China as a peace-loving country

Note: Some lines are broken due to unavailable data: government work reports were delivered in only some
   of the years; survey questions did not always contain perception data of a given image.
* China as a peace-loving country was coded as: 1 = positive, 0 = neutral, −1 = negative

as peace loving (figure 4.3); instead, they frequently regard China as militant. They seldom see China as an international operator; rather, in their
view, China is an obstructive force (figure 4.10). They have not given much
thought to whether China is an autonomous actor, but to the extent they
have, their conclusion has been negative (figure 4.11). Finally, the American public has by and large ignored China's self-depiction as a bastion of
revolution (figure 4.6), while it strongly holds an image not projected by the
Chinese government—that is, the image of China as an authoritarian state
(figure 4.12).

   What explains these patterns? Why are American images of China sometimes similar to, but often at odds with, China's projected images? Part of the
answer lies in the type of image involved. Some images are about more-or-

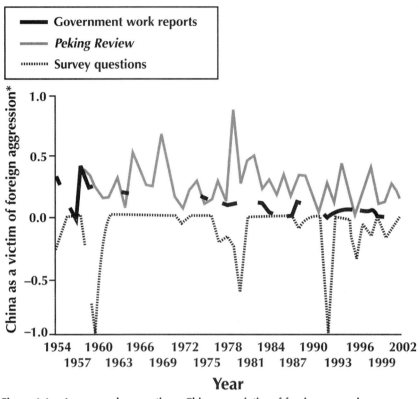

Figure 4.4. Images and perceptions: China as a victim of foreign aggression

Note: Some lines are broken due to unavailable data: government work reports were delivered in only some of the years; survey questions did not always contain perception data of a given image.
* China as a victim of foreign aggression was coded as: 1 = positive, 0 = neutral, −1 = negative

less objective attributes and thus leave little room for interpretation. China's images as a developing country and a major power fall into this category. China's backward economy and low living standards are rather straightforward indicators of its development status. Its size, population, permanent membership on the UN Security Council, and possession of nuclear weapons are all clear signs of its major power status. In such cases, it is not hard for American perceptions and China's projections to converge. Other images require subjective judgments and are thus more controversial. China's images as a socialist country, an antihegemonic force, a peace-loving nation, a victim of foreign aggression, an international cooperator, a bastion of revolution, and an autonomous actor belong to this more subjective category.

What, then, explains when and why American perceptions converge with, or diverge from, China's projected images on the more subjective issues? One

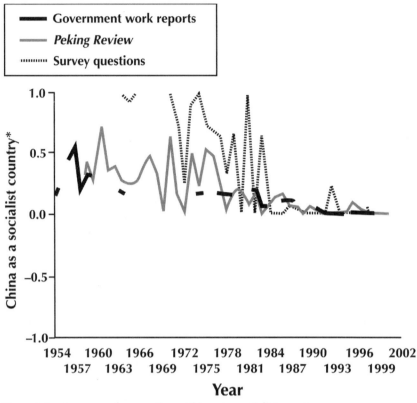

Figure 4.5.　Images and perceptions: China as a socialist country

Note: Some lines are broken due to unavailable data: government work reports were delivered in only some of the years; survey questions did not always contain perception data of a given image.

* China as a socialist country was coded as: 1 = positive, 0 = neutral, −1 = negative

factor may be found in the differences between the images and Chinese be-havior. If China substantiates its words with deeds, then American percep-tions will likely concur with the images. For instance, it is hard for Americans to concur with China's self-portrayal as a peace-loving nation when it uses or threatens force against its neighbors. It is no wonder that American percep-tion of China as a warlike country intensified during the early 1960s after the Sino-Indian War; during the late 1970s and early 1980s, around the time of the Sino-Vietnamese War; and during the early 1990s, when China dramati-cally increased its military budget and engaged in some alarming weapons deals, including the purchase of fighters from the former Soviet Union and the alleged negotiation over an aircraft carrier from Ukraine.

However, even when China's behavior is consistent with its projected im-ages, American perception may still differ greatly from those images. For ex-

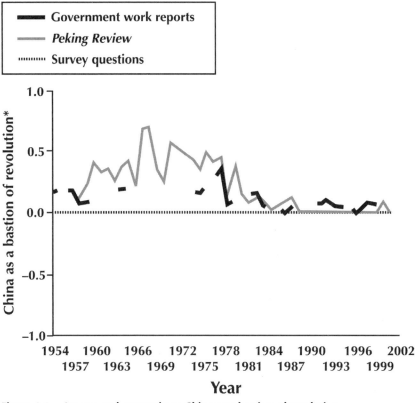

Figure 4.6. Images and perceptions: China as a bastion of revolution

Note: Some lines are broken due to unavailable data: government work reports were delivered in only some of the years; survey questions did not always contain perception data of a given image.
* China as a bastion of revolution was coded as: 1 = positive, 0 = neutral, −1 = negative

ample, by most standards, it is clear that the Chinese government has become much more cooperative with the international community in the past twenty years or so. Ironically, the American perception of China has moved the other way. In the past ten years, in particular, Americans have become increasingly negative about China in this area.

To explain this phenomenon, it is helpful to turn to psychological theories of perception (and misperception). Psychologists have long noticed that people do not treat all incoming information equally. People accept information that is consistent with their existing perceptions much more than they do information that is contradictory. In fact, they even misinterpret information that contradicts familiar patterns as information consistent with those patterns.[18] Similarly, in policy making, "decision-makers tend to fit incoming information into their existing theories and images."[19] Extending

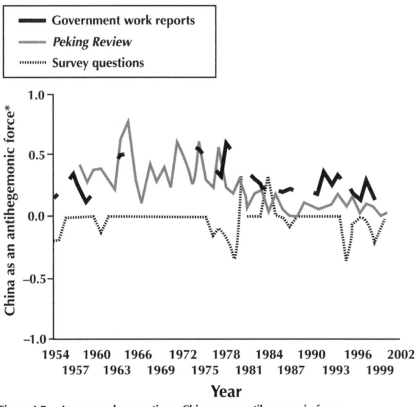

Figure 4.7.   Images and perceptions: China as an antihegemonic force

Note: Some lines are broken due to unavailable data: government work reports were delivered in only some
of the years; survey questions did not always contain perception data of a given image.
* China as an antihegemonic force was coded as: 1 = positive, 0 = neutral, −1 = negative

this perspective to intergroup perceptions, social psychologists find that
people tend to use character-based attributions to explain an out-group's undesirable behaviors and use situational attributions to explain the group's
desirable behaviors.[20] In international relations, this means that if a rival
country acts cooperatively, it is seen as forced to do so by situation; if the
rival country acts aggressively, its action is seen as dispositional.[21] Combining these insights, one could draw the following inferences: First, the
likelihood is high that people will accept a negative image of a rival country if the image is consistent with existing images of that country. Second,
it is somewhat likely that people will accept a negative image of a rival
country even if the image challenges existing images of that country. Third,
it is somewhat likely that people will accept a positive image of a rival
country if the image is consistent with existing images of that country.

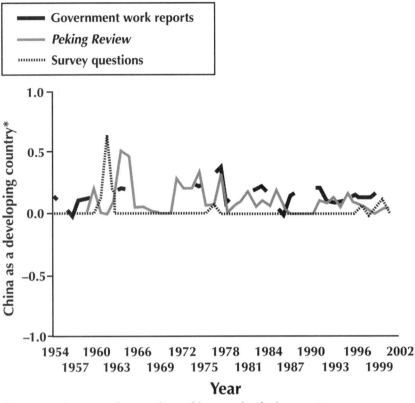

Figure 4.8.   Images and perceptions: China as a developing country

Note: Some lines are broken due to unavailable data: government work reports were delivered in only some of the years; survey questions did not always contain perception data of a given image.
* China as a developing country was coded as: 1 = positive, 0 = neutral, −1 = negative

Fourth, the likelihood is low that people will accept a positive image of a rival country if the image contradicts existing images of that country (see table 4.2).

These inferences about perception between rivals shed light on the convergence and divergence of American perception of China and China's projected national images.[22] We begin with the case of convergence. The image of China as a socialist country corresponds with the existing American perception since the founding of the PRC. Furthermore, in the ideological context of the United States, this is a negative image. Not surprisingly, Americans easily accept this image.

The images of China as an antihegemonic force and victim of foreign aggression are mixed cases. The antihegemonic image is not particularly consistent with the traditional American view of the Middle Kingdom. Thus, it

Figure 4.9.   Images and perceptions: China as a major power

Note: Some lines are broken due to unavailable data: government work reports were delivered in only some of the years; survey questions did not always contain perception

is not surprising that most of the time American perceptions of China have gone in the opposite direction. However, to the United States, which is a hegemonic power, an antihegemonic force is as much a negative image as a positive one. Thus, the American public did not always reject this image of China.

Next, we turn to the cases of divergence. The image of a peace-loving nation is a positive one that every country in the world seeks for itself. Furthermore, it contradicts the American stereotype of communist countries, including the PRC. Thus, it has been a hard sell to the American public. The same is true of China's image as a victim, an international cooperator, and to a lesser extent an autonomous actor. Thus, the American public has by and large rejected these images.

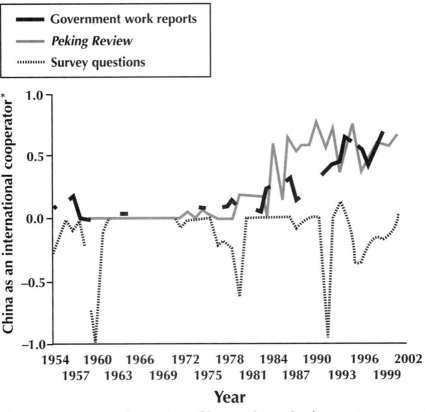

Figure 4.10. Images and perceptions: China as an international cooperator

Note: Some lines are broken due to unavailable data: government work reports were delivered in only some of the years; survey questions did not always contain perception data of a given image.
* China as an international cooperator was coded as: 1 = positive, 0 = neutral, −1 = negative

The image of China as a bastion of revolution has been neither accepted nor rejected but simply ignored by the American public. The reason is that such language is so alien to American foreign policy culture that it has failed to engage the American public altogether. Finally, the image of China as an authoritarian state is a negative image that fits well with the American stereotype of communist countries. It is thus not surprising that Americans hold this perception of China, even though it is not an image projected by the Chinese government.

What lessons can the Chinese government learn from this record? First, it is worth taking into account the variation among images along the objective–subjective spectrum. Generally speaking, national images toward the objective

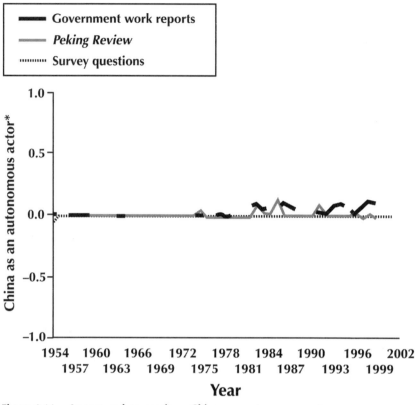

Figure 4.11. Images and perceptions: China as a autonomous actor

Note: Some lines are broken due to unavailable data: government work reports were delivered in only some of the years; survey questions did not always contain perception data of a given image.
* China as an autonomous actor was coded as: 1 = positive, 0 = neutral, −1 = negative

end are relatively clear-cut, leaving little room for the art of image building. However, national images toward the subjective end are more subject to cultivation. Second, while building images, it is important to substantiate words with deeds. Image building is likely to produce desirable perceptions when action conforms with the projected images, though such positive outcomes are, of course, never guaranteed. Third, it is important to recognize that although it is easy to maintain an old negative image or gain a new negative image, it is extremely difficult to build a new positive image. In other words, it is easy to damage national images but very hard to repair them. Finally, projection of China's images abroad needs to take foreign cultures into consideration. If the Chinese government uses concepts or language that are alien to a targeted audience, as it has done so frequently, its image building is bound to fail.[23]

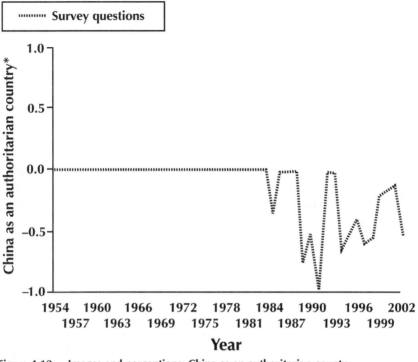

Figure 4.12.   Images and perceptions: China as an authoritarian country

* China as an authoritarian country was coded as: 1 = positive, 0 = neutral, −1 = negative

IMAGE BUILDING AND BEHAVIOR

Just as the PRC government should be concerned about the convergence or divergence of others' perceptions of China and its own projected images of China, other countries interacting with China should be interested in the impact of China's projected images on its actual behavior. If China's projected images have some bearing on its behavior, then they could be seen as one indicator of the likely range of Chinese behavior. Furthermore, if images can affect behavior, outsiders can try to influence Chinese behavior by influencing the kinds of national images China pursues.

I see four possible types of image–behavior relationships. First, there may be a big gap between China's projected images and its foreign policy behavior. In this scenario, the images and behavior are "decoupled" and have almost nothing to do with each other.[24] Second, the government may use various national images to justify its foreign policies to the domestic public and the international community. In this scenario, images may seem

Table 4.2.   The Psychology of Image Building

	Negative Images	Positive Images
Stereotype Confirming	Highly likely to be accepted	Somewhat likely to be accepted
Stereotype Challenging	Somewhat likely to be accepted	Unlikely to be accepted

to be consistent with the behavior but have no causal effect on foreign policy behaviors. Instead, they are afterthoughts aimed at assisting foreign policies chosen on other grounds. Third, the government may calculatingly engage in foreign policy behavior according to its projected images to give credibility to the latter. Fourth, the government may unthinkingly choose its foreign policies according to its projected images because these images indeed reflect the leadership's conception of China's role in international affairs.

We will not discuss the first two types of image–behavior relationships because neither involves any causal effect of images on behaviors. Instead, we shall focus on the third and fourth types of image–behavior relationships, where projected images have a causal impact on foreign policy behaviors. Generally speaking, if a projected image is strategic, it can have a *constraining* effect on behavior. If a projected image is internalized, it is likely to have a *constitutive* effect. Therefore, before looking into the image–behavior relationships, it is helpful to distinguish strategic national images and internalized national images.

A simple and seemingly reasonable way to judge whether an image is strategic or internalized is to see if it is projected consistently across time and to various audiences. Those images projected consistently are probably internalized, whereas those invoked variably across time or audiences are likely to be strategic and thus not internalized. Going back to figures 4.1 and 4.2, we can see that four national images have been projected most consistently across time and audiences—China as a peace-loving nation, as a victim, as an antihegemonic force, and as a developing country. We can conclude with some confidence that these projected images are more than strategic, that they reflect the leadership's strongly held self-images of China.[25] The other images are likely to be strategic.

How do we know when strategic images have a causal impact on foreign policy behavior? There are two methods to establish this relationship. One is to look for direct evidence that the Chinese government takes a foreign policy action because it sees the action as consistent with the strategic image it is trying to project. The other is to look for indirect evidence that a foreign policy action is not taken because of any immediate material gains and that it is consistent with a projected national image.[26] Direct evidence is not easy to find since Chinese policy making has been for the most part secretive. So here we have to rely primarily on indirect evidence.

First, we examine some strategic national images and their constraining effect on Chinese foreign policy. The most salient of such images during the Maoist period was that of China as a bastion of revolution. As figure 4.6 shows, the Chinese government emphasized this image from the late 1950s to the mid-1970s, a period when the PRC was more or less estranged from both the United States and the Soviet Union. During this time, the Chinese government saw the Third World as its greatest political opportunity and believed that a revolutionary image would help increase China's political influence in Asia, Africa, and Latin America.[27] While there is no doubt that the image of a bastion of revolution was an instrument serving China's national interest, it sometimes had a constraining impact on Chinese foreign policy. To boost its credentials, China spent valuable resources supporting revolutionary forces when no immediate economic, military, or political interest was at stake. This was especially true during the Cultural Revolution, when the Chinese government strenuously projected China's revolutionary image. According to one scholar, during that time "Peking committed itself to various avowedly radical groups in Africa, India, and the Persian Gulf in whose victory or defeat China had little to gain."[28] The absence of material payoffs in these cases constitutes indirect evidence that China's foreign policy behavior was aimed primarily at national image building.[29]

A salient example can be found in China's relations with Southeast Asia. From the 1950s to the early 1970s, Mao's government provided military and political training, propaganda support as well as arms to rebellious groups in Southeast Asia. China's assistance to these revolutionary activities did not promise tangible returns. In fact, not only did this cost China resources, but it also badly undermined China's relations with the governments of those countries.[30] China's revolutionary diplomacy thus only makes sense if it is seen as part of China's national image-building efforts.

Not only did considerations of national image building lead to China's providing military and political support to revolutionary groups, but they also played a role in shaping China's foreign economic aid behaviors during the Maoist era. China under Mao was the only country in the world that regularly gave aid to other countries with higher per capita gross national product (GNP) than its own.[31] The Chinese saw their assistance to socialist countries and countries that were former colonies as part of their commitment to the struggle against colonialism and imperialism. By and large, China's aid lived up to its declared purpose—to help the recipient countries become economically independent. Not only were the financial terms generous, but the aid programs were also designed to enable recipient countries to gradually free themselves from having to export cheap raw materials and import expensive finished products. According to one student of Chinese foreign aid, "Beijing wanted to use aid for propaganda purposes and thus sought to emphasise differences between its aid and that provided by the West."[32]

The most important strategic national image in the post-Mao period has been that of China as an international cooperator. As figure 4.10 shows, since the mid-1980s the Chinese government has gone out of its way to portray China as eager to cooperate with other countries in the world. This image has been part of China's overall strategy to establish a friendly international environment for its modernization project. It, too, has had a constraining impact on Chinese foreign policy behavior under some conditions. An important case in point is China's signing of the Comprehensive Test Ban Treaty (CTBT) in 1996. This was a dramatic departure from the previous Chinese position. For years the Chinese government had called for the United States and Russia to substantially cut down their nuclear weapons before China would limit its own development of nuclear weapons. This is understandable given the small size of China's nuclear arsenal and its importance as a symbol of China's great power status and ultimate guarantor of China's national security. Since the CTBT puts a number of explicit restrictions on China's nuclear development plan, the treaty—from a Chinese point of view—would freeze China's inferior position vis-à-vis Russia and the United States and thus seriously undermine its national security and national power. What, then, made the Chinese government change its policy and accept the CTBT? According to informed scholars, the government's concern for China's international image was a major factor.[33] After the CTBT moved on to the arms control agenda in 1993, China was compelled to negotiate despite deep reservations, because not doing so would contradict decades of Chinese rhetoric of disarmament and badly damage the country's image. The Chinese government does not deny its concern over international pubic opinion. In a statement about China's decision to sign the treaty, the Chinese government noted that it was in part "a response to the appeal of the vast number of non-nuclear-weapon states."[34]

Another case is China's foreign exchange policy in the aftermath of the Asian financial crisis of 1997. In July of that year, the currencies of a number of Asian economies collapsed due to international speculation and domestic corruption. As the crisis spread from one country to the next, the world turned its attention to China, to see if it would devalue the renminbi (RMB). China had good economic and political reasons to do so. The depreciation of regional currencies threatened to undermine Chinese exports and the inflow of foreign direct investment (FDI)—the twin engines of economic growth in

China. This, in turn, would further undermine the country's political stability, which was already fragile because of increasing layoffs in the cities and the deterioration of rural living standards. However, despite these considerations, the Chinese government decided not to resort to a yuan devaluation. Instead, it promised the world that it would uphold the value of its currency because it was the right thing to do for a "responsible great power" (*fuzeren de daguo*). For the next couple of years, Chinese leaders repeatedly emphasized that its exchange policy represented its willingness and ability to contribute to the well-being of the international community.[35] Chinese policy analysts explicitly linked China's exchange-rate policy to its desire to improve China's image on the international stage.[36]

The constraining effect of images is quite consistent with the neoliberal institutionalist approach to international relations. This approach stresses the importance of reputation in the conduct of foreign relations. In the words of Robert Keohane, "To a government that values its ability to make future agreements, reputation is a crucial resource; and the most important aspect of an actor's reputation in world politics is the belief of others that it will keep its future commitments even when a particular situation, myopically viewed, makes it appear disadvantageous to do so."[37] Sometimes, achieving a credible reputation with rivals as well as allies requires behavior that may not be in the immediate interests of a state. If policy makers regard reputation as sufficiently important, they will engage in behavior that they otherwise would avoid. For example, to demonstrate resolve in its confrontation with the Soviet Union and the Eastern bloc, the United States became involved in the Vietnam War, which generated enormous political, economic, and military losses with no obvious material returns.[38] Likewise, Scandinavian countries and the European Union devote considerable economic resources to aid poor countries, which does not necessarily result in immediate financial or strategic gains but does establish and reinforce their altruistic images.[39] Similarly, since World War II, Japan has significantly limited its military capabilities to ameliorate its militarist reputation and establish a trustworthy image among its Asian neighbors.[40]

While strategic national images can constrain foreign policy behavior, internalized national images often have a constitutive effect on the latter. As discussed, internalized images include China as a peace-loving nation, a victim of foreign aggression, an antihegemonic force, and a developing country.[41] We examine each image in turn.

First, we begin with the image of China as a peace-loving nation and victim. Figures 4.3 and 4.4 show that the Chinese government has pursued these images with remarkable consistency. On the surface, these images seem to be at odds with China's foreign policy conduct. In fact, the PRC has been more prone to use force against others than other major powers. According to the Correlates of War Project, between 1950 and 1992, there were twenty-two interstate wars.[42] China was party to four of these wars, more than any other country except Israel (see table 4.3). But a careful look yields a different conclusion. Although the image and self-image of China as a peace-loving nation and victim has not led the Chinese government to a particularly peaceful and humble approach to foreign relations, it has significantly shaped the way Chinese policy makers perceive and define international problems. Given its firm belief that China is a peace-loving nation and a victim, the Chinese government—in situations of conflicts and through the mechanism of cognitive balance—invariably sees the other side as the aggressor. Once the situation is defined as foreign aggression against China, the Chinese government often feels compelled to take resolute action. One can see this pattern in numerous cases, from the Korean War to the Sino-Vietnamese war, and from the multiple Taiwan Strait crises to the disputes in the South China Sea. In each situation, the internalized image of China as a peace-loving nation and victim ultimately led to self-righteousness and intransigence on the part of China's foreign policy.[43]

What about the image of China as an antihegemonic force? Figure 4.7 shows that it has been a constant theme in Chinese national image building. The constitutive effect of this image can be seen in the Chinese position vis-à-vis international conflicts involving asymmetric powers. For instance, as noted, the Correlates of War Project records twenty-two interstate wars between 1950 and 1992. Of the eighteen that did not involve China, the Chinese government expressed support for, or sympathy with, the weaker party in ten cases, or 56 percent of the time, and sided with the stronger party in only one case, or 5 percent of the time (see table 4.3). Further research is likely to show similar patterns of Chinese behavior regarding other types of asymmetrical international conflicts, including incidents of international tension short of war, economic quarrels, and political arguments.

Furthermore, the internalized image of China as an antihegemonic agent, like the images of China as a peace-loving nation and victim, colors the way Chinese leaders perceive China's interactions with other countries. It makes it possible and likely for the Chinese government to reject, in a knee-jerk reaction, any characterization of China ever threatening anyone else. When others find China overbearing, Chinese policy makers are bound to view this reaction as a misunderstanding or, worse, a deliberate distortion. For instance, when China went to war with Vietnam in 1979, China was obviously the stronger party. But given China's self-image, it was not possible for the Chinese government to see its own behavior as hegemonic. Instead, it believed that Vietnam had acted hegemonically in Indochina. China was simply teaching the Vietnamese a lesson.

Table 4.3.   Interstate Wars, 1950–1992

Wars	China[a]	China–WP[b]	China–SP[c]
1. Korean (1950–1953)	√		
2. Russo-Hungarian (1956)			√
3. Sinai (1956)		√	
4. Sino-Indian (1962)	√		
5. Vietnam (1965–1975)		√	
6. Second Kashmir (1965)		√	
7. Six Day (1967)		√	
8. Israel Egyptian (1969–1970)		√	
9. Football (1969)			
10. Bangladesh (1971)			
11. Yom Kippur (1973)		√	
12. Turco-Cypriot (1974)			
13. Vietnam-Cambodia (1975–1979)		√	
14. Ethiopia-Somalia (1977–1978)		√	
15. Uganda-Tanzania (1978–1979)			
16. Sino-Vietnamese (1979)	√		
17. Iran-Iraq (1980–1988)			
18. Falkland Islands (1982)		√	
19. Israel-Syria (1982)		√	
20. Sino-Vietnamese (1985–1987)	√		
21. Gulf (1990–1991)			
22. Azeri-Armenian (1992)			

Source: J. David Singer and Melvin Small, *Correlates of War Project: International and Civil War Data, 1816-1992*, ICPSR 9905 (Ann Arbor, Mich.: Interuniversity Consortium for Political and Social Research, 1994).
[a] Wars involving China
[b] Wars where China sided/sympathized with weaker party
[c] Wars where China sided/sympathized with stronger party

Finally, we turn to the image of China as a developing country. Figure 4.8 shows this to be another image that the Chinese government has projected steadfastly. The constitutive effect of this self-image can be seen in China's interactions with the developed countries in the world. During the early years of the People's Republic of China, the Chinese government was a junior ally of the Soviet Union. Although Mao could not tolerate Soviet domination of China, the Chinese government—having defined itself as a developing country—was perfectly comfortable being a recipient of Soviet economic and military aid. In fact, Chinese policy makers took such aid for granted. By the late 1950s and early 1960s, when the Soviet Union reduced and then withheld aid, despite China's repeated requests for assistance, the Chinese were bitterly disappointed. This issue played an important part in the breakup of the Sino-Soviet alliance.[44]

The internalized image of China as a developing country has also had a constitutive effect on its relations with Western industrialized countries. For example, for years China has been one of the largest recipients of Japanese foreign aid. Recently, the Japanese public expressed reluctance to continue the same level of assistance to China. In addition to Japan's own fiscal problems, the Japanese were concerned about China's growing military and economic strengths. In 2000, a Japanese foreign ministry panel suggested reducing Japan's aid to China. Chinese officials dismiss the view that China is becoming powerful and thus should do what it can for itself. They make clear that China is still poor and still needs Japanese assistance. In fact, they define Japanese financial assistance as an important part of the bilateral relationship, implying aid reduction would undermine Sino-Japanese relations. China's internalized image of a developing country has similarly shaped its reaction to other industrialized nations as well as to international human rights, environmental, and trade regimes.

These four national images—a peace-loving nation, a victim of foreign aggression, an antihegemonic force, and a developing country—reflect China's self-conception in international affairs. They are as much assertions of China's identity as they are public relations scripts for foreign consumption. The impact of these images on Chinese foreign policy behavior is consistent with the contention of the constructivist perspective of international relations. This perspective emphasizes the constructed nature of national interest, among other things, arguing that the means and ends of a country's foreign policy are shaped by its identity. For example, American foreign policy in the early years, Soviet foreign policy at the end of the Cold War, and Japanese and German foreign policy since the end of World War II are all "abnormal" from a structural–realist point of view but can be better understood in light of national self-images.[45]

It is worth noting that over time, even a strategic image can become a self-image and thus have a constitutive effect on a country's behavior. As psychologists demonstrate in their study of individuals, various considerations can lead people to take actions that are inconsistent with, or directly contradictory to, their beliefs. But once they engage in these actions, a number of psychological mechanisms—self-attribution, self-persuasion, and dissonance reduction—may intervene and remold their beliefs.[46] In other words, if people consistently abide by a norm, they may internalize the norm over time, even if they do not believe in it at the beginning. Assuming that the same process takes place among national leaders, it seems quite possible that as they seek to establish a certain kind of image by engaging in behavior consistent with that image, that image may in time become an internalized self-image. In that case, it is likely to have a constitutive effect on future foreign policy behavior.

To summarize, projected national images can have a causal impact on foreign policy behavior. Thus, it would be a mistake simply to dismiss China's projected images as being pure deception and having nothing to do with Chinese foreign policy behavior. Instead, such images provide useful clues. Sometimes, they can help predict the range of behavior on the part of China. Sometimes they can help understand Chinese interpretations of international situations. With these clues, one can gain a more nuanced picture of Chinese foreign policy behavior than that portrayed by a simple structural theory such as neorealism. Furthermore, the findings here suggest that outsiders can influence Chinese behavior by influencing the kinds of images that China pursues. Once the Chinese government decides to build a certain type of image, that image can have a constraining effect on China's policy choices. Evidence suggests that during the Asian financial crisis in the late 1990s, the social rewards that the international community bestowed on China played an important role in encouraging the Chinese government to pursue an image of a "responsible great power." This in turn led China to adhere to a cooperative policy of no devaluation. Moreover, if this image becomes internalized over time, it may even have a constitutive effect on Chinese behavior.

CONCLUSION

In this chapter I have taken a modest step toward understanding China's national image building as part of Chinese foreign policy. I have reported findings about the types of images that the Chinese government has sought to project, the discrepancies between China's projected images and others' perceptions of China, and the impact of projected images on Chinese foreign policy behavior. Much more remains to be done. First, as noted, in comparing China's projected images and others' perceptions of China, I have only examined the public opinion in the United States, which may not have been the intended audience until the past twenty to thirty years. In the future, it will be useful to study the perceptions of China on the part of European and Third World countries. Second, as I also noted, in exploring the possible impact of China's image building on its foreign policy behaviors, I have primarily used indirect evidence. Detailed case studies are necessary to find direct evidence of the role of image considerations in foreign policy making, including how such considerations interact with other factors. Finally, this chapter does not deal with the sources of China's projected images and their evolution. I have provided some preliminary answers to this question elsewhere,[47] but it is an area that certainly deserves further research.

NOTES

An earlier version of this chapter was delivered at the annual meeting of the American Political Science Association, Boston, August 29–September 1, 2002. The author is grateful to Xueyi Chen for her dedicated and competent research assistance. This chapter first appeared in *China: An International Journal* 1, no. 1 (March 2003): 46–72. It is reprinted with permission.

1. Jeffrey Parker, "New Propaganda Office Pledges 'True Image' of China," United Press International, June 13, 1991.
2. Marcy Gordon, "China Fighting to Change Image as Crucial Trade Vote Nears," Associated Press, July 9, 1991.
3. Xinhua News Agency, "President Calls for Further Propaganda Work to Enhance China's Image Abroad," BBC Worldwide Monitoring, February 28, 1999.
4. For an elaboration on national images in international relations, see Michael Kunczik, *Images of Nations and International Pubic Relations* (Mahwah, N.J.: Lawrence Erlbaum Associates, 1997).
5. The topic of perceptions (and misperceptions) has been a central theme in the study of Chinese foreign relations. Scholarly work on this subject has yielded important insights into the formation of China's perceptions of others and others' perceptions of China, as well as the impact of mutual perceptions. See, for example, David Shambaugh, *Beautiful Imperialist: China Perceives America, 1972–1990* (Princeton, N.J.: Princeton University Press, 1991); and Jianwei Wang, *Limited Adversaries: Post–Cold War Sino-American Mutual Images* (New York: Oxford University Press, 2000). But this literature does not directly address China's national image building.
6. The literal Chinese translation of "national image" is *guojia xingxiang*. While this phrase appears in Chinese publications, more often used is the phrase *guoji xingxiang* (international image), which emphasizes the international community as the target of image projection.
7. For instance, in late 1990, China's top leaders presided over an important meeting on overseas publicity. The meeting called for Chinese from all walks of life to help project a favorable image of China to the rest of the world. It required propaganda workers to study the differences between foreigners (and overseas Chinese) and people in China and to distinguish methods of propaganda for these two audiences. In early 1998, Premier Li Peng wrote to the national overseas publicity conference, calling for improvement in this area of work. At a similar conference in early 1999, President Jiang Zemin called for massive publicity efforts to raise China's international stature. He emphasized that the departments in charge of the work should be equipped with advanced information technology and facilities. He asked CCP committees and governments at all levels to provide support for the publicity work.
8. In 1998 the Party Propaganda Department changed its English name to Publicity Department, even though its Chinese name remained the same.
9. One study shows that foreign countries using American public relations firms have seen their national images improve in the United States. See Jarol Manheim and Robert Albritton, "Changing National Images: The International Public Relations and

Media Agenda Setting," *American Political Science Review* 78, no. 3 (1984): 641–57. But I have not seen systematic data on China's use of these firms or their results in shaping foreign public opinion.

10. Elisabeth Rosenthal, "China's U.S. Road Show," *New York Times*, August 23, 2000, A3.

11. Many scholars of imperial China have written about its images as the "Middle Kingdom" and a benign hegemon, although they disagree on the extent to which these images were consistent with reality. See, for example, John King Fairbank, ed., *Chinese World Order: Traditional China's Foreign Relations* (Cambridge, Mass.: Harvard University Press, 1968); Mark Mancall, *China at the Center: 300 Years of Foreign Policy* (New York: Free Press, 1984); Alastair Iain Johnston, *Cultural Realism: Strategic Culture and Grand Strategy in Chinese History* (Princeton, N.J.: Princeton University Press, 1995); and Warren Cohen, *East Asia at the Center: Four Thousand Years of Engagement with the World* (New York: Columbia University Press, 2000).

12. Other official publications aimed at image building include the *China Daily*, *China Reconstructs*, and the *People's Daily*. However, none of them seems suitable for the task at hand. *China Daily* was first published in the late 1970s and thus does not offer data for earlier years. *China Reconstructs* focuses mainly on domestic development in China and does not shed much light on China's desired images in international relations. *People's Daily* aims primarily at the domestic audience and covers a wide range of issues. A random sampling of a reasonable size may or may not produce much information on China's image building vis-à-vis the international community.

13. This is stated on the official *Beijing Review* website: www.bjreview.com.cn (December 2002).

14. My focus here is what images the Chinese government has tried to build of China rather than what images have reached the intended audience. Therefore it is not my concern whether or how many foreigners actually read these documents.

15. I used different coding units for the *Peking Review* and for the government work reports—paragraphs for the former and sentences for the latter. For both, the unit of analysis was each projected image. Before the formal coding, my research assistant and I did a preliminary test. For the nine image variables, we achieved a high intercoder agreement, with an average coefficient of agreement of 0.96.

16. The Roper Center for Public Opinion Research in Storrs, Connecticut, was founded immediately following World War II and maintains a database of public opinion surveys conducted by academics, media organizations, and commercial pollsters dating back to 1935.

17. For example, I coded the following question as perceiving China as socialist, militant (opposite to peace loving), and a major power: "Red China has exploded another atomic bomb. Do you think we should try to negotiate an atomic test-ban treaty with them?" I coded the following question as perceiving China as militant, obstructive (opposite to cooperative), and socialist: "Do you agree that the U.S. should come to the defense of Japan with military force if it is attacked by Soviet Russia or Communist China?"

18. For an early discussion of this, see Jerome Bruner and Leo Postman, "On the Perceptions of Incongruity: A Paradigm," in *Perception and Personality*, ed. Jerome Bruner and David Krech (Durham, N.C.: Duke University Press, 1950).

19. Robert Jervis, "Hypotheses on Misperception," *World Politics* 20, no. 3 (1968): 455.

20. These findings can be found in Donald Taylor and Vaishna Jaggi, "Ethnocentrism and Causal Attribution in a South Indian Context," *Journal of Cross-Cultural Psychology* 5, no. 2 (1974): 162–71; and Thomas Pettigrew, "The Ultimate Attribution Error: Extending Allport's Cognitive Analysis of Prejudice," *Personality and Social Psychology Bulletin* 5, no. 4 (1979): 461–76.

21. On this point, see Jonathan Mercer, *Reputation and International Politics* (Ithaca, N.Y.: Cornell University Press, 1996).

22. Since September 11, 2001, Americans have changed their view of the world in important ways. The conceptual global realignment in the minds of American policy makers may have changed China's status from a member of the out-group to that of the in-group. If this pattern holds, it may well change the underlying dynamics of U.S. perception of China. I thank Yong Deng and Fei-ling Wang for this insight.

23. China's public relations czar Zhao Qizheng seems to understand this point very well. See an interview with Zhao in *Huasheng Yuebao*, July 2000. However, China's publicity workers have changed little in that direction.

24. The "decoupling" of images and behavior may reflect the lack of seriousness on the part of the government about its projected images. It may also result from a lack of coordination between the government agencies in charge of image building and other agencies pursuing their own goals.

25. These self-images overlap but differ from what Wang Gungwu identifies as the several layers of Chinese self-perceptions—a socialist market economy, a developing economy, a modern nation, a historic empire, a civilizational challenge, and a potential global power. See Wang Gungwu, "China's New Paths for National Reemergence," in *China's Political Economy*, ed. Wang Gungwu and John Wong (Singapore: Singapore University Press), 95–148. The absence of a socialist market economy, modern nation, historic empire, and civilizational challenge on my list of China's self-images is probably due to my narrow focus on China's images as an international actor rather than its general national images. That aside, my analysis agrees with Wang Gungwu's on China's self-perception as a developing country. We differ in that my data point to China's self-images of a peace-loving nation and an antihegemonic force, while Wang Gungwu emphasizes China's self-perception as a potential global power.

26. Two points are worth noting here. First, I emphasize *immediate* material gains because analytically it is hard to separate long-term material interests from image building. Today's good image often translates into tomorrow's material gains. Second, my focus here is on cases where image-making considerations produce different behavior than do short-term material considerations. This is not to negate the many instances where these two sets of considerations go hand in hand and lead to the same behavior. I do not deal with the latter type of cases because there it is difficult to single out the effects of image-building considerations.

27. See Peter Van Ness, *Revolution and Chinese Foreign Policy: Peking's Support for Wars of National Liberation* (Berkeley: University of California Press, 1970), 15; and Yan Xuetong, *Zhongguo Guojia Liyi Fenxi* [An Analysis of China's National Interest], 2nd ed. (Tianjin, China: Tianjin Renmin Chubanshe, 1997), 38.

28. Jay Taylor, *China and Southeast Asia: Peking's Relations with Revolutionary Movements* (New York: Praeger Publishers, 1976), 389.

29. An alternative explanation may attribute such behavior to Marxist ideology. I find that explanation less than convincing because, despite its rhetoric, the Chinese government has often departed from Marxism in its domestic and foreign policies.

30. See Melvin Gurtov, *China and Southeast Asia—The Politics of Survival: A Study of Foreign Policy Interaction* (Baltimore: Johns Hopkins University Press, 1975); Taylor and Jaggi, "Ethnocentrism"; and Edwin Martin, *Southeast Asia and China: The End of Containment* (Boulder, Colo.: Westview Press, 1977). Similar behavior was present in China's foreign relations elsewhere in the world. The cost of such behavior is made clear by the political and strategic gains after China toned down its rhetoric of world revolution. In 1970, at the height of China's radical foreign policy practices, only fifty-three countries had diplomatic relations with China. By early 1974, the number had grown to ninety. See Gurtov, *China and Southeast Asia*, 180.

31. This is pointed out by Teh-chang Lin, "Beijing's Foreign Aid Policy in the 1990s: Continuity and Change," *Issues and Studies* 32, no. 1 (1996): 32–56; and Ping Ai, "From Proletarian Internationalism to Mutual Development: China's Cooperation with Tanzania, 1965–1995," in *Agencies in Foreign Aid: Comparing China, Sweden and the United States in Tanzania*, ed. Goran Hyden and Rwekaza Mukandala (New York: St. Martin, 1999), 156–201.

32. Lin, "Beijing's Foreign Aid Policy," 34.

33. See Alastair Iain Johnston, "Prospects for Chinese Nuclear Force Modernization: Limited Deterrence Versus Multilateral Arms Control," *China Quarterly* (1996): 548–76; and Bates Gill and Evan Medeiros, "Foreign and Domestic Influences in China's Arms Control and Nonproliferation Policies," *China Quarterly* (2000): 66–94.

34. Gill and Medeiros, "Foreign and Domestic Influences," 70.

35. For a detailed discussion, see Hongying Wang, "Crisis and Credibility: China's Exchange Rate Policy in the Aftermath of the Asian Financial Crisis," in *Monetary Order: Ambiguous Economics, Ubiquitous Politics*, ed. Jonathan Kirshner (Ithaca, N.Y.: Cornell University Press, 2002), 153–71.

36. See, for example, Liu Jinhua, "Zhongguo Guoji Zhanlue: Xiangguan Lilun yu Xianshi Sikao" [China's international strategy: Relevant theories and reflections], *Guoji Jingji Pinglun* 3–4 (1999): 57–60; Shi Yinhong, "Guanyu Zhonguo de Daguo Diwei Jiqi Xingxiang Sikao" [Thoughts on China's great power status and its image], *Guoji Jingji Pinglun* (September–October 1999): 43–44; and Shen Jianing, "APEC Shanghai Huiyi yu Zhongguo de Guoji Xingxiang" [APEC meeting in Shanghai and China's international image], *Guoji Zhengzhi Yanjiu*, no. 1 (2002): 115–18. In an argument parallel to the one made here, Rosemary Foot contends that because the Chinese government cares about its international image (though she does not discuss what kind of an image), it is capable of being shamed for violating international human rights standards. China's image consciousness has been a major factor underlying its incremental concessions to

the international human rights regime. See Rosemary Foot, *Rights Beyond Borders: The Global Community and the Struggle over Human Rights in China* (Oxford: Oxford University Press, 2000).

37. Robert Keohane, *After Hegemony* (Princeton, N.J.: Princeton University Press, 1984), 116.

38. For such a perspective of American involvement in Vietnam, see Stephen Krasner, *Defending the National Interest: Raw Materials Investment and U.S. Foreign Policy* (Princeton, N.J.: Princeton University Press, 1978).

39. O. Stokke, "Development Assistance: Prospects and Priorities," *Development Dialogue* 2 (1995): 21–33; and Christian Freres, "The European Union as a Global 'Civilian Power': Development Cooperation in EU–Latin American Relations," *Journal of Interamerican Studies and World Affairs* 62, no. 2 (2000): 63–85.

40. This argument is made by Paul Midford, "The Logic of Reassurance and Japan's Grand Strategy," *Security Studies* 11, no. 3 (2002): 1–44.

41. I make no claim that these internalized images are uniquely Chinese. For instance, many countries probably see themselves as peace-loving nations.

42. J. David Singer and Melvin Small, *Correlates of War Project: International and Civil War Data, 1816–1992*, ICPSR 9905 (Ann Arbor, Mich.: Interuniversity Consortium for Political and Social Research, 1994). Data derived from the Correlates of War Project are widely used in studies of war.

43. In a parallel argument, Andrew Scobell points out that the Chinese elite holds three core beliefs dearly—that the Chinese are a peace-loving people, are not aggressive or expansionist, and only use force in self-defense. These beliefs, however, do not constrain China's use of military force. See Andrew Scobell, "The Chinese Cult of Defense," *Issues and Studies* 37, no. 5 (2001): 100–127.

44. This is made clear by Shuguang Zhang, *Economic Cold War: America's Embargo against China and the Sino-Soviet Alliance, 1949–1963* (Stanford, Calif.: Stanford University Press, 2001).

45. See Mlada Bukovansky, "American Identity and Neutral Rights from Independence to the War of 1912," *International Organization* 55, no. 3 (1997): 553–88; Peter Katzenstein, *Cultural Norms and National Security: Police and Military in Postwar Japan* (Ithaca, N.Y.: Cornell University Press, 1996); Robert Herman, "Identity, Norms, and National Security: The Soviet Foreign Policy Revolution and the End of the Cold War," in *The Culture of National Security: Norms and Identities in World Politics*, ed. Peter Katzenstein (New York: Columbia University Press, 1996): 271–316; and Thomas Berger, "Norms, Identity, and National Security in Germany and Japan," in *The Culture of National Security*, 317–56. Another theoretical perspective that emphasizes the constitutive impact of internalized national images can be found in the foreign policy literature on "national role conception." See Stephen Walker, ed., *Role Theory and Foreign Policy Analysis* (Durham, N.C.: Duke University Press, 1987).

46. For an elaboration, see Philip G. Zimbardo and Michael R. Leippe, *The Psychology of Attitude Change and Social Influence* (Philadelphia: Temple University Press, 1991): 87–125.

47. See Hongying Wang, "National Image Building: A Case Study of China" (paper presented at the International Studies Association Meeting, Hong Kong, July 2001).

5

Nationalism and Chinese Foreign Policy

Peter Hays Gries

What motivates Chinese foreign policy? Rationalist international relations (IR) theorists have despaired of ever directly understanding Chinese intentions, so they have sought to infer them indirectly from China's position in the international balance of power and from China's economic and military capabilities—but both data sources are subject to interpretation. Pro-China analysts point to China's low per capita gross national product (GNP) and the undeniable inferiority of the People's Liberation Army (PLA) in comparison to the U.S. military to argue that China is no threat to the global balance of power. Henry Kissinger, for instance, argues that "China is no military colossus" and has "the best of intentions."[1] Those suspicious of Chinese intentions, in contrast, point to recent Chinese arms acquisitions from Russia and elsewhere to argue that China is aggressively seeking to upset the East Asian balance of power. For example, Arthur Waldron of the American Enterprise Institute argues that "China seeks to combine targeted military capabilities with diplomatic and economic measures in order to weaken American presence and resolve in Asia."[2] In the end, such rationalist analyses are frequently reductionist, reducing the complex issue of Chinese intentions to a crude debate over material capabilities. Furthermore, these arguments usually tell us more about the optimism or pessimism of the analyst than they do about China.[3]

This chapter argues that human motivation is invisible, complex, and multiple and that nationalism is a key—if not *the* key—motivator of Chinese foreign policy. After a brief unpacking of the concept of motivation, I make two arguments about the impact of nationalism on Chinese foreign policy making. First, a social psychological approach to nationalism can reveal how complex and multiple motives drive Chinese nationalists. Nationalism is not an irrational emotionalism to be juxtaposed against the cool pursuit of China's national interest. Instead, nationalist behaviors are often simultaneously emotional and instrumental. Second, against the common view of China as a unitary actor that can coolly calculate its national interest, I contend that foreign policy making in China is increasingly a "two-level game," with Chinese diplomats keeping one eye on domestic nationalists, even as they negotiate with their foreign counterparts. Popular nationalism is increasingly constraining the making of Chinese foreign policy. The chapter concludes with a few thoughts on the implications that this analysis of nationalism and Chinese foreign policy might have for the making of U.S. China policy.

Intentions are not directly observable; they can only be inferred indirectly by triangulating from the things that people say and do. But words and deeds are not transparent either and must be interpreted very carefully. First, we humans are strategic animals and frequently disguise our true intentions through the use of deception. As Bob Jervis and other IR theorists have shown, states can and frequently do use deceptive signaling (diplomatic statements as well as military posturing) to disguise their true intentions from other states and thus achieve advantage.[4] Second, we are also social animals and frequently disguise our true motives from others—and even from ourselves. As Italian sociologist Vilfredo Pareto noted almost a century ago, although we frequently act irrationally, we are masters at the art of ex post facto rationalizations of our behaviors.[5] For instance, although aggressive displays of force are generally motivated by emotions such as pride or anger, foreign policy makers usually rationalize them with the instrumental language of deterrence.

Human motivation is not just invisible; it is also complex. For instance, anger is an emotion that frequently drives our behaviors, but not all anger is the same. Following the May 1999 U.S. bombing of the Chinese embassy in Belgrade, Chinese protestors frequently wrote and spoke about strong feelings of *fennu* or *qifen* but rarely of feeling *shengqi*. All can be translated as "anger," but they are actually very different emotions. The former two are higher forms of anger, or "righteous indignation," that stem from feelings of injustice and ethical desires to right a wrong; the latter, a lower or visceral form of anger, or even "blind fury," is little more than a personal psychological satisfaction.[6] Given their understanding of the Belgrade bombing as an intentional assault on Chinese sovereignty, another in a long line of Western aggressions against China, it is little wonder that many Chinese were indignant.[7] The distinction between "ethical" and "visceral" forms of anger is no mere academic nuance; the accurate interpretation of other states' motivations is vital to states as they formulate their policy responses.

Finally, human motivation is frequently multiple. In the West, we typically juxtapose reason against emotion as if they exist in a zero-sum relationship: any increase in emotionality entailing a decrease in rationality, and vice versa. Our behaviors, however, are often motivated by reason *and* emotion. For instance, actions designed to "save face," or restore honor, frequently have both instrumental and emotional dimensions. When Chinese diplomats raise the "war card" in negotiations with the Japanese, they seek to gain instrumental advantage. But raising the issue of wartime victimization also implicates cherished self-identifications—challenging the very meaning of being "Chinese" or "Japanese." This helps explain why World War II continues to be an extremely sensitive issue in Sino-Japanese relations.

Interestingly, both Americans and Chinese tend to deny the multiplicity of their own motives—but each tends to privilege diametrically opposite intentions. Americans, like most post-Enlightenment Westerners, tend to depict their own behaviors as driven solely by reason and enlightened self-interest—and will passionately deny being driven by "irrational" emotions. The Chinese, in contrast, tend to depict their own behaviors as driven by emotions such as compassion and benevolence—and will passionately deny being motivated by "selfish" (*zisi*) interests. Thus, although both Americans and Chinese are driven by considerations of sense and sensibility, Americans tend to privilege the former whereas the Chinese privilege the latter in their ex post facto rationalizations of their own behaviors. Attributions of each other's motives are also influenced by this normative difference. For instance, American China-bashers and Chinese America-bashers frequently hurl insults at each other that fail to hit their mark, with the Americans accusing the Chinese of being overly emotional and with the Chinese belittling American foreign policies as being selfish.[8] I doubt many nationalists on either side of the Pacific lose much sleep over such accusations.

Human motivation, in sum, is invisible, complex, and multiple. Rather than project onto China preexisting "gut feelings," analysts must carefully infer Chinese intentions from the things that Chinese actually say and do. We must, furthermore, interrogate the nuances of various motives and explore their relative weight in driving behavior.

MAINTAINING *MIANZI* IN CHINESE FOREIGN POLICY

Nationalism, which I define here as any behavior designed to restore, maintain, or advance public images of the nation,[9] may well be the most important determinant of Chinese foreign policy. The Chinese Communist Party (CCP) came to power on the basis of anti-Japanese peasant nationalism and has staked its legitimacy on its nationalist credentials ever since.[10] Under Mao Zedong, Chinese nationalism was expressed in a "victor narrative" of heroic Chinese victories over Western and Japanese imperialism. Under Jiang Zemin and now Hu Jintao, however, Chinese nationalists are increasingly constructing a "victimization narrative" of the Chinese suffering at the hands of Western and Japanese imperialists during the "Century of Humiliation" (*bainian guochi*).[11] This has created strong and widespread desires to "erase" (*xixue*) the national humiliation by restoring China to the position of dominance in East Asia that most Chinese imagine China to have enjoyed before its defeat to the British in the first Opium War, 1839–1842. This nationalist goal of strengthening China is shared by virtually all Chinese.[12] In this sense, nationalism is the metamotive driving Chinese political behavior. It is only on the means to the common ends of a strong China that the Chinese disagree. For instance, where Chinese during the Maoist era saw communism as the key to strengthening China, Chinese today have turned to capitalism as the proper means toward economic development. Both approaches were likely right: where the underdeveloped Chinese economy of the 1950s and 1960s required a planned economy to allocate scarce resources for industrialization, China's economy today is more developed and complex and thus more suitable to market-driven development. The relative ease of the Chinese people's acceptance of the economic transition from plan to market suggests that these developmental strategies were never seen as ends in themselves but rather as means to the nationalist ends of strengthening China.

In China, nationalist desires to protect and advance China's "international image" (*guoji xingxiang*) are often expressed in the language of *mianzi*, or "face," the "self revealed before others."[13] Due to its Orientalist origins, the English figurative "face" has pejorative overtones, as in "two-faced." Following sociologist Erving Goffman, father of the Western study of face, I see the idea of *face* as neither uniquely Chinese nor inherently bad. It is a cultural universal, although it is expressed in widely different manners across time and place. For the twenty-first-century American reader, it might be helpful to think of *face* in the value-neutral language of "honor" and "dishonor."[14]

Nationalist desires to maintain China's international *mianzi* frequently have instrumental and emotional dimensions.[15] For instance, during the ten days of "apology diplomacy" that followed the April 1, 2001, plane collision incident, Chinese diplomats were driven by an instrumental concern to maintain China's position in the evolving East Asian hierarchy of power and by equally powerful emotions that sought to restore Chinese self-respect. Considerations of power and passion thus informed Chinese (and American) apology diplomacy.

Apologies are about power relations. Offenses to the social order threaten established hierarchies. One way that the aggrieved can regain social position is vengeance. As sociologist J. M. Barbalet writes, "Vengefulness is an emotion of power relations. It functions to correct imbalanced or disjointed power relationships. Vengefulness is concerned with restoring social actors to their rightful place in relationships."[16] Apologies are another means of restoring threatened social hierarchies. The form an apology takes depends critically on the relative status of the parties involved. The kind of apology necessary to rectify an offense an inferior commits against a superior is greater than that required of an offense committed between equals. For instance, a son who insults his father publicly must give an extended and public apology. Privately insulting his brother, however, requires a lesser kind of apology. An apology may not be possible, therefore, if there is disagreement over the relative status of the parties involved. If both parties claim to be the superior in a hierarchical relationship with each other, there can be no agreement on the extent of the apology necessary to rectify the offense.

The politics of apology is not just about relative status and material power, however; it is also about equally powerful passions. A public offense causes the aggrieved to lose face and is therefore far more offensive than one made in private.[17] As noted, vengeance and apologies can help reestablish power relations; they can also help restore self-esteem. As sociologist Barrington Moore writes, "Vengeance means retaliation. It also means a reassertion of human dignity or worth, after injury or damage. Both are basic sentiments behind moral anger and the sense of injustice."[18] Social psychologists have convincingly demonstrated that derogating the offender can restore the collective self-esteem of the offended. In one arresting experiment, American women actually lost national self-esteem when they were shown a clip from an altered *Rocky IV* in which the American boxer (played by Sylvester Stallone) loses to the Russian. Self-esteem was restored, however, when the subjects were subsequently allowed to denigrate Russians.[19] By righting a wrong, apologies can similarly restore the self-esteem of the aggrieved. However, if an offense is felt to be too hurtful, it may be impossible to even consider an apology.

On April 1, 2001, a Chinese F-8 jet fighter and an American EP-3 surveillance plane collided over the South China Sea. The EP-3 made it safely to China's Hainan Island; the F-8 tore apart and crashed, and Chinese pilot Wang Wei was killed. A few days later, Chinese foreign minister Tang Jiaxuan and president Jiang Zemin demanded an American apology. Americans balked: viewing the aggressiveness of the Chinese jet as the cause of the collision, Americans did not feel responsible. As Senator Joseph Lieberman said on CNN's *Larry King Live,* "When you play chicken, sometimes you get hurt."[20]

The impasse was only broken after eleven days of intensive negotiations. American ambassador Joseph Prueher gave a letter to Foreign Minister Tang:

"Please convey to the Chinese people and to the family of pilot Wang Wei that we are very sorry for their loss. . . . We are very sorry the entering of China's airspace and the landing did not have verbal clearance."[21] Having extracted an "apology" from Washington, Beijing released the twenty-four American servicemen being held on Hainan Island.

Psychological research on collective self-esteem can shed light on Chinese and American reactions to the plane collision incident. To the extent that we identify with a group, our self-esteem is tied to the group's fate. Both the Chinese and the Americans viewed the events of early April 2001 as a threat to their self-esteem. In China, many perceived American callousness toward the fate of Wang Wei as a humiliating loss of face. In the United States, Robert Kagan and William Kristol, of the conservative *Weekly Standard,* similarly declared the Bush administration's handling of the affair "a national humiliation": Bush's "groveling" was a degrading "loss of face."[22] Concern for face is not uniquely Oriental; it clearly drove both Chinese and American reactions to the incident.

Some Chinese and Americans responded to this identity threat by going into denial. Although the incident was a disaster for the bilateral relationship, many on both sides quickly claimed victory—a clear sign of face-saving self-deception. Gloating that "We won!" allowed many Chinese and American nationalists to save face. In Beijing, many boasted of how President Jiang had planned America's humiliation from the start and had "taught Bush Jr. a lesson."[23] Qinghua University's Yan Xuetong, for instance, declared that "China stuck to principle" and "did a better job of dealing with the incident."[24] Meanwhile, in Washington, Bush was widely praised for having handled the situation masterfully, winning the day. For instance, the *Nelson Report* circulated a parody of the American "we're sorry" letter: "We're sorry the world is now seeing your leaders as the xenophobic, clueless thugs that they really are. We're sorry you are losing so much face over this."

Others responded to the threat to their self-esteem not with denial but by venting a rage designed to restore national self-respect—to save face. For instance, by publicly calling Bush a "coward" (in a letter from Wang Wei's wife), Beijing sought to gain *face* for China at Washington's expense. And with the release of the American crew on April 11, American hawks quickly began screaming for vengeance. Secretary of Defense Donald Rumsfeld, who had been muzzled during the sensitive negotiations, immediately held a Pentagon news conference to present additional incriminating evidence against Chinese pilot Wang Wei.

The apology diplomacy that followed the 2001 plane collision was no mere emotional matter. China and the United States were jockeying for position in the post–Cold War hierarchy of power in East Asia. But because apologies also implicate collective self-esteem (in this case national dignity), both the Chinese and the Americans were extremely sensitive over the issue, prompting both sides to engage in a brief but dangerous game of chicken. Ironically, it was the face-saving, self-deceptive victory claiming of hawks on both sides that helped to defuse the crisis.

POPULAR NATIONALISM AND ELITE FOREIGN POLICY MAKING

Democracies, according to a well-established argument, are constrained by elections and public opinion and are thus at a disadvantage in foreign policy making. Authoritarian governments, conversely, are seen as free of domestic constraints and are thus at a diplomatic advantage. As Kant put it, autocrats may "resolve on war as on a pleasure party for the most trivial reasons."[25] In the mid-nineteenth century, Alexis de Tocqueville was forceful: "I have no hesitation in saying that in the control of society's foreign affairs democratic governments do appear decidedly inferior to others."[26] During the Cold War, U.S. Secretary of State Dean Acheson concurred: "In the conduct of their foreign relations, democracies appear to me decidedly inferior to other governments."[27] As IR theorist Randall Schweller recently put it, "Due to the strength of public opinion, the policies of a democratic state, in contrast to those of an autocracy, must ultimately conform to the moral values of that society."[28]

Popular opinion, in this view, can compel aggression and appeasement—against the will of elite foreign policy makers in democratic states. The USS *Maine* and "Munich" episodes serve as useful shorthand for these twin arguments. The sinking of the USS *Maine* in Havana Harbor (mistakenly attributed to Spanish subterfuge) and the popular outrage over Spanish atrocities against the Cubans forced President McKinley to launch the Spanish–American War of 1898, "a war which he did not want," according to Ernest May, "for a cause in which he did not believe."[29] "Munich" is short for Britain and France's 1938 acquiescence to the German annexation of Czechoslovakia. A pacifist British and French public is frequently blamed for prime ministers Chamberlain and Daladier's decision to appease Hitler. In sum, in democracies popular opinion can undermine the national interest, compelling governments toward both war and peace.

The democratic-disadvantage/authoritarian-advantage logic continues to drive American visions of Chinese foreign policy in the post–Cold War world. Viewing China as a "communist tyranny," many Americans today hold that the CCP, unlike the U.S. government, can calmly construct China's foreign policies unfettered by domestic constraints. For example, in the summer of 2002 the bipartisan United States–China Security Review Commission

(USCC) submitted its first annual report to the U.S. Congress. The report expresses concern that while America's China policy lacks consistency, beset by rivalries between Congress and the Bush administration within and by conflicts among various interest groups without, China's U.S. policy is driven by a coherent set of expansionist goals. Free of domestic constraints, Chinese foreign policy makers are seen as better able to pursue their goals, which, according to Commissioner Arthur Waldron, involve excluding the United States from Asia and threatening and coercing neighboring states.[30]

The emerging role that popular nationalism is playing in Chinese foreign policy making challenges the "democratic disadvantage" view. Lacking the procedural legitimacy accorded to democratically elected governments and facing the collapse of communist ideology, the CCP is increasingly dependent on its nationalist credentials to rule.[31] Thomas Christensen expressed this point succinctly in an influential *Foreign Affairs* article: "Since the Chinese Communist Party is no longer communist, it must be even more Chinese."[32] Popular nationalists may therefore come to play a *greater* role in foreign policy decision making in China than in the United States.

What role do popular nationalists play in the negotiation of the CCP's nationalist legitimacy? Chinese nationalist politics today exhibits the claim–response dynamic central to the negotiation of legitimacy in all political systems.[33] Not only do popular nationalists support and challenge the state's claims to legitimacy, but they also issue their own rival nationalist claims. The party suppresses *and* responds to such challenges to its nationalist credentials. The suppression of legitimate nationalist claims, however, makes the party lose face and authority before the Chinese people. Such suppression signals a reversion to coercive forms of power, undermining regime stability. Successful responses to popular nationalist demands, by contrast, allow the party to gain *face* before nationalist audiences, solidifying regime legitimacy.

The thirty-something "fourth generation" producers of popular Chinese nationalist discourse today may support or challenge the state's foreign policies.[34] For instance, in the 1997 best seller *The Plot to Demonize China*, Liu Kang argues that the U.S. government, big business, and the media conspire to make China lose face before world opinion.[35] *The Plot* clearly seeks to support the party. The 1996 anti-American sensation *China Can Say No* also supported the party's America policy.[36]

Other products of popular nationalism, however, challenge the party's legitimacy, claiming it has failed to maintain China's national *face*. For instance, in an open letter sent to the party leadership in February 1998, Chinese dissident Lin Xinshu argued that Li Peng not be given Qiao Shi's job as chairman of the National People's Congress. His argument, significantly, was not just about Li's "incompetence" but also that Li—tainted by his role in the

Tiananmen massacre—would tarnish "China's image in the world."[37] In other words, Li would be unable to maintain *face* for China.

The party elite suppress and respond to such assaults on its status. For example, following the 2001 spy-plane collision, the *People's Daily* sought to censor extreme nationalist postings on its online chatroom Strong Country Forum (*qiangguo luntan*). Many Chinese cyber-nationalists responded by moving to chatrooms at private sites such as Sina.com, where they fervently decried the state's suppression of their nationalist views.

But the story does not, as the Western media so frequently suggests, end with censorship and repression. The elite also responds to popular nationalists by seeking to gain *face* for China. It has begun, for example, an active campaign of promoting Chinese culture abroad. In 1998 the New China News Agency announced an official website designed to promote China's cultural image, introducing "China's 5,000-year-old culture on the Internet, promoting commercial performances and exhibitions. . . . Cultural activities that might degrade the country's dignity, however, will be banned."[38] Similarly, in September 2000—and in response to *The Plot to Demonize China* and to other popular nationalists' concerns that the American media makes China lose face before international opinion—the Chinese government organized a nine-city tour of the United States to directly introduce Chinese culture to ordinary Americans.[39] I suggest, however, that their real audience was on the other side of the Pacific: by promoting Chinese culture and upholding China's dignity, the party was making a claim to nationalist legitimacy. Such actions demonstrate its belief that crude repression is not enough: the party must gain *face* for China before international society to earn the support of nationalist audiences at home.

Regime legitimacy hinges on the combination of strategies that the Communist Party and popular nationalists choose during their encounters and how such strategies evolve over time. I have argued elsewhere that the party responded to the Diaoyu Islands protests of 1996, the *China Can Say No* sensation of 1996 and 1997, and the Belgrade bombing protests of May 1999 with a different combination of suppression and co-optation, largely suppressing Diaoyu protestors, seeking to co-opt and utilize the *China Can Say No* fever, and striving just to respond to the angry demands of Belgrade bombing demonstrators.[40] This movement away from suppression and toward co-optation reflects the emergence of a popular nationalism that is increasingly challenging the party-state.

Struggling just to keep up with popular nationalist demands, the party is slowly losing its autonomy in foreign policy making. For instance, Shen Jiru's 1998 *China Should Not Play "Mr. No"* sought to counter the parochial nationalism of the "say no" sensation with a more moderate nationalism—and to urge popular nationalists to entrust the CCP with the making of China's foreign policy. Shen is a researcher at the Institute of World Economics and Politics at the Chinese Academy of Social Sciences (CASS), and CASS vice president Liu Ji wrote the foreword to his book. *China Should Not Play "Mr. No"* is arguably an official response to the popular *China Can Say No* books.[41] Shen is clearly a nationalist—"As a great nation, China should participate in constructing a new post–Cold War order"—and he praises the "righteous anger" (*yifen*) of fourth-generation popular nationalists. But he rejects the extremism of many naysayers in favor of a more mature attitude toward foreign policy: "China's 21st century international strategy must not be a parochial nationalist, uncooperative stream of 'nos.' . . . 21st century China and the world require understanding, reconciliation, and cooperation—not antagonism." Shen wields the specter of the former Soviet Union as an admonition against those who advocate confrontation: "The Soviets were nicknamed 'Mr. No' for using their veto in the UN Security Council all the time. We do not need to play a second 'Mr. No.'" He then asks, "Is the only way that Chinese can prove their independence and strength by daring to say 'no'?" Shen admonishes popular nationalists that "emotion cannot substitute for policy."[42] It is the elite, in other words, who must coolly construct China's foreign policy.

China's popular nationalists do not appear to have heeded Shen's advice. John Keefe, who was special assistant to U.S. ambassador to China Joseph Prueher during the April 2001 spy-plane incident, later related that, during the negotiations in Beijing, American diplomats "saw a Chinese government acutely sensitive to Chinese public opinion."[43]

During 2001 through 2002, a pop-up appeared on the main page of the Ministry of Foreign Affairs (MFA) Chinese-language website. It solicited the opinions of ordinary Chinese, linking the reader to a page where he or she could e-mail the MFA and read the transcripts of electronic chats now held regularly between senior MFA officials and concerned Chinese "netizens."[44] The MFA, it seems, does not just direct its attention at the international community; it also has an eye on the demands of domestic nationalists.

Bottom-up popular pressures are playing an increasingly central role in nationalist legitimation today—and those pressures tend to be of the aggressive USS *Maine* variety, not the pacifist "Munich" type. Chinese nationalism can therefore no longer be described as a purely "state" or "official" top-down affair. Aware that popular nationalists now command a large following, the MFA is actively seeking to appease them. China's foreign policy makers, it appears, do not gain a "nondemocratic advantage" over their counterparts in democratic nations; as they make policy, they too must be responsive to domestic opinion. Western policy makers ignore this new influence on Chinese foreign policy making at their own peril.

IMPLICATIONS FOR U.S. CHINA POLICY

What lessons might Western analysts and policy makers draw from this brief discussion of nationalism and Chinese foreign policy?

I have argued that since human motivation is not directly observable, analysts must carefully infer intentions from what people say and do. One implication of this argument is that Western analysts must be extremely careful not to simply project onto China their preexisting "gut feelings." How much do our various assessments of China as a "cuddly panda" or a "fierce dragon" reflect Chinese realities? And how much do they reflect deep-rooted feelings about China, communism, or the nature of the world system (a Kantian heaven or a Hobbesian hell)?

A second implication of this argument that intentions are invisible is that analysts need to devote more attention to the careful interrogation of Chinese words and deeds. We cannot be content to simply infer Chinese intentions from Chinese capabilities or from China's position in the balance of power. Against structural realists such as Robert Ross, I contend that there is still an acute need for the analysis of perceptions and images in United States–China relations; the work of Bob Jervis remains highly relevant.[45] The question remains: When the PLA acquires a new weapons system, is it evidence of an aggressive Chinese nationalism that seeks to upset the regional balance of power, or is it evidence of a status-quo China seeking to protect its position in the region? Rationalist analyses alone cannot answer such a question. To understand Chinese intentions, we still need to critically examine Chinese rhetoric and behavior.

I have also argued that human motivation is complex. Not all anger, for example, is the same. One implication of this argument is that Western analysts and policy makers must be careful to avoid simply projecting their own understandings of human motivation onto the Chinese. For instance, during the 2001 apology diplomacy discussed earlier, Americans tended to assume that the Chinese understood the situation the same way that we did—that since the fault lied with Wang Wei and his F-8, the United States had nothing to apologize for. Americans thus tended to attribute extreme motives to Chinese demands for apologies. Chinese were either overly emotional, deformed by cruel Chinese traditions, or highly instrumental in seeking to utilize the incident to extract concessions from the United States.[46] A greater awareness of the complexity of human motivation may have helped Westerners recognize that, for many Chinese, culpability was not the issue. Cross-cultural psychologists have demonstrated that the Chinese tend to have a more consequentialist view of responsibility than do Americans.[47] In this case, a Chinese citizen was dead, and an apology was therefore necessary to restore the bilateral relationship. When Americans initially refused to apologize, this created a higher, or more ethical, anger that sought to correct this injustice. The American failure to recognize the nuances of this Chinese view aggravated an already difficult situation.[48]

I have also argued that human motivation is frequently multiple. One implication of this argument, especially important for Americans who tend to valorize the idea of enlightened self-interest, is that we should be wary of reducing Chinese intentions to the instrumental pursuit of China's national interest. Despite a rugged individualist lore, Americans care greatly about their various social identities—including their national identity. The passionate American reaction to September 11, 2001, clearly revealed that Americans care greatly about being "American." The invasions of Afghanistan and Iraq revealed that Americans are willing to bear significant instrumental costs to protect their cherished self-identifications. Chinese are no different. While Chinese nationalists are frequently motivated by instrumental goals, such as growing China's economy or increasing the strength of the PLA, they are often simultaneously moved by desires to restore, maintain, or improve China's "international image." China's decision to invade Vietnam in the late 1970s, for instance, was motivated in part, as Deng Xiaoping put it, by a desire to "teach little brother a lesson." After all of China's aid to the Vietnamese communists during the Vietnam War, Chinese such as Deng were outraged by the view that "little brother" Vietnam would repay this Chinese kindness by betraying China with an alliance with China's enemy the Soviet Union. Righteous indignation was a big reason that China's leaders decided to invade Vietnam. Similarly, China's Japan policy today is often driven by emotion. To be sure, the Chinese want Japanese aid, but the symbolic politics of what it means to be "Chinese" or "Japanese" often takes precedence.[49] Indeed, the furious 2003 debate over the "new thinking on Japan" revealed that anti-Japanese sentiment is increasingly undermining China's interest in improving relations with Japan.[50]

Finally, I have argued that Chinese foreign policy, like American foreign policy, is a two-level game: China is not a totalitarian regime in which diplomats can calmly construct their foreign policies free from domestic constraints. One implication of this argument is that American diplomats must recognize that their Chinese counterparts do not have the autonomy previously assumed; popular nationalism has become a major constraint on Chinese diplomats. Popular pressures on Chinese foreign policy makers were apparent during the fall of 2003. Following the Qiqihar mustard-gas incident, in which one Chinese died and dozens were injured upon discovering abandoned Japanese chemical weapons from World War II, cyber-nationalists gathered over one million signatures on an anti-Japanese petition circulated on the Internet. The Foreign Ministry had a genuine dilemma: either champion the Chinese position and placate popular nationalists, or maintain China's lucrative trade relations with Japan. Foreign Ministry officials ably walked the tightrope, allowing petition organizers to present their petition to the Japanese embassy in Beijing on September 18, the seventy-second anniversary of the Mukden incident of 1931, which led to the Japanese occupation of Manchuria; but they rejected the nationalists' application for a protest march in Beijing. "So it seems to me," Beijing analyst Liu Junning later told the BBC, "the petition is something of significance between the Chinese government and its people rather than between China and Japan."[51] Chinese citizens are demanding a larger say in Chinese foreign policy, and the MFA has its hands full accommodating their demands. Popular nationalism is increasingly binding the hands of China's foreign policy makers.

A second implication of this argument that Chinese foreign policy is now a two-level game is that American China policy makers should devote greater attention not just to substance but also to presentation. There are real conflicts of material interests in United States–China relations. The substantive content of U.S. policies is therefore extremely sensitive. But how the Chinese public perceives American words and deeds also has a major impact on the direction of Chinese nationalism and Chinese foreign policy in the twenty-first century. China bashing may be emotionally gratifying for journalists such as the *Washington Times*'s Bill Gertz, pundits such as American Enterprise Institute's Arthur Waldron, and statesmen such as Secretary of Defense Donald Rumsfeld—but doing so is extremely dangerous. American China-bashing begets Chinese America-bashing, and vice versa. In a bilateral relationship already dangerously short on mutual trust, such trans-Pacific diatribes could become a self-fulfilling prophecy, leading to a United States–China conflict.

NOTES

1. See Henry Kissinger, "The Folly of Bullying Beijing," *Los Angeles Times*, July 6, 1997.

2. See Arthor Waldron, "Why China Could Be Dangerous," *American Enterprise* 9, no. 4 (July/August 1998).

3. Indeed, one article that sides with the optimists about Chinese nationalism even concludes by citing Kant's "spirit of hopeful determination to make the best of history." See Thomas A. Metzger and Ramon H. Myers, "Chinese Nationalism and American Policy," *Orbis* 42, no. 1 (1998): 37.

4. On signaling in foreign policy, see Robert Jervis, *The Logic of Images in International Relations* (Princeton, N.J.: Princeton University Press, 1970).

5. See Vilfredo Pareto, *Treatise in General Sociology*, part I (Firenze, Italy: G. Barbera, 1916).

6. As sociologist Charles Cooley put it over a century ago, "A man in a rage does not want to get out of it. . . . An enduring hatred may also be a source of satisfaction to some minds." See Cooley, *Human Nature and the Social Order* (New York: Scribners, [1902] 1922), 284.

7. On Chinese reactions to the Belgrade bombing, see Peter Hays Gries, "Tears of Rage: Chinese Nationalism and the Belgrade Embassy Bombing," *China Journal*, no. 46 (July 2001): 25–43.

8. For instance, nationalist Li Fang castigates the West as a "selfish civilization" to praise Chinese civilization as "harmonious." See Li Fang, "Chongjian Zhongguo youxi guize" [Rewriting China's rules of the game], *Zhongguo ruhe shuobu* [How China Should Say No] special 1996 issue of *Zuojia tiandi* [Writer's World], 29.

9. This definition is largely social psychological. Following Henri Tajfel's description of "social identity" as "that part of an individual's self-concept which derives from his knowledge of his membership in a social group. . . together with the value and emotional significance attached to that membership," I define national identity as that aspect of an individual's self-concept that derives from his or her perceived membership in a national group. Nationalism is here understood as the commitment to protect, restore, and enhance national identity. See Henri Tajfel, *Human Groups and Social Categories: Studies in Social Psychology* (Cambridge: Cambridge University Press, 1981), 255.

10. For the classic statement of the "peasant nationalism" thesis, see Chalmers Johnson, *Peasant Nationalism and Communist Power: The Emergence of Revolutionary China* (Stanford, Calif.: Stanford University Press, 1962).

11. For an extended discussion of the victor and victim narratives of the "Century of Humiliation," see Peter Hays Gries, *China's New Nationalism: Pride, Politics, and Diplomacy* (Berkeley: University of California Press, 2004), chaps. 3–5.

12. As Paul Heer puts it, "On foreign policy, the common denominator is a genuine commitment to Chinese nationalism." See "A House United: Beijing's View of Washington," *Foreign Affairs* 79, no. 4 (July/August 2000): 20.

13. Chinese views of *face* should be understood at the two levels of *lian* and *mianzi*. Sociologist Hu Hsien-chin defines the former as "decency" or "good moral reputation" and the latter as an "extra reputation" achieved through social accomplishments. Andrew Kipnis similarly argues that *lian* is of "first order visibility" while *mian* is of "second order visibility": the former is "directly knowable" whereas the latter depends on a "third-party audience." My discussions of *face* in the Chinese context refer to the more social *mianzi*. See Hu Hsien-chin, "The Chinese Concepts of 'Face,'" *American Anthropologist* 46 (1944); and Andrew B. Kipnis, "'Face': An Adaptable Discourse of Social Surfaces," *Positions* 3, no. 1 (1995): 126.

14. For more on *face* and honor, see Gries, *China's New Nationalism*, 21–29.

15. My approach thus differs from the mainstream "party propaganda" view of Chinese nationalism, which ignores the emotional in favor of the instrumental. For instance, Zhao Suisheng, who has written extensively on Chinese nationalism, has argued that two of the key features of today's "pragmatic nationalism" are that it is "state-led" (read: party) and "instrumental" (read: propaganda). Although he recognizes emotions of "deep bitterness at China's humiliation," Zhao nevertheless insists

that nationalism in China is "national-interest driven," based on a "calculation of benefits and costs." Like most analysts, Zhao highlights Chinese nationalist's instrumental motivations. See Zhao Suisheng, "Chinese Nationalism and Its International Orientations," *Political Science Quarterly* 115, no. 1 (2000): 1–33.

16. J. M. Barbalet, *Emotion, Social Theory, and Social Structure: A Macrosociological Approach* (New York: Cambridge University Press, 1998), 136.

17. In his *Confessions*, for instance, Jean-Jacques Rousseau admits his fear of discovery after falsely accusing a maidservant of theft: "When she appeared my heart was agonized, but the presence of so many people was more powerful than my compunction. I did not fear punishment, but I dreaded shame: I dreaded it more than death. . . . I felt no dread but that of being detected, of being publicly and to my face declared a thief, liar" (quoted in Cooley, *Human Nature and the Social Order*, 291). The emotional intensity of the moment is palpable and clearly context dependent. Should his secret be exposed publicly, Rousseau's social credit among his peers would be depleted. The instrumental stakes of a more private confrontation, however, would not be so great and would not likely elicit such strong emotions.

18. Barrington Moore, *Injustice: The Social Bases of Obedience and Revolt* (Boston: Beacon Press, 1978), 17.

19. Nyla R. Branscombe and Daniel L. Wann, "Collective Self-Esteem Consequences of Outgroup Derogation When a Valued Social Identity Is on Trial," *European Journal of Social Psychology* 24, no. 6 (November–December 1994): 641–57.

20. "Lieberman: China Played 'Aggressive Game of Aerial Chicken,'" CNN, April 4, 2001. The following draws from Peter Hays Gries and Peng Kaiping, "Culture Clash? Apologies East and West," *Journal of Contemporary China* 11, no. 30 (February 2002): 173–78.

21. The full text of the "two I'm sorrys" letter is available online at www.cnn.com/2001/WORLD/asiapcf/east/04/11/prueher.letter.text (accessed August 15, 2003).

22. Robert Kagan and William Kristol, "A National Humiliation," *Weekly Standard*, April 16–23, 2001, 11–16.

23. Willy Wo-Lap Lam, "Behind the Scenes in Beijing's Corridors of Power," CNN, April 11, 2001.

24. "Experts Praise China's Handling of Jet Collision Incident," *Liaowang*, no. 16 (April 16, 2001): 6–8; translated in FBIS-CHI-2001-0426.

25. Immanuel Kant, cited in Joanne Gowa, "Democratic States and International Disputes," *International Organization* 49, no. 3 (Summer 1995): 516. My thanks to Fei-ling Wang and Yong Deng for the Gowa cite.

26. Alexis de Tocqueville, *Democracy in America* (Chicago: University of Chicago Press, 2000), 228; cited in Dan Reiter and Allan C. Stam, *Democracies at War* (Princeton, N.J.: Princeton University Press, 2002), 2–3. My thanks to Steve Chan for this reference.

27. Michael Pearlman, *Warmaking and American Democracy: The Struggle over Military Strategy, 1700 to the Present* (Lawrence: University Press of Kansas, 1999), 10; cited in Reiter and Stam, *Democracies at War*.

28. Randall L. Schweller, "Domestic Structures and Preventative War: Are Democracies More Pacific?" *World Politics* 44 (January 1992): 245.

29. Ernest R. May, *Imperial Democracy: The Emergence of America as a Great Power* (New York: Harcourt, Brace, and World, 1961); cited in Schweller, "Domestic Structures and Preventative War," 245.

30. Waldron does not disclose his sources revealing nefarious Chinese intent. Commissioners Kenneth Lewis and June Teufel Dreyer nonetheless concurred with Waldron's opinion. See U.S.–China Security Review Commission, "Report to Congress of the U.S.–China Security Review Commission: The National Security Implications of the Economic Relationship between the United States and China" (Washington, D.C., 2002), available online at www.uscc.gov/anrp02.htm (accessed August 15, 2003).

31. John Fitzgerald has presented the "state nationalism" thesis the most eloquently: "In the Chinese revolution, the state was not just midwife at the birth of the nation but in fact its sire. So the founder of the Nationalist Party, Sun Yat-sen, is appropriately remembered as the 'father of the country' (*guofu*)." It is Zheng Yongnian, however, who has advanced the "state nationalism" argument the most recently. In *Discovering Chinese Nationalism in China,* Zheng maintains that the emergence of nationalism in China today is best understood as a statist response to the decentralization of state power that occurred under Deng's reforms. See John Fitzgerald, "The Nationless State: The Search for a Nation in Modern Chinese Nationalism," in *Chinese Nationalism,* ed. Jonathan Unger (Armonk, N.Y.: M. E. Sharpe, 1996), 58; and Zheng Yongnian, *Discovering Chinese Nationalism in China: Modernization, Identity, and International Relations* (Cambridge: Cambridge University Press, 1999).

32. See Thomas Christensen, "Chinese Realpolitik," *Foreign Affairs* 75, no. 5 (1996): 37.

33. On legitimacy dynamics, see Reinhard Bendix, *Nation-Building and Citizenship: Studies of Our Changing Social Order,* new enl. ed. (Berkeley: University of California Press, 1977); and Max Weber, *The Theory of Social and Economic Organization* (New York: Free Press, 1964).

34. As Xu Ben has recently noted, "Nationalism in China is . . . a junction and node of contradiction, interaction, and integration between state and society." See "Chinese Populist Nationalism: Its Intellectual Politics and Moral Dilemma," *Representations* 76, no. 1 (2001): 120–40.

35. Li Xiguang and Liu Kang, *Yaomohua Zhongguo de beiho* [The Plot to Demonize China] (Beijing: Zhongguo shehui kexue chubanshe, 1996).

36. Song Qiang, Zhang Zangzang, and Qiao Bian, *Zhongguo keyi shuobu* [China Can Say No] (Beijing: Zhonghua gongshang lianhe chubanshe, 1996). For an English-language review, see Peter Hays Gries, review of *Zhongguo keyi shuobu* [China Can Say No], *Zhongguo haishineng shuobu* [China Still Can Say No], and *Liuxue Meiguo* [Studying in the USA], *China Journal* 37 (1997): 180–85.

37. Wu Fang and Ray Zhang, "Dissident Called the Chinese Premier 'Incompetent,'" *China News Digest* (1998).

38. "China Gets Wired as Cultural Blitz Planned," *China News Digest* (1998). This project also suggests that the Internet in China is not the realm of a civil society set against the state; rather, the Internet is another site for nationalist politics, with actors both for and against the state vying for authority.

39. David Briscoe, "China Trying to Improve Image with Ordinary Americans, Still Wary of Government," Associated Press, August 30, 2000.

40. See Gries, *China's New Nationalism*, chap. 7.

41. For a concurring interpretation of the official nature of *China Should Not Play "Mr. No,"* see Joseph Fewsmith, "Historical Echoes and Chinese Politics: Can China Leave the Twentieth Century Behind?" in *China Briefing 2000: The Continuing Transformation*, ed. Tyrene White (Armonk, N.Y.: M. E. Sharpe, 2000), 21.

42. Shen Jiru, *Zhongguo budang "bu xiansheng"—dangdai Zhongguo de guoji zhanlue wenti* [China Should Not Play "Mr. No": The Problem of China's Contemporary International Strategy] (Beijing: Jinri Zhongguo chubanshe, 1998), 2–3, 56, 57.

43. John Keefe, "Anatomy of the EP-3 Incident, April 2001" (Center for Naval Analysis, Alexandria, Va., 2001), 10.

44. The MFA's Chinese-language webpage is at www.fmprc.gov.cn/chn. The pop-up led to http://bbs.fmprc.gov.cn/index.jsp. The English-language site is at www.fmprc.gov.cn/eng (all accessed on August 19, 2002; although the pop-up has since been deactivated, the interactive page remains).

45. Citing Jervis, Ross writes that "common arguments about misperceptions in policymaking. . . do not apply to the U.S.-China conflict." See Robert S. Ross, "Introduction," in *Re-Examining the Cold War: U.S.–China Diplomacy, 1954–1973*, ed. Robert S. Ross and Jiang Changbin (Cambridge, Mass.: Harvard University Press, 2001), 395n7.

46. Writing in the *New York Times*, Fox Butterfield located the cultural roots of China's demand for an American apology in "Chinese child-rearing practices" and the "old Confucian tradition of conformity." A cruel Confucian culture, Butterfield argues, lies at the heart of communist tyranny. The *Financial Times*'s James Kynge went to the opposite extreme, writing that Jiang Zemin "seized on the incident to demand a halt to U.S. air surveillance missions near the Chinese coastline." Chinese, Kynge argues, are not crazy; they are simply cold and calculating. See Fox Butterfield, "China's Demand for Apology Is Rooted in Tradition," *New York Times*, April 7, 2001; and James Kynge, "China Calls for Apology over Collision," *Financial Times*, April 4, 2001, 12.

47. For a pair of fine recent overviews of this research, see Peng Kaiping, Daniel Ames, and Eric Knowles, "Culture and Human Inference: Perspectives from Three Traditions," in *Handbook of Cross-cultural Psychology* (Oxford: Oxford University Press, 2001); and Richard E. Nisbett, *The Geography of Thought: Why We Think the Way We Do* (New York: Free Press, 2003).

48. Of course, the Chinese also failed to recognize that Americans have a more culpability-oriented view of responsibility. On the psychological dimension of the spy-plane incident, see Peter Hays Gries and Peng, "Culture Clash? Apologies East and West."

49. Allen Whiting is right that negative images of Japan have thwarted China's interest in closer relations with its Asian neighbor. See *China Eyes Japan* (Berkeley: University of California Press, 1989).

50. See Ma Licheng, "Duiri guanxi xinsiwei" [New thinking on relations with Japan], *Zhanlue yu guanli* [Strategy and Management], no. 6 (2002); Shi Yinhong,

"ZhongRi jiejin yu 'waijiao geming'" [Sino-Japanese Rapprochement and the "Diplomatic Revolution"], *Zhanlue yu guanli* [Strategy and Management], no. 2 (2003). For an analysis of the 2003 academic and popular debate over Japanese policy, see Peter Hays Gries, "China's 'New Thinking on Japan,'" *China Quarterly*, forthcoming 2005.

51. Tim Luard, "Anti-Japan Protests Worry China," BBC News Online, September 18, 2003, available at http://news.bbc.co.uk/2/hi/asia-pacific/3118850.stm (accessed September 22, 2003).

6

Chinese Foreign Policy in the Age of Globalization

Thomas G. Moore

This chapter examines globalization as an increasingly salient context for understanding China's foreign relations. In their public statements, China's leaders have repeatedly asserted that globalization has had a profound influence on their reform priorities, development strategies, and foreign policy positions. Although Beijing's rhetoric has not always been matched by action, there is considerable evidence that globalization is an important lens through which China's leaders view a variety of tasks facing their country. Domestically, China has taken significant steps toward the creation of a modern economy that can compete effectively in a world economy that is expected to be even more interconnected in the future. Internationally, China has become increasingly active in regional and global multilateral institutions, especially in economic affairs. Beijing's accession to the World Trade Organization (WTO) in 2001 was the culmination of a fifteen-year odyssey, one that holds tremendous long-term importance for China and the world economy. In East Asia, Beijing's active participation in the ASEAN plus Three (APT) process, including its leadership in forging the landmark ASEAN–China Free Trade Agreement, raises issues at the nexus of regionalism and globalization. (APT consists of the ten members of the Association of Southeast Asian Nations [ASEAN] plus China, Japan, and South Korea.) Bilaterally, China has pursued cooperative relations with great powers and small powers alike, in East Asia and worldwide. Of particular note, Beijing enjoys burgeoning commercial relations that would have been almost unthinkable a decade ago, let alone during the Mao Zedong era.

The first section of this chapter provides a detailed examination of Beijing's official rhetoric on the subject of globalization. This approach is taken

for two reasons. First, previous studies on globalization have typically focused on either the nature of China's deepening economic ties to the world
economy or the implications of globalization for China's economic reforms
(and domestic change generally).[1] In addition, some studies have examined
the views of globalization held by Chinese scholars and policy analysts.[2] By
contrast, the increasing thematic attention paid to globalization in China's official policy statements has received only passing scholarly attention.

The second and far more important reason for this approach is that official
thinking on globalization has evolved significantly over the past decade.
Even as applied narrowly to the economic realm, globalization is now the
subject of several distinct discourses related to domestic and foreign policy.
For example, an analysis of leaders' speeches and other policy statements reveals that economic globalization can mean any (or, in some cases, all) of the
following: increasing cross-national flows of goods, capital, and technology;
a process of win–win (*shuangying*) competition in which countries cooperatively pursue development as equals; and a more zero-sum form of competition, rooted in the struggle for comprehensive national power (*zonghe guoli*),
in which states vie over the means to create wealth within their territories.
While economic factors still enjoy pride of place in China's globalization discourse, the range of foreign policy issues analyzed through the lens of globalization now includes traditional security threats, such as the proliferation of
weapons and weapons technology, and nontraditional security threats, such as
refugee crises, environmental degradation, overpopulation, ethnic and religious unrest, terrorism, drug trafficking, illegal immigration, energy short-
ages, and infectious disease.

The second section of the chapter examines the impact of globalization on
Chinese behavior. Beijing has pursued policies designed to improve not only
China's own participation in the world economy but also the international
management of globalization processes. For example, China's leaders expect
that WTO membership will give them more influence, at least in the long
run, over the shape of the world trading system. Beijing's efforts to shape the
new trade and monetary regionalism emerging in East Asia should also be
seen in this light. Underlying this approach is the apparent belief among
China's leaders that economic globalization—as guided by appropriate national policies—affords latecomers the chance to achieve significant development by integrating themselves into dynamic transnational production and
financial structures. Because economic modernization is viewed as an imperative for domestic stability and regime survival as well as for long-term
national power and security, Beijing has continued to accept higher levels of
interdependence with the outside world. Indeed, "reform and opening"
(*gaige kaifang*) seems to be the most viable option, given that China still

lacks the indigenous investment capital, advanced technology, and human expertise necessary to compete successfully in world product markets. With respect to the strategic implications of this development strategy, which are critical given the unipolarity found in the international system, Beijing seems to be pursuing a strategy that aims to constrain the exercise of American power by "democratizing" international relations. In lieu of a classical balancing strategy, which would face several obstacles at present, China seeks instead to restrain the United States in the webs of deepening interdependence spun by globalization—for example, dense economic ties and strengthened multilateral institutions.

CHINA'S GLOBALIZATION DISCOURSE

Globalization (*quanqiuhua*) has a fairly short history in China's diplomatic lexicon.[3] Although there were occasional references to the term in academic writings in the early 1990s, the first official reference to *quanqiuhua* appeared in China's statement during the general debate of the United Nations General Assembly (hereafter, UN statement) in 1996. In this address, then–foreign minister Qian Qichen commented that "world economic globalization" (*shijie jingji quanqiuhua*) "presents a rare opportunity to both developed and developing countries."[4] Previously, Chinese officials had preferred generic statements, such as the often-repeated observation that economic factors were playing a "greater role" in post–Cold War international relations.[5] After Qian introduced the term, *quanqiuhua* found its profile further raised by a political report by then-president Jiang Zemin to the Fifteenth National Congress of the Chinese Communist Party (hereafter, Party Congress) in September 1997, in which he provided the following statement on the relevance of globalization to China's domestic and foreign policy agendas:

> Opening to the outside world is a long-term basic state policy. Confronted with the globalization trend in economic, scientific, and technological development, we should take an even more active stance in the world by improving the pattern of opening up in all directions, at all levels and in a wide range, developing an open economy, enhancing our international competitiveness, optimizing our economic structure and improving the quality of our national economy[6]

In an effort to convey not just the scale of change but also the increasing speed of change that was occurring in the 1990s, globalization essentially replaced internationalization in Chinese diplomatic parlance. For its part, interdependence remained a separate, albeit related, concept important to Chinese discourse on international affairs. Especially at first, analysis of globalization did not focus on the power relationships that flow from deepening economic interaction between countries. According to a definition provided in a 1997 *Xiandai Guoji Guanxi* article, economic interdependence is "an order in which actions between countries are characterized by mutual influence."[7] By contrast, a *People's Daily* article published in 1998 defined globalization as

> the free circulation and rational allocation of the key elements in production on a global scale and the gradual elimination of various kinds of barriers and obstructions, with a resulting continual strengthening of economic ties and interdependence between states. It is the inevitable result of development toward high levels in productive forces and international division of work.[8]

As this quotation suggests, globalization was understood initially to involve only economic, rather than political, dynamics. The rationale at the time was that China could deepen its participation in the world economy without economic globalization becoming a transmission belt for social, cultural, ideological, or security globalization. Until 2001, when references to "globalized security" were introduced into China's official rhetoric, Beijing had in fact only publicly acknowledged economic globalization. Although the prefix "economic" (i.e., *jingji quanqiuhua*) appeared more often over time, presumably to distinguish this dimension of globalization from other (still unspecified) aspects of transnational interconnectedness, Chinese officials continued to explain that economic globalization should be seen as an "inevitable outcome of world economic development and scientific and technological progress."[9] In 2000, Jiang reiterated that globalization is an "objective requirement and inevitable outcome of the development of social productive forces and science and technology."[10]

Ever since acknowledging that the scope of globalization includes security as well as economic affairs, Chinese leaders have stuck by this view, lest the increased flows of capital, goods, and technology—which they regard as being central to their development goals—become unnecessarily embroiled in debates over U.S. hegemony, Westernization, and other contentious topics. In 2001, for example, Qian argued that economic globalization remains fundamentally "driven by the new technology revolution."[11] This explanation is consistent with his original description in 1996, when he described globalization as involving a "rapid advance of science and technology" that has led to the "vigorous expansion of international trade and investment."[12] By consistently emphasizing these factors as the underlying dynamic fueling economic globalization, China's leaders have tried to keep the identity of economic globalization analytically separate from other dimensions of globalization.

Managing the Process of Economic Globalization

A growing theme in China's foreign policy discourse has been that developing countries are at a significant disadvantage relative to developed countries in navigating the fast-paced economic currents associated with globalization. When *quanqiuhua* first entered China's diplomatic lexicon, Qian mentioned only how it provided an opportunity for world economic growth and wider prospects for international cooperation. The attendant challenges, which would later become the other side of an oft-cited "double-edged sword," were conspicuously missing. Qian offered the usual warning about the evils of trade protectionism in developed country markets, but he identified no dangers in globalization itself. With the passage of time, and the onset of the Asian financial crisis (AFC) in particular, Beijing's official rhetoric increasingly suggested that the long-term effects of globalization would ultimately depend on how the process was handled.

Given the fallout from the AFC, globalization received unprecedented attention in China's 1997 and 1998 UN statements. In 1997, shortly after the crisis began, Qian offered support for globalization, characterizing as "good" the fact that "economic links and mutual penetration among countries and regions are on the constant increase." At the same time, he also warned of the "highly globalized" nature of international financial markets in citing the need for greater international cooperation.[13] As these comments suggest, the AFC was already creating an analytical distinction in Chinese thinking between growing economic ties (good) and the globalization process itself (potentially dangerous if not handled properly). A year later, when the ravages of the AFC were more fully apparent, then–foreign minister Tang Jiaxuan resolutely declared that "the world of today is a world of interdependence." With regard to Beijing's own policies, Tang observed: "In today's world, where the economy is increasingly globalized, countries must pursue an open policy in order to achieve economic growth. . . . As a huge emerging market, China will strive to keep abreast of the trend of economic globalization and be even more active in opening up to the world."[14] To this end, he reiterated China's commitment to proceed with reform and opening and to join the WTO.

Although this evolution in rhetoric took a while to unfold, by 2000 Jiang used his annual speech at the Asia–Pacific Economic Cooperation (APEC) forum to provide a detailed discussion of the "negative effects of economic globalization," such as a widening "gap of wealth between North and South" and the fact that already "disadvantaged developing countries face new challenges to their economic sovereignty and economic security." The message was that while globalization remained an opportunity, the accompanying challenges had been underestimated. In particular, Jiang argued that the "phenomenal advancement of high and new technologies spearheaded by IT [information technology] and bio-technology" in the 1990s had led to growing (and, in some cases, new) imbalances between developed and developing countries, imbalances that would require concerted international cooperation to redress.[15] Although globalization brought "challenges" as well as "opportunities," uneven development and other perils in the world economy were primarily the result, in Jiang's words, of an "improper handling" of the globalization process, rather than of dangers inherent in deepening ties among national economies per se (as defined by flows of capital, goods, and technology).[16] The fault, then, lay more with inequities in the existing international economic order than with globalization as such: "While the old economic pattern remains basically unchanged, developing countries are generally in a highly disadvantaged position in the course of economic globalization."[17]

In this sense, globalization has long been understood to be separate from the international economic system per se. In his 1998 APEC speech, Jiang observed that "the trend of economic globalization is emerging and developing in a context where there is no fundamental change in the inequitable and irrational old international economic order."[18] From this perspective, globalization is virtually synonymous with scientific and technological advance, the expansion of market forces in the world economy, and the new industrial revolution associated with the rise of the so-called knowledge economy. While these developments are surely thought to be a product of the international economic system at some level, an important distinction is made in Beijing's official rhetoric between the trend of globalization itself and the existing international order. For example, in a 1999 Asia–Europe Meeting (ASEM) speech, Tang's discussion of the post-AFC international situation distinguished between "challenges posed by the trend towards economic globalization" and "the defects of the current international financial system."[19] In the same vein, Chinese officials have studiously avoided blaming globalization for the economic woes of developing countries. In 1995, Jiang argued that the "current backwardness and poverty [of developing countries] are caused mainly by the past colonial rule and the present unfair and irrational international economic system."[20] Seven years later, in a speech to the Asian Development Bank (ADB), he still maintained that "the root cause for the uneven global development lies in the absence of a fair and reasonable international economic order." What seems to be "objective" and "inevitable" about globalization, therefore, is the advance of science and technology and the resulting increase in interaction among national economies. In this sense, the "economics" of economic globalization is fairly straightforward. The nettlesome issue, rather, is the "politics" of economic globalization. That said, Beijing's rhetoric generally offers hope that globalization can be managed effectively.

Just as economic globalization is understood to be separate from the international economic system, so too is economic globalization generally distinguished analytically from U.S. hegemony as a force in world affairs. In leadership speeches and media statements, it is "hegemonism and power politics" (*baquan zhuyi he qiangquan zhengzhi*) rather than globalization that is ritualistically identified as the main threat to peace and development. With few exceptions, Beijing has consciously sought not to establish a connection between U.S. hegemony and globalization. The most notable exception was a speech during Jiang's September 1999 visit to Thailand, in the wake of the AFC and the May 1999 bombing of China's embassy in Belgrade, in which he declared that "hegemonism and power politics still exist and have even developed in the international political, economic, and security fields. The new 'Gunboat Policy' and economic neo-colonialism pursued by some big powers have severely undermined the sovereign independence and development interests" of many countries. Jiang proceeded to argue that "no country should be allowed to make use of its advantages to seek privileges and impair other countries' interests in the process of economic globalization."[21]

In China's annual UN statement later that month, Tang echoed that warning, asserting that "no country should prejudice other countries' economic security and development by virtue of its economic, technological, and financial advantages." He further argued that "developing countries have the right to equal participation in world economic decision-making and the formulation of relevant rules." Interestingly, however, the term "globalization" was not used in this section of Tang's speech. The only reference to *quanqiuhua* came later when Tang proposed that the UN "hold a special conference . . . to discuss the globalization of the world economy," calling the world economy an "interrelated and indivisible whole." In this connection, Tang urged that increased technological and financial assistance be provided for developing countries as the world copes with pressing global issues such as environmental degradation, overpopulation, poverty, and debt.[22]

Although Chinese leaders have certainly implied that globalization could be harnessed to U.S. purposes, such as when Jiang declared in 2000 that some countries "have tried to force their own values, economic regime, and social system on other countries by taking advantage of economic globalization," the strongest statements have been reserved for the Chinese media.[23] For example, the official news agency *Xinhua* observed in August 1999 that globalization "provides an opportunity for the United States to pursue its hegemonic strategy." At the same time, however, the article also argued that "as an objective trend, globalization is actually a 'double-edged sword' which also brings about major constraining factors for the United States' pursuit of its hegemonic strategy."[24] Although certain advantages accrue to the United

States as the world's superpower, most observers in China still believe that "economic globalization makes it impossible for any country to keep its scientific and technological achievements from benefiting others."[25] Consistent with this perspective, the *Xinhua* analysis concluded that "to maintain its hegemonic position, the United States must try hard to prevent the appearance of other superpowers. However, globalization will make it hard for the United States to achieve this intention."[26]

As illustrated by the AFC, economic globalization was understood to entail significant risks—economically, socially, politically, and strategically. That said, Beijing concluded that the long-term prospects of enhancing China's comprehensive national power (CNP) were bleak unless more intense efforts were made to seize the developmental opportunities associated with globalization while simultaneously minimizing the accompanying dangers by better safeguarding the country's economic security. As discussed later, this decision sheds much light on China's subsequent domestic and foreign policies. Despite serious misgivings about U.S. primacy and heightened awareness of the tradeoffs involved in China's deepening participation in the world economy, Beijing reiterated its commitment to reform and opening as the country's basic development strategy and addressed its longstanding bid to gain WTO membership with renewed dedication. At the same time, Beijing also realized that reform and opening would not alone suffice as a means for making China rich and strong. The main modification to Chinese thinking on economic globalization was greater linkage to the promotion of politically oriented objectives such as the "democratization of international relations" (hereafter, democratization of IR) and the "establishment of a fair and rational new international political and economic order" (hereafter, new international order). By focusing on the nature of international decision making, both of these policies are implicitly aimed at restraining the exercise of U.S. hegemony.

As explained by Jiang, the democratization of IR (*guoji guanxi de minzhuhua*) means that the "affairs of each country should be decided by its own people, affairs between countries should be handled through consultations among them as equal members, and global challenges should be taken on by all countries working in close cooperation."[27] On another occasion, Jiang referred to this mode of state-to-state conduct as the "spirit of development through multilateral cooperation."[28] When first introduced in 1998, the democratization of IR placed considerable emphasis on respecting national diversity and ensuring the right of countries to choose their own developmental path, as one might expect in the immediate aftermath of the AFC, when economic security and political sovereignty were seen as imperiled.[29] While that theme remains, the focus has shifted over time to a more broad emphasis on international decision making, with democratic consultation implicitly contrasted with hegemonic governance.[30] *China's National Defense in 2002*, a white paper, concluded that "democracy in international relations remains elusive, and there are new manifestations of hegemonism and power politics."[31] In China's 2003 UN statement, Foreign Minister Li Zhaoxing described democratization as a process in which "all countries, big or small, rich or poor, strong or weak, are treated as equals, and no country has the right to impose its will on others."[32] Hu Jintao, Jiang's successor, has repeatedly argued that each country has the "right to participate as an equal in decisions on international affairs."[33]

Calls for a new international order have been a staple of China's diplomatic discourse since its 1997 UN statement.[34] In their speeches, Chinese leaders have closely associated the promotion of a new international order with globalization and the democratization of IR. The political goal of globalization, so to speak, is a "balanced development" in which all countries not only benefit materially but also participate on the basis of democratic consultation.[35] Unless the nature of economic cooperation is transformed to include all countries equally—on the basis of such principles as mutual benefit, complementarity, consensus, flexibility, and respect for diversity—the process of globalization is seen as incomplete and the goal of a new international order is unfulfilled. In a May 2003 speech in Moscow, Hu invoked the imagery of a "global village" in calling for a new international order in which "global economic balance" would be a leading priority.[36]

Beijing has long voiced its concern about the persistence of inequities in the world economy. In so doing, Chinese officials have also consistently called for change: "The international economic system should be reformed in such a manner as to accommodate the needs of developing countries, reflect their interests as much as possible, and promote the common development of all nations."[37] In his 2002 APEC speech, Jiang argued that the Doha Development Agenda of the WTO should place priority on the "needs of developing countries, enabling the new round of negotiations to become the true 'development' round."[38] Along these lines, Beijing has also expressed a desire, in the words of then–prime minister Zhu Rongji, to "deepen and expand South–South cooperation and improve the standing of the developing countries in North–South dialogue so as to facilitate the establishment of a fair and rational new international political and economic order."[39] Claiming that globalization can be properly "handled" through appropriate national and international policy making, China's leaders have deliberately cultivated the idea that there is no logic to globalization that makes any particular outcome inevitable. As described by Jiang at the APEC summit hosted by Shanghai in 2001:

> There are two possible development scenarios for the process of economic globalization and trade liberalization. If the process moves along a rational

track, it may not only allocate world resources more effectively and fairly and
expand the productive forces of all countries, but also promote the establishment of a global multilateral trading system and of a new, just and rational
international economic order to the benefit of people of all countries. But if
it should be allowed to proceed along an irrational way, it may aggravate the
uneven distribution of world resources and an unbalanced economic development, widen the gap between the North and the South, sharpen the polarization between the rich and the poor and cause further environmental degradation.[40]

In this way, China's increasing participation in multilateral processes such as
the WTO, APEC, and APT is designed to allow Beijing to exert greater influence over the course of economic globalization. In fact, Chinese officials
have in recent years emphasized the "management of the globalization
process" (*quanqiuhua jincheng de guanli*) in their public statements.[41] In his
speech to the UN Millennium Summit in 2000, Jiang averred that there is an
"imbalance in world development" in which "not all countries have become
beneficiaries of the progress of modern science and technology and economic
globalization." Accordingly, he called for increased technological, financial,
and managerial assistance for developing countries "so that they may share
the fruits of economic globalization and scientific and technological progress
alongside the developed countries."[42] That said, Jiang and other Chinese officials have always taken care not to blame globalization itself for development woes at home or abroad. In this vein, Tang summed up Beijing's position well in China's 2001 UN statement:

> In recent years, anti-globalization activities in many parts of the world have in-
> creased. In fact, globalization is neither a panacea for development nor a mon-
> ster causing disaster. The appropriate response to globalization should maximize
> its advantages and minimize its disadvantages so that all countries can come out
> winners and prosper side by side. Globalization should benefit all people from
> all social strata in all countries.[43]

Globalization and the Rejuvenation of China

One consistent theme expressed by Chinese leaders in recent years has
been the relationship between efforts to meet the challenges of economic
globalization and the goal of restoring China to its historic greatness.
Building on Deng Xiaoping's depiction of Mao's China as backward economically and weak internationally, and therefore in need of national rejuvenation (*minzu fuxing*), Jiang placed China's reform in a much more explicitly global context. Whereas Deng focused more narrowly on economic

modernization, Jiang expressed China's national identity squarely in terms of global economic competition and China's aspiration to achieve its rightful place in "the family of the world's advanced nations."[44] On numerous occasions, Jiang noted China's current "underdevelopment" as a way of stressing the imperative of pursuing economic modernization. In his speech at the Fifteenth Party Congress, for example, he explicitly contrasted China's "underdevelopment" with the "advanced world standard" that serves as the target of the country's ambitions. Referring to the primary stage of socialism, Jiang described it as "a stage in which we will gradually narrow the gap between our level and the advanced world standard and bring about a great rejuvenation of the Chinese nation on the basis of socialism."[45]

Rather than try to suppress nationalism, Jiang invoked it creatively by associating success in a globalizing, interdependent world with the underlying goal of making China rich and strong. In a 2002 speech marking the eightieth anniversary of the Chinese Communist Youth League, Jiang argued that "this kind of patriotism [rejuvenating the nation] puts the future destiny of China in the context of global structures, and closely combines the development of Chinese society with the advancement of the entire human society." To act on this vision, Jiang argued, the Chinese people "must grasp the general trend of global development" in order to properly "take up the historical mission of modernization."[46] In this connection, it should be noted that Beijing has long tried to rally the Chinese diaspora to the cause of rejuvenating China, thereby allowing the country to stand up as an equal in the world of states.[47]

Chinese leaders have been remarkably consistent over the last few years in their acceptance of globalization as a fact of economic life, one that the country can ignore only at its own peril. In an October 2001 speech commemorating the ninetieth anniversary of the 1911 Revolution, Jiang noted that Sun Yat-sen had also called on China to adapt itself to "world trends" in trying to catch up to advanced countries. Jiang quoted Sun as saying, "The tide of world events is mighty. Those who follow it prosper, whereas those who resist it perish."[48] To reestablish itself as a great nation, China must therefore meet the challenge of globalization by succeeding through openness. In one of Hu's first speeches as chairman of the Chinese Communist Party (CCP), his argument for continued economic reform referred for nationalist inspiration to the "wide gap between our country's economic strength, strength in science and technology, and strength in national defense and those of the world's advanced level."[49] Just as the CCP itself must advance with the times, as enshrined in Jiang's doctrine of the "three represents," so too must China adapt to globalization.

The State and International Competition in the Age of Globalization

Although the nonstate dimension of globalization is widely acknowledged by Chinese observers, the dominant view is still one in which the state remains a robust actor. Despite well-documented increases in cross-border flows of goods, capital, and technology, globalization is not considered to be synonymous with the deterritorialization of world economic activity. In fact, globalization is depicted primarily as a national challenge in which intensifying economic competition determines which countries will be rich and strong. Accordingly, Beijing rejects the view that state sovereignty, not to mention the viability of the nation-state itself, is significantly imperiled by globalization. Policy autonomy may be constrained, but globalization has not resulted in any fundamental change in the interstate nature of world politics. The instruments of state power are changing to some degree, and the basis of national power certainly depends more on economic factors than it did previously, but states still wield significant influence to shape events. In this sense, China's leaders seem convinced that economic globalization can empower the state if handled properly.

Although economic activity is global—in the sense that economic structures and processes are now increasingly transnational in character—industrial restructuring is seen as being shaped less by the invisible hand of global markets than by the visible hand of global production networks organized by multinational corporations. More specifically, the profound changes in the international division of labor, which Beijing regards as providing a substantial opportunity for China to accelerate its own industrial transformation, are understood to be the product of ongoing synergies between corporate-based hierarchies and state-based hierarchies. Chinese officials have devoted considerable attention in their public statements to the implications of this dynamic for contemporary development strategies. Beijing's thinking, as summarized here by Long Yongtu when he was deputy foreign trade minister and chief negotiator for international economic affairs (including China's WTO accession), is worth quoting at length:

> In the past, when the speed of enhancing production technology and upgrading products was comparatively slow, the developing countries, especially countries with relatively large domestic markets, could carry out nationalization under the protection of state policies, establish their own industrial systems, and catch up with the advanced world levels by importing advanced technology. In an era when new things in science and technology are appearing every day, . . . we must develop these industries in an environment of opening up to the world, and the short cut is to use foreign investment and to cooperate with multinational companies that have ample capital and technology, to become the foreign pro-

duction bases of these companies and a link in their entire global production line and a part of their international sales network. . . . This is an opportunity that was not available to Japan and Korea in the 1960s and 1970s.[50]

If one element is missing from this explanation, it is Beijing's oft-stated awareness of how fast-changing and unforgiving the world economy has become in recent years. As Qian observed in 2001, "Economic restructuring in a global scope is advancing at a quicker and quicker pace. . . . The international competition is getting more and more intense."[51] For his part, Jiang made nearly identical statements at the Fifteenth and Sixteenth Party Congresses about the acute nature of international competition and the accompanying pressure China faces due to economic, scientific, and technological gaps that separate it from developed countries. In another major address, his 2001 speech marking the eightieth anniversary of the founding of the CCP, Jiang noted that "competition in terms of overall national strength is becoming increasingly fierce" in the era of economic globalization.[52] This theme was echoed in Hu's speech during a 2002 visit to Malaysia, in which he asserted that "international economic competition will further intensify amid economic globalization."[53] The emphasis on fierce international competition expressed by China's leaders also allows them to portray their desired domestic policies (e.g., economic reforms) as a national imperative for improving the country's performance in world markets. Similarly, it also has the virtue of validating the role of the party-state in the age of globalization. Just as Deng insisted that China's expanding participation in the world economy earlier in the post-Mao era had to take place under strict party rule, so too have Jiang and Hu emphasized that national rejuvenation in the globalization era requires the leadership of the CCP.[54]

As stated by then–vice premier Wen Jiabao in 2001, "Globalization does not mean lessening government responsibilities and functions." Specifically, Wen argued that a central role for the government was critical to "maintain macroeconomic stability, push forward the strategic economic structural adjustment, and guarantee the country's economic security." With respect to social issues, Wen noted a particular role for the state in regulating income distribution, expanding employment, perfecting the social security system, narrowing the urban–rural gap, providing clean and honest government, and strengthening the legal system.[55] On the domestic front, the government is therefore an indispensable gatekeeper in safeguarding the well-being and stability of the country as China's participation in the world economy deepens. Internationally, the government is seen as playing a strategic role in managing the globalization process, working to accelerate those aspects consistent with the country's interests while slowing the advance of changes inimical to

Chinese interests. As this discussion suggests, the state retains its critical role because of, rather than in spite of, globalization.

Globalization and Multipolarization: Toward a Synthesis

The evolving relationship between globalization (*quanqiuhua*) and multipolarization (*duojihua*) has been increasingly critical to China's foreign policy discourse in recent years.[56] When the subject of economic globalization was first broached, official statements indicated that it would enhance the trend toward multipolarity.[57] Foreshadowing this, Jiang had earlier asserted that "sound economic development" could be used by the countries of the world to "effectively resist hegemonism and outside interference, safeguard their independence . . . and secure a firm foothold in the community of nations."[58] That said, the discourses about multipolarization and globalization were carried on quite separately at first. While the multipolarization discourse centered on the nature of the post–Cold War international security environment and China's role in a world characterized by U.S. primacy, the discussion on globalization focused on issues such as the implications of technological changes for world economic activity, the desirability of WTO membership, and the proper course for domestic economic reform. Over time, however, these separate discourses were largely merged into a single discourse identified by a new formulation—"multipolarization and globalization"—which first appeared in China's UN statement in 1998. In 1999, Jiang and other Chinese officials began to use the pairing with regularity.[59] Although the two phenomena are still occasionally analyzed in isolation, depending on the topic under consideration, as "trends" they are typically discussed together.

Although this reformulation had several noteworthy effects on China's foreign policy discourse, one particularly significant implication concerned China's conceptualization of multipolarity itself. In the past, the discourse on multipolarity considered China's international objectives largely in terms of the distribution of power in the international system. In the new pairing, however, multipolarization is much more closely associated with the democratization of IR than with polarity as such. Indeed, references to multipolarization now emphasize a world in which diversity, pluralism, and multiple paths to economic and political development prevail over a world in which one mode of life is imposed by a superpower. In this sense, it is not so much the quantifiable gap in CNP among "poles" as much as the conduct of relations among states that is at issue. Overall, the tenor of China's public statements and diplomatic interactions has focused less on restoring a balance of power (the old conceptualization of multipolarization) than on the proper management of relations among states (the new conceptualization of multipolarization as paired with globalization).

To emphasize the complementary and mutually reinforcing nature of the pairing, Chinese officials sometimes refer explicitly to "political multipolarization and economic globalization."[60] Compared to the 1990s, when the effect of globalization (relative gains for the United States) seemed to undermine the trend toward multipolarization (as understood in terms of power distribution), this position provides a coherent foreign policy discourse in which concepts associated with political multipolarization (e.g., China's advocacy of a "new security concept" in its relations with ASEAN) fit well alongside concepts associated with economic globalization (e.g., China's advocacy of economic and technical cooperation, or Ecotech, in APEC and ASEM). In his report delivered at the Sixteenth Party Congress in November 2002, Jiang quite effectively captured the broader agenda that supports the pairing of "multipolarization and globalization" in a single formulation:

> We stand for maintaining the diversity of the world and are in favor of promoting democracy in international relations and diversifying development models. Ours is a colorful world. Countries having different civilizations and social systems and taking different roads to development should respect one another and draw upon one another's strong points through competition and comparison and should develop side by side by seeking common ground while shelving differences. The affairs of each country should be left to the people of that country to decide. World affairs should be determined by all countries concerned through consultations on the basis of equality.[61]

In seeking the democratization of IR, Beijing pursues a new type of state-to-state relations in which multipolarity refers more to the nature of international decision making than to the distribution of material power. In fact, China has most recently placed greater emphasis on multilateralism than multipolarity. Several foreign policy speeches by Hu and Wen have failed to mention, let alone promote, multipolarization.[62] While the term has certainly not disappeared from China's diplomatic lexicon, its absence from bilateral accords such as the Sino-French Joint Declaration issued in January 2004 is notable, especially since the statement signed by Hu and president Jacques Chirac did explicitly promote multilateralism.[63]

Security Globalization

In China's 2001 UN statement, Tang Jiaxuan broke new ground in China's globalization discourse by characterizing "the question of security" as "becoming increasingly multifaceted and globalized."[64] While there had been occasional observations previously about "common security" and the need for greater "security cooperation," Tang's reference to "globalized" security represented the beginning of a new stage in official rhetoric. In China's 2002 UN statement, Tang further declared that "security is no longer a zero-sum game. Its mutuality is obviously on the increase, as countries have to come to realize that they have common security interests and feel a greater sense of interdependence." Tang also argued that "security is no longer a purely military concern. It has permeated politics, economics, finance, science, technology, culture, and many other areas."[65] The first comment implied that security has only recently become a positive-sum game, while the second comment suggested that security threats have become increasingly diversified. That Tang and other Chinese officials now discuss issues as wide ranging as weapons proliferation, drug trafficking, and cyber-crime in terms of globalized security underscores the increased importance of globalization as an actual phenomenon and, equally important, as a lens through which Chinese policy makers view the internal and external challenges facing their country.

Beijing has long proclaimed that China's economic development cannot be separated from the world's development. By 2003 Chinese leaders had begun to make the same argument about security matters: "In today's world, as countries become increasingly interdependent, the best guarantee for security is common security."[66] While no public statement has yet argued that the concept of national security is becoming an anachronism, Beijing's new rhetoric does suggest that globalization processes have made international security unprecedentedly vital to Chinese interests. Simply put, China cannot enjoy security unless other states enjoy security too. According to *China's National Defense in 2002*, "Threats to world security have come in multiple forms and assumed global dimension, which has increased the common interests of countries on the issue of security."[67] In his 2002 speech to the ASEAN Regional Forum (ARF), Tang referred to a "new development in the global security situation in which traditional and non-traditional security factors are intertwined, with the latter on the rise. . . . Under the new circumstances, security links between countries have become closer and cooperation in international relations has visibly expanded. Countries are even more aware of the need for properly dealing with globalization and striving for coexistence and win–win situations."[68]

As Tang's analysis suggests, nontraditional security threats have been an especially important impetus to China's evolving views on globalized security. Although the spread of lethal technologies, such as those for weapons of mass destruction, also constitute a security threat closely related to globalization, the rise of nontraditional security threats seems to have made a particular contribution to the leadership's growing sense of security interdependence. In Tang's 2002 ARF speech, he declared that nontraditional security issues "are now a real threat we face and a pressing subject we must cope with. Transnational or transregional in nature, most of these issues are difficult for one or a few countries to deal with. Multilateral cooperation is the only way to tackle them."[69]

Although Chinese officials have long identified issues such as refugee crises, drug trafficking, and terrorism as "scourges" that "impede global stability and development," they were seen as "problems" rather than threats.[70] Accordingly, these observations were not made in the context of security affairs, as this discourse was reserved for what Beijing now distinguishes as "traditional" security issues. Several factors have been important in the evolution of China's thinking about the relationship between globalization, nontraditional problems, and security threats. One such factor was the September 11, 2001, attacks on the United States and the accompanying war on terrorism launched by Washington.[71] Specifically, Beijing sees terrorism as a dimension of globalization that affects the country's interests in several ways. First, as Jiang and other Chinese officials have repeatedly pointed out, China considers itself a victim of terrorism due to the activities of "East Turkistan splittist forces."[72] Second, terrorism is understood to be an increasingly widespread threat to peace, thereby jeopardizing not just international security but also the regional and global stability regarded as being so vital for China's continued economic development. Third, counterterrorism, and particularly the global effort led by the United States, has serious implications for Chinese interests. Although a detailed analysis of this complex issue lies beyond the scope of this chapter, the link to globalization is worth identifying. The United States–led war on terrorism illustrates how the framework of "globalizing security" invoked by Chinese officials applies not only to the diversifying types and sources of threats faced in the world today but also to the nature of state responses to those threats. Beijing recognizes that national security requires greater international cooperation, as described by Jiang in an April 2002 speech:

> As countries increase their interdependency and common ground on security, it has become difficult for any single country to realize its security objective by itself alone. Only by strengthening international cooperation can we effectively deal with the security challenge worldwide and realize universal and sustained security.[73]

Implicit in this same comment, however, is a concern about the basis on which international cooperation will be carried out. Indeed, Jiang proceeded to observe that "in cracking down on terrorism, it is necessary to abide by the goals and principles of the UN Charter and universally recognized norms of international relations and bring into full play the role of the United Nations and its Security Council." Perhaps most revealing, Jiang went on to express implicit concern about U.S. unilateralism by warning that "no other political agenda having an impact on world and regional stability and development should be promoted in the name of counter-terrorism." Elsewhere in the speech, Jiang appealed for greater democratization in IR as a requirement for satisfactorily resolving contemporary security problems: "History has time and again proven that global issues need to be jointly resolved by various countries, and global challenges need to be dealt with through cooperation by various countries. No country or force can solve or is capable of solving this task single-handedly. . . . International matters require consultations by various countries on an equal footing."[74]

As this brief discussion illustrates, the expansion of the globalization discourse to security matters is consistent with increasing emphasis on the democratization of IR and the establishment of a new international order. Just as Beijing's analysis of economic globalization has increasingly focused on achieving "balanced development" in the world economy, the emerging discourse on security globalization emphasizes the so-called new security concept (*xin anquan guan*).

Globalization, the Economic–Security Nexus, and China's Foreign Policy Discourse

China's discourse on globalized security has been accompanied by reinvigorated efforts to promote the new security concept (NSC), an innovation that reflects Beijing's desire to circumvent Washington's well-established alliance networks in East Asia by associating those structures with a "Cold War mentality" (*lengzhan siwei*) ill-suited to a new era in which security is a positive-sum game requiring mutual cooperation rather than the "bloc politics" (*jituan zhengzhi*) of the past.[75] In the place of alliance structures, the NSC foresees the creation of a more progressive security order in which bilateral relations and multilateral institutions are characterized by mutual trust and benefit, equality, and cooperation, all to reduce "insecurity and safeguard global strategic equilibrium and stability."[76] Not surprisingly, the NSC has been closely associated with calls for the democratization of IR. Similarly, globalization is cited by Chinese officials as having increased the need for the NSC:

> Economic globalization has led to the mingling of economic and security interests. . . . The connotation of security has expanded from the military and political to economic, scientific and technological, environmental, cultural and many other fields. For this, we propose a new security concept, with the emphasis on

building mutual trust through dialogue, settling disputes through negotiation, and seeking security through cooperation.[77]

Consistent with this viewpoint is China's recently expressed willingness to expand the focus of ostensibly economic forums, such as APEC and APT, to include political and security cooperation. This is especially true in APT, where China proposed and ultimately organized a regional meeting on transnational crime as part of its campaign to place greater emphasis on nontraditional security issues. Within APT, China's boldest initiatives have involved its relations with ASEAN. In November 2002, for example, Beijing signed a joint declaration with ASEAN to increase cooperation on a variety of nontraditional security issues. On the heels of that agreement, an emergency China–ASEAN summit was convened in April 2003 to address the severe acute respiratory syndrome (SARS) crisis. At that meeting, which was Wen Jiabao's first overseas trip as premier, Beijing signed a joint declaration pledging unprecedented information sharing to combat the further spread of the disease.

Continuing its trend of promoting deeper regional cooperation, China proposed in June 2003 that a new "ARF Security Policy Conference" should be established in which military as well as civilian personnel would participate. Consistent with the NSC, Beijing's reported goal was the development of a security pact in which ARF countries would reaffirm principles such as the peaceful resolution of international disputes through negotiation and noninterference in the internal affairs of other countries.[78] Toward this end, in October 2003 China acceded to the Treaty of Amity and Cooperation, ASEAN's nonaggression pact, a step that further signaled Beijing's intention to forge a more comprehensive regional economic and security partnership based on the incipient ASEAN–China free trade agreement. In fact Beijing, at the same set of meetings in Bali, Indonesia, signed a joint declaration with ASEAN that called for, among other things, the establishment of a security dialogue among the "ten plus one" countries—that is, the ten ASEAN countries and China. Although most of China's attention has focused on ASEAN, Beijing used the "Plus Three" meeting in Bali to finalize the "Joint Declaration on the Promotion of Tripartite Cooperation among China, Japan, and South Korea." This initiative identifies areas of cooperation ranging from commerce (trade, investment, and tourism) to traditional and nontraditional security issues (antiproliferation, environmental protection, and infectious disease). Notably, the statement explicitly called for a strengthening security dialogue among the three countries.

The origin of these developments can be traced back to 2001, when Zhu proposed in his speech at the annual APT summit that "efforts should be made to gradually carry out dialogue and cooperation in the political and security field."[79] As recently as the 1999 summit, Zhu had explicitly stated that APT should focus on cooperation in the economic, financial, and scientific and technological fields. Although Beijing has limited its new enthusiasm thus far mainly to discussion of nontraditional security issues, Tang did note in his 2002 ARF speech that "traditional and nontraditional security factors are intertwined."[80] In a 2002 position paper on nontraditional security issues, Beijing explained that traditional security problems can be exacerbated, or even triggered, by nontraditional security issues ranging from ethnic unrest and development imbalances to terrorism and natural resource disputes.[81] Moreover, China's concerted diplomatic efforts since 2003 to resolve the North Korean nuclear crisis suggest an increasing recognition of the threat posed to its own interests by the spread of lethal technologies. All told, China's rhetoric and behavior demonstrate that it now takes a less-compartmentalized view of international cooperation than it did even a few years ago.

One factor instrumental in breaking down the previously formidable conceptual barriers between economic and security affairs has been the emergence of economic security (*jingji anquan*) as a concept central to China's foreign policy discourse. Economic security has in fact long occupied a prominent spot on China's list of nontraditional security threats. Moreover, many of the specific issues associated with the nontraditional security dimension (e.g., energy security; information security; environmental security; infectious disease; and transnational crimes such as drug trafficking, money laundering, and piracy) relate directly to the concept of economic security. Especially since the AFC, the idea of economic security has been routinely invoked by China's leaders in making a range of arguments about various imperatives in domestic and foreign policy, especially those regarding globalization. In his 1998 APEC speech, Jiang argued that economic globalization has "presented to countries, developing ones in particular, a new subject to tackle, that is how to ensure the economic security of a country."[82] In China's 1999 UN statement, Tang invoked the pursuit of national and global economic security in calling for reform of the international economic system.[83] In his report to the Sixteenth Party Congress, Jiang warned: "In opening wider to the outside world, we must pay great attention to safeguarding our national economic security."[84]

As this discussion suggests, the economic–security nexus has become central to China's foreign policy discourse. Moreover, dynamic interaction between economic and security affairs is viewed increasingly through the lens of globalization. As China's participation in the world economy has deepened, security issues are seen as directly affecting developmental prospects. For example, various forms of strife and instability short of major war—such as local wars, regional conflicts, and terrorist activities—are seen as security threats carrying enormously negative economic potential.[85] Nontraditional security threats, which Beijing regards as the fastest-growing variety of security threats, are viewed as particularly worrisome in their economic implications. Indeed, these threats are arguably feared within China mainly for their economic impact.

At the same time, economic factors are widely regarded as being critical to the regional and global security environment. As Tang put it in his 2002 ARF speech, "The economic factor is increasingly becoming an important factor for the maintenance of Asia-Pacific security."[86] *China's Position Paper on the New Security Concept*, which was released at the 2002 ARF, hailed economic cooperation in APT as an important contribution to regional security. This line of argumentation dates back to China's 1997 UN statement, during the early stages of the AFC, in which Qian identified a narrowing of the North–South gap as "the economic foundation for global and regional security."[87] For traditional security issues (e.g., proliferation) and for nontraditional security threats (e.g., terrorism), Beijing regularly cites connections between issues of economic security—and globalization more generally—and prospects for regional and global stability.

Less conventionally, Chinese officials have begun to cite improved prospects for economic cooperation as a compelling argument for trying to increase political and security cooperation, especially regionally. In his 2001 ARF speech, Tang noted that "increased political and security dialogue . . . will provide more favorable conditions for further economic cooperation." By reversing the usual logic that economic cooperation can improve political trust and thereby create opportunities for security cooperation, Tang suggested that prospects for further economic cooperation— which he argued will be necessary "as economic globalization picks up speed"—may depend on whether political and security dialogue can be advanced.[88] In his speech at the 2002 summit of the Shanghai Cooperation Organization (SCO), Jiang observed that "security cooperation and economic and trade cooperation complement and promote each other. They are the two wheels that drive regional cooperation and SCO development."[89] Jiang's comment raises a final point on the economic–security nexus, especially as it relates to the management of globalization. More than in the past, China's foreign policy discourse offers consistent points of reference for the dual pursuits of development and security. With respect to the democratization of IR, the idea of a new security concept, and the establishment of a new international order, economic and security issues share a common vision.

CHINA'S GLOBALIZATION BEHAVIOR

This chapter cannot fully survey the myriad ways in which globalization has influenced China's declared foreign policies and actual international behavior.

Instead, this section focuses on three objectives. First, it provides a simple framework within which to consider the different types of impact that globalization can have on policy positions and external behavior. Second, it provides a preliminary assessment concerning how well Chinese policy and behavior matches Beijing's rhetoric on globalization. Finally, the chapter concludes by placing globalization issues within the broader context of China's grand strategy.

Globalization and Chinese Foreign Policy: A Framework for Analysis

To make our consideration of Chinese foreign policy more systematic, it is useful to identify three distinct types of "impacts" associated with globalization: decisional, institutional, and structural.[90] Decisional impacts refer to the ways in which globalization processes influence outcomes by increasing or decreasing the costs of certain policy choices. Consider, for example, China's currency policy in recent years. By most accounts, Beijing's calculation of costs and benefits in deciding not to devalue the renminbi during the AFC was significantly affected by forces associated with globalization.[91] Likewise, the international furor since 2003 over the proper valuation of the renminbi further demonstrates the interdependent nature of China's currency relations. In formulating its policy, Beijing must consider international as well as domestic factors.

The notion of institutional impacts goes beyond the effects of globalization on policy preferences as they pertain to a particular decision; such impacts allow one to consider the ways in which globalization reconfigures "the agenda of decision-making itself and, consequently, the available choices which agents may or may not realistically make."[92] According to this conceptualization, globalization processes structure (or, perhaps more accurately, restructure) the range of policy options available, often widening as well as narrowing the agenda.[93] Applied to the Chinese case, this notion of institutional impacts is consistent with an idea I have developed elsewhere about the "global logic" of China's reform and opening.[94] In essence, the argument is that China (and other similarly situated developing countries) face powerful incentives to adopt certain kinds of (primarily liberalizing) economic policies, institutional changes, and foreign policy strategies in an era of rampant globalization. Wielded as an ideal type, the global logic argument asserts that China's foreign and domestic policies are best understood as a function of the country's position in the international political economy. Conceptually, it focuses on the opportunity costs of insufficient opening, such as failing to participate fully in the transnational manufacturing networks that have become so decisive in shaping world economic activity.

In word and deed, it is clear that China's leaders now view the country's economic challenges (and, therefore, its policy options) within the larger context of global industrial restructuring. In his speech to the Sixteenth Party Congress, Jiang highlighted the utility of the "bringing in" and "going out" strategies, arguing that China must "actively participate in international economic and technological cooperation and competition and open wider to the outside world."[95] For evidence of the leadership's commitment, one need look no further than the timing and circumstances of Beijing's agreement with Washington over its WTO accession. Specifically, Beijing had to overlook a series of tensions in the bilateral relationship, including Washington's closer relationship with Taipei in the extended wake of the 1995–1996 Taiwan Strait crisis, the strengthening of United States–Japan defense guidelines in 1996 and 1997, and the United States–led NATO intervention in Kosovo (and the resulting bombing of the Chinese embassy in Belgrade in May 1999). The fact that the Chinese leadership delivered politically not once but twice in 1999 (April and November) in sealing a WTO deal with the United States underscores the depth of Beijing's commitment. Indeed, most analysts have concluded that the key factor in overcoming "mounting domestic opposition" to China's WTO entry was "the commitment of Jiang Zemin and Zhu Rongji to globalization and a fundamental restructuring of Chinese industry."[96] According to this view, globalization is an increasingly salient context—and, arguably, the most important external context—for decision making in China, one that induced (or at least reinforced) reform and opening as the centerpiece of Beijing's development strategy. As stated resolutely by Zhu, "Reform and opening up are the only way to modernization for China."[97]

Especially as manifested in AFC, globalization has contributed to the adoption of a more comprehensive concept of national security in China. As long as economic security is defined primarily in terms of robust economic growth achieved by maintaining stable or expanding access to the developmental resources of the world economy, China will have a powerful incentive to nurture constructive relations with as many countries as possible. As discussed previously, China's leaders have used their public statements to define the national identity increasingly in terms of meeting the challenge of globalization through deeper participation in the world economy, even if doing so results in higher levels of interdependence.[98] As they depict the global situation, China is locked in a fierce race for CNP, a race that intensifies day by day. As Jiang succinctly put it in his speech to the Sixteenth Party Congress, "Reform and opening up are ways to make China powerful."[99] In sum, globalization can be said to have an institutional impact by shaping the decision-making agenda China's leaders face.

Structural impacts concern the influence that globalization processes can have on domestic structure, broadly understood to include economic, social, and political structure. Given this book's focus on foreign policy, it is well beyond the scope of this chapter to consider the impact of globalization on China's economic and social structures. In passing, however, it is worth reiterating the enormous influence that transnational economic activity has had on the extensive restructuring of China's economy and society during the post-Mao era.

To date, the impact of globalization on political change has been modest. All told, China's leaders have harnessed economic globalization quite effectively to the objective of political stability. While there has been speculation that China's experience with the SARS crisis may have long-term effects on political change by demonstrating the need for greater transparency and accountability, this remains to be seen. As far as the country's external affairs are concerned, globalization has transformed the conduct of China's foreign relations in important ways. Even if we restrict our focus to economic affairs, it would be difficult to overstate the significance of expanding person-to-person contacts, commercial exchange, and interaction with intergovernmental bodies and nonstate actors. In this way, the policy-making environment has been broadened to include new actors, new interests, and new identities, even as the formal structure of the foreign policy system remains relatively unchanged. Especially in terms of policy feedback and policy implementation, a proliferating set of forces now shapes the conduct of China's foreign relations. To a more limited extent, this may also be true in policy formulation. Globalization has unquestionably played a substantial role in this pluralization process.[100]

Reconciling Rhetoric and Behavior:
Is China a Status Quo Economic Power?

China has long cultivated an identity as a leader of the developing world, although that tradition did weaken somewhat during the post-Mao era as Beijing's priorities of reform and modernization led it to place greater emphasis on economic relations with advanced industrial countries. With the advent of international debates over globalization, however, Beijing was provided with a seemingly tailor-made platform from which to restore its longstanding role as a spokesman for the world's disadvantaged. To this point, there has been a gap between China's words and deeds on globalization as they relate to the interests of developing countries. Beijing's rhetoric has in fact seized the opportunity to defend the rights of the world's poor and weak. To a lesser extent, China's declared policies have aimed to promote more balanced development across the international community. In its actual behavior, however, China cannot be characterized as seriously challenging the status quo.

As Margaret Pearson has examined at length, China has for the most part played by the "rules of the game," resisting the norms, principles, and rules of the liberal international economic system no more than most other developing countries.[101] The terms of China's WTO accession constitute Beijing's most formal acceptance of this system, as well as of the legitimacy of the multilateral economic institutions (MEIs) themselves and the capitalist world economy more generally. Indeed, Beijing's relatively cooperative behavior in world affairs, and its de facto validation of the international economic system in particular, reflects the apparent conviction of China's leaders that the existing interstate system is a viable one for meeting China's central goals, such as economic development and increased CNP. This, of course, represents a major departure from the Mao era, during which China did in fact advocate revisionist arrangements.

However dissatisfied China may be with various inequities in the international economic system, it seeks neither to undermine specific regimes nor to weaken their norms in any substantial way. For example, there is scant evidence from China's initial behavior in the WTO that it intends to challenge the decision-making procedures and structures of that body, to say nothing of the organization's basic norms and ideology.[102] Although Beijing's WTO honeymoon lasted less than two years, as evidenced by mounting frustration—mainly in the United States but also in Europe—over an alleged loss of momentum in the implementation of China's WTO obligations, these ups and downs were to be expected. Given the lengths to which Beijing went to gain membership, arguments that China seeks to undermine the WTO are premature at best. If anything, the early record suggests that Beijing sees the WTO as an effective mechanism for defending its interests. For example, China was one of several countries that won a ruling against the United States for its imposition of steel tariffs in 2002. Long the world's most frequent target of antidumping actions, China has itself recently begun to use this instrument of trade policy, which is allowed under WTO rules, to safeguard its manufacturing sector from imports.

More broadly, China's policies toward the Doha Development Agenda—the round of global trade negotiations launched at a 2001 conference in Doha, Qatar—reflect a belief that WTO processes can (and should) be used to achieve a better balance between the needs of developing countries and further trade liberalization. On the surface, one could infer from China's participation in the Group of 22 (G-22) at the September 2003 WTO Ministerial Conference in Cancun, Mexico, that it prefers to block a new agreement.

Quite to the contrary, Washington praised Beijing afterward for working assiduously to broker a deal under difficult circumstances. By all accounts, China proceeded pragmatically while Brazil and India served as the main leaders of the G-22. Although Beijing insists that any new agreement must deliver on the development-oriented pledges made in Doha, especially in light of broken promises from the Uruguay round of the 1990s, China also stands to benefit considerably from various aspects of the liberalization agenda under negotiation. Presumably this is why WTO director general Supachai Panitchpakdi called on Beijing to "use its influence to be a bridge between developed and developing countries" in the wake of the collapse of the Cancun meeting.[103] This direct appeal to Chinese leaders, in which Supachai acknowledged that China is a "developing nation" and an "emerging superpower," reflects Beijing's growing influence in shaping the economic order from which it already benefits handsomely. To that end, China has recently expressed a willingness to play a more "active and constructive role" in reinvigorating the WTO talks that stalled in Cancun.

China's behavior in the WTO is broadly consistent with the pattern it has established in other MEIs, as well as in the United Nations and other regional and global bodies. Writing about the 1980s, Samuel Kim has argued that "Beijing became more interested in what the U.N. system could do for China's modernization and less interested in what China could do to reform the United Nations."[104] With little modification, this characterization would also describe China's relationship with the international economic system during the post-Mao era, in its ties with formal institutions and in its interactions with nonstate actors such as multinational corporations. Using Kim's three ideal types as a point of reference, China's approach to international economic relations in the current era certainly cannot be characterized as "system transforming" since it shows no overt signs of wishing to overturn the system. In its rhetoric, China's approach is sometimes "system reforming." Behaviorally, however, China's approach is still better characterized as "system maintaining" given the relative lack of action Beijing has taken in support of its public statements about effecting change in international economic relations.

Even on Ecotech, where China has been a long-standing advocate, Beijing has used venues such as APEC, APT, WTO, IMF (International Monetary Fund), and ADB to promote (and provide limited financial support for) initiatives on human resource development, infrastructure building, and scientific and technological cooperation. Even more striking than this multilateral approach is the fact that China has consistently portrayed Ecotech as a complement to (rather than a substitute for) trade and investment liberalization. Jiang first presented this view in his 1995 APEC speech:

Trade and investment liberalization and economic and technical cooperation should be given equal emphasis. . . . They are important means to narrow economic disparities among members and to achieve common prosperity. Economic and technical cooperation can also help turn potential markets into real ones which in turn will accelerate the pace of trade and investment liberalization. Trade and investment liberalization and economic and technical cooperation are like two wheels carrying the cart of APEC. The two should complement and promote each other.[105]

Even at the height of the AFC, Beijing never advocated that MEIs should abandon their agenda of trade and investment liberalization. For example, in his 1998 APEC speech, Jiang simply called for a "timely readjustment of the priority areas for cooperation so as to better meet the needs of the developing members."[106] Indeed, the most recognizable theme of China's economic diplomacy over the past decade has been that developed and developing countries need each other for continued prosperity. Consequently, Beijing has consistently argued that no one's interest is served by a widening digital divide or by persistent income gaps between North and South. As Jiang put it in his 2001 APEC speech, "Globalization will grow smoothly and the world economy will develop in a sustained and steady manner only when most members of the international community can reap the benefit."[107]

The positive-sum analysis that infuses Chinese thinking is noteworthy. Although disparities between developing and developed countries persist, Chinese leaders do not subscribe to dependency theory, modern world system theory, or other perspectives from which a more revisionist (or inward looking) approach to international economic relations might emerge. Intense economic competition is a defining feature of Chinese views on globalization, but there is no logic whereby developing countries must suffer adverse consequences for developed countries to enjoy continued prosperity.

For all of Beijing's commentary about various irrationalities in the international economic system, China's development needs are, on balance, well-served by economic globalization. Although Chinese leaders might prefer a more equitable distribution of benefits across the world economy, this goal has not been made a priority of Chinese foreign policy. By most accounts, China sees itself as one of globalization's leading beneficiaries.[108] Not surprisingly, there is ample evidence that Beijing intends to pursue its own interests rather than undertake actions on behalf of other developing countries, actions that might weaken the international order on which China's continued modernization seemingly depends. In 2003, for example, China became a member of the WTO's Information Technology Agreement, a goal Beijing had long targeted as a means "to become part of the multinational companies' global base for IT products."[109] As a signatory, Beijing must eliminate tariffs and other duties on certain information technology imports from other WTO members. As this case illustrates, Beijing pragmatically supports liberalization that expands overseas markets for Chinese goods or facilitates the flow of international capital and technology to Chinese soil.

Even if China's rhetorical solidarity with developing countries is not generally matched by action, it still serves several purposes. First, it allows Beijing to retain some voice as a leader of the developing world. Second, expressions of Chinese concern for the plight of developing countries reflect a larger diplomatic effort to refute the "China threat" theory in which Beijing's rising economic power is seen as a growing regional and global challenge to the interests of ASEAN, Mexico, and others. Finally, Chinese criticism of the international economic system as "unfair" and "irrational" allows Beijing to convey its antihegemonic concerns without directly challenging the interests of the United States. Indeed, China's greatest reservation about the globalization process involves, not economic policy, but the inadequacy of "democratic consultation" in international decision making.

Globalization as the Twenty-First-Century Context of China's Grand Strategy

Which is a more important context for understanding Chinese foreign policy, globalization or the distribution of international power? Much of Beijing's rhetoric and behavior suggests that globalization is likely to prove more important to China's long-term prosperity and security than the distribution of power. From this perspective, China's future well-being is seen as depending less on the number of poles in the international system than on the country's ability to take advantage of the opportunities (and avoid the dangers) associated with increasing transnational flows of capital, information, and technology.[110] By most measures, China is not following the classical balancing strategy (internal mobilization or external military alliances) against the United States as expected by traditional great power theories. Indeed, Beijing's decision to eschew balancing arguably owes much to the thickening context of globalization in which Chinese decision makers formulate the country's foreign policy. For example, economic globalization is widely thought to have inhibited the emergence of a multipolar distribution of power in the 1990s, thereby making balancing a less-practical approach.[111] Along the same lines, the importance of relative gains is often thought to be greatest when differences in power are small. To the extent that the gap in CNP between China and the United States has failed to narrow due to economic globalization, it could be argued that Beijing has been dissuaded from trying to engage in peer competition with Washington.[112] Likewise, the virtual developmental imperative of participating vigorously in the globalizing world economy has placed huge opportunity costs in the path of a balancing strategy, a strategy in which China would have to divert large sums of scarce resources to an arms buildup, establish military alliances against Washington, and withdraw from (and perhaps even undermine) the liberal international economic system.

China's domestic focus on economic construction, with an accompanying emphasis on developing and maintaining cooperative relations with as many countries as possible, reflects a belief that the primary determinant of long-term national power and security is the ability to generate wealth. Therefore, the significance of economic globalization is that the objective of making China rich and strong can be achieved only by increasing its interdependence with other countries. As Jiang has explained it, economic globalization is a "natural outcome of world economic development as well as the external environment for the economic development of all countries in the future."[113] Even during the darkest days of the AFC, Jiang never wavered from this bedrock position:

> Economic globalization, being an objective tendency of the development of the world's economy, is independent of man's will and cannot be avoided by any country. The world today is an open world and no country can develop its own economy if isolated from the outside world. We must firmly implement the policy of opening up, keep in line with economic globalization, energetically take part in international economic cooperation and competition, and make full use of various favorable conditions and opportunities brought by economic globalization.[114]

As discussed earlier, globalization can be conceived as having decisional and institutional impacts on Chinese foreign policy by altering the costs and benefits of certain choices and restructuring the range of available strategies, respectively. The argument, in essence, is that while China still pursues it own interests, this pursuit of self-interest leads Beijing to accept policies that entail unprecedented levels of interdependence. In the process, state interests themselves may be reconfigured. With each passing year, China's interests are more intertwined with those of its major economic partners, in East Asia and across the world. Although international commercial ties may at first have been pursued narrowly as a means for pursuing economic development, the reality of interdependence shapes China's interests all the same. To the extent that globalization has contributed significantly to the deepening interdependence that now characterizes interstate relations, it has influenced Chinese behavior in important ways.

In this respect, economic globalization provides the means by which China can pursue an alternative strategy for coping with U.S. hegemony in lieu of the classical balancing strategy many observers had expected Beijing to adopt during the post–Cold War era. Unable to compete with the United States in CNP for the foreseeable future, China instead seeks to restrain Washington through a growing reliance on formal and informal mechanisms of interdependence. Even if heightened interdependence has not replaced increased CNP as the ultimate strategic goal pursued by Beijing, expanding Sino-American economic ties have emerged as a vital stabilizing force in the bilateral relationship. According to this perspective, burgeoning commercial relations with the United States serve as an informal mechanism of interdependence that will weaken any American impulse to view China as a rival that needs to be contained. For example, Washington's penchant for overseas borrowing offsets, at least in part, China's dependence on the United States as an export market. By virtually any measure, Chinese holdings of U.S. debt, such as Treasury securities, dwarfs U.S. investment in Chinese factories. The result is a historically unusual relationship in which the rising power (a developing China) provides exports and loans to the superpower (an industrialized United States). Some analysts argue more broadly that Beijing long ago adopted a conscious strategy of developing constituencies in the United States that will favor continued engagement policies toward China even if noneconomic aspects of the relationship sour.[115]

As far as formal mechanisms of interdependence are concerned, globalization has served as a powerful impetus for institutionalized multilateralism at the regional and global levels. The public statements of China's leaders routinely acknowledge that globalization—mainly economic globalization but now also security globalization—encourages broad participation in multilateral institutions.[116] Across an increasingly wide range of issue areas, China's behavior reflects an understanding of the benefits that can accrue from greater cooperation in multilateral institutions. Although Beijing's case-by-case approach to multilateralism is still best characterized as, in Samuel Kim's words, "incremental and conditional," its formerly unyielding skepticism about formal modes of international cooperation has dissipated significantly.[117] In China's 2003 UN statement, Li placed unprecedented emphasis on multilateral cooperation, arguing that it should be the "principal vehicle in the handling of international affairs." He further asserted that global challenges require "globalized cooperation" (*quanqiuxing de hezuo*).[118] To the extent that the opportunities and challenges associated with economic-cum-security globalization have in fact induced this change in thinking about multilateralism, they may also be partly responsible for China's relatively status quo orientation toward the international system.

While there is much for Chinese leaders to dislike about American dominance in world affairs, the United States–led globalized world is also widely seen as having provided the stable and open international environment essential for China's remarkable economic success. Any alternative to the status quo carries with it risks of significant geoeconomic fragmentation and reduced international stability in general, neither of which would suit China's pressing development needs. Moreover, there is also the prospect that the United States may become increasingly restrained by the very same institutions it helped to create. On a range of issues important to China's trade interests, from steel tariffs to textile quotas, the WTO may prove to be an important means by which Beijing protects itself from American unilateralism. Similarly, global and regional institutions have provided a measure of support as China's leaders have tried to resist pressure to revalue the renminbi on U.S. terms. In November 2003, for example, the IMF's majority assessment was that the Chinese currency was not substantially undervalued. Two months earlier, members of ASEAN undermined the Bush administration's drive to issue a statement on Beijing's currency policy at a meeting of APEC finance ministers. If other countries work to strengthen regional and global multilateral cooperation, as China itself now seems inclined to do with greater commitment than in the past, the United States may find its range of action increasingly (albeit unevenly and incompletely) constrained by a new institutional context.[119]

While the foregoing analysis could be interpreted as supporting a view that globalization has now eclipsed the international distribution of power in importance as a context for understanding Chinese foreign policy, it would be more accurate to say that globalization now largely defines the circumstances within which China responds to the international distribution of power. As discussed, one of globalization's most profound effects has been to transform the geoeconomic context within which states compete for CNP. It may be that states increasingly pursue their interests through participation in transnational economic structures and multilateral institutions, but relative power is still highly valued by most countries. China may be deepening its embrace of globalization and multilateralism, but the evidence is mixed about whether the value Beijing attaches to interdependence now exceeds that placed on competing values such as independence and sovereignty. Consider, for example, the compromises on policy autonomy that accompanied China's WTO accession. These were accepted primarily as a means for advancing specific state interests related to economic modernization. Indeed, Beijing's logic was that the protection of China's sovereignty actually required further reform and opening, as expressed in the following statement by Jiang:

> Modern technology is advancing rapidly and industrial and economic restructuring on a global scale is speeding up. Competition based on overall national strength will increasingly become the leading factor deciding a country's future

and destiny. We are facing rare development opportunities as well as grim challenges. Only by constantly improving our economic strength, national defense strength, and national cohesiveness, can we remain invincible amidst increasingly intensive international competition and truly safeguard our national sovereignty and national pride.[120]

This is not to say that China does not value interdependence for its own sake.[121] As this chapter has attempted to show, China's policies and behavior suggest a preference for advancing state interests—albeit interests still defined significantly in terms of national power—through the deepening economic and security interdependence of the existing international system. The fact that Beijing now assigns independent weight to interdependence as a goal of Chinese foreign policy raises the possibility that China's leaders may have begun to pursue a fundamentally different approach to great power politics, one that improves prospects for peaceful change in the international system.[122] While that question will not be answered soon, it is already clear that globalization has cast a long shadow over China's rise.

NOTES

1. On China's participation in the world economy, see Nicholas Lardy, *Integrating China into the Global Economy* (Washington, D.C.: Brookings, 2002). On the general implications of globalization for China, see Stuart Harris, "China and the Pursuit of State Interests in a Globalizing World," *Pacifica Review* 13, no. 1 (February 2001): 15–29; and Thomas G. Moore, "China and Globalization," in *East Asia and Globalization*, ed. Samuel Kim (Lanham, Md.: Rowman & Littlefield, 2000), 105–31.

2. See, for example, Banning Garrett, "China Faces, Debates, the Contradictions of Globalization," *Asian Survey* 41, no. 3 (May/June 2001): 409–27.

3. Parts of this chapter draw on and update Moore, "China and Globalization."

4. Qian Qichen, speech to UN General Assembly, September 25, 1996, UN document A/51/PV.8.

5. One example appeared in Jiang Zemin's speech to the Second APEC Informal Leadership Meeting, November 15, 1994, in which he declared that the "economic factor is, indeed, increasingly playing the overriding and pivotal role in international relations." The text of this speech is available at www.fmprc.gov/cn/eng/5122.html.

6. Jiang Zemin, "Hold High the Great Banner of Deng Xiaoping Theory, Carrying the Cause of Building Socialism with Chinese Characteristics to the 21st Century," *Xinhua*, September 21, 1997, FBIS-CHI-97-266. Throughout this chapter, the abbreviation FBIS-CHI stands for Foreign Broadcast Information Service–China (Internet version).

7. Zhang Yiping, "A New View of Post–Cold War World Security," *Xiandai guoji guanxi* (February 1997), FBIS-CHI-97-091.

8. Gu Yuanyang, "Economic Globalization and the 'Rules of the Game,'" *Renmin ribao*, June 10, 1998, FBIS-CHI-98-167.

9. Shi Guangsheng, "To Intensify China-Africa Cooperation for a Brilliant Future," October 11, 2000, available at www.fmprc.gov/cn/eng/5374.html.

10. Jiang Zemin, speech at the Eighth APEC Informal Leadership Meeting, November 16, 2000, available at www.fmprc.gov/cn/eng/6004.html.

11. Qian Qichen, speech to the Asia Society, March 20, 2001, available at www.fmprc.gov/.cn/eng/9319.html.

12. Qian, speech to UN General Assembly, 1996.

13. Qian Qichen, speech to UN General Assembly, September 24, 1997, UN document A/52/PV.9.

14. Tang Jiaxuan, speech to UN General Assembly, September 23, 1998, UN document A/53/PV.11.

15. Jiang, speech at the Eighth APEC Informal Leadership Meeting, 2000.

16. Jiang Zemin, "Striving for Development and Prosperity through Cooperation," October 18, 2001, available at www.fmprc.gov/cn/eng/18923.html.

17. "Jiang: Asian Nations Need to Enhance Cooperation," *Renmin Ribao*, February 26, 2001.

18. Jiang Zemin, speech at the Sixth APEC Informal Leadership Meeting, November 18, 1998, available at www.fmprc.gov/.cn/eng/5192.html.

19. Tang Jiaxuan, "Asia and Europe Work Together to Create a Better Future," March 29, 1999, available at www.fmprc.gov/.cn/eng/5186.html.

20. Jiang Zemin, speech at the Third APEC Informal Leadership Meeting, November 19, 1995, available at www.fmprc.gov/.cn/eng/5194.html.

21. Jiang Zemin, "Enhance Good-Neighborliness and Friendship and Build a Better Future Together," *Xinhua*, September 3, 1999, FBIS-CHI-1999-0903.

22. Tang Jiaxuan, speech to UN General Assembly, September 22, 1999, UN document A/54/PV.8.

23. Jiang, speech at Eighth APEC Informal Leadership Meeting, 2000.

24. Both quotes from *Xinhua*, August 10, 1999, FBIS-CHI-1999-0822.

25. Yan Xuetong, "The Rise of China in Chinese Eyes," *Journal of Contemporary China* 10, no. 26 (February 2001): 33.

26. *Xinhua*, August 10, 1999, FBIS-CHI-1999-0822.

27. Jiang Zemin, "Unity and Cooperation in Asia for Peace and Development in the World," May 10, 2002, *Xinhua*, FBIS-CHI-2002-0510.

28. Jiang Zemin, "Striving for Development and Prosperity through Cooperation."

29. For an earlier reference, see Tang, speech to UN General Assembly, 1998.

30. See, for example, Jiang, speech at Eighth APEC Informal Leadership Meeting, 2000.

31. Available online at http://news.xinhuanet.com/zhengfu/2003-02/27/content_748657.htm.

32. Li Zhaoxing, speech to UN General Assembly, September 24, 2003, available online at www.un.org/webcast/ga/58/statements/chinaeng030924.htm.

33. See, for example, Hu Jintao, "Generations of Neighborly Friendship, Developing and Prospering Together," May 28, 2003, *Xinhua*, FBIS-CHI-2003-0528.

34. Qian, speech to the UN General Assembly, 1997. Although the English translations used by Beijing have varied somewhat over the years, the Chinese phrasing of

this formulation (*jianli gongzheng heli de guoji zhengzhi jingji xin zhixu*) has remained consistent. For an official statement, see "China's Position on Establishing a New International Political and Economic Order," available online at www.fmprc .gov.cn/eng/4493.html.

35. See, for example, Jiang, "Unity and Cooperation in Asia," and Dai Xianglong, "China's Position in International Economic and Financial Affairs," *Ta Kung Pao* (Hong Kong), FBIS-CHI-2002-0423.

36. Hu Jintao, "Generations of Neighborly Friendship, Developing and Prospering Together."

37. "Speech by Foreign Minister Tang Jiaxuan at Forum on China-Africa Cooperation," October 10, 2000, available at www.fmprc.gov.cn/eng/5838.html.

38. "Full Text of Jiang Zemin Speech at 10th APEC Leaders' Informal Meeting," October 27, 2002, *Xinhua*, FBIS-CHI-2002-1027.

39. Zhu Rongji, "Strengthen Solidarity, Enhance Cooperation, and Pursue Common Development," October 12, 2000, available at www.fmprc.gov.cn/eng/ 5233.html.

40. Jiang Zemin, "Striving for Development and Prosperity through Cooperation."

41. See, for example, Tang Jiaxuan, speech to the UN General Assembly, September 13, 2002, UN document A/57/PV.5.

42. Jiang Zemin, speech to the UN General Assembly, September 6, 2000, UN document A/55/PV.3.

43. Tang Jiaxuan, speech to UN General Assembly, November 11, 2001, UN document A/56/PV.46.

44. Jiang Zemin, quoted in "Knowledge Economy and Learning Society," *Renmin Ribao*, July 7, 1998, FBIS-CHI-98-201.

45. Jiang, "Hold High the Great Banner of Deng Xiaoping Theory."

46. "Text of Jiang Zemin Speech at CYL 80th Anniversary Rally," *Xinhua*, May 15, 2002, FBIS-CHI-2002-0515.

47. See, for example, Zhu Rongji, speech to the World Chinese Entrepreneurs Convention, September 19, 2001, FBIS-CHI-2001-0919.

48. "Jiang's Speech at Meeting Marking 90th Anniversary of 1911 Revolution," *Xinhua*, October 9, 2001, FBIS-CHI-2001-1009.

49. "Hu Jintao's Xibaibo Speech on Plain Living, Hard Stuggle," *Xinhua*, January 2, 2003, FBIS-CHI-2003-0102.

50. Long Yongtu, "On Economic Globalization," *Guangming ribao*, October 30, 1998, FBIS-CHI-98-313.

51. Qian Qichen, speech at the Inauguration of the Boao Forum for Asia, February 27, 2001, *Xinhua*, FBIS-CHI-2001-0227.

52. "Jiang Zemin's Speech Marking the 80th CCP Founding Anniversary," July 1, 2001, *Xinhua*, FBIS-CHI-2001-0701.

53. "Hu Jintao Speaks at Malaysia Meeting on Asian Economic Development," April 24, 2002, *Xinhua*, FBIS-CHI-2002-0424.

54. For a good primer on the Deng era, see Christopher Hughes, "Globalization and Nationalism: Squaring the Circle in Chinese International Relations Theory," *Millenium* 26, no. 1 (1997): 103–24.

55. "Wen Jiabao's Speech at Opening Ceremony of 'China Development Forum 2001,'" March 25, 2001, *Renmin Ribao*, FBIS-CHI-2001-0328.

56. For an excellent overview of this relationship, see Yong Deng, "Economic Globalization and Multipolarization in Chinese Foreign Policy," *Harvard China Review* 4, no. 1 (Fall 2003): 18–22.

57. See, for example, Qian Qichen, speech at the ASEM Foreign Ministers Meeting, February 5, 1997, available at www.fmprc.gov.cn.eng/4943.html.

58. Jiang Zemin, "Carrying Forward Generations of Friendly and Good-Neighborly Relations and Endeavoring Towards a Better Tomorrow for All," December 2, 1996, available at www.fmprc.gov.cn.eng/4288.html. A year earlier, Jiang explicitly linked the revitalization of developing countries to the furtherance of multipolarization. See Jiang, speech at the Third APEC Informal Leaders Meeting, 1995.

59. See, for example, Jiang Zemin, "Promote Disarmament Process and Safeguard World Security," March 26, 1999, available at www.fmprc.gov.cn.eng/4074.html.

60. See, for example, Qian, speech at the inauguration of the Boao Forum for Asia, 2001, and "Foreign Minister Tang Jiaxuan Addresses Shanghai Five Foreign Ministers' Meeting 29 April 2001," available at www.fmprc.gov.cn.eng/10082.html.

61. Jiang Zemin, "Build a Well-Off Society in an All-Round Way and Create a New Situation in Building Socialism with Chinese Characteristics," November 8, 2002, available at www.chinadaily.com.cn/highlights/party16/news/1118full.htm.

62. Examples include Hu's speech to the Australian Parliament in October 2003 and Wen's speeches to the Boao Forum and the China–Africa Cooperation Forum in November and December 2003, respectively.

63. For a text of the declaration, see January 27, 2004, *Xinhua*, FBIS-CHI-2004-0127.

64. Tang, speech to UN General Assembly, 2001.

65. Tang, speech to UN General Assembly, 2002.

66. Wu Bangguo, "Create a Hundred Years of Peace in Asia, Jointly Build Sustained Development of Asia," September 1, 2003, FBIS-CHI-2003-0901.

67. *China's National Defense in 2002* is available at http://news.xinhuanet.com/zhengfu/2003-02/27/content_748657.htm.

68. Tang Jiaxuan, speech at the Ninth ARF Foreign Ministers Meeting, July 31, 2002, available at http://fmprc.gov.cn/eng/33228.html.

69. Tang Jiaxuan, speech at the Ninth ARF Foreign Ministers Meeting, 2002.

70. See, for example, Qian, speech to the UN General Assembly, 1996.

71. "China's Position Paper on the New Security Concept," July 31, 2002, available at www.fmprc.gov.cn/eng/33227.html.

72. See, for example, Jiang Zemin's speech at the Conference on Interaction and Confidence Building Measures in Asia, June 4, 2002, *Xinhua*, FBIS-CHI-2002-0604.

73. Jiang Zemin, "Together Create a New Century of Peace and Prosperity," April 10, 2002, *Xinhua*, FBIS-CHI-2002-0410.

74. Jiang Zemin, "Together Create a New Century of Peace and Prosperity."

75. According to Tang Jiaxuan's speech at the Ninth ARF Foreign Ministers Meeting, July 31, 2002, the new security concept was formally introduced to China's ARF

interlocutors in 1996. For a recent detailed explanation of the concept, see Tang, speech to the UN General Assembly, 2002.

76. Jiang Zemin, "Together Create a New Century of Peace and Prosperity."

77. Tang, speech at the Ninth ARF Foreign Ministers Meeting, 2002.

78. For an official statement of these principles, see "China's Position Paper on the New Security Concept."

79. Zhu Rongji, "Strengthening East Asian Cooperation and Promoting Common Development," November 5, 2001, available at www.fmprc.gov.cn/eng/21861.html.

80. Tang, speech at the Ninth ARF Foreign Ministers Meeting, 2002.

81. "China's Position Paper on Enhanced Cooperation in the Field of Non-Traditional Security Issues," May 29, 2002, available www.fmprc.gov.cn/eng/30439.html.

82. Jiang, speech at the Sixth Informal APEC Leadership Meeting, 1998.

83. Tang, speech to the UN General Assembly, 1999.

84. Jiang, "Build a Well-Off Society."

85. See, for example, Wen Jiabao, speech at the World Food Summit, June 10, 2002, available at www.fmprc.gov.cn/eng/31040.html.

86. Tang, speech at the Ninth ARF Foreign Ministers Meeting, 2002.

87. Qian, speech to the UN General Assembly, 1997.

88. Tang Jiaxuan, speech at the Eighth ARF Foreign Ministers Meeting, July 25, 2001, available at http://fmprc.gov.cn/eng/16580.html.

89. Jiang Zemin, "Amplify the 'Shanghai Spirit' and Promote World Peace," June 7, 2002, *Xinhua*, FBIS-CHI-2002-0607.

90. This framework is borrowed from David Held, Anthony McGrew, David Goldblatt, and Jonathan Perraton, *Global Transformations* (Stanford, Calif.: Stanford University Press, 1999).

91. For more detail on this case, see Thomas G. Moore and Dixia Yang, "Empowered and Restrained: Chinese Foreign Policy in the Age of Economic Interdependence," *The Making of Chinese Foreign and Security Policy in the Era of Reform, 1978–2000*, ed. David M. Lampton (Stanford, Calif.: Stanford University Press, 2001), 191–229.

92. Held et al., *Global Transformations*, 18.

93. For a lengthier discussion on how external forces have restructured policy options as China's participation in the world economy has grown, especially in the context of specific industries, see Thomas G. Moore, *China in the World Market: Chinese Industry and International Sources of Reform in the Post-Mao Era* (New York: Cambridge University Press, 2002).

94. For a recent overview of this idea, see Moore and Yang, "Empowered and Restrained." The notion of a global logic was first examined in Thomas G. Moore, "China as a Latecomer: Toward a Global Logic of the Open Policy," *Journal of Contemporary China* 5, no. 12 (Summer 1996): 187–208.

95. Jiang, "Build a Well-Off Society."

96. See, for example, Samuel S. Kim, "China's Path to Great Power Status in the Globalization Era," *Asian Perspective* 27, no. 1 (2003): 65.

97. Zhu Rongji, speech at the ASEM Science and Technology Ministers Meeting, October 14, 1999, available at www.fmprc.gov.cn/eng/5188.html.

98. For more on this theme, see George T. Crane, "Imagining the Economic Nation: Globalisation in China," *New Political Economy* 4, no. 2 (July 1999): 215–32.

99. Jiang, "Build a Well-Off Society."

100. Moore and Yang, "Empowered and Restrained." This theme is explored at length throughout Lampton, *The Making of Chinese Foreign and Security Policy in the Era of Reform, 1978–2000.*

101. Margaret M. Pearson, "The Major Multilateral Economic Institutions Engage China," in *Engaging China: The Management of an Emerging Power*, ed. Alastair Iain Johnston and Robert S. Ross (London: Routledge, 1999), 207.

102. Margaret M. Pearson, "China's Multiple Personalities in Geneva: Constructing a Template for Future Research on Chinese Behavior in WTO," paper cited in Alastair Iain Johnston, "Is China a Status Quo Power?" *International Security* 27, no. 4 (Spring 2003): 23.

103. Rebecca Buckman, "WTO Head Asks China to Help Revive Talks," *Asian Wall Street Journal*, November 11, 2003, A3.

104. Samuel S. Kim, "China and the United Nations," in *China Joins the World: Progress and Prospects*, ed. Elizabeth Economy and Michel Oksenberg (New York: Council on Foreign Relations, 1999), 46.

105. Jiang, speech to the Third APEC Leaders Informal Meeting, 1995.

106. Jiang, speech to the Sixth APEC Informal Leaders Meeting, 1998.

107. Jiang Zemin, "Strengthen Cooperation and Meet New Challenges Together in the New Century," speech at the Ninth APEC Informal Leadership Meeting, October 21, 2001, available at www.fmprc.gov.cn/eng/19010.html.

108. On these points, see the survey of views contained in Garrett, "China Faces, Debates, the Contradictions of Globalization."

109. Long, "On Economic Globalization."

110. For reasoning along these lines, see Johnston, "Is China a Status Quo Power," especially 35–36.

111. For a related discussion, see Garrett, "China Faces," 414.

112. This analysis would be consistent with William C. Wohlforth, "The Stability of a Unipolar World," *International Security* 24, no. 1 (Summer 1999): 5–41.

113. Jiang Zemin, "Address to the 21st Century Forum," FBIS-CHI-2000-0613.

114. "Jiang Zemin, Zhang Wannian Meet Diplomats," *Xinhua*, August 28, 1998, FBIS-CHI-98–242.

115. For two perspectives on this issue, see Liu Fei, "Economic and Trade Ties Are the 'Ballast Tank' for Stabilizing Sino-U.S. Relations," *Liaowang*, October 21, 2002, FBIS-CHI-2002-1030; and Phillip Saunders, "Supping with a Long Spoon: Dependence and Interdependence in Sino-American Relations," *China Journal* 43 (2000): 55–81.

116. On economic affairs, one example is Jiang, speech to Eighth APEC Informal Leaders Meeting, 2000. On security affairs, see Tang, speech at the Ninth ARF Foreign Ministers Meeting, 2002.

117. Kim, "China's Path to Great Power Status in the Globalization Era," 69.

118. Li, speech to UN General Assembly, 2003.

119. Thomas G. Moore, "In Pursuit of Open Markets: U.S. Economic Strategy in the Asia-Pacific," *Asian Affairs* 28, no. 3 (Fall 2001): 179. Deng, "Economic Globalization and Multipolarization" makes a similar argument.

120. Jiang Zemin, "Strengthen Confidence, Deepen Reform, Create a New Situation in Development of State-Owned Enterprises," *Xinhua*, August 12, 1999, FBIS-CHI-1999-0817.

121. For statements linking interdependence to global and regional stability, respectively, see Jiang, speech at the Eighth APEC Informal Leadership Meeting, 2000; and Qian, speech at Inauguration of Boao Forum for Asia, 2001.

122. See Yong Deng and Thomas G. Moore, "China Views Globalization: Towards a New Great Power Politics?" *Washington Quarterly* 27, no. 3 (Summer 2004): 117–36.

7

China's Multilateral Diplomacy in the New Millennium

Jianwei Wang

In the existing literature of Chinese foreign policy, China is often portrayed as a reluctant and suspicious participant in multilateral diplomacy, particularly in the domain of security multilateralism. As a staunch advocate of the Westphalia international system of nation-state and national sovereignty, China is more comfortable dealing with other nations bilaterally rather than multilaterally.[1] Indeed as late as 1999, some Chinese élite still regarded multilateral diplomacy as a taboo that should not be touched.[2] Yet, the beginning of the twenty-first century has witnessed China's increasing embrace of multilateralism in its foreign policy and a flurry of new initiatives and practice of multilateral diplomacy: the first summit of the permanent members of the UN Security Council, the active promotion of economic integration in Southeast Asia and East Asia, the launch of a new regional organization in Northeast Asia and Central Asia, and endorsement of a multilateral framework for conflict resolution on the Korean Peninsula. China's participation in multilateral intergovernmental and nongovernmental organizations has also steadily increased in the post-Maoist period, and China has also shown greater willingness to sign multilateral international treaties.[3]

By examining these new practices of multilateralism and related conceptual evolution in China's foreign policy in recent years, I attempt to make the following three arguments in this chapter. First, shifting from passive response to active participation and even initiation, multilateral diplomacy has increasingly become an integral part of Chinese foreign policy in general and regional diplomacy in particular. Second, China no longer perceives security multilateralism as a taboo; rather, it has gradually recognized the legitimacy of the multilateral approach in resolving international and regional security issues, and it has actively explored new forms of multilateralism in security relations with other countries. Third, China's multilateral diplomacy does not merely serve the traditional function of external balancing or utility generating; it also indicates Beijing's growing interest in establishing a less-instrumental, more rule- and norm-based international order, particularly around its periphery.

CONCEPTUAL EVOLUTION ON MULTILATERALISM

China's accelerated pace in global and regional multilateral diplomacy is not just a kind of ad hoc, short-term reaction to outside stimulus. It also reflects its overall assessment of the nature and trends of the international system and the international environment, its evolving concepts of national security, and its deepening understanding of the function of multilateral diplomacy under new circumstances.

Irrespective of the tragic events of the September 11 terrorist attack against the United States in 2001, Beijing's overall estimation of international situation by and large remains upbeat. The official analyses argue that although the international situation changed dramatically in 2001, peace and development are still the main themes of our times, and the trend toward a multipolar world remains unchanged."[4] In the aftermath of the terrorist attack, Jiang Zemin pointed out that, while wars, tension, and unrest continue to plague certain regions of the world, the world in general remains peaceful, stable, and calm.[5] On various occasions, Chinese leaders summarized the post–September 11 international situation as that of "overall peace and local warfare, overall relaxation and local tension, and overall stability and local turbulence."[6]

Although China faces new challenges under such circumstances, its overall international environment is still one that provides "more of opportunity than of challenge."[7] Therefore, the Chinese leadership has concluded that the first two decades of the twenty-first century form "a period of the important strategic opportunities" that China "must seize and which offer bright prospects."[8] The sanguine predication about "a fairly long period of peace in the world and a favorable climate in areas around China"[9] set a stage for active multilateral diplomacy at global and regional levels.

Beijing's understanding and analysis of the nature and features of international relations have also undergone significant changes. With the traditional vocabulary of describing international politics—such as *national sovereignty, territorial integrity, hegemony,* and *power politics*—Chinese analyses have increasingly applied new phrases, such as *interdependence, globalization, win–win diplomacy, cooperative security, common interest,* and *coordination.*

These analytic terms demonstrate that at least at the normative level, the traditional hard-core realist paradigm in the Chinese international thinking has been remolded by something much closer to more liberal and cooperative international relations theories.

It has become a consensus of the Chinese leadership and foreign policy élite that economic globalization, and the global issues that arise from it, has made the interests of various countries increasingly interdependent. No single nation or regional group alone can handle these global issues.[10] Interdependence among nations is not just limited to economic issues; indeed, interdependence in security among nations is also deepening. Human beings, including the Chinese, "live in a new era when losses and gains of all countries are co-shared side by side."[11]

With such an unprecedented degree of interdependence, China's understanding of security has been experiencing some noticeable changes. Starting in 1996, China has strongly advocated and consciously cultivated the so-called "new concept of security" on various occasions. The elaboration of the new concept of security in the official documents and speeches has been more systematic and articulate in recent years. It "has become an important component of China's foreign policies."[12]

According to the Chinese official interpretation, the core of such a new security concept is characterized by mutual trust, mutual benefit, equality, and coordination.[13] While these terms are not new in the Chinese diplomatic vocabulary to define interstate relations, they are new in that they are used to define security—a domain that used to be considered quite sensitive and only related to terms such as *military, strength, power,* and *force.*

As one senior Chinese official put it, the new security concept takes the best from various security concepts: common security, mutual security, cooperative security, comprehensive security, and collective security.[14] More specifically, the new security concept first and for most means "common security," which transcends the traditional one-sided security. It is based on common interest.[15] Second, the new security concept also means "cooperative security," namely, seeking security through cooperation. Under the condition of interdependence and globalization, the security of all states is interdependent. Without international cooperation, no state can maintain its security single-handedly no matter how powerful the country is.[16] Therefore "dialogue and cooperation are indispensable."[17] Third, the new security concept means that a county's security is no longer one-dimensional; rather, it is meant to be multifold, including not only military and political security, but also economic, scientific, technological, environmental, and cultural as well as many other areas of nontraditional security.[18] In other words, the new security concept means "comprehensive security" and is no longer military centered. Fourth, related to the "comprehensive security," the new security concept also emphasizes the importance of nontraditional security. The September 11 terrorist attack, as well as the SARS (severe acute respiratory syndrome) epidemic, fully exposed the vulnerability of individual nations to nontraditional threats, including terrorism, drug trafficking, weapon proliferation, the spread of disease, and environmental degradation.[19] These nontraditional security threats are often intertwined with one another, making the security situation more complicated and imposing bigger challengers to global security.[20]

To deal with these new challenges, China should come up with new approaches to seek security. First, military means are not the only way, probably not even the most important way, to achieve security. The means to seek security are being diversified. Force is not always the most effective way to do the job. "The security concept and regime based on the use of force and the threat to use force can hardly bring lasting peace."[21] The traditional means of maximizing security, such as military alliance, should be abandoned. International cooperation in the fields of economics, the environment, and social affairs can also promote China's security.[22] In recent years, Beijing has gradually shifted its focus from security policy to economic exchange and interactions, particularly in the peripheral area, as it regards economic diplomacy as "an important avenue to a lasting security in its surrounding area."[23] Second, the cooperation under the new security concept should be flexible and diversified in form and model. It could be a multilateral security mechanism of relatively strong binding force, or it could be a forum like a multilateral security dialogue, a confidence-building bilateral security dialogue, or an academic, nongovernmental dialogue.[24] Third, since the security among nations is interdependent rather than one-sided, international politics is no longer a zero-sum game and the security policy of a country should seek win–win results rather than unilateral advantages.

Under the new international circumstances, and with a new understanding of international security situation, multilateralism has been increasingly regarded as a more effective means to address China's security concerns. Instead of just reacting or responding to the call of multilateralism by others, China "should vigorously promote multilateralism."[25] The justification for a more multilateral approach in Chinese foreign policy, however, does not just result from the changes in objective circumstances; it also reflects the change of China's position in international relations. First of all, China's growing national strength during the past two decades provides a solid material foundation for its multilateral diplomacy. Second, a multilateral thrust in Chinese foreign policy is also a natural consequence of China' further integration into the international community. As a result of these changes, China feels much more confident and comfortable in carrying out a more multilateral-oriented foreign policy, departing from its traditional bilateral-focused diplomacy. Multilateralism therefore is seen by some Chinese commentators as testimony of "more maturity and self-confidence" in China's overall foreign policy.[26]

Of course, China's strong advocacy of a new security concept and multilateralism, just like that of other major powers, does not merely indicate China's vision of what the world should be but also contains instrumental elements that are more closely related to what the perceived world is and to China's own foreign policy objectives. On the one hand, multilateralism is increasingly perceived as a more effective tool to counterbalance the U.S. hegemonism or unilateralism at global and regional levels. On the other hand, multilateralism has been applied as a more-charming and less-threatening form of exercising China's influence in the world and in the region.

One of the major Chinese foreign policy objectives in the post–Cold War era is multipolarization. While multipolarization in the past was often regarded as a function of the shifting balance of power, China now has more closely associated multipolarization with multilateralism on a global scale. In other words, multilateralism is instrumental to the formation of multipolarization because multilateralism is often associated with another term China has used quite frequently in foreign policy statements: democratization of international relations. Multilateralism is useful in promoting democracy in international relations in a sense that it could "bring about a new regime in which all countries are equal and no country has the right to impose its will on others."[27] The political implication for China is quite clear: while the post–Cold War unipolar power structure in which the United States enjoys unchallenged power as a sole superpower is unlikely to be changed in the foreseeable future, multilateralism might put some checks and balance on the American power. In a multilateral system, China's freedom of action might be constrained, but so is that of the United States.

After the Bush administration came to power, China increasingly defined its diplomatic strategy as multilateral to contrast the perceived U.S. unilateralism. Chinese observers tend to characterize the debate in the United Nations after September 11 as "multilateralism vs. unilateralism" in which the United States appears to be isolated.[28] The American unilateralism is logically correlated with its objection to multilateralism as indicated by its withdrawal or invalidation of a series of international multilateral treaties. The U.S. preemptive attack against Iraq is the climax of the unilateral thrust in its foreign policy, which "costs it the sympathy from the whole world after the September 11 and alienated it from the international community."[29] In doing so, the United States is fighting the world multilateral institutions it helped establish in the first place. Chinese analysts observed with relief that key multilateral institutions—such as the United Nations (UN), World Trade Organization

(WTO), World Bank (WB), International Monetary Fund (IMF)—are not on the side of the American unilateralism. In terms of economic matters, the WTO, WB, and IMF are not necessarily dominated by the United States to serve its interest of global hegemony. In terms of politics, the UN refused to bow to the demands of the United States as it used to do. Even NATO is refusing to accept the United States' unilateral stance.[30]

In contrast to the United States, China has moved much closer to the international multilateral system and regime.[31] China acceded to the WTO despite the strong odds at home and abroad. It has been on board of many of the multilateral international treaties that the United States withdrew from, and it has championed the irreplaceable position of the UN in handling international conflict. At the regional level, China turns out to be even more enthusiastic about taking multilateralism as its main diplomatic approach. China observed at the global level how unwise use of predominant power by the United States could alienate or even incur resentment from the international community. Fully aware of the anxiety and suspicion that its rapidly growing power has created in the region, Beijing is determined to minimize the side effect accompanying its rise through multilateralism—not just economic multilateralism but increasingly security multilateralism as well. It has become a more harmless channel for China to project its international clout and exert its influence in the region.[32] China's regional multilateral diplomacy, such as ASEAN+1 (Association of Southeast Asian Nations plus China) and the Shanghai Cooperation Organization (SCO), has therefore been construed as the main forum in which to practice the new security concept discussed here.[33]

CHINA'S GLOBAL MULTILATERALISM—UNITED NATIONS

One indicator for China's increasing embrace of multilateralism at the global level is its strong advocacy of the core role of the UN in the post–Cold War international order and conflict resolution.[34] Since entering the UN in 1971, China's perception of the UN, particularly its function of collective security in international and domestic conflict resolution, has experienced some significant changes, from being suspicious and nonparticipatory to being passively involved with reservations to being a more active and conscious advocate of multilateralism and the UN.[35]

Chinese leaders in recent years, particularly after September 11, have repeatedly emphasized the irreplaceable position of the UN in international affairs. They called for further consolidation of the authority of the UN Security Council in dealing with international crisis.[36] In his speech to the Australian parliament in Canberra in October 2003, Chinese president Hu Jintao urged the world to give full support to the UN in solving security issues.[37] Beijing's evaluation of the United Nation has become more and more positive. Chinese foreign minister Li Zhaoxing described the UN as "the most universal, most representative and most authoritative international organization in the world today" and that "the hope of the world rests on a strong UN."[38]

While China tended to be reactive to UN multilateral diplomacy in the past, it began to take initiative at the highest level. In September 2000, at China's request, the heads of state from all five permanent members of the UN Security Council held a summit, the first ever in the UN's fifty-five-year history, highlighting the unity and importance of the "big five" in post–Cold War international affairs. Chinese president Jiang Zemin used the podium to preach for "a new concept of security" and an end of the "Cold War mentality." He made a particularly pointed criticism about those whose approach to the UN is "use it when it is needed and abandon it when it is not."[39]

One important mechanism of the UN's collective security is peacekeeping. Originally suspicious about the legitimacy of the operation, China broke the taboo in 1990 by sending military observers to peacekeeping operations. Its endorsement of UN peacekeeping operations reached a milestone in 1992 with its participation in the most "intrusive" peacekeeping operation by then— UNTAC (United Nations Transitional Authority in Cambodia). China not only underwrote the operation politically and financially, it also for the first time sent a sizable military unit (an engineering battalion) to Cambodia. China as well suffered its first casualties in UN peacekeeping operations.[40] Since then, China has continued its more active involvement in the peacekeeping operations. In January 2000, the Chinese government dispatched fifteen civilian policemen to the UN Transitional Authority in East Timor. This was the first time that China sent civilian policemen to UN peacekeeping operations. By 2002, China had sent more than 650 military observers, 800 engineering troops, and 198 civilian policemen to take part in ten UN peacekeeping operations. In 2003, China agreed to deploy a contingent of 550 troops to Liberia as part of the UN peacekeeping mission. In 2004, Beijing decided to send 125 police officers to Haiti to support the UN-led international effort to stabilize the country. China's peacekeeping forces have suffered casualties, with five killed and dozens wounded. In 1997, the Chinese government decided to take part, in principle, in the UN's standing-by arrangements. Then, in 2002, China formally participated in the class A stand-by arrangements mechanism for the UN peacekeeping operations and agreed to provide those operations with engineering, medical, transportation, and other logistical support teams at appropriate times. China is able to provide these operations with one UN-standard engineering battalion, one UN-standard medical team, and two UN-standard transportation companies.[41]

But compared with that of other major powers, the level of China's participation in UN peacekeeping operations is still relatively low.[42] In particular,
China has not, as of 2004, sent any combat troops to peacekeeping operations.
That reflects China's reluctance of being directly involved in military conflict
in other countries. China is still more cautious and reserved about the UN
peace-enforcement operations invoking Chapter VII of the UN Charter. China
repeatedly warned that the Security Council should be very careful in authorizing enforcement operations. The enforcement measures should be reserved
to deal with gross violations of peace, such as aggression. Excessive use of
enforcement measures will only damage the reputation of the UN.[43] In most
of the 1980s and 1990s, China often abstained on UN resolutions that authorized the use of force for peace enforcement. In the case of Cambodia in
the early 1990s, China strongly opposed to change the UN mission from a
strictly peace-keeping Chapter VI mission to an active war-stopping, peace-
enforcing Chapter VII role. Even in such a clear-cut case of the Iraqi invasion
of Kuwait in 1990, China did not vote to support the U.S. military operation
to drive Iraq out of Kuwait in 1991. Over years, China tried to convince the
Security Council that the enforcement actions should be limited to protect the
security of UN troops in peacekeeping operations. This became customary in
many Security Council resolutions to authorize peacekeeping operations.[44]
This more-reserved attitude toward UN peace enforcement has significantly
changed after the September 11 terrorist attack. For the first time since China
entered the UN in 1971, China voted to endorse an American use of force
against a sovereign country (Afghanistan) in the UN Security Council. Although China opposed the United States–led war against Iraq in 2003—as did
France, Russia, and Germany—it nevertheless endorsed an intrusive UN Security Council resolution to disarm Iraq, another sovereign country.

REGIONAL MULTILATERALISM—THE SOUTHWARD DRIVE

China's embrace of multilateralism, however, has been more forcefully reflected in its regional foreign policy. Ever since the Western sanction against
Beijing in the aftermath of the Tiananmen incident in 1989, China has implemented the so-called peripheral diplomacy, or good-neighbor policy, to break
the post-Tiananmen diplomatic isolation. While initially a tactical measure to
counter the Western pressure after Tiananmen, the peripheral diplomacy has
gradually gained strategic significance in the entire Chinese foreign policy.[45]
This strategic adjustment was first implemented by traditional bilateral diplomacy, through improving relations with the former Soviet Union and later
Russia as well as through establishing diplomatic relations with a number of

Southeast Asian countries. Starting from the late 1990s, however, multilateral diplomacy has increasingly obtained its salience in China's peripheral or regional strategy. There has emerged a consensus among the Chinese foreign policy establishment that multilateralism, particularly economic multilateralism, might be the most effective means to mitigate the suspicions of China's Asian neighbors, maintain good relations with China's neighbors, and increase its influence in the region. Some scholars advocate that China's Asia strategy should be the so-called flexible multilateralism.[46]

This "flexible multilateralism" means that China will not pursue a single model of multilateralism in the region. Instead China will take different approaches of multilateralism according to different geopolitical and geoeconomic conditions. Since the late 1990s, and particularly since the dawn of the new century, China has launched a regional offense of multilateral diplomacy toward the South and the North. However, the approaches and methods applied are not necessarily the same.

Toward the South, China applied a strategy that can be summarized as "economic multilateralism first and security multilateralism second." Some scholars point out that China's participation in global multilateral economic regimes, as exemplified by its accession to WTO, has to be supplemented by its participation in regional multilateral economic regimes. Global economic multilateralism and regional economic multilateralism are "the two wheels of one cart."[47] Indeed because the economic integration in the Asia–Pacific region is not as developed as that in other regions, such as Western Europe, China could play a more important role in the game of regime- and rule-building. Moreover, it is not sufficient to participate in the existing economic integration mechanism—namely, the Asia–Pacific Economic Cooperation (APEC). For one thing, it is difficult for APEC to raise the level of economic integration, as it has too many members with too wide a range of economic development. Therefore China should strive to establish smaller but more highly integrated multilateral economic frameworks, such as the framework of "subregional economic integration." Such an endeavor is not only of economic importance but of political and strategic significance as well.[48]

In building such a framework of subregional economic integration, China's relations with ASEAN are key.[49] Among other reasons, ASEAN has long been a strong advocate of regional multilateralism, not just to engage ASEAN members, but also to do so with outside countries, particularly the major powers in the region. Over years, ASEAN has initiated a series of multilateral consulting mechanisms, such as the ASEAN Post-ministerial Conference, the ASEAN Regional Forum, the Asia–Europe meeting, ASEAN+3 (Association of Southeast Asian Nations plus China, Japan, and Republic of Korea), and so forth.[50] It can be said that China's regional multilateral diplomacy started with its interaction with ASEAN.

Since its normalization of diplomatic relations with all ASEAN countries in the early 1990s, China's interaction and integration with ASEAN has been on a steady rise. The official relations between China and ASEAN started in 1991, when China became a consultative partner of ASEAN and began to attend the ASEAN Post-ministerial Conference (PMC). In 1996, China was upgraded to a full dialogue partner of ASEAN. In 1997, the first informal China–ASEAN summit was held, thus establishing a new mechanism of consultation that has been regularized and institutionalized ever since. During this process, China established a network of multilayer, multilevel dialogue and consultation with ASEAN. While initially economically oriented, the range of issues covered by the China–ASEAN dialogue gradually expanded from economic issues to security issues, including promotion of confidence-building measures, peacekeeping, maritime search and rescue, preventive diplomacy, and nonproliferation.[51]

Entering the new century, China–ASEAN relations have been gradually moving from "dialogue cooperation" to "institutionalized cooperation."[52] If China often reacted to ASEAN's push for multilateralism in the past, Beijing has now become increasingly proactive, sometimes taking initiatives in promoting institutionalization of the China–ASEAN cooperation.

In the economic domain, China began to pay more attention to regional economic integration after it joined the WTO in December 2001. China's initial interest in regional trade liberalization was stimulated by the 1997 Asian financial crisis. The idea of the China–ASEAN Free Trade Area (CAFTA) was first discussed in Chinese academic circles, and then it moved up to the policy-making level in 1999. In 2000, Chinese premier Zhong Rongji proposed a feasibility study of CAFTA at the fourth ASEAN+3 informal summit. Subsequently, at the ASEAN–China leaders meeting in November 2001, China and ASEAN formally agreed to establish a free trade area within ten years.[53] This was the first time that China was committed to a free trade area with other countries. The initiative surprised many people and caught other ASEAN regional partners, such as Japan, South Korea, and the United States, off guard. Following Beijing's footsteps, these countries, as well as India and Russia, suddenly all talked about establishing the free trade area with ASEAN, thus triggering a new wave of trade liberalization negotiations in East Asia.

In May 2002, formal negotiations to establish CAFTA began. Merely six months later, the two sides signed the Framework Agreement on China–ASEAN Comprehensive Economic Cooperation, which is now considered a landmark in China–ASEAN economic relations. According to the framework,

CAFTA will be complete in 2010. Both sides will offer mutual tariff cuts on imported goods and finally lift tariff barriers. In implementation, China took a practical and gradual approach and has engaged with each ASEAN member to create differential trade liberation timetables according to each nation's level of economic development. China agreed to give preferential treatment to some economically less-developed ASEAN members under the "early harvest package." For example, it gives Laos, Cambodia, and Myanmar favorable tariff rates, and it grants those non-WTO ASEAN nations most-favored-nation treatment. In June 2003, China and Thailand signed an agreement in Beijing to impose zero tariffs on nearly two hundred categories of fruits and vegetables in bilateral trade, and the agreement became effective in October 2003.[54] Tariff cuts on selected farm products between the two countries started in 2004.[55] At the ASEAN+3 summit in 2002, China announced that it would waive all or part of the debt owned by Vietnam, Laos, Cambodia, and Burma. China would also give exports from Laos, Cambodia, and Burma the zero-tariff treatment.[56]

The formation of CAFTA will form a huge tariff-free market in a region that has a population of 1.7 billion, a $2.0 trillion gross domestic product, and a $1.2 trillion trade volume. At present, trade volume between the two sides accounts for less than 10 percent of their total foreign trade. The mutual exports will increase by 50 percent when CAFTA is set up.[57] The prospect of CAFTA has triggered a new wave of interest in Southeast Asia, not just among the Chinese academic circles, but also among Chinese entrepreneurs, as they position themselves to benefit from the trade liberalization. As a new stimulant, CAFTA has already increased trade volume between China and ASEAN.[58]

China's economic initiatives toward ASEAN are not just a result of pure economic calculation. They have broad political and strategic significance. First of all, the Asian financial crisis in 1997 made the Chinese realize the importance of the economic stability in the Southeast Asia to China's peripheral environment. From the perspective of the comprehensive security discussed earlier, the economic prosperity of ASEAN countries is conducive to China's regional economic security. To help ASEAN countries get out of economic sluggishness is therefore perceived as in China's national interest. When CAFTA was proposed in 2000, it was aimed at accelerating ASEAN's weak economic recovery after the financial crisis.[59] Second, Beijing is fully aware that China's rapid economic growth and its widened market openness after entering the WTO provide opportunities as well as challenges to the ASEAN countries. They are nervous and worried about the increasing Chinese economic might in the region. To create a win–win situation, Beijing needs to turn "China opportunity" into a "China–ASEAN common opportunity."[60]

Long Yongtu, who led the negotiations for China's entry into the WTO, made it very clear: "China's policy is to make her neighbors richer by letting them share the benefits of China's development."[61] By offering preferential trade policy to various ASEAN countries, China is to some extent committed to unilaterally opening its market to ASEAN countries. Doing so also helps improve the investment environment of ASEAN countries to increase the confidence of outside investors.[62] China's move toward a free trade area was therefore considered by U.S. trade representative Robert Zoellick a "thoughtful move" that "institutionalized what these countries now recognize: that China's growth is a benefit to them."[63] In doing so, China is taking a leading role in subregional economic integration.[64] China's preferential trade policy toward ASEAN also increased mutual trust that was often lacking in the relationship in the past. Promising economic ties have laid a more solid foundation for political, security, and other functional relations between China and ASEAN.

One sticky issue in China–ASEAN security relations is the territorial dispute in the South China Sea. For a long time, China preferred to deal with ASEAN countries on this issue on a bilateral basis and was quite reluctant to put the issue under the context of multilateral consultation, let alone seek a multilateral solution. China was not responsive to ASEAN's appeal to form a code of conduct in the South China Sea. In the mid-1990s, China's perceived unilateral and assertive action in the Spratly Islands (e.g., the Mischief Reef incident in 1995) raised a lot of concerns among ASEAN countries about Beijing's long-term intention, and it reinforced the growing perception of a China threat in the region. Since the establishment of the ASEAN+1 mechanism in 1997, however, China's attitude toward the South China Sea has become increasingly more reconciliatory and cooperative. Beijing began to be more willing to discuss the issue in the annual China–ASEAN senior official consultation. In 1999, the Philippines proposed to establish a regional code of conduct to govern activities in the South China Sea, and China responded favorably. The process of negotiation took more than three years due to disputes over the wording and the area it would cover—disputes not just between China and ASEAN but more so among ASEAN members.[65] In November 2002 China and ASEAN signed the Declaration on the Conduct of Parties in the South China Sea at the sixth ASEAN–China summit. In the declaration, China and ASEAN reaffirmed their commitment to the purpose and principles of the UN Charter, the 1982 UN Convention on the Law of the Sea, the Treaty of Amity and Cooperation in Southeast Asia, the Five Principles of Peaceful Coexistence, and other universal principles of international law. The declaration commits the concerned parties to resolve their territorial and jurisdictional disputes by peaceful means, without resorting to force, through friendly consultations and negotiations by sovereign states directly concerned. The parties concerned agreed to exercise self-restraint in the conduct of activities that would complicate or escalate disputes and affect peace and stability, including refraining from action of inhabiting on the presently uninhabited islands, reefs, shoals, cays, and other features. They also agreed to respect freedom of navigation in- and overflight above the South China Sea. In addition, the declaration stipulates some important confidence-building measures, such as dialogue between defense and military officials, just and humane treatment of all persons in danger, notifying other parties of any joint or combined military exercise. Pending a comprehensive and durable settlement of the disputes, the parties concerned could explore or undertake cooperative environmental marine protection, scientific marine research, search and rescue, and the combating of transnational crime.[66] Although it is a nonbinding document and falls short of the original goal of having a detailed and binding code of conduct,[67] it is nevertheless the first political document concluded between China and ASEAN over the South China Sea issue[68] and an important step to defuse potential conflict in the region.[69]

Taking the momentum of the South China Sea accord, the new Chinese leadership after the Sixteenth Party Congress accelerated its efforts to build mutual confidence and advance its political and strategic relations with ASEAN in 2003. ASEAN for a long time has hoped that China would accede to the Treaty of Amity and Cooperation (TAC) in Southeast Asia, which was signed in 1976 as a guiding document for conflict management among ASEAN members. In June 2003, China's highest legislative body, the National People's Congress (NPC), approved China's accession to the TAC treaty. In October 2003, China formally joined the TAC treaty at the seventh ASEAN+1 summit meeting in Indonesia, becoming the first non–Southeast Asian major power to sign the treaty. Similar to its handling of CAFTA, China took the lead, and its action was expected to be followed by India, Japan, South Korea, and other non-ASEAN regional powers.[70] The treaty commits all sides to use peaceful means to resolve disputes, including territorial conflicts. In adopting the treaty, China and ASEAN countries have agreed not to "participate in any activity which shall constitute a threat to the political and economic stability, sovereignty, or territorial integrity" of other signatory states.[71]

In addition to signing the TAC, the new Chinese premier Wen Jiabao also signed a historic document to forge "a strategic partnership for peace and prosperity" with ASEAN countries. This "strategic partnership" is comprehensive and forward looking to include cooperation in politics, economy, social affairs, security, and international and regional affairs. Just as in the case of TAC, China has become the first strategic partner of ASEAN, and ASEAN is the first regional grouping with which China has formed such a partnership, indicating a new and higher stage of mutual political and strategic relations.[72] This strategic partnership is another example of what China calls a new type of interstate relations; namely, it is "non-aligned, non-military, and non-exclusive, and does not prevent the participants from developing their all-directional ties of friendship and cooperation with others."[73]

China's intensified multilateral diplomacy toward ASEAN in recent years has borne fruits. Among other things, ASEAN countries' perception of, and attitude toward, China has been changing for the better. The rise of China has been perceived by ASEAN countries more as an opportunity than as a threat. Former Pilipino president Ramos wanted China to be "a big brother" of the Asian family, not only providing a huge market for Asian countries, but also acting as a major force in the settlement of conflicts within the "family."[74] Beijing's conciliatory and nonpushy diplomacy seems to be a sharp contrast with George Bush's "cowboy" style diplomacy.[75] Chinese officials confidently declared that the once quite prevalent talk of a China threat has gone bankrupt in Southeast Asia.[76] As an American analyst pointed out, given the historical animosity and suspicion between China and ASEAN and the natural tendency for smaller countries to fear the rise of a powerful neighboring country, the change in ASEAN's attitude toward China represents "a significant success for Chinese diplomacy."[77]

Taking its relations with ASEAN as a platform, China's multilateral diplomacy has radiated to the broader Asia–Pacific region. China today has been thoroughly enmeshed in the increasingly thickening and multilayered web of multilateral organizations, regimes, and consultation mechanisms.[78] Compared to the situation in the 1980s, China's overall attitude toward these multilateral networks has changed significantly, from being passive to more active, reserved to more open, reluctant to more enthusiastic, and uneasy to more comfortable. Initially, Beijing was more receptive to economic multilateralism and more suspicious about security multilateralism.[79] While China is still more cautious about security multilateralism, it no longer shies away from actively participating in multilateral mechanisms on security issues.

China's attitude toward APEC—the most inclusive and highest-level transregional economic consultative mechanism—has gone through some subtle changes. China was initially cautious about the institutionalization of APEC. It insisted that APEC was a governmental forum solely for the purpose of regional economic cooperation. China therefore opposed the American idea of changing "cooperation" into "community." China also did not want APEC to evolve into a political forum or organization to discuss regional political and security issues.[80] However, over years and through practice, China's attitudes have been evolving. First of all, China has attached more and more importance to APEC. Chinese leaders call APEC "one of the most important economic forums in the region and even in the world."[81] Chinese analysts concluded that through the development of one decade, APEC has transformed from a general regional economic forum at the beginning to the highest-level intergovernmental economic cooperative mechanism in the Asia–Pacific.[82]

China supported the APEC goals of achieving trade and investment liberalization by 2010 for developed members and by 2020 for developing members, which were set in the Bogor Declaration issued at the second informal meeting of APEC leaders, in 1994. At the APEC meetings, China has advocated that APEC should persistently open to the region and not turn it into a closed trade group. When implementing trade and investment liberalization, APEC should take into consideration the members' different levels of economic development and their specific situations. China also took some unilateral actions to achieve trade liberalization. Chinese president Jiang Zemin declared that China would drastically lower its tariff rate at the 1995 Osaka meeting. From 1996, China has reduced its tariff level several times, and the average tariff on China's imported commodities dropped to 15 percent by 2000. It has planned to further drop its average tariff on industrial goods to 10 percent by 2005. While acknowledging the importance of trade liberalization, Chinese leaders have tended to emphasize the importance of economic and technological cooperation; they have also argued that trade and investment liberalization should be balanced by economic and technological cooperation and have proposed several initiatives in this regard.[83]

After the Asian financial crisis, China tended to be more positive and receptive toward establishing more institutionalized regional multilateral economic cooperative mechanisms. For example, China strongly supported the establishment of the regional currency cooperative mechanism. Beijing was instrumental in reaching the Chiang Mai agreement on currency cooperation in May 2000.[84] After the September 11 terrorist attack, China also realized that it was unrealistic for the only Pan-Asia-Pacific mechanism not to discuss political and security issues at all. Immediately after the attacks, China hosted the Ninth APEC Economic Leaders Meeting in Shanghai—it was the first time that China had ever hosted the meeting. One inevitable consequence of the terrorist attack was the expansion of the agenda items from pure economic and technological cooperation to political and security issues. China handled the situation in a creative way by discussing the issue of terrorism informally, at the breakfast of foreign ministers and at the lunch of leaders, without the participation of Taiwan and Hong Kong. An antiterrorism declaration was then issued by the summit. This practice became known as "Shanghai method." It was followed in next few years by the APEC summit to discuss international terrorism as well as the North Korea issue.[85] Needless to say, while China supported these efforts, it still wanted to maintain APEC as mainly an economic organization rather than a comprehensive regional organization. In doing so, Chinese leaders advocated the so-called APEC approach, which is characterized by respects for "differences, equality, mutual benefit, voluntarism, and consensus."[86]

It can be said that at the level of the broadly defined Asia–Pacific, China still prefers, in most cases, loosely structured consultative multilateralism rather than highly institutionalized multilateralism. This preference is more typically reflected in its attitudes toward the only regionwide multilateral security mechanism—the ASEAN Regional Forum (ARF). China was not very interested at first, as it was somewhat "dragged into" it, signaling the initial Chinese uneasiness with security multilateralism.[87] But gradually, China got used to participating in this security consultation mechanism and began to view AFR in a more positive way.[88]

Over years, China has insisted that the development of ARF should never be out of touch with reality. According to the Chinese, the reality in the region is that ARF comprises countries of different sizes and that they differ in values and social systems and do not share exactly the same security interests and concepts. The main issue affecting security in the region is lack of trust among nations.[89] Therefore, confidence building should be the core function of ARF. The central task of ARF for the foreseeable future should be to enhance mutual understanding and trust and remove misgivings and worries.[90]

For that kind of purpose, a high degree of institutionalization of a security regime is not necessary. Although Beijing does not oppose a regional multilateral security institution in the long run,[91] that time certainly has not yet come, and ARG should maintain its nature as a forum rather than as an institution.[92] Beijing has serious reservations about strengthening military alliances in the Asia–Pacific by the United States in the post–Cold War era and wants to make sure that ARF would not turn into a similar institution that could be used by some dominant countries to deal with a perceived enemy.[93] In the operation and development of ARF, the Chinese advocated the so-called ARF approach, which is featured by "equal participation, consensus-making, seeking common ground while shelving differences and incremental progress."[94] To avoid ARF's being dominated by other major powers, such as the United States and Japan, China supports ASEAN to play a leading role in this forum.[95]

Starting from 1996, China has tried very hard to sell its "new thinking" in security affairs to ARF. In 1996, China made a call for the first time at an ARF foreign ministers meeting for the abandonment of the "Cold War mentality" and for the introduction of a "new security concept" that is based "neither on military build-up nor on military alliances" but is grounded in "mutual trust and common interests."[96] This is obviously an attempt to offset the perceived security concepts of the United States and shape new normative norms for ARF. In 2002, China submitted to the ARF foreign ministers meeting a position paper on the new security concept, systematically articulating its views on international security affairs.[97] It could be said that such an effort to shape conceptual underpinnings of a regional security mechanism is seldom seen in Chinese diplomacy.

China has not been short of making proposals and initiatives at ARF, but most of them do not deal with traditional core security issues. Beijing has also been resistant to discussing those security issues directly involving China's interest, such as the South China Sea and the Taiwan issue. In other words, Beijing wants to see ARF sever the function of norm setting and confidence-building but not really that of really problem solving. For example, China has advocated multilateral cooperation in military medicine, military law, and the conversion of military technologies and facilities for civilian use within the framework of ARF. It has proposed to establish an ARF marine information and data center, encourage exchange of high-level military visits and port calls by naval vessels, as well as advocate for exchanges of military personnel; it has also supported cooperation in emergency rescue and disaster relief, safety in maritime navigation, and environmental marine protection.[98] Furthermore, China has started to sponsor and hold multilateral security dialogues and consultation in Beijing.[99]

After the September 11 terrorist attack, China suggested that ARF's focus should be switched to the nontraditional security issues. China held that most of these issues were difficult for one or a few countries to deal with. Multilateral cooperation is the only way to tackle them.[100] At 2001's ARF foreign ministers meeting, China put forward a proposition for ARF to launch cooperation on nonsecurity issues.[101] At the ARF senior officials conference held in May 2002, China submitted its position paper on enhanced cooperation in the field of nontraditional security issues.

To further promote mutual trust and confidence, China proposed at the 2001's ARF foreign ministers meeting that ARF members should notify each other well in advance and invite other ARF members to participate as observers before conducting any bilateral or multilateral joint military exercises with other ARF members or with non-ARF members. China is ready to send its observers to those military exercises that are designed to enhance cooperation in nontraditional security.[102] Related to this new thinking regarding foreign and multilateral military exercises, Chinese started sending military officers to observe military exercises sponsored by Singapore, Japan, the United States, and Thailand. It also intends to "selectively and gradually" participate in more multilateral joint military exercises in the nontraditional fields of security.[103] More recently, China proposed to hold an ARF security policy conference to facilitate the participation of defense officials from member states.[104]

Besides APEC and ARF, China has been fully involved in other auxiliary multilateral economic and security mechanisms derived from ASEAN, APEC, ARF, and other regional groupings at different levels.

One important regional multilateral mechanism deriving from ASEAN is ASEAN+3, which was born in 1997, when the ASEAN+1 dialogue was put into place. Starting in 2000, the ASEAN+3 annual meeting has been upgraded from an informal dialogue to a formal East Asia summit, thus becoming a key part of the ASEAN annual gatherings, which include the ASEAN Foreign Ministerial Meeting (AMM), ARF, and PMCs. Some Chinese scholars consider ASEAN+3 "the last and the best chance for realizing regional integration in East Asia."[105] Therefore Beijing has showed unusual enthusiasm toward this multilateral mechanism. It has not just passively reacted to the proposals from other countries, but it recently has also actively made new initiatives to turn this ASEAN+3 into a main framework of East Asia regional cooperation. For example, after the Asian financial crisis, China proposed to hold meetings of financial officials from the thirteen economies in ASEAN+3. As a result of these consultations, ASEAN+3 reached an agreement on the Asian money-swap scheme known as the Chiang Mai Initiative.[106] China has signed bilateral currency swap agreements with Thailand, Japan, and South Korea; and it has begun consultations with other countries in the region. China has also held four training courses for the ASEAN+3 financial and central bank officials, and another four are to be held in the two years to come.[107] Almost every year since 2000, Chinese leaders tried to provide conceptual guidance, as well as make concrete proposals, at the ASEAN+3 summit. In 2000, Chinese premier Zhu Rongji suggested that ASEAN+3 could become the main channel of East Asia regional cooperation through which regional cooperation frameworks of finance, trade, and investment are to be gradually established thus achieving further regional economic integration. In 2001, Zhu further elaborated China's vision for ASEAN+3 in the new century. While emphasizing economic cooperation, ASEAN+3 could gradually expand its dialogue and cooperation to political and security fields starting with the cooperation in the nontraditional areas.[108] The next year he made twenty-seven proposals and initiatives at the ASEAN+1 and ASEAN+3 summits and signed fifteen agreements and documents.[109] In 2003, Chinese premier Wen Jiabao proposed to study feasibility of an East Asian free trade area. He also advocated to strengthen political and security dialogue among member states.[110] China formally submitted its concept paper on building a network of East Asia think tanks.[111] Some Chinese scholars advocated a plan to turn ASEAN+3 into a genuine regional organization—Organization of East Asia Cooperation with a secretariat and various functional committees.[112]

Beginning in 2000, the leaders of China, Japan, and South Korea have met separately at ASEAN+3, forming a new trilateral consultative mechanism of major powers in East Asia—for the first time in history. At China's initiative, the three countries issued the Joint Declaration on the Promotion of Tripartite Cooperation in October 2003. This became the first document on tripartitie cooperation among China, Japan, and the Republic of Korea.[113]

REGIONAL MULTILATERALISM—THE NORTHWARD DRIVE

Another major thrust of China's regional multilateral diplomacy is in Northeast Asia and Central Asia. Unlike Southeast Asia, where ASEAN has been the main engine of multilateralism, Northeast Asia has had little tradition of multilateralism to begin with, due to the polarizing effect of the Cold War. In other words, in this subregion, multilateralism has to develop from scratch. In this region, China has taken an approach of multilateralism that is quite different from its Southeast Asia multilateral strategy. Instead of small country-driven multilateralism, as in the case of ASEAN-led multilateralism, the multilateralism in Northeast Asia and Central Asia is more driven by the major powers. Compared with Southeast Asia, China is more in the driver's seat. However, China's multilateralism in this area is more an unintended result of practice rather than a result made by design. Due to the unique geopolitical pattern in the region, the initial bilateral interaction between China and the former Soviet Union gradually evolved into a new regional organization that no party, including China, has foreseen—Shanghai Cooperation Organization (SCO).

SCO originated from the military confidence-building measures (CBMs) between China and Russia as well as the other three former Soviet republics with whom China shares common borders: Kazakhstan, Kyrgyzstan, and Tajikistan. In 1996, the presidents of the five countries met for the first time, in Shanghai, to sign the landmark treaty of CBMs in the border region. The presidents also decided that they would hold a regular summit every year, thus indicating the establishment of the "Shanghai Five" mechanism. In 1997, another treaty featuring a mutual reduction of military force in the border region was signed in Moscow. These two treaties were aimed at building trust and confidence and reducing tension in the border area by downsizing troop levels, reducing military activities, limiting the deployment of weapons, and increasing security transparency. From 1998 on, the summit of the Shanghai Five began to expand the scope of its agenda to include other security issues, such as the three antis (antiterrorism, antiseparatism, and antiextremism), and nonsecurity issues such as economic cooperation and cultural exchanges. Each summit resulted in a signed agreement or statement dealing with major security issues in the region as well as expressing common positions on major international issues. At the fifth summit, held in July 2000, the joint statement explicitly stated that all parties would work to turn the Shanghai Five into a regional mechanism to conduct multilateral cooperation in all areas. Eventually the Shanghai Five mechanism evolved into a formal regional organization—the SCO, in June 2001, at the sixth summit meeting. Uzbekistan was admitted as the new founding member of SCO, thus expanding Shanghai Five to Shanghai Six.

SCO provides an interesting case from which to study the change and continuity in Chinese multilateral diplomacy from policy and theoretical perspectives. SCO is the first regional multilateral cooperative organization born in the twenty-first century. But more important, it is the first multilateral security organization largely promoted by China and one in which China has played a leading role from the very beginning.[114] This can be easily seen from the fact that it is named after a Chinese city. In addition, the permanent body of SCO—the secretariat—was set up in Beijing. A Chinese diplomat was appointed as the first secretary-general of the organization. All of these are remarkable and unprecedented events in China's foreign policy in general and its multilateral diplomacy in particular.

As discussed earlier, Beijing has long preferred bilateralism rather than multilateralism in its diplomacy. It is even more skeptical about multilateralism in security fields. In its Southeast Asian multilateral diplomacy, the Chinese often argued that it is unnecessary and undesirable to establish a formal and institutionalized security regime in the Asia–Pacific region. Multilateral security dialogue and consultation will be sufficient to address countries' security concerns. No student of Chinese foreign policy predicted that China would so soon embrace a formal security-oriented regional organization with its former enemies in Northeast Asia.

Indeed, the Shanghai Five was initially designed to be bilateral rather than multilateral. The first two CBM agreements mentioned earlier were signed between China as one side and Russia and three Central Asian countries as the other side. So it was a bilateral negotiation of five countries. During the process, however, the bilateral mechanism gradually transformed into a multilateral mechanism, as the agenda of the summit moved away from pure border management. At the summit in 1998, the bilateral talk became multilateral talk among five countries rather than two sides. At first, China was satisfied with the Shanghai Five remaining as solely a meeting mechanism. But in recent years, China became the driving force pushing for the institutionalization of the Shanghai Five, partially departing from its long-claimed position of not forming alliances with other countries.

The organizational and functional evolution of SCO is unique; traditional functionalism cannot explain its development. Unlike the European Union, which started with "low politics"—economic cooperation and then gradual expansion into security and foreign policy domain—SCO was security oriented from the outset. In other words, SCO put functionalism upside down. It was the function of a highly successful cooperation in security areas that eventually "spilled over" into other nonsecurity areas, such as foreign policy coordination, economic, and cultural cooperation. The scope of security cooperation widened gradually. Initially, the focus of the Shanghai Five was quite narrow: maintenance of stability and peace in the border area. After territorial disputes among the five had basically been settled, the Shanghai Five moved to addressing broader security issues, such as terrorism and separatism. Before SCO was formed in 2001, it became obvious that security alone was not enough to sustain the momentum of institution building. Therefore the mandate of SCO is defined as promoting comprehensive cooperation in all domains among members rather than just security issues. Chinese president Jiang Zemin described security cooperation and economic cooperation as two indispensable wheels of SCO. They are equally important and mutually reinforcing. In short, SCO developed from a one-dimensional security-consulting mechanism to a comprehensive formal regional organization.[115]

Related to the pattern of security first, economy second, another interesting feature in the development of SCO is that it took a top-down rather than bottom-up approach. It started with the summit in which top leaders of five countries were committed to the Shanghai Five mechanism. Then, foreign ministers, defense ministers, and ministers of internal security—and now prime ministers and ministers of cultural affairs—began to meet on a regular basis, thus creating a multiple-layer, multiple-area consulting mechanism. In terms of institutionalization, the development of SCO is also somewhat different from that of another regional organization, ASEAN. The formation of ASEAN was declared in 1967, but it did not institutionalize until ten years later. The formation of SCO, however, was quickly followed by further measures of institutionalization. It could be argued that, compared to ASEAN, SCO has a more solid basis, as it had accumulated five years of practice before the formation.

At each stage of SCO's development—from bilateral to multilateral, from informal to formal, from security to comprehensive—China and other members tried to identify a core issue of common interest to sustain the momentum or find a "bright spot": territorial disputes, three vices, economic cooperation, and so forth.

Less than three months after the establishment of the organization, the viability of SCO was put under a serious test in the aftermath of the September 11 terrorist attack. The attack dramatically changed the geopolitical configuration in the region. As a consequence of the war on terror, the United States, for the first time since World War II, has established significant military and political presence in Central Asia. With a series of geopolitical changes, SCO seemed to have been sidelined. The United States–Russia relations dramatically improved. Other, smaller members of SCO took, in various degrees, more pro-Western policies. Uzbekistan, Kyrgyzstan, and Tajikistan, for example, allowed the United States to establish military bases and deploy military forces on their territories. The three countries strengthened their antiterrorist cooperation with the United States through bilateral channels rather than through SCO. In light of these developments, Chinese analysts worried that the United States might turn its temporary antiterror arrangements with the central Asian states into a formal United States–dominant regional security mechanism,[116] thus making SCO irrelevant. Consequently China's strategic position "has eroded substantially" in Central Asia.[117] Western observers have predicted a possible early demise of this infant multilateral organization.[118]

China, Russia, and other SCO members realize the danger and have made an effort to offset the adverse effect of the U.S. war on terror on SCO. Among other things, they attempted to make SCO more relevant in the war against terror. Indeed, the Shanghai Five is the earliest regional multilateral organization calling for cooperative actions against terrorism in Central Asia. SOC took on international terrorism as its major target at the very time of its establishment. The Shanghai Convention against Terrorism, Separatism and Extremism signed on June 15, 2001, already predicted an intensified struggle against terrorism in Central Asia and laid down a legal base for member states to combat terrorism.[119] Immediately after September 11 attacks on the United States, prime ministers who were attending the prime ministers conference of the SCO at the Alma-Ata, Kazakhstan, issued a joint communiqué on September 14, in which they denounced the terrorist attacks while expressing sympathy and condolence for the American people. The joint communiqué declared that the SCO was ready to closely unite with all countries and international organizations and that effective measures would be taken to wage an unremitting struggle for eradicating all global risks brought about by terrorism.[120] However, because of the lack of a coordinating mechanism, SCO was unable to take more forceful and concerted actions against terrorism. SCO proposed to establish an antiterrorist center long before September 11 and as early as 1999. But the material progress of this initiative was stalled due to the different interests of member states. Some SCO members did not want to see too much militarization of the organization fearing the apprehension of the United States and Western countries.[121] The September 11 terrorist attack gave this antiterrorist initiative new momentum. SCO members realized an urgency of setting up such a mechanism. China pushed hard for the institutionalization of a regional antiterrorism center. In early 2002, Chinese president Jiang Zimin declared it "the most urgent thing at present."[122] The agreement signed in June 2003 to establish the SCO Regional Antiterrorism Structure in Bishkek[123] materialized China's intention. The agreement stipulates that this center should become operational no later than January 2004. Furthermore, Beijing would like to see SCO members' antiterrorist cooperation with the United States conducted in the framework of SCO.[124]

To further substantiate the SCO antiterrorist cooperation, China pioneered a joint military exercise among SCO members. The Chinese troops conducted joint military exercise with the Kyrgyz forces in October 2002. At the Moscow summit in May 2003, pushed by the SCO leaders, the SCO defense ministers signed a memorandum on joint military exercises to be carried out in autumn 2003.[125] The first multilateral antiterrorist military exercise of SCO was thus conducted in August 2003. The drill had two phases carried out, respectively, in Kazakhstan and China and included war games against terrorists and a hostage-rescue operation. For China, the significance of this military exercise goes beyond SCO. It is the first large-scale multilateral antiterrorist exercise that the Chinese army has participated in, and it is also the first time that China has invited foreign armies into its territory. The Chinese military subsequently set a precedent for conducting missions in other countries during peacetime when they participated in the China–Kyrgyzstan bilateral antiterrorist drill.[126] Related to the talk of antiterrorism, Chinese leaders emphasized the function of SCO to manage nontraditional security threats, such as drug trafficking, weapon smuggle, transnational monetary crimes, and so forth.[127]

The setting up of the antiterrorism mechanism and joint military exercises made some analysts call SCO by and large a military alliance. According to one of the unpublished terms of the SCO, China could send troops to Central Asia to combat Islamic extremism, if requested to do so.[128] SCO and the Shanghai Five were initially conceived as a nonmilitary organization aimed primarily at solving political issues such as border delimitation. While it still cannot be called a full-fledged military alliance, SCO nevertheless contains some military elements.

The endorsement of the SCO regional antiterrorist mechanism was part of China's push for the further institutionalization of SCO. China was convinced that "internal institutional building is an important way to strengthen cohesiveness and enhance its vitality of the organization."[129] Chinese premier Zhu Rongji, while attending the first SCO prime ministers conference, in Alma-Ata, Kazakhstan, in 2001, suggested that SCO should put its emphasis on two tasks: finish drafting the SCO charter as soon as possible and step up the establishment of the antiterrorism center.[130] To make the SCO more functional before the charter and permanent agency of SCO have been put into place, SCO foreign ministers agreed, in January 2002, to some transitional measures during the SCO foreign ministers meeting. The joint statement issued after the meeting established a contingency mechanism that included the emergency meeting of foreign ministers and the statement of foreign ministers to express the common position of the SCO members.[131]

The first step was to draft various legal documents to bind member states together and increase the normative stake for possible defection. At the second summit of SCO, held in St. Petersburg on June 7, 2002, the six members approved a series of documents, including the charter of the SCO, an agreement on the establishment of a regional antiterrorism agency, and the declaration of presidents of SCO members. The charter provides purposes, principles, structure, and operation rules of the organization, laying a legal foundation for its construction and development. The agreement is the legal basis for members to launch substantial cooperation in the field of security, thus offering an effective means to resolutely fight terrorism, separatism, and extremism.[132]

The successful summit meeting at St. Petersburg in June 2002 suggests to some extent that SCO regained vitality under a new situation. Jiang Zemin noted in his meeting with Kazakh president Nazarbayev that SCO has vitality in that it conforms to the practical needs of the region, the interests of the SCO member countries, and the trend of development of history. As Kyrgyz president Akayev put it, SCO has withstood the test over the past year.[133] At the Moscow summit in May 2003, Chinese president Hu Jingtao emphasized that institutional building was the top priority of SCO. He urged member states to work even harder to make sure that the secretariat could be operational by 2003 and that the antiterror center should be created as soon as possible.[134] The six leaders signed a declaration to confirm the legal standing of the SCO charter and to indicate the common position on major international issues. The summit also approved the appointment of Chinese ambassador to Russia, Zhang Deguang, as the first SCO secretary-general and urged that this permanent institution of the SCO be launched before January 2004.[135] As the host country of the SCO secretariat, the Chinese government decided to provide free office facilities for the secretariat in Beijing.[136] Russian president Vladimir Putin said that the summit marked the first time the SCO has become an international cooperation organization "in a real sense."[137] On January 15, 2004, SCO secretariat was formally launched in Beijing, as scheduled. At the same time, the SCO's Regional Antiterrorism Center was opened in Tashkent, Uzbekistan. The two organs have an annual budget of $3.5 million. China and Russia each pays 24 percent of the budget.[138]

Another way to sustain SCO is to add the economic dimension to the organization. Economic and trade relations among SCO members have been underdeveloped compared with the security relations. Even before September 11, the Chinese came to the conclusion that for SCO to become a viable regional organization, security multilateralism was insufficient. Without substantial economic multilateralism, SCO is likely to be "hollowed out."[139] The economic benefits from SCO are particularly needed by four Central Asian countries. They are actually more interested in economic, rather than security or military, cooperation. It is predicted that promoting economic cooperation will constitute a new growth point to increase the coherence of SCO; but in reality, compared with that of Southeast Asia, the level of economic integration in SCO is much lower. Among other things, the Chinese business community is not particularly interested in the region; therefore, the member governments need more political will to take actions that will support some major projects and thereby increase the member states' stake of economic interdependence within the organization.[140] At the SCO summit in Moscow in May 2003, the importance of economic cooperation was particularly emphasized. The Chinese president made a strong push for an early focus on building transportation infrastructure through multilateral treaties.[141] At the SCO prime ministers meeting in September 2003, the member countries signed a framework agreement on multilateral economic cooperation. Similar to its initiative to ASEAN, Chinese premier Wen Jiabao proposed to establish a free trade area among SCO members.[142] With security and economic cooperation as two main pillars, SCO has become increasingly comprehensive. It is committed to "expand cooperation among the member states in political, economic and trade, cultural, scientific and technological and other fields."[143]

As in the case of its participation in ASEAN, APEC, and AFR (but to greater extent than all), SCO reflects Beijing's interest in establishing a norm- and rule-based security order in the region. Just like any other international organization, SCO does have its instrumental function, either to manage border disputes in the narrow sense or offset the U.S. influence in Central Asia in the broad sense. The Western media described SCO as Beijing and Russia's attempt to establish a condominium in Central Asia and a mini-NATO to counterbalance U.S. dominance.[144] There is some truth in such an argument, but it is hardly the only or even the most important motivation. Indeed the initiation of the Shanghai Five mechanism has nothing to do with external balancing;

thus, the Shanghai Five and the SCO point to the gradual evolution from an instrumental order to a normative–contractual order in this specific subregion.[145] Chinese president Jiang Zemin made it very clear in 2000 that the purpose of SCO was not just to find a way to promote friendly cooperation among member countries, but more important, it was an experiment to explore "new interstate relations, new security concept and new model of regional cooperation" beyond the Cold War mentality.[146]

In terms of the nature of the organization, China advocated that SCO follow the principle of nonalignment, not targeting against any third country or region, but opening to all, including nonmembers.[147] In terms of norms governing the relationship among member states, China emphasized that SCO is underlined by the so-called Shanghai spirit. At the St. Petersburg summit in June 2002, Jiang defined the Shanghai spirit in the following terms: mutual trust, mutual advantages, equality, joint consultation, respect for cultural diversity, and the desire for common development.[148] It was summarized by a Chinese scholar as the five Cs: confidence, communication, cooperation, coexistence, and common interest.[149]

These norms are consistent with the new conceptions of security discussed earlier. As Jiang Zemin indicated, China wants to use SCO as a catalyst to promote a new type of international relations, based on these new concepts of security. These norms, needless to say, are still closely attached to the Westphalia international system as well as to the realist framework. But it could be argued that the realism embedded in SCO is at least not the hard-core Hobbesian version as described by some scholars as "particularly acute" in Chinese foreign policy.[150] In addition, by the practice of SCO, China is advocating some post–Cold War norms that are different from what Beijing perceived as the outdated Cold War mentality manifested by the American post–Cold War foreign policy.

Among other things, Beijing attempts to demonstrate through SCO that first, countries with different civilizations and social systems could coexist in peace without democratizing domestic systems, as the democratic peace advocates would argue. Second, the era of "either enemy or allies" is gone, as declared by Chinese vice president Hu Jintao in his visit to the United States in early 2002. Interstate relations could be something between these two ends. SCO, unlike NATO, is not an alliance. It strives for a relationship among members that is neither confrontational nor collusive. It is called a "partnership without alliance."[151] In Beijing's opinion, this is a right approach to maintain regional stability and peace and to avoid repetition of the polarization. Third, Beijing intends to develop a model of cooperation in which major powers and smaller powers can collaborate on equal footing. One mechanism for such equality is consensus building in decision making that gives all members virtually the veto power. The SCO charter legalized this mechanism. While Chinese scholars admit that these norms still sound idealistic under current circumstances, such norms could nevertheless play a constructivist role in molding the behavior of member states.[152] Some evidence shows that the norms of the Shanghai spirit are being increasingly accepted by the member states.[153] In fact, it was formally adopted by the Declaration of Shanghai Cooperation Organization. Overall the Shanghai Five–SCO mechanism has been instrumental to the security order and stability in the region. As one Chinese scholar put it, "We can say without any exaggeration, if there were no 'Shanghai Five'–SCO mechanism, the Afghan conflict would already have spread to Tajikistan and Uzbekistan, and maybe to Pakistan as well."[154]

China's multilateral diplomacy in Northeast Asia is not just limited to institution building and conflict prevention. It also, for the first time, applied multilateralism to conflict resolution on the Korean Peninsula—the most explosive flashpoint left by the Cold War. The Korean nuclear crisis heated up again in October 2002, after U.S. assistant secretary James Kelly visited Pyongyang and alleged that North Korea had acknowledged its covert enriched-uranium program for nuclear weapons. From the very beginning the hard-line Bush administration refused to have face-to-face negotiations with North Korea and insisted that its nuclear program is a regional problem that must be settled through multilateral diplomacy. The belligerent North Korea, however, insisted that the only way of solving the problem was to conclude a nonaggression treaty with legal binding force through bilateral direct talks.

While China and the United States shared the same objective of a nuclear-free Korean Peninsula, they initially did not see eye to eye on the approach to realize this goal. The United States firmly believed that this was a "multilateral" issue. In secretary of state Colin Powell's words, "It's China's matter, Japan's matter, Russia's matter, the matter of the UN and the International Atomic Energy Agency, and also the U.S.'s matter."[155] China was initially reluctant to get involved, indicating that this is the matter between the United States and the DPRK and did not approve of the United States' call for a multilateral talk. Indeed China thought it was largely an issue of America's own making and that the United States should "untie the bell," taking initiatives to resolve the crisis.[156] The most effective way to break the deadlock and ease the tension was for the United States to open direct dialogue with North Korea on an equal footing.[157]

But with the pressure from the United States mounting, Beijing gradually realized that multilateral talks might be a way for both the DPRK and North Korea to get out. In early 2003, China began to shift its position. In a telephone conversation between Chinese president Jiang Zemin and U.S. president Bush,

Jiang declared that the form of dialogue is not the most important; the key is whether both sides have sincerity, whether the dialogue has substantial content and result."[158] China began to perceive its role as a mediator to "promote dialogue" and "cool both sides down."[159]

China played a pivotal role in breaking the impasse in the United States–DPRK nuclear standoff. Beijing first tried something between bilateral and multilateral diplomacy. Providing a good office, China brokered and hosted a trilateral talk among the United States, the DPRK, and China in April 2003. The trilateral talk was a compromise between the United States' wish for multilateral talks and the DPRK's insistence on bilateral negotiation. Then further moving toward a truly multilateral approach, China mediated the six-party talk among the United States, North Korea, Japan, South Korea, Russia, and China. To bring all the parties to the table, Chinese diplomats engaged in an unusual flurry of "shuttle diplomacy" between Pyongyang, Washington, Seoul, and Moscow in July 2003. Eventually Kim Jong II accepted the multilateral format of the talk.[160] Consequently the first truly multilateral talk on the North Korean nuclear issue was held in August 2003 in Beijing. An official Chinese commentator declared that "China has been a great influence on the DPRK's agreement to participate in the multilateral talks it had once resolutely opposed."[161] About six months later, Beijing hosted the second round of six-party talks on the Korean Peninsula nuclear issue. Despite no breakthrough on substantial issues, the second round produced some important consensus in a form of chairman's statement.[162]

In these multilateral talks, China has played a proactive leading role as facilitator and mediator. This is in sharp contrast to its traditional low-profile position in international security affairs. Before the first round of talks formerly kicked off, Chinese officials, as hosts, had been busy consulting with five other diplomatic groups since their arrival in Beijing. The Chinese even took great pain to make a special layout designed for the multilateral talks.[163] The talk witnessed a frenzy of bilateral, trilateral, and multilateral diplomatic activities. Under the multilateral framework, the United States and the DPRK held direct talk. China helped shape two primary common goals of the six parties: the denuclearization of the Korean Peninsula and the peaceful solution to the nuclear crisis.[164] This pattern also applied to China's diplomacy leading to the second round. To make it happen, China held sixty more meetings in a flurry of shuttle diplomacy to make arrangements.[165] Before and during the negotiations, China successfully pushed the participating countries to issue a written statement and set up a permanent working group. China was also willing to provide energy assistance to North Korea, as were South Korea and Russia.[166] China's new profile in regional conflict was widely credited by the parties involved.[167]

Through the mediation of the North Korean nuclear issues, China realized the utility of multilateral diplomacy in conflict resolution in the Asia–Pacific region. It indeed might be a better way to deal with difficult issues. Some Chinese scholars even argued that a bilateral approach was probably the wrong solution to the nuclear issue in the first place. One problem with the 1994 Framework Agreement is that it is bilaterally based. One Chinese analyst pointed out that the United States and North Korea needed a third independent force that could balance and constrain the two sides and thus stop any extreme situation. Moreover, once a compromise is reached between the two countries, the third party should monitor whether the promises made are fulfilled.[168] In other words, a multilateral framework could restrain the DPRK and the United States due to the pressure from the international community.[169]

From initially resisting the multilateral talk on the issue to concluding that it is the only solution to the problem is indeed a "great leap forward." This change partially resulted from conceptual changes regarding the nature of the North Korean nuclear issue. According to the Chinese analysis, after Pyongyang formally declared that it would possess nuclear weapons, the DPRK nuclear issue became "one of the regional security problems instead of a bilateral issue."[170] In their meetings with North Koreans, Chinese officials declared that the DPRK issue was a security concern for all nations involved. More than that, some Chinese scholars and analysts even hoped that a successful multilateral approach to resolve the nuclear issue would establish a new "mechanism for security and cooperation in Northeast Asia" and thus lay a foundation for a regional security mechanism in the future.[171] Indeed, during the second round of six-party talks, Chinese diplomats strongly advocated the institutionalization of the consultation by setting up a working group and by stationing specialists from all parties in Beijing on a permanent basis.[172]

CONCLUSION

China has gone a long way in adopting multilateralism in its foreign policy. Initially suspicious and resistant, it has experienced a learning curve of reacting, adapting, initiating, and advocating. At the global level, China has become a full-fledged member of the international multilateral political, economic, and security regimes centered on the UN. China's conceptual and behavioral changes regarding multilateralism at the regional level are even more remarkable. It can be said that multilateralism has increasingly become the main thrust of China's periphery foreign policy strategy. In certain areas, such as economic liberalization and integration, China has been playing a leading role.

Like other major powers, China's multilateral diplomacy is mainly motivated by instrumental considerations. It is perceived as a more-effective and less-alarming way to advance China's national interest and project China's influence. In the UN, China's advocacy of multilateralism is closely related to its opposition to the perceived U.S. hegemonism and unilateralism. Indeed, multilateralism might be a pathway that more effectively leads to multipolarity.[173] China's active involvement in ASEAN, APEC, ARF, and SCO is also aimed at creating a more peaceful and favorable regional environment for China's economic development; raising Beijing's positive profile and dispelling misgivings and concerns about China's growing economic and military might; and offsetting the influence of outside as well as indigenous major powers, such as the United States and Japan. Nevertheless, China's multilateral diplomacy is driven by more than just practical or utility calculations. It reflects China's intention to coordinate interstate relations and establish order on the basis of "generalized" principles of conduct.[174] China firmly believes that the new reality of world politics needs some norms and principles that are different from those that regulated interstate relations during the Cold War period. China is determined to have a say in formulating these new norms and principles. Its tireless advocacy of "new security concepts"—as well as the configuration of these concepts in forms of the Shanghai spirit, the APEC approach, and the ARF approach—points to the increasing weight of norm- and rule-making in China's foreign policy.

In pursuing multilateralism in the region, China has not followed a unified model; rather, it has adopted approaches based on each situation's context. In its southward multilateral diplomacy, Beijing took an economics first, security second approach. Trade liberalization as exemplified by free trade areas is a driving force behind China's multilateral diplomacy, particularly in Southeast Asia. Further economic integration is supposed to provide a cushion for political and security cooperation. This is the conventional functional approach for regional integration and cooperation. In its northward multilateral diplomacy, China took a neofunctional approach in a sense that it started from the high politics of security multilateralism and then gravitated to economic and other functional cooperation after a large-enough reservoir of goodwill and trust had been nurtured among member states. However, in either direction, the Chinese concluded that further economic integration is the key for the survival and longevity of regional multilateralism. This reveals a new dynamics for the post–Cold War regional multilateralism: a mere security rationale featured by a threat or enemy is not enough to sustain multilateralism.

Another difference in China's approaches toward multilateralism in the South and North lies in the degree of institutionalization of multilateralism. China has favored a kind of loosely structured, open-ended multilateralism in the Asia–Pacific and generally regarded a high degree of institutionalization particularly in the security area as unnecessary and even undesirable. While this by and large remains true for China's multilateral diplomacy in Southeast Asia, China has led the push for institutionalization in the case of the Shanghai Five–SOC. Although SCO is still in its formative stage and cannot be labeled a full-fledged military alliance, the mere fact that China has turned out to be a founding member of such a regional organization indicates a considerable departure from its past clear-cut policy of nonalignment. It seems that China is more ready to endorse institutionalization of subregional multilateralism rather than the institutionalization of the regionwide multilateral mechanism, particularly in the security domains. As some Chinese scholars argued, the interest and concerns of the countries involved are just too diverse to ask for a high degree of institutionalization for a broadly based regional mechanism such as APEC and ARF. Relatedly, China has been more enthusiastic about indigenous multilateral initiatives, such as East Asia's ASEAN+3, and more cautious about regional multilateral mechanism involving outside major powers.[175] For example, China has no problem joining the trilateral mechanism among China, Japan, and South Korea, but it has remained noncommittal to the proposed trilateral dialogue among China, the United States, and Japan unless the talk is conducted at the unofficial level.

The weight of bilateral and multilateral diplomacy in China's foreign policy calculus has been definitely shifting. As its policy changes on the South China Sea and DPRK nuclear issue show, China is more ready to recognize multilateral diplomacy as the legitimate and viable pathway for conflict resolution and order building, particularly with regard to those so-called nontraditional security issues. The growing visibility of multilateralism in Chinese foreign policy of course does not mean that the traditional bilateral diplomacy has lost its validity. Some sensitive issues, such as Taiwan, are still off-limits for multilateral consultation, irrespective of its broad regional impact. Indeed bilateral and multilateral diplomacy are mutually reinforcing in China's international behavior. In its dealing with ASEAN and SCO, China often applies bilateral diplomacy to build up momentum for realizing multilateral objectives. China's trade relations with Thailand in the case of CAFTA and its military relations with Kyrgyzstan in case the of the SCO antiterrorism mechanism are examples to the point.

Overall, China's more active and dynamic multilateral diplomacy has brought it tangible and intangible benefits. Among other things, Beijing's willingness to get involved in an ever-thickening multilateral network in the region and subject itself to the influence and restrains of various multilateral mechanisms help change China's image in the world as a non–status quo power, particularly in the Asia–Pacific region. "A new, more benign view of

China is emerging" in the area. Some of China's international behavior, such as its effort to settle the Korean nuclear crisis in a multilateral framework and its considerate treatment of some ASEAN members in the process of trade liberalization, won the hearts and minds of Asian countries. They perceive that "China is trying to do its best to please, assist, accommodate its neighbors." As a result "Asian countries look toward China as the increasingly vital regional power, political and business leaders in Asia."[176]

NOTES

1. Among others, see Amitav Achary, *Regionalism and Multilateralism* (Singapore: Times Academic Press, 2002), 278; Hongying Wang, "Chinese Culture and Multilateralism," in *The New Realism, Perspectives on Multilateralism and Word Order*, ed. Robert Cox (Tokyo: United Nations University Press, 1997), 158; Jing-dong Yuan, "Culture Matters: Chinese Approaches to Arms Control and Disarmament," in *Culture and Security, Multilateralism, Arms Control and Security Building*, ed. Keith Krause (London: Frank Cass, 1999), 99. To the extent that China does participate in multilateral diplomacy, various authors tend to emphasize its "realist, instrumental, and peripheral" nature. See David Lampton, "China's Foreign Policy and National Security Policy-making Process: Is It Changing and Does It Matter?" in *The Making of Chinese Foreign and Security Policy in the Era of Reform, 1978–2000*, ed. David Lampton (Stanford, Calif.: Stanford University Press, 2001), 29; Hongying Wang, "Multilateralism in Chinese Foreign Policy: The Limits of Socialization?" in *China's International Relations in the 21st Century, Dynamics of Paradigm Shifts*, ed. Weixing Hu, Gerald Chan, and Daojiong Zha (Lanham, Md.: University Press of America, 2000), 85.

2. A Chinese scholar of international relations mentioned an interesting anecdote in his article on multilateralism. A general of the Chinese Defense University warned him: "China should not get involved in multilateral diplomacy. It is not suitable for China. You scholars could do a lot in other areas, but don't touch this subject. In any case, for China, multilateralism will do more harm than good." Wang Yizhou, "China in the New Century and Multilateral Diplomacy," *Pacific Journal*, no. 4 (2001): 3.

3. See Alastair Iain Johnston, "China's International Relations: The Political and Security Dimensions," 67; and Samuel Kim, "Northeast Asia in the Local-Regional-Global Nexus: Multiple Challenges and Contending Explanations," in *The International Relations of Northeast Asia*, ed. Samuel Kim (Lanham, Md.: Rowan & Littlefield, 2004), 16.

4. "Premier Zhu's Government Work Report, Fifth Session of the Ninth National People's Congress on March 5, 2002," Xinhua News Agency, March 16, 2002.

5. "Chinese Diplomacy Aims to Maintain World Peace and Development," Xinhua News Agency, November 14, 2002.

6. "Premier Zhu's Government Work Report, Fifth Session of the Ninth National People's Congress on March 5, 2002," Xinhua News Agency, March 16, 2002.

7. "Premier Zhu's Government Work Report, Fifth Session of the Ninth National People's Congress on March 5, 2002," Xinhua News Agency, March 16, 2002.

8. "Full Text of Jiang Zemin's Report at the 16th Party Congress," Xinhua News Agency, November 17, 2002.

9. "Chinese Diplomacy Aims to Maintain World Peace and Development," Xinhua News Agency, November 14, 2002.

10. "Global Problems Call for Global Answers: Chinese FM," *People's Daily*, January 18, 2002.

11. Statement by Ambassador Hu Xiaodi, head of the Chinese delegation, at the First Committee of the Fifty-eighth Session of the United Nations General Assembly, October 7, 2003, New York.

12. "China's Position Paper on the New Security Concept," August 6, 2002.

13. "China's Position Paper on the New Security Concept," August 6, 2002.

14. Xiong Guangkai, "The New Security Concept Advocated by China, a Speech at the London Institute of International Strategic Studies," May 22, 2002, *Study of International Strategy*, no. 3 (2002): 2.

15. "China's Position Paper on the New Security Concept," August 6, 2002.

16. Statement by Ambassador Hu Xiaodi, head of the Chinese delegation, at the First Committee of the Fifty-eighth Session of the United Nations General Assembly, October 7, 2003, New York.

17. "Global Problems Call for Global Answers: Chinese FM," *People's Daily*, January 18, 2002.

18. "China's Position Paper on the New Security Concept," August 6, 2002.

19. "To Enhance the Role of the United Nations, in Promotion of Peace and Development," statement by Chinese foreign minister Li Zhaoxing at the general debate of the Fifty-eighth Session of the United Nations General Assembly, September 24, 2003, at http://un.fmprc.gov.cn/eng.56633.html.

20. Li Zhaoxing, "To Enhance the Role of the United Nations"; statement by Ambassador Hu Xiaodi, head of the Chinese delegation, at the First Committee of the Fifty-eighth Session of the United Nations General Assembly, October 7, 2003, New York.

21. "China's Position Paper on the New Security Concept," August 6, 2002.

22. "Chinese Foreign Policy after the 16th CPC National Congress," *China Daily*, July 18, 2003.

23. "China's Position Paper on the New Security Concept," August 6, 2002.

24. "China's Position Paper on the New Security Concept," August 6, 2002.

25. Statement by Ambassador Hu Xiaodi, head of the Chinese delegation, at the First Committee of the Fifty-eighth Session of the United Nations General Assembly, October 7, 2003, New York.

26. "China's Foreign Policy Matures," *China Daily*, November 29, 2002.

27. "U.S. Policy Reeking of Unilateralism," *China Daily*, April 1, 2003.

28. Director of the Russian Studies Center at the East China Normal University, "Changing Characteristics of Global Power Relations," translated by Zheng Guihong, September 17, 2002, at http://service.china.org.cn/link/wcm/Show_Text?info_id=43207&p_qry=multilateral.

29. "U.S. Policy Reeking of Unilateralism," *China Daily*, April 3, 2003.

30. Director of the Russian Studies, "Changing Characteristics of Global Power Relations."

31. As a Chinese scholar declared, "While Bush adopts a unilateral approach, we label ours as multilateral." Tim Shorrock, "China's Shift to Multilateralism," Inter Press Service, Globalvision News Network, June 11, 2003, at www.goneuo.net/html/opinion/alert688.html.

32. One analyst points out that "multilateral diplomacy is becoming an important platform on which China's influence is being built." "Chinese Foreign Policy after the 16th CPC National Congress," at China.org.cn, translated by Zheng Guihong, December 18, 2002.

33. "China's Position Paper on the New Security Concept," August 6, 2002.

34. "Chinese Foreign Policy after the 16th CPC National Congress," at China.org.cn, translated by Zheng Guihong, December 18, 2002.

35. See my discussion in "Managing Conflict: Chinese Perspectives on Multilateral Diplomacy and Collective Security," in *In the Eyes of the Dragon: China Views the World*, ed. Yong Deng and Fei-Ling Wang (Lanham, Md.: Rowman & Littlefield, 1999), 75–81.

36. "Chinese, Russian Leaders Call for Strengthened UN Authority," Xinhua News Agency, September 25, 2003.

37. "Hu Urges More Support for UN," CNN.com, October 24, 2003.

38. "To Enhance the Role of the United Nations, in Promotion of Peace and Development," statement by Chinese foreign minister Li Zhaoxing at the general debate of the Fifty-eighth Session of the United Nations General Assembly, at http://un.fmprc.gov.cn/eng/56633.html.

39. Statement by H. E. Jiang Zemin, president of the People's Republic of China, at the Millennium Summit of the United Nations, September 6, 2000.

40. See Wang, "Managing Conflict," 76–77.

41. This information is drawn from China's *National Defense in 1998, China's National Defense in 2000,* and *China's National Defense in 2002* (Beijing: Information Office of the State Council of the People's Republic of China, 1998, 2000, and 2002); "China's Peacekeeping Forces Leave for Liberia," *People's Daily* online, December 10, 2003, at http://english.peopledaily.com.cn/200312/09/html; "China to Send Anti-riot Peacekeepers for Haiti," Xinhuanet, June 4, 2004, at http://news.xinhuanet.com/english/2004-06/04/content_1509032.htm; Tang Yongsheng, "China and the UN Peacekeeping Operations," *World Economics and Politics*, no. 9 (2002): 40.

42. Some Chinese scholars advocated more active participation in UN peacekeeping operations and argued that this is a responsibility of China as a major power. See Tang Yongsheng, "China and the UN Peacekeeping Operations," 41–42.

43. See Chen Weixiong, *My Experience in the UN Security Council* (Beijing: Economic Daily Press, 2001), 103.

44. This practice was later named "Chinese model," Chen, *My Experience in the UN Security Council*, 103–4.

45. Jiang Zemin defined this strategy at the Sixteenth Party Congress as "building a good neighborly relationship and partnership" with China's neighbors. "Full Text of

Jiang Zemin's Report at the 16th Party Congress," Xinhua News Agency, November 17, 2002.

46. Pang Zhongying, "China's Asian Strategy: Flexible Multilateralism," *World Economy and Politics*, no. 10 (2001): 30–35. He argues that although China's Asian neighbors always want to use multilateral mechanism to check China, China should not be afraid of multilateralism and should not reject it. Rather China should positively and actively pursue multilateralism in the region to safeguard China's national interest and security.

47. Zhang Baili, "Strengthening the Economic Integration between China and East Asia," in *The Thinking of the New Century*, ed. Ling Rong (Beijing: CPC Central Party School Press, 2002), 104–5.

48. Zhang Baili, "Strengthening the Economic Integration between China and East Asia," in Ling, *The Thinking of the New Century*, 108.

49. Beijing holds that ASEAN plays an extremely important role in China's peripheral stability, economic development, and omnidirectional diplomacy. Therefore strengthening its relations with ASEAN is one of China's strategic directions. "A Study Report on China's Policy towards ASEAN," *Contemporary International Relations*, no. 10 (2002): 5.

50. "ASEAN Cooperation Surges Ahead," *China Daily*, January 6, 2002.

51. For more detailed discussion, see Wang, "Managing Conflict."

52. Zhang Yunling, "East Asian Cooperation and the Construction of China–ASEAN Free Trade Area," *Contemporary Asia-Pacific*, no. 1 (2002): 8.

53. Some analysts point out that this is the first time in Chinese history that it has found common interest to engage all the Southeast Asian countries constructively to talk about cooperation, instead of quarrelling on issues such as the rival claims in the Spratly Islands. Sheng Lijun, "FTA with Asean a Safety Cushion for China," *Straits Times*, November 8, 2002.

54. Sun Cheng, "Road to CAFTA," *Beijing Review*, August 28, 2003, 43.

55. Xu Ningning, "Trends in China–ASEAN cooperation," *Beijing Review*, September 4, 2003.

56. "Building a Good-Neighborly Relationship and Partnership—an Interview with Fu Ying, Director-General of Asian Bureau, Chinese Ministry of Foreign Affairs," *Chinese diplomacy*, no. 3 (2003): 27.

57. Sun Cheng, "Road to CAFTA," *Beijing Review*, August 28, 2003, 44.

58. Chinese prime minister Wen Jiabao urged Southeast Asia nations to achieve $100 billion worth of trade with China in two years, nearly double the current $55 billion volume in 2003. If achieved, this will be very close to the $120 billion that the U.S. traded with ASEAN in 2001. Jane Perlez, "Asian Leaders Find China a More Cordial Neighbor," *New York Times*, October 18, 2003.

59. Some Chinese analysts point out that China has twice served as a propelling force to bail ASEAN out. The first time was China's commitment not to devalue its currency during the financial economic crisis. The second time was China's proposal of China–ASEAN FTA. "ASEAN Cooperation Surges Ahead," *China Daily*, January 6, 2002.

60. Sun Cheng, "Road to CAFTA," *Beijing Review*, August 28, 2003, 45.

61. "Forum Set to Promote Regional Integration," *China Daily*, November 1, 2003. A senior Chinese diplomat summarized such a policy as "making neighbors friendly, stable, and rich." Wang Yi, "Strengthening Mutual Trust and Cooperation and Promoting Common Security," a speech delivered at the "Security Cooperation in East Asia Conference," Qinghua University, December 13–14, 2003, *Global Times*, December 14, 2003.

62. "ASEAN Cooperation Surges Ahead," *China Daily*, January 6, 2002.

63. Perlez, "Asian Leaders Find China a More Cordial Neighbor."

64. As former president of the Philippines points out, China is playing a crucial role in promoting regional integration because it provides a huge market for Asian countries. "Forum Set to Promote Regional Integration," *China Daily*, November 1, 2003.

65. "ASEAN to Work with Beijing on South China Sea Accord," Agence France-Press, July 20, 2002; "China, RP Vow Peaceful Talks on South China Sea," Agence France-Press, September 30, 2002.

66. "Declaration on the Conduct of Parties in the South China Sea," November 4, 2002, at www.aseansec.org/13165.htm.

67. David Wiencek, "South China Sea Flashpoint Revisited," *China Brief* 2, no. 24 (December 10), at www.jamestown.org/bubs/view/cwe_002_024_002.htm; Ralf Emmers, "Asean, China and the South China Sea: An Opportunity Missed," Institute of Defense and Strategic Studies, Nanyang Technological University, Singapore, at www.ntu.edu.sg/idss/Perspective/Research_050228.htm.

68. "China, ASEAN Sign Code of Conduct on South China Sea," *Xinhuanet*, November 4, 2002.

69. Chinese premier Zhu Rongji declared that the accord marks "a higher level of political trust between the two sides and will contribute to regional peace and stability." Francesco Sisci, "The Spratlys Pact: Beijing's Olive Branch," November 6, 2002, at www.atimes.com/atimes/printN.html.

70. "China Joins Treaty of Amity, Cooperation in Southeast Asia," *People's Daily*, October 9, 2003.

71. Alan Boyd, "South China Sea: Pact Won't Calm Waters," July 2, 2003, at www.atimes.com/atimes/printN.html.

72. "ASEAN, China Forge Strategic Partnership," *People's Daily*, October 9, 2003.

73. "China Joins Treaty of Amity, Cooperation in Southeast Asia," *People's Daily*, October 9, 2003.

74. "Forum Set to Promote Regional Integration," *China Daily*, November 1, 2003.

75. One Singapore businessman observed that China is trying to help its neighbors while the United States "is perceived as a country involved more and more on its own foreign policy agenda, and strong-arming everyone onto that agenda." Perlez, "Asian Leaders Find China a More Cordial Neighbor."

76. "China and ASEAN Forge a Strategic Partnership," *Ming Pao*, October 7, 2003.

77. Dennis Roy, "China and Southeast Asia: ASEAN Makes the Best of the Inevitable," *Asia Pacific Security Studies Series* 1, no. 4 (November 2002), at www.apcss.org/Publications/APSSS/China%20and%20Southeast%20Asia.pdf.

78. For example, just look at Chinese foreign minister Li Zhaoxing's itinerary of his visit to Cambodia and Thailand in June 2003: he went there to the attend the For-

eign Ministers Meeting of the ASEAN, China, Japan, and the Republic of Korea (ASEAN+3); the Tenth Foreign Ministers Meeting of the ASEAN Regional Forum (ARF); the ASEAN Post-Ministerial Conference (PMC); the ASEAN–China (ASEAN+1) Dialogue; the Second Informal Meeting of the Foreign Ministers of China, Japan, and the Republic of Korea; and the Asian Cooperation Dialogue (ACD). "Foreign Ministry Official Briefs Overseas Journalists on Foreign Minister Li Zhaoxing's Upcoming Attendance of ARF and Other Meetings," June 5, 2003, at www.chinaembassy.org.tr/eng.50964.html.

79. See Wang, "Managing Conflict," 82–84.

80. Cai Penghong, "China and APEC," *International Review*, no. 4 (2001): 11–12.

81. "APEC Makes Remarkable Achievements," Xinhua News Agency, October 17, 2001.

82. "Change and Continuity—APEC Has Been Moving Forward," Xinhua News Agency, October 21, 2003.

83. "Commentary: Promoting APEC Development on 'Two Wheels.'" *People's Daily*, October 15, 2001.

84. Gao Lianfu, "East Asia Regional Cooperation Entered the Stage of Institutionalization," *Pacific Journal*, no. 2 (2001): 25.

85. Wang Xiaolong, "The Asia-Pacific Economic Cooperation and the Regional Political and Security Issues," *Contemparary Asia-Pacific*, no. 4 (2003): 52–53.

86. Speech by president of the People's Republic of China, H. E. Hu Jintao, at the Eleventh APEC Economic Leaders Meeting, October 20, 2003.

87. Li Nian, "China's Foreign Policy Agenda and the PLA's New Mission," Institute of Defense and Strategic Studies, Nanyang Technological University, Singapore, August 2002, at www.ntu.edu.sg/idss/Perspective/research_050213.htm.

88. China defined ARF as "the sole governmental-level channel for security dialogues in the Asia-Pacific region . . . playing an ever-greater role in enhancing mutual confidence among Asian-Pacific countries and promoting regional peace and stability." Address by H. E. Tang Jiaxuan, minister of foreign affairs of the People's Republic of China, at the Fifth ARF Ministerial Meeting, Manila, July 27, 1998. It is "the largest official multilateral security consultative and cooperative channel in the Asia-Pacific region" and "has played an irreplaceable role in maintaining regional peace, security and stability, and promoting regional development." "Forum Enhances Cooperation," *China Daily*, June 23, 2003.

89. "China Urges ARF to Focus on Confidence Building," *People's Daily*, July 27, 1999.

90. Opening statement by H. E. Qian Qichen, vice premier and minister of foreign affairs, People's Republic China, ASEAN Regional Forum, Subang Jaya, July 27, 1997.

91. Chinese foreign minister Tang Jiaxuan believes that "based on vigorous exploration and practice, a multilateral security and cooperation framework will eventually take shape." Speech by Chinese foreign minister Tang Jiaxuan at the Ninth ARF Foreign Ministers meeting, July 31, 2002.

92. "Foreign Ministry Official Briefs Overseas Journalists on Foreign Minister Li Zhaoxing's Upcoming Attendance of ARF and Other Meetings," June 5, 2003.

93. Chinese vice premier Qian Qichen makes it very clear that the purpose of ARF

"is not to defuse a common threat, but rather to achieve a common goal, that is, regional peace and stability." Opening statement by H. E. Qian Qichen, vice premier and minister of foreign affairs, People's Republic of China, ASEAN Regional Forum, Subang Jaya, July 27, 1997.

94. Address by H. E. Tang Jiaxuan, minister of foreign affairs of the People's Republic of China, at the Fifth ARF Ministerial Meeting, Manila, July 27, 1998.

95. "China Backs ASEAN's Leading Role in Regional Forum: Tang," *People's Daily*, July 25, 2001.

96. Opening statement by H. E. Qian Qichen, vice premier and minister of foreign affairs, People's Republic of China, ASEAN Regional Forum, Subang Jaya, July 27, 1997.

97. See the discussion in the first section of this chapter.

98. *China's National Defense in 2000,* http://english.pladaily.com.cn/special/book/c2000/17.htm.

99. Among others, China has participated in the Conference on Interaction and Confidence Building in Asia (CICA); the Council on Security Cooperation in the Asia-Pacific Region (CSCAP); the Northeast Asia Cooperation Dialogue (NEACD); and the Academic Symposium of China, the United States, and Japan. By 2002, China had hosted, successively in Beijing, the ARF Seminar on Tropical Hygiene and Prevention and Treatment of Tropical Infectious Diseases; the ARF Professional Training Program on China's Security Policy; the Fourth ARF Meeting of Heads of Defense Colleges; the ARF Seminar on Defense Conversion Cooperation; the ARF Seminar on Military Logistics Outsourcing Support; and NEACD. *China's National Defense in 2000*, at http://english.pladaily.com.cn/special/book/c2000/17.htm; *China's National Defense in 2002*, at http://english.pladaily.com.cn/special/book/c2002/06-1.htm.

100. Speech by Chinese foreign minister Tang Jianxuan at the Ninth ARF Foreign Ministers meeting, June 8, 2002.

101. "China's Position Paper on Enhanced Cooperation in the Field of Nontraditional Security Issues," May 29, 2002.

102. "China's Position Paper on Enhanced Cooperation in the Field of Nontraditional Security Issues," May 29, 2002.

103. *China's National Defense in 2002,* at http://english.pladaily.com.cn/special/book/c2002/06-1.htm.

104. Wang Yi, "Strengthening Mutual Trust and Cooperation and Promoting Common Security," a speech delivered at the "Security Cooperation in East Asia Conference," Qinghua University, December 13–14, 2003, *Global Times*, December 14, 2003.

105. Tang Shiping, "Last Chance for East Asia Integration," *Strait Times*, November 18, 2002.

106. Li, Jingyu and Wang Jun, "The Prospect of East Asian Economic Development under the Cooperative Framework of 10+3," *Peace and Development Quarterly*, no. 2 (2001): 4.

107. "China Actively Supports Asian Cooperation: Chinese FM," *People's Daily*, July 31, 2002.

108. Hu Zhaoming, "The Present and Future of East Asian Cooperation," *Study of International Issues*, no. 1 (2001): 22, 25.

109. "Building a Good-Neighborly Relationship and Partnership—an Interview with Fu Ying, Director-General of Asian Bureau, Chinese Ministry of Foreign Affairs," *Chinese Diplomacy*, no. 3 (2003): 27.

110. "ASEAN+China, Japan, ROK Summit Held," *People's Daily*, October 8, 2003.

111. "Foreign Ministry Official Briefs Overseas Journalists on Foreign Minister Li Zhaoxing's Upcoming Attendance of ARF and Other Meetings," June 5, 2003, www .chinaembassy.org.tr/eng.50964.html.

112. Liu Xiaoxue, "Summary of the International Seminar on East Asian Cooperation," *Contemporary Asia-Pacific*, no. 10 (2002): 64.

113. "ASEAN, China Forge Strategic Partnership," *People's Daily*, October 9, 2003.

114. Yu Jianhua, "The Development of SCO and the Exploration of New Interstate Relations," *Chinese Diplomacy*, no. 7 (2003): 28.

115. Chinese scholars hold that this security-driven multilateralism has a merit of building up trust among parties involved first and then spreading cooperation to other functional areas. Pang Guang, "An Analysis of the Prospect of 'Shanghai Five,'" in *Thinking of the New Century*, ed. Ling Rong (Beijing: Chinese Central Party School Press, December 2002), 111.

116. Zhao Huasheng, "The changing situation in Central Asia and SCO," *International Politics Monthly*, no. 2 (2003), 115.

117. David Sands, "China Counters U.S. Influence," January 11, 2002, at www .mail-archive.com/mutti-1@taklamaka.org/msg01027.html.

118. Here are some of descriptions about SCO's state of affairs after the September 11 attacks: "The SCO has cracked at the first serious test." "The SCO went into cardiac arrest." "SCO stood as exposed as irrelevant." SCO is a "stillborn" organization, and "the SCO will lose viability as a regional security and political forum." See Sean L. Yom, "Geopolitics in Central Asia: The SCO and Its Future," *Journal of World Affairs and New Technology* 5 (October 2002), at http://world-affairs .com/54sco.htm; *Monitor* (Jamestown Foundation) 7, no. 217 (November 27, 2001), at http://russia.jameston.org/pubs/views/mon_007_217_000.htm; *Russia's Week* (Jamestown Foundation) 7, no. 2 (January 16, 2002), at http://russia.jamestown.org/ pubs/view/bul_007_002_001.htm.

119. "Shanghai Convention on combating terrorism, separatism, and extremism," Shanghai Cooperation Organization, June 15, 2001, at www.sectsco.org/news_ detail.asp?id=93&LanguageID=2.

120. *Kazakhstan News Bulletin,* September 14, 2001.

121. Pang Guang, "SCO under New Circumstances: Challenge, Opportunity and Prospect for Development," *Journal of International Studies*, no. 5 (2002): 40.

122. "Jiang Zemin Calls for Regional Anti-terrorism Mechanism between SCO," January 7, 2001, at http://genevamissiontoun.fmprc.gov.cn/eng/23370.html.

123. The location of the center was later moved to Tashkent of Uzbekistan. "SCO Foreign Ministers Converge in Tashkent," *Muslim Uzbekistan,* September 6, 2003, at www.muslimuzbekistan.com/eng/ennews/2003/09/ennews06092003_2.html.

124. Some Chinese analysts argue that the SCO plays a particularly important role in the U.S. antiterrorism strategy and that such a role cannot by entirely replaced by any other organization. Therefore it is necessary for the United States to cooperate with SCO to deal with international terrorism. Bei Zhou, "After the St. Petersburg Summit," *Beijing Review*, July 4, 2002, 8–9.

125. Xu Tao, "SCO: Example for the World," *Beijing Review*, June 12, 2003, 27.

126. Xu Tao, "Exercising for Regional Defense Fitness," *Beijing Review*, August 21, 2003, 42–43.

127. "SCO Foreign Ministers Release Communiqué," *People's Daily*, November 25, 2002.

128. "Shanghai Grouping a 'Military Alliance,'" *Strait Times*, July 21, 2001.

129. Xu Tao, "SCO: Example for the World," *Beijing Review*, June 12, 2003, 27.

130. Pang Guang, "The Development of Sino-Russian Relations and the SCO under the New Situation," *Chinese Diplomacy*, no. 4 (2003): 40.

131. Pang Guang, "The Development of Sino-Russian Relations and the SCO under the New Situation," *Chinese Diplomacy*, no. 4 (2003): 41.

132. Bei Zhou, "After the St. Petersburg Summit," *Beijing Review*, July 4, 2002, 8.

133. "St. Petersburg Summit of SCO Concludes with Rich Fruit," Xinhua News Agency, June 8, 2002.

134. "Chinese President Urges Great Efforts to Fight Terrorism," *People's Daily*, May 30, 2003.

135. Xu Tao, "SCO: Example for the World," *Beijing Review*, June 12, 2003, 27.

136. "Hu Jintao's Speech at the SCO Moscow Summit," May 29, 2003, *People's Daily*, May 30, 2003.

137. Xu Tao, "SCO: Example for the World," *Beijing Review*, June 12, 2003, 26.

138. "SCO Major Force in International Counter-terrorism," Xinhua News Agency, January 16, 2004.

139. Pang, "An Analysis of the Prospect of 'Shanghai Five,'" 115.

140. Pang, "An Analysis of the Prospect of 'Shanghai Five,'" 115.

141. "Hu Jintao's Speech at the SCO Moscow Summit," May 29, 2003, *People's Daily*, May 30, 2003.

142. "China Proposes Free Trade Zone between SCO Members," *China Daily*, September 24, 2003.

143. "Declaration of Shanghai Cooperation Organization," June 15, 2001.

144. Willy Wo-Lap Lam, "Beijing's NATO' Hits Stumbling Block," CNN.com, May 16, 2002. Some alarmists even see the SCO as China's Warsaw Pact. Western intelligence circles describe the SCO as merely a synergistic tool and framework for Russia and China to court Central Asian countries and to establish the strategic Sino-Russian condominium over Central Asia against NATO. Matthew Oresman, "The SCO: A New Hope or to the Graveyard of Acronyms?" PacNet newsletter, no. 21, May 22, 2003, at www.csis.org/pacfor/pac0321.htm; Yom, "Geopolitics in Central Asia."

145. For discussion of instrumental and normative-contractual order, see Muthiah Alagappa, "Constructing security order in Asia: conception and issues," in *Asian Security Order, Instrumental and Normative Features*, ed. Muthiah Alagappa (Stanford,

Calif.: Stanford University Press, 2003), 41–52.

146. See Yu Jianhua, "The Development of SCO and the Exploration of New Interstate Relations," *Chinese Diplomacy*, no. 7 (2003): 29.

147. "Declaration of Shanghai Cooperation Organization," June 15, 2001.

148. "Shanghai Cooperation Organization Approves Center of Anti-Terror," *China Daily*, June 8, 2002.

149. Lu Zhongwei, "The Evolution of the Geo-Strategic Structure in Eurasia" in *Shanghai Cooperation Organization—New Security Concept and New Mechanism*" (Beijing: Current Affairs Press, 2002), 10.

150. Thomas Christensen, "Pride, Pressure, and Politics: The Roots of China's Worldview," in Deng and Wang, *In the Eyes of the Dragon*, 240.

151. Wang Jincun, "An Advance of Historical Significance—from 'Shanghai Five' to 'Shanghai Cooperation Organization,'" *World Economics and Politics*, no. 9 (2001): 80.

152. Xu Tao, "Shanghai Cooperation Organization under New Situation," *Contemporary International Relations*, no. 6 (2002): 13.

153. As Russia's foreign ministry spokesman pointed out, the SCO is based on the principles of equality and consensus. It does not necessarily follow one country's leader, and it does not have "leading" members or nations to be "led." Sergei Blagov, "Shanghai Cooperation Organization Prepares for New Role," *Eurasia Insight,* April 29, 2002, at www.eurasianet.org/departments/insight/articles/eav)42902.shtml.

154. Pan Guang, "China-Central Asia-Russian Relations and the Role of SCO in the War on Terrorism," paper presented at Stanford University, University of California–Los Angeles, RAND, Monterey Institute of International Studies, University of Cambridge, and Carleton University, 2002, 4.

155. "China Urges U.S. to Open Direct Dialogue with DPRK," Xinhua News Agency, February 26, 2003.

156. "Ball in U.S. Court over DPRK Issue" *China Daily*, February 27, 2003.

157. "Chinese FM Calls for Dialogue between U.S., DPRK," Xinhua News Agency, February 24, 2003.

158. "Jiang, Bush Talk over Phone on DPRK, Iraq Issues," Xinhua News Agency, March 10, 2003.

159. "China Willing to 'Mediate, Promote Dialogue' on DPRK Nuclear Issue," Xinhua News Agency, February 28, 2003.

160. This was a huge concession made by Pyongyang from its previous firmly held stance for direct bilateral talks with the United States, as it once said that it would never participate in any multilateral talks on the nuclear matter. "DPRK Reiterates Demand for Non-aggression Pact with U.S.," Xinhua News Agency, January 29, 2003.

161. Zhou Bian, "China Practices Shuttle Diplomacy," *Beijing Review*, August 21, 2003, 40.

162. Among other things, six parties agreed in principle to hold the third round of the six-party talks no later than June and to set up a working group to continue the discussion on a permanent basis. "Full Text of Chairman's Statement for Six-Party Talks," *People's Daily*, February 28, 2004.

163. Six delegations surrounded, in alphabetic order, a giant hexagonal table, cov-

ered with dark green felt. DPRK diplomats were sitting to the left of the U.S. delegation and opposite the Seoul team. "Handshakes and Smiling Faces Kick Off Six-Way Talks," Xinhua News Agency, August 27, 2003.

164. "Separate Talks Highlight Second Day of Six-Party Talks," Xinhua News Agency, August 29, 2003.

165. "China Seeks Progress as Host of Nuke Talks," Associated Press, February 23, 2004.

166. "China, Russia, ROK Agree to Offer DPRK Energy Aid," *People's Daily*, February 26, 2004.

167. As a senior official of the U.S. delegation commented, China was not only a "participant" but also a "facilitator" and has done an "exceptional job." "Six-Party Talks Conclude as Disagreements Exist," *People's Daily*, February 28, 2004.

168. Shi Yongming, "The Beijing Talks: A Difficult Beginning," *Beijing Review*, May 1993.

169. Shi Yongming, "Advantage Found in Compromise," *Beijing Review*, August 21, 2003, 41.

170. Shi Yongming, "Advantage Found in Compromise," *Beijing Review*, August 21, 2003, 40.

171. "Hope Grows amid Nuclear Crisis," *China Daily,* August 13, 2003.

172. "Six-Party Talks Should Become Mechanism: FM Spokeswoman," *People's Daily*, February 24, 2004.

173. As one Chinese scholar put it, a nonconfrontational multilateral diplomacy is a positive and feasible way to make the United States say good-bye to hegemonism. Shen Jiru, "About the Mutual Adaptation between China and APEC," *World Economics and Politics*, no. 5 (2002): 14.

174. John Gerard Ruggie, "Multilateralism: The Anatomy of an Institution," *International Organization* 46, no. 3 (Summer 1992): 561–98.

175. As one Chinese scholar points out, the ASEAN+3 mechanism is the first time that East Asia countries can independently discuss regional cooperation without the influence of outside powers, particularly the United States. Tiang Zhongqing, "East Asia Cooperation and China's Strategic Interest," *Contemporary Asia-Pacific*, no. 5 (2003): 41.

176. Perlez, "Asian Leaders Find China a More Cordial Neighbor."

8

China's U.S. Policies

John W. Garver

This chapter analyzes the broad structure of People's Republic of China (PRC) policies toward the United States. It identifies as the major determinant of those policies the deep dependence of China's highly successful post-1978 development drive on U.S. input and goodwill. It also argues that China's leaders have sought through a mix of punitive sanctions and positive inducements to mitigate U.S. inclination and ability to use China's dependency to pressure Beijing on key issues, especially on Taiwan and the control of the Chinese Communist Party (CCP) over Chinese society. This chapter also analyzes the dependency of China's development drive on the United States and reviews the several policy instruments Beijing has used to countervail U.S. pressure. This chapter views China's U.S. policies as the result of a two-level bargaining process. On the one hand, China's leaders attempt to influence Washington to sustain and increase U.S. support for China's development drive while foiling U.S. demands antithetical to China's core interests. On the other hand, China's leaders are not of one mind about the nature of China's interests vis-à-vis the United States or about the proper mix of rewards and sanctions ("carrots" and "sticks") in dealing with the United States. Thus, China's U.S. policies arise from various perspectives within China's élite and out of bargaining between adherents of those perspectives.

DENG XIAOPING'S FOREIGN POLICY REVOLUTION

When Deng Xiaoping became China's paramount leader in December 1978, he undertook a systematic and deliberate break with the foreign policy line of Mao Zedong. Mao had presided over a bold, assertive, and high-risk foreign policy designed to revolutionize China and the global order. That policy cost China dearly. Mao's revolutionary activism helped cast the Chinese people into the dire poverty that was their lot in the 1970s. Deng concluded that for now and a considerable period, China should concentrate on economic development, on lifting its people out of poverty, and on modernizing its economy. Unless this was done, Deng postulated, the CCP would have no future, and China would not achieve the position of power and respect in the world that it deserved. This position pointed toward a broadly cooperative relation with the United States. Deng believed that a successful drive to modernize China would require a cooperative and nonconfrontational relation with the power that, for better or worse, dominated the global system— the United States. Broadly speaking, Deng's strategy was to draw on the resources available via the global capitalist system to make socialist China wealthy and powerful. Deng's approach was profoundly pragmatic. He characterized his line as "peace and development," in distinction to Mao's line of "war and revolution."

During his first decade as paramount leader, Deng Xiaoping scraped the support for revolutionary movements in Southeast Asia, South Asia, and Africa that China had provided during the Mao era. He ditched the tiny Maoist communist parties scattered around the world, which Maoist China had nurtured and courted to prove the helmsman's revolutionary brilliance. He abandoned the revolutionary rhetoric that had decorated Chinese foreign policy under Mao. Deng brought China into the major institutions of world capitalism—the International Monetary Fund and the World Bank. Deng also normalized diplomatic relations with the United States (beginning as of January 1, 1979) and worked closely with the United States to counter the expansionism of the Brezhnev-era Soviet Union. Deng continued the policies of exploiting the strategic triangle to China's advantage developed by Mao Zedong and Zhou Enlai but gave China's triangular diplomacy a new strategic content. The PRC and the United States would now cooperate not only to counter Soviet expansionism, as had been the case since 1972, but to develop China's economy. Deng hoped that the common struggle against the Soviet Union would provide a strategic basis for a supportive, positive American attitude toward China's development drive. This was indeed the case for the first decade of Deng's leadership, until 1989.

The Cold War provided an excellent situation for Deng to secure U.S. support for China's development. In that protracted, global rivalry with the Soviet Union and its allies, the United States profited from a strong China and from China's assistance in the global anti-Soviet struggle. Following the Soviet-supported Vietnamese occupation of Cambodia (then called Kampuchea) in

December 1978, China and the United States worked together to force Vietnam's withdrawal. A year later, when Soviet forces occupied Afghanistan, Beijing and Washington joined to support the anti-Soviet Afghan mujahadeen fighters resisting Soviet occupation and to jointly guarantee Pakistan's security, allowing that country to offer sanctuary to the Afghan mujahadeen. The Reagan administration (which took office in January 1981) was determined to confront Moscow with insurmountable pressures designed to force a fundamental reorientation of Soviet policies, and it welcomed the contribution that China could make in this regard.[1] In the late 1970s and early 1980s, China was often viewed as a "quasi ally" in Washington. Then as Sino-Soviet rapprochement advanced after Michael Gorbachev's rise in Moscow, Deng was careful to keep Sino-American relations several steps ahead of Sino-Soviet relations.

The end of the Cold War destroyed the Soviet–United States–Chinese strategic triangle that had underpinned American support for China's development during the 1980s. The traumatic conjunction of the upheaval against CCP rule in China in 1989, with the collapse of communist regimes in Eastern Europe and the Soviet Union in the 1989–1991 period, produced a strong push within the CCP élite to distance China from the United States. The ideological apostasy and "class betrayal" of the Communist Party of the Soviet Union (CPSU) meant that the Chinese Communist Party should assume leadership of the world revolutionary movement, according to these newly energized CCP leftists. Recent events in China, Eastern Europe, and the Soviet Union indicated to these leftists that the United States was embarked on an extremely dangerous course of subverting socialist societies from within, a strategy they dubbed "peaceful evolution." It was necessary to wage renewed "class struggle" to thwart the U.S. strategy. Internationally, the CCP should issue a series of polemics exposing the "errors" of the CPSU and the counterrevolutionary "peaceful evolution" strategies of the United States. Domestically, the CCP should wage class struggle against the "new bourgeois class" that had emerged during the course of post-1978 reform in China and that constituted the "class basis" for the "restoration of capitalism" and the "overthrow of proletarian state power" that had taken place in Eastern Europe and the Soviet Union.[2]

Deng vetoed such a course, dictating that China maintain a low profile. It would make a sharp distinction between its "internal" beliefs and its "external" statements. Internally (within the CCP and within China) the CCP would indeed wage resolute struggle against "peaceful evolution" and associated "bourgeois ideologies." Externally, however, China would abstain from ideological debates and would pursue cooperative relations with all countries, regardless of ideological differences—even with Boris Yeltsin's anticommunist Russian Federation and the peaceful evolution–promoting United States. In

April 1990 Deng issued an authoritative twenty-four-character directive that epitomized his cautious and pragmatic approach:

> Observe the situation calmly, stand firm in our position, respond cautiously, conceal our capabilities and await an opportune moment to make a comeback, be good at guarding our weaknesses, never claim leadership.

At the Fourth Plenum in late June 1989 Jiang Zemin was designated Deng's new successor (the third, after Hu Yaobang and Zhao Ziyang). Jiang's situation in CCP élite politics was delicate and would influence his handling of U.S. policy during the 1990s. Retaining Deng Xiaoping's support and goodwill was essential to Jiang's successful succession to Deng as paramount leader. The understanding was that until Deng's death (which occurred in September 1997) Deng would remain paramount leader and could remove or override Jiang whenever he wished. This meant that Jiang needed to demonstrate to Deng his faithful adherence to Deng's cautious, low-profile foreign-policy line. Yet to expand his influence with the People's Liberation Army (PLA), with pro-plan ideologues led by Chen Yun, and with law-and-order hard-liners led by premier Li Peng, Jiang Zemin needed to demonstrate that he was able and willing to wage a tough "struggle" against the United States whenever necessary. Jiang had to prove he was tough enough to stand up to the United States. This, too, was essential to validating Jiang's standing as a nationalist and a true successor to Mao and Deng.

By the early 1990s Jiang positioned himself as heir and continuator of Deng's foreign policy line of maintaining a stable, cooperative relation with the United States. Indeed, correct management of China's relationship with the United States became one of Jiang's key claims to status as Deng's legitimate and true successor, and a key basis for his successful claim to remain the de facto "power behind the curtain" after transferring formal front-rank power to Hu Jintao in late 2002. The high points of Jiang's guiding of China's relationship with the United States included visits by Jiang to the United States in October–November 1997 and again in October 2002 — the latter visit including a visit to president George W. Bush's private ranch in Crawford, Texas. Jiang's 1997 state visit was the first summit meeting since president George H. W. Bush's visit in February 1989 and the first by a PRC leader since president Li Xiannian's visit in 1985. Both of Jiang's visits were carefully choreographed by both sides to symbolize renormalization of PRC–U.S. relations. On the American side, Jiang's 1997 visit reflected a decision for renewed cooperation with China after several years' chastisement by Beijing's exercise of punitive pressure (a matter discussed in a later section). There were also visits by presidents William J. Clinton in June 1998 and George W. Bush in October 2001 and February–March 2002. Each of these exchanges was given extensive publicity in China, with abundant television and newspaper coverage and even special movies, video programs, and photo albums being produced for some of them. The key point made by this publicity was that under Jiang Zemin's guidance, as under that of Deng Xiaoping, China's vital relation with the United States was stable and healthy. The people of China could be reassured that their country's post-1978 advance would continue.

THE UNITED STATES AND CHINA'S DEVELOPMENT DRIVE

As they embarked on China's "second liberation," in 1978, Deng and his comrades were aware of the astounding success of the East Asian countries in industrializing through a combination of export promotion plus absorption of foreign capital and technology. Japan had emerged from the catastrophe of 1945 via this path. Taiwan, South Korea, Singapore, and Hong Kong—"newly industrialized countries" that had reached quite comfortable levels of development by the 1970s—had also followed this path. All of those countries were culturally similar to China. Deng's reformers wondered: could China follow their path? Of course, the developmental success of those other East Asian countries was predicated on U.S. support; all were allies or at least friendly toward the United States. Deng did not shy away from the logic of this conclusion. To replicate the developmental success of the East Asian countries, China too would have to forge and sustain a friendly, cooperative relation with the United States.

One key component of China's post-1978 development drive was export promotion. Following the experience of the earlier East Asian developmental successes, China's reform-minded leaders targeted exports of labor-intensive goods to the rich developed countries. This would generate hard currency revenue that the state could use to import machinery and technologies to meet developmental objectives, while also creating higher-paying jobs that were not funded out of state budgets. To achieve this, access to the vast and highly open markets of the United States was vital.

According to Chinese statistics, the United States consumed about 7.7 percent of all China's exports in 1987. As table 8.1 indicates, the percentage consumed by the United States had risen to 10.1 percent by 1992. By 1996, the year before the onset of the Asian financial crisis, the U.S. share had risen to 17.1 percent. The decline of several Asian economies after 1997 led to diminished Chinese exports to the countries of those affected economies. This further boosted the percentage of total Chinese exports taken by the United States. By 1998 the figure had increased to 20.7 percent and remained nearly unchanged over the next several years.

Table 8.1.   United States as Consumer of Chinese Exports (in U.S. dollars)

Year	Total PRC Exports	Exports to U.S.	U.S. as % of Total
1987	39,440,000,000	3,037,470,000	7.7
1988	47,520,000,000	3,380,030,000	7.1
1989	52,540,000,000	4,409,780,000	8.4
1990	62,090,000,000	5,179,460,000	8.4
1991	n.a.	n.a.	
1992	84,940,000,000	8,593,800,000	10.1
1993	91,740,000,000	16,964,690,000	18.5
1994	121,010,000,000	21,461,030,000	17.8
1995	148,780,000,000	24,711,330,000	16.6
1996	151,050,000,000	26,683,100,000	17.7
1997	182,790,000,000	32,694,800,000	17.9
1998	183,710,000,000	37,975,870,000	20.7
1999	194,930,000,000	41,946,910,000	21.5
2000	249,200,000,000	52,099,220,000	20.9

Sources: *China Statistical Yearbook*, 1998 (Beijing: China Statistical Press, 1998), 628. *China Statistical Yearbook, 1996* (Beijing: China Statistical Press, 1996), 588. *China Statistical Yearbook, 1999* (Beijing: China Statistical Press, 1999), 585. *China Statistical Yearbook, 1991* (Beijing: China Statistical Press, 1991), 622. *China Statistical Yearbook, 1989* (Beijing: China Statistical Press, 1989), 638. *Yearbook of China's Foreign Economic Relations and Trade, 1994,* 474.

In sum, 21 percent of a country's total exports is a hefty share. The real share may however be considerably more. China does not count as exports to the United States Chinese goods exported to Hong Kong that are then reexported to the United States. The U.S. government does. When U.S. data for imports into the United States from China is used, as is done in table 8.2, the result indicates that in 2000 the United States consumed a huge 40.1 percent of Chinese exports—a staggering amount.

It is important to note that markets for exports are far more difficult to acquire than alternate sources of imports. There are many willing suppliers of most industrial equipment and technologies (excluding military-sensitive items) in France, Germany, Sweden, Japan, Italy, and Canada. But were China to lose its rich export markets in the United States, no other country, or even all other countries collectively, could soak up more than a small portion of the Chinese goods excluded from U.S. markets. While other countries might serve as alternatives to the United States as suppliers of Chinese imports of technology, they simply could not replace the United States in terms of purchase of Chinese exports. Were China to lose U.S. markets for its exports, tens of thousands of factories all along the China coast would shut down; China's economy be thrown into severe recession; and the economic development drive sustained since 1978 would suffer a severe setback.

A number of measures—all deriving from U.S. goodwill and support for China's economic development drive—facilitated the expansion of China's

Table 8.2. U.S. Consumption of Chinese Exports, 2000: United States versus PRC

	Total PRC Exports	Exports to U.S.	U.S. as % of Total
PRC Data	$249,202,550,000	$52,099,220,000	20.90%
U.S. Data		$100,018,400,000	40.10%

Sources: *China Statistical Yearbook, 2001* (Beijing: China Statistical Press, 2001), 591–93. U.S. Bureau of Census, at www.census.gov/foreign-trade/alance/c5700.html (accessed January 29, 2003).

exports to the United States. The establishment of normal diplomatic relations in 1979 led to the swift creation of legal and institutional bases for normal trade relations. In 1979 the United States granted China most-favored-nation (MFN) status. This critical move delinked treatment of China from treatment of the Soviet Union (which *never* won MFN status from the United States) and opened the way for major increases in Chinese exports to the United States. Without MFN status, Chinese goods would have faced prohibitively high tariffs. Then in 1980 and 1983 Beijing persuaded Washington to grant generous textile quotas. In effect, Washington agreed to allow China's cotton textile exports to expand at the expense of traditional suppliers of the U.S. market: Hong Kong and Taiwan. In 1980 China's cotton textile exports to the United States were 5 percent of Hong Kong's cotton textile exports to the United States and 71 percent of Taiwan's. By 1987 they were 7 percent above Hong Kong's and 6.8 times those of Taiwan.[3] China's textile export industry, an industry that played a leading role in the industrialization of many countries, was allowed to occupy the crucial U.S. market. Traditional East Asian suppliers were forced to move up the value-added ladder. The steady expansion of bilateral contacts at all levels with normalization and opening, the attraction of foreign investment (much of which was export oriented), and the successful negotiation of World Trade Organization (WTO) entry in 2001 all contributed to the expansion of Sino-American trade. The key point here is that the willingness of the U.S. government to open U.S. markets to China was a major factor allowing China's exports to grow so rapidly in the twenty-four years between 1978 and 2002. Conversely, were that goodwill to be replaced by ill will, China's exports could collapse.

After 1982 China's exports to the United States were growing much more rapidly than China's imports from the United States. This produced a very large surplus for China. Due to differing statistical methods, the two governments disagree on the size of that trade imbalance. They both agree, however, that it is large and growing. Were protectionist sentiment to mount in Washington, leading to measures limiting China's ballooning exports to the United States, China's development drive could be hobbled.

In 1994 Beijing and Washington set up a bilateral trade-statistics expert working group to reconcile the widely disparate trade statistics. The group, composed on the U.S. side of experts from the Census Bureau of the Department of Commerce, spent more than a year comparing 1992 and 1993 statistical data from China, the United States, and Hong Kong. The group issued its report in October 1995.[4] The report concluded that the major cause of the discrepancy in trade figures derived from trade transshipped by intermediaries, especially via Hong Kong, constituted two-thirds of trade discrepancy between the United States and the PRC. China often did not know the final destination of goods shipped to Hong Kong and thus recorded that area as their final destination. The United States, however, attributed to China the total value of all China-origin goods, even though there was often a substantial markup in value in Hong Kong.

Two years later, in March 1997, China's State Council issued a white paper on the trade imbalance.[5] That white paper used a perhaps slanted interpretation of the working group report to bolster the Chinese case. The white paper argued that U.S. figures overstated the trade imbalance by as much as 70 percent. First, U.S. data counted as PRC exports those which had value added in and were shipped from Hong Kong. Second, U.S. data understated U.S. exports to China by excluding a hefty portion of U.S. goods exported to Hong Kong and then reexported to China. Third, since U.S. exports, unlike imports, are not taxed by the U.S. government, U.S. statistics do not catch all exports to China. The white paper also argued that a major cause of the trade imbalance was U.S. restrictions of technology exports to China—a matter discussed shorty.

The objective relative merits of the two sides of the trade imbalance issue are not our prime concern here. Many U.S. elected officials and legislators, business leaders, and labor union leaders are convinced that multiple nontariff barriers (such as an undervalued currency) form the major reason for China's limited purchases of American goods and services. Given these beliefs, the trade imbalance rouses considerable concern and anger in the United States. Were that anger and concern to coalesce into the adoption of a managed-trade strategy, China's export growth and generation of foreign currency would suffer a severe setback.

Drawing on U.S. and Western capital was still another component of China's post-1978 development effort. The architects of that effort concluded that China was a capital-poor but resource-rich country. The shortage of capital had constituted, they believed, a critical bottleneck on China's earlier development efforts. The solution was to tap global capital markets, combining foreign capital with Chinese land, labor, and materials, thus breaking the bottleneck and producing more rapid development.

Throughout the post-1978 period, the United States was consistently one of the top suppliers of foreign investment to China. As indicated by table 8.3, between 1978 and the end of 1982, the United States supplied a whopping 39.1

Table 8.3.   U.S. Role as Supplier of Direct Foreign Investment for China

Period	1978-1982	1988	1996	2000
U.S. as % of Total FDI	39.10%	7.40%	8.30%	10.80%
U.S. Ranking as Investor	2	3	4	2
Countries Outranking U.S.	Hong Kong	Hong Kong	Hong Kong	Hong Kong
		Japan	Japan	
			Taiwan	

Sources: *Almanac of China's Foreign Economic Relations and Trade, 1997–1998,* 686–89. *China Statistical Yearbook, 2001* (Beijing: China Statistical Press, 2001), 604–6. *China Statistical Yearbook, 1999* (Beijing: China Statistical Press, 1999), 555.

percent of all China's foreign capital, ranking second only to Hong Kong, which supplied 44.3 percent of all foreign capital during that period. The absolute amounts invested during those years were not large—$55 million for the United States and $62 million for Hong Kong—but they did play a vital role in China's initial marketization. During the 1980s, as businesses from other countries invested in China, the percentage supplied to the United States fell to 7.4 in 1988. The U.S. role remained fairly stable over the next decade, rising to 8.3 percent in 1996 and 10.8 percent in 2000. By the latter year, the Virgin Islands had emerged as the third-largest supplier of foreign investment in China, ranking well ahead of Japan and not too far behind the United States in that regard. A substantial proportion of Virgin Islands investment is actually U.S. capital seeking tax relief. This conduit could easily be shut by U.S. legislation were Sino-U.S. relations to become hostile.

Development of China's human capital is every bit as important as augmentation of physical capital. In this regard, access to U.S. higher education is another important input for China's development drive. Table 8.4 compares official Chinese statistics on "personnel of all sorts going abroad for study" (*gelei chuguo liuxue renyuan*) with the number of PRC students enrolled at U.S. universities and colleges as reported by those schools.[6] While the two data sets are not strictly comparable (the Chinese data are for calendar years and the U.S. data are for academic years), the two sets suffice to make clear the extremely important role of U.S. universities in educating China's higher-level human capital. After a modest beginning in 1979, Chinese enrollment at U.S. universities began to climb rapidly, reaching a peak in 1991. In the 1991–1992 academic year, 14.8 times as many Chinese were studying at U.S. universities and colleges, as were listed as "going abroad" by the Chinese government in 1991. In the seven years after that high point, the role of the United States declined, yet the yearly average of Chinese who were studying at U.S. universities and colleges was still 3.15 times as many, as counted as "going abroad" by the Chinese government.

Table 8.4.   The Role of the United States in China's Overseas Higher Education Effort

Years	Number of PRC Students Sent Abroad[a] (gelei chuguo liuxue renyuan)	Number of PRC Students Studying in the U.S.[b]	Number Studying in U.S. as % of All Students Sent Abroad
1978	860	28	3
1979	1,777	1,000	56
1980	2,124	2,770	130
1981	2,922	4,350	149
1982	2,326	6,230	268
1983	2,633	8,140	309
1984	3,073	10,100	329
1985	4,888	13,980	286
1986	4,676	20,030	428
1987	4,703	25,170	535
1988	3,786	29,040	767
1989	3,329	33,390	1000
1990	2,950	39,600	1342
1991	2,900	42,940	1481
1992	6,540	45,126	690
1993	10,742	44,139	411
1994	19,071	39,403	207
1995	20,381	39,613	194
1996	20,905	42,503	203
1997	22,410	46,958	210
1998	17,622	51,001	289

[a] *Comprehensive Statistical Data and Materials on 50 Years of New China* (Beijing: China Statistics Press, 1999), 99.
[b] Institute of International Education (IIE), at Opendoors.iienetwork.org. Data for the years 1978–1992 were supplied by IIE by special arrangement. IIE data are for academic years rather than calender years.

Other countries have universities, of course, but none combines the large enrollments, degree of openness to foreign students, and the high level of financial support available to foreign students provided by universities and colleges in the United States. There is also the consideration that in many areas of science, engineering, medicine, and business—areas favored by most Chinese students going abroad—the United States is a world leader. Largely for these reasons, the United States has been the overwhelmingly favored destination for Chinese seeking advanced training abroad, although the Chinese preference for the United States diminished somewhat with the introduction of tougher U.S. visa requirements following the September 11, 2001, attacks on the United States.

Were China to lose this access because of a deterioration of Sino-American relations, the result would not be as immediate as loss of U.S. investment or merchandise trade markets. Over the longer run, however, the loss of this source of highly trained human capital would sap China's continued growth. Even though a majority of these Chinese students do not return to China when their studies are finished, those that do provide a valuable source of human capital. Moreover, those who opt to remain in the United States often serve as bridges between China and the United States, promoting collaborative research or business operations.

Access to U.S. and global technology is yet another important input to China's development drive. During the ambitious industrialization drives of the 1950s and 1960s, China expanded production by building more factories and machines, employing more workers, and pumping more energy and raw materials into production—an approach known as *extensive development*. There were important improvements in productivity, as Soviet and East European machinery was introduced, then copied, and those Chinese copies disseminated across broad swaths of China's economy. Improvements in factor productivity and efficiency due to better technology soon stagnated, however, and were in any case inadequate to compensate for the ravenous consumption of inputs of all sorts by China's planned industry. Under a planned economy, managers simply had too few incentives to use resources efficiently and had too many incentives to squander them. Moreover, as the size of the industrial sector expanded, achieving desired increments of growth required ever-greater input, which imposed severe, ever-greater constraints. Table 8.5 illustrates China's low factor productivity at the end of the Mao era, when Deng set China in a new direction. If China had continued to pursue extensive development, it would have had to choose between expansion of industry and improvements in the lives of the Chinese people via greater investment in consumer goods and infrastructure. Deng and his reform comrades believed that unless the people's standards of living were quickly and substantially improved, there would be rebellion or a deepening apathy. Deng was unwilling to countenance a slowdown of industrial development, yet he believed that major improvements in standards of living were absolutely vital for political stability. Broad import and absorption of advanced foreign technology leading to improvements in factor productivity, a pathway known as *intensive development,* offered a way to achieve both objectives.

China's technology imports have boomed since 1978, greatly improving productivity. Table 8.6 shows China's technology imports as a percentage of total imports. These data indicate that imports of machinery and equipment (a customs category that captures most technology imports) constituted a generally larger percentage of total imports over the course of the post-1978 period. Industrial machinery and transportation equipment expand a nation's production and distribution base. An ability to import more of these relative to other commodities is an accurate indicator of a country's industrialization. It means

Table 8.5. Factor Productivity in China's State-owned Industry Circa 1978

Measure	1952	1957	1978
Net Output	37.6	100	673.3
Labor Input	68.2	100	406.6
Capital Input	44.3	100	948.7
Labor Productivity	55.1	100	165.6
Capital Productivity	84.9	100	71
Total Factor Productivity	69.8	100	89.6

Source: World Bank, *China: Long-Term Development Issues and Options* (Baltimore: Johns Hopkins University Press, 1985), 111.

that the nation's production capacity is expanding. Moreover, since imported machinery and equipment are typically superior to domestically available equipment—especially in China's current state of development—additions of foreign machinery equipment typically yield increases in productivity. For purposes of this chapter, the important point is that the PRC has been quite successful in acquiring foreign technology and that persuading Washington to relax export controls, while exploiting differences between the United States and Europe, has formed important underpinnings of that success.

As noted earlier, the United States was not the only supplier of advanced industrial technologies. For most technologies, there are global markets based purely on pursuit of profit. Yet during the Cold War, the United States exerted great influence over the technology sales of other members of the Western alliance system, which included most of the advanced industrial states of Europe. During the Cold War, the United States, as leader of the Western alliance system, presided over the creation of an alliance-wide system restricting the transfer of technologies to communist countries. This technology-control system, known as the Control Committee (COCOM), was never leak-proof, but it was generally quite effective. In fact, it greatly restricted the transfer of Western technology to the Soviet Union, the PRC, and other communist countries. Restrictions imposed on China under this regime were much more severe than those for the Soviet Union—a function largely of the Korean and Vietnam wars. Abolishing the 1972 "China differential" (which had placed stricter controls on China than on the Soviet Union) and placing it in the same category as the Soviet Union marked a major advance in the U.S. policy of rapprochement with China.

Once again China's strategic partnership with the United States against the Soviet Union in the late 1970s and early 1980s paid off. In 1980 China was decoupled from the Soviet Union and placed in a special one-country COCOM category. In the same year Washington authorized sale of dual-use goods to China (i.e., those having civilian and military uses). In 1983 the PRC was des-

Table 8.6.   China's Imports of Machinery and Equipment (M/E)

Year	M&E Imports (US$ 100 millions)	Total Imports (US$ 100 millions)	M&E as % of Total
1978	19.03	109.9	17.5
1979	39.57	156.7	25.5
1980	51.19	200.2	25.6
1981	58.66	220.2	26.6
1982	32.04	192.9	10.9
1983	39.88	213.9	18.6
1984	72.45	274.1	26.4
1985	162.39	422.5	38.4
1986	167.81	429.1	39.1
1987	146.07	432.1	33.8
1988	166.97	552.7	30.2
1989	182.07	591.4	30.8
1990	168.45	533.5	31.6
1991	196.01	637.9	30.7
1992	313.12	805.9	38.9
1993	450.23	1039.6	43.3
1994	514.67	1156.1	44.5
1995	526.42	1320.8	39.9
1996	547.63	1388.3	39.4
1997	527.74	1423.7	37.1
1998	567.86	1401.7	40.5
1999	694.53	1656.9	41.9
2000	919.31	2250.9	40.8

Sources: *Comprehensive Statistical Data and Materials on 50 Years of New China* (Beijing: China Statistics Press, 1999), 60, 62. *China Statistical Yearbook, 2001* (Beijing: China Statistical Press, 2001), 588. *Zhongguo duiwai jingji maoyi nianjian* (Beijing: Zhongguo zhanwang chubanshe, 1989), 309.

ignated as a "friendly, nonallied country" under COCOM regulations. Further moves to expand technology exports to China came in 1985, when the Western countries simplified approval procedures governing technology exports to China. The final move came in March 1994, when the Clinton administration abolished COCOM, a move that roused considerable criticism by critics in the U.S. Congress who charged that this allowed China to acquire technologies that could be used to substantially enhance PLA military capabilities.

With the disappearance of the Soviet threat to Western Europe, European countries became much less willing to follow Washington's lead on technology controls toward China. The simple fact is that these countries did not face the prospect of possible military conflict with China via a responsibility to protect Taiwan and other East Asian countries. Because of its security treaties and roles in the Western Pacific, the United States *does* face the real possibility of military conflict with China, and thus it has an interest in maintaining a distinct qualitative edge over the PLA in that region. The Western European countries simply did not share this interest, though they were to some degree sympathetic of the concerns of their U.S. ally. The outcome was that Western European capitals were willing to accept formal Chinese guarantees promising the nonmilitary diversion of advanced technologies. The United States, however, was unwilling to rely primarily on Chinese promises and insisted on more elaborate verification procedures: prelicensing inspection of the site where the technology was to be used, inspections after the unloading of the imported goods, round-the-clock surveillance, and uncontested random checks.[7] These measures were difficult for China to accept, in the understated words of China's 1997 white paper on Sino-U.S. trade.

Beijing turned to European suppliers for advanced technologies. In consequence, as Beijing's 1997 white paper pointed out, "the European Union member countries are not only free of any trade deficit, but have enjoyed an average annual trade surplus worth several billion U.S. dollars with China. This comparison between [the] EU and the United States speaks aloud on the different effects on bilateral trade balance brought [about] by different export policies toward China." The way to eliminate the Sino-U.S. trade imbalance, Beijing's 1997 white paper said, was "to relax or even cancel the current discriminatory export control policies against China so as to usher in a healthy and balanced Sino-U.S. trade relationship." "China needs to import advanced machine tools, thus providing good trade opportunities for U.S. manufacturers. But the U.S. government's strict export control has forestalled normal business with China." Nuclear energy technology, integrated circuits, and program-controlled switching boards are other blocked technologies specified by the 1997 white paper. "It makes no sense for the United States to play up trade deficits against China on the one hand, and continue its export control on the other."

Implicit in Beijing's position is the proposition that the United States should abandon efforts to restrict the growth of Chinese military capabilities. This implies, further, that the United States should abandon any idea of intervention in a cross–Taiwan Strait conflict. Another somewhat more remote implication is that the United States will need to accept that, in the fullness of time, Chinese military capabilities in the East Asian and Western Pacific regions will grow to exceed those of the United States. The United States should accept this as natural and inevitable and thus accommodate itself to it.

There is a close relation between China's efforts to develop its national power on the one hand and acquire foreign technology, expand exports, and attract foreign investment on the other. Militarily, quality of technology is a major determinant of combat effectiveness. This was a lesson taught repeatedly to China during its "century of national humiliation," when smaller but technologically superior foreign military forces inflicted painful defeats on larger but technologically inferior Chinese forces. China's leaders from Chiang Kai-shek to Mao Zedong tried to compensate in various ways for this technological inferiority, and these efforts were not without some success. Nevertheless, fighting from a position of technological inferiority was not the preferred solution. China's leaders, or at least those who rallied around Deng Xiaoping, favored catching up with, or better yet technologically surpassing, powers who were hostile or potentially hostile to China. This was incorporated into the PLA war-fighting doctrine of waging victorious partial wars under high-tech conditions, a doctrine adopted in the mid-1980s.[8] A country's level of economic development also determines its level of wealth, which in turn has a direct relation to that country's ability to mobilize resources to influence events abroad. A wealthier country is more able than a nonwealthy country to pay for such instruments of national influence as foreign aid, diplomatic activity, collection of foreign intelligence, cultural activities designed to win friends and influence people, and military instruments of national power. A wealthier country also offers a more attractive model to other countries.

In sum, the success of the developmental drive launched by Deng Xiaoping and his followers in 1978 has been highly successful and offers the prospect of raising the Chinese people to a midlevel of prosperity by the middle of the twenty-first century. It offers the prospect of reestablishing China to its long-lost but rightfully deserved position of high international status, finally blotting out the "century of national humiliation" that began with the Opium War in 1839. To return to the proper topic of this chapter, achieving this requires maintaining friendly, cooperative relations with the United States.

THE STRATEGIC PROBLEM OF MITIGATING CHINA'S DEPENDENCY ON THE UNITED STATES

The large role played by the United States—and by United States–influenced markets, capital, technology, and higher education in China's post-1978 development drive—gave Washington potentially great leverage over Beijing. As U.S. president William Clinton explained repeatedly during 1993 while making the case for his policy of linking China's continued enjoyment of most-favored-nation status and China's human rights conditions, China then had an annual $15 billion trade surplus with the United States making its stake in trade with the United States much larger than the American stake in trade with China.[9] Or again, as the prominent American academic Chalmers Johnson wrote a few years later while arguing for the United States to adopt a policy of "managed trade" that would link U.S. sales on PRC markets to PRC sales on U.S. markets, "The United States potentially has a very strong

hand when it comes to dealing with China. Precisely because the United
States purchases so much of what China produces, even a partial loss of access to the American consumer market would be a crushing blow to Chinese
economic expansion."[10] Beijing's strategic problem with the United States
since 1989 has been preventing Washington from using its economic leverage with Beijing.

The long-run solution to China's strategic vulnerability vis-à-vis the United
States is the diminution of the relative economic and political role of the
United States in the world. As other centers of economic power (Europe,
Japan, Russia, perhaps South East Asia and China itself) grow relative to the
United States, and as the influence of the United States over those other centers of economic power declines, China will have more alternatives to cooperation with the United States. Such a desirable future state, in which China
will be less vulnerable to the United States, is called a *multipolarity* by Chinese international affairs analysts. Multipolarity was lauded throughout the
Deng era, especially after 1989, as the desirable goal for the evolution of the
international order.

A key problem for Beijing is that events did not move the global order in
the direction of multipolarity but in fact toward ever-greater American domination. The collapse of the Soviet Union and the dramatic U.S. military victory over Iraq in 1991; the continuation of the NATO alliance and the expansion of that alliance into Eastern Europe; the NATO military intervention in
the Balkans; and by the mid-1990s, the economic stagnation of Japan and Europe compared with continued U.S. economic growth—all pointed toward a
greater, not a weaker, degree of unipolarity. The aspect of growing U.S. dominance that formed the greatest concern to China's leaders was China's deepening dependence on U.S. markets and capital. As the analysis in the first section of this chapter indicates, China's dependency on U.S. markets and capital
increased as Deng's program of opening and reform advanced. Moreover, as
foreign-linked and foreign-invested Chinese enterprises grew with reform
and thus became a larger portion of China's economy, and as more autarkic
state-owned enterprises withered, securing access to foreign markets became
ever more important for China's continuing economic prosperity.

Equally grievous for Beijing was the end to the division of Europe in 1989
and the collapse of the Soviet Union in 1991 that combined with the upheaval
in China in 1989 to destroy the anti-Soviet strategic basis for Sino–United
States cooperation. The Soviet challenge had made U.S. leaders and the public more willing to overlook China's human rights shortcomings. After the
1989–1991 period, this was no longer the case. Human rights began to weigh
more heavily with Americans.[11] About the same time, Taiwan was undergoing a profound but peaceful political revolution, transforming the island

polity of twenty-three million people into a genuine and vibrant liberal democracy. Democratic Taiwan increasingly contrasted with the sternly repressive order in the PRC. The United States' support for China's post-1978 development drive was partially predicated on belief that such support would make China more free, pluralistic, governed by rule of law, and ultimately democratic. These beliefs may have been a way of making U.S. moral beliefs congruent with U.S. economic interests, but they were nonetheless important U.S. beliefs. When the dramatic repressive actions by the PRC government in 1989 suggested that this core U.S. expectation might be wrong, U.S. leaders, especially in Congress, were sometimes dismayed and thus inclined to ratchet down U.S. support for China's development. Critics declared that making a repressive dictatorship stronger served neither the interests of the United States nor the Chinese people.

Human rights, U.S. access to China's markets, and Taiwan became, after 1989, the major areas in which Washington pressured Beijing and, consequently, areas in which Beijing had to countervail U.S. pressure. Regarding human rights, U.S. policy frequently pressed China's CCP rulers to conform—on pain of loss of U.S. support—to what Washington believed were international norms regarding toleration of political dissent, freedom of labor-union organization, religious freedom, and rights of ethnic minorities. The boldest, most sweeping instance of this type of U.S. pressure came during William Clinton's first two years as president, when he embraced congressional efforts to link continued Chinese enjoyment of most-favored-nation status to fundamental improvements in China's human rights record.

As for U.S. economic demands, as China's trade surplus with the United States ballooned in the 1990s (surpassing Japan's in 1996) access for U.S. goods, services, and capital to China's markets became an increasingly difficult area of pressure and Chinese counterpressure. From the standpoint of many of China's leaders, U.S. human rights demands and economic pressures threatened the CCP's control over China's domestic affairs. Many of these hard-line leaders suspected that such an outcome was precisely the intent of the United States. They wondered, was Washington trying to collapse and fragment the PRC state as it had so successfully done to the Soviet Union?

Regarding Taiwan, a common U.S. belief was that China's need for U.S. support would force Beijing to acquiesce to upgrading the United States–Taiwan relationship. For example, in 1981 and 1982 during the early Reagan administration, secretary of state Alexander Haig attempted to use the prospect of the United States' transferring key military-related dual-use technologies to China to secure Chinese acquiescence to enhanced U.S. arms sales to Taiwan. A decade later, as Congress began to press the Clinton administration in 1994 and 1995 to upgrade relations with Taiwan, the idea that Chinese dependency on

U.S. markets would lead China to acquiesce to unpalatable U.S. moves played a key role inspiring congressional moves.[12] The expanded arms sales of the second Bush administration and the further elevation of United States–Taiwan ties during 2001 through 2004 were once again predicated, though to a lesser degree, on the belief that Beijing's reaction would be constrained by China's ultimate need for U.S. goodwill.

Beijing did not, of course, reject any and all of Washington's demands. Indeed, in many areas (e.g., protection of intellectual property rights, greater access to China's markets) Beijing accepted some, or even most, of U.S. demands. China's ultimate acceptance of U.S. demands regarding the terms of its entry into the WTO in 2001 represented a striking Chinese accession to the United States, an accession both sides chose to understate to avoid embarrassing China's reformers before domestic hard-line critics. In the area of human rights, Beijing frequently made well-timed and sometimes well-negotiated marginal but symbolic concessions to the United States. But what concerns us here is the area of U.S. demands that were unacceptable to Beijing and the means used by Beijing to foil those demands.

CHINESE INSTRUMENTS OF LEVERAGE WITH THE UNITED STATES: THE "CARROTS"

China uses positive rewards, or inducements, and negative coercive sanctions to influence U.S. policy—in other words, "carrots" and "sticks." Carrots demonstrate to Washington the benefits of cooperation with China, whereas sticks make clear the potential costs of noncooperation and confrontation with China. Let's begin with the carrots.

One positive inducement is cooperation with Washington in dealing with regional and global issues. Through such cooperation Beijing demonstrates to Washington that strong ties with China help the United States get things done and serve U.S. interests. Willingness to cooperate with the United States also demonstrates that China is not necessarily hostile to the United States and that the United States need not fear China's growing power.

Undoing Iraq's seizure of Kuwait in 1990 and 1991 was the first major post-1989 instance of Chinese cooperation with the United States. Starting with the first UN Security Council resolution in August 1990, China supported all eleven resolutions condemning Iraq's invasion of Kuwait, implementing an embargo of Iraq until it withdrew from Kuwait, nullifying the annexation of Kuwait, calling on UN members to supply naval vessels to enforce the embargo, and banning air traffic with Iraq. On resolution 678 in November 1990—the one authorizing the use of force against Iraq—Beijing abstained, after tough bargaining with Washington over the lifting of post–June 1989 U.S. sanctions against China. After Iraq accepted the UN's cease-fire terms, China agreed to dispatch a group of soldiers to help oversee implementation of those terms.

In 1991 China again worked with the United States and through the United Nations to end the civil war in Cambodia, disarm and disband the murderous Khmer Rouge, hold open elections, and establish a stable moderate government in Cambodia. Since the Khmer Rouge commanded the largest nongovernment armed force in Cambodia, and since China had long been the Khmer Rouge's only foreign supporter, pressure from Beijing played a crucial role in persuading the Khmer Rouge to accept a UN-sponsored peace accord in October 1991. China then dispatched a contingent of eight hundred military engineers as part of the UN's peacekeeping force that presided over elections in Cambodia, implementation of a new constitution, and, in September 1993, inauguration of a government headed by restored Prince Sihanouk.

During the crises over North Korea's nuclear weapons program in 1994 and 2003 to 2004, Beijing worked in parallel with Washington, although not nearly as close as it had on other regional problems. The first crisis began in mid-1994, when North Korea disclosed its intent to begin refueling its Yongbyong nuclear reactor and withdraw from the International Atomic Energy Agency. Beijing was resolutely opposed to the nuclearization of the Korean Peninsula, and it conveyed this sentiment privately to North Korea's leaders while Washington mobilized support in the United Nations for an embargo. Beijing was strongly opposed to the use of United States–proposed economic sanctions against North Korea, but it did not take up the cause of opposition to U.S. efforts in the Security Council. The exact content of Beijing's communications to North Korea is still not clear, but U.S. leaders believed that Beijing had played a positive, constructive role in persuading North Korea to suspend its nuclear effort. But Beijing also made clear that it would not accept U.S. coercion, especially military coercion, of small friendly neighbors of China. The United States' use of military means against countries far away from China was one thing; its targeting of China's friendly neighbors was quite another.

The second round of the Korean crisis began in October 2002, when the Bush administration presented evidence that North Korea, by processing uranium, had violated the 1994 Agreed Framework. Pyongyang responded by firing up a previously dormant five-megawatt nuclear plant, thereby producing more plutonium for reprocessing. Pyongyang also announced (on January 10, 2003) its immediate withdrawal from the Nuclear Nonproliferation Treaty, becoming the first nation ever to withdraw from that treaty. Pyongyang simultaneously cancelled all inspection arrangements with the International Atomic Energy Agency.[13]

Securing China's cooperation in pressuring North Korea to abandon its nuclear weapons programs was a major part of the Bush administration's response to Pyongyang's actions. The United States had periodically intervened in the past to help keep Japan, Taiwan, and South Korea from developing nuclear weapons; now it was China's turn to act likewise, U.S. representatives urged China.[14] Moreover, the consequences of North Korean nuclearization would adversely affect China's own interests, quite possibly leading to Japan's, South Korea's, and even Taiwan's nuclear weaponization—a development that would leave China almost completely surrounded by nuclear weapons states (following the 1998 Indian and Pakistani nuclearization).

U.S. representatives believed that Beijing had substantial leverage with Pyongyang, which it could use if it so chose. By 2002 China provided North Korea with an average annual assistance of $1.3 billion. This was one-third of China's total foreign aid expenditures.[15] Moreover, Chinese–North Korean trade expanded rapidly in 2002. During the year, two-way trade increased 30 percent, with Chinese exports of grain and vegetables doubling. China also supplied 70 percent of North Korea's petroleum.[16] Chinese oil met one-third of all North Korea's energy needs, while Chinese grain accounted for one-half of North Korea's grain requirements.[17] Washington believed that because no other country had such substantial leverage with Pyongyang, Beijing should use that leverage to push Kim Jong Il to abandon his nuclear weapons programs via the modality of multilateral talks involving both Koreas plus China, Japan, Russia, and the United States.

In October 2002, assistant secretary of state James Kelly made Beijing the first stop on a multination tour of Asia and Europe. Kelly urged China to join Japan, South Korea, and the United States in pressuring Pyongyang. "North Korea needs to feel the pressure across the board, from the people who have supported it in the past and those they want to improve relations with in the future," said a senior administration official of Kelly's talks in Beijing.[18] Bush further lobbied Jiang Zemin on Korea during their meeting at Bush's Crawford, Texas, ranch in October 2002. Jiang would only proclaim his support for a nonnuclear Korea and promise to work with the United States, while avoiding any commitment to participate in economic sanctions against North Korea and rejecting the notion that China had much influence over Pyongyang.[19] Bush again lobbied Jiang via telephone in early February 2003. Bush told Jiang that it was the "joint responsibility" of China and the United States to make the Korean Peninsula nuclear-free, a goal they had agreed on when they met at Crawford the previous October.[20] Privately, administration officials complained that Beijing should do more to pressure Pyongyang.

Beijing initially rejected United States' urging. Resorting to economic sanctions violated long-standing Chinese taboos for dealing with North Korea. Beijing instead merely reiterated its "principled" support for a nonnuclear Korea while endorsing Pyongyang's demand for purely bilateral United States–North Korean talks. As a spokesman of China's foreign ministry said early in 2003, "There's a saying in Chinese: 'a lock can only be opened by one key.' I think that as long as the relevant sides feel that the resumption of direct dialogue between the United States and North Korea is the crux of the matter, then I think all concerned parties should continue to make efforts to push them to resume talks."[21] A more straightforward statement of Chinese thinking had been given by the blunt-speaking premier Zhu Rongji in April 1999: "North Korea is a sovereign state, so it is none of our business whether North Korea develops a missile or whether it researches and develops nuclear weapons."[22]

In March 2003 Beijing shifted course and began active cooperation with Washington. In early March the pipeline carrying Chinese oil to North Korea closed down for three consecutive days. Technical problems were given as the reason for the closure, but the move was widely interpreted as a strong Chinese signal to Pyongyang that continued provocations with its nuclear weapons program could lead to a reduction of Chinese economic support.[23] About the same time that the oil pipeline was closed, Beijing sent its most senior diplomat, Qian Qichen, to Pyongyang to deliver the message that North Korea had to stop its gratuitous provocations and start talking to Washington.[24] Shortly afterward, Beijing for the first time publicly, if only implicitly, criticized North Korea for reneging on the 1994 Agreed Framework. China supported the denuclearization of the Korean Peninsula according to the principles set out in the Agreed Framework, which "should be maintained," a foreign ministry spokeswoman said. "We believe that the relevant parties should do more that may help restore dialogue at an early date."[25] As Brent Scowcroft wrote in the *New York Times*, the "Chinese role has changed. In response to United States requests, China has gone from its more familiar posture of sitting on the sidelines . . . to playing an active and constructive role."[26]

In South Asia as well, Beijing has cooperated with the United States. In that region China used its considerable influence with Pakistan, and its far lesser influence with India, in tandem with the United States to avert a major India–Pakistan war. In 1990 during an India–Pakistan confrontation precipitated by Pakistani support for insurgents in India's Punjab state, and again in 1999 during a confrontation precipitated by seizure of a strategic mountaintop at Kargil by Pakistani infiltrators, Beijing and Washington worked in parallel to avert an India–Pakistan war. During the 1999 confrontation—when first the Pakistani foreign minister and then the prime minister visited Beijing during the Kargil crisis in June—foreign minister Tang Jiaxuan, premier Zhu Rongji, and president Jiang Zemin all urged them to reduce tension with India, end military conflict, and seek to resolve the Kashmir issue through talks.[27] Washington undertook similar efforts. Beijing and Washington coordinated their approaches to Islamabad and New Delhi to persuade the two South Asian powers to pull back from the brink of war.[28] During the India–Pakistan confrontation of 2002 (following a terrorist attack on the Indian parliament) China once again played a similar, moderating role. During the 2000 confrontation, Sino–United States cooperation was far less close than in the two earlier cases, but this was due not to China's decisions but to a U.S. decision to distance itself from China for the sake of improved India–United States relations.

In none of these instances was Beijing's only objective, or even necessarily its most important objective, to curry American appreciation of China. Beijing desired peace and stability in the Persian Gulf, South East Asia, Korean Peninsula, and South Asia for reasons other than those having to do with currying U.S. goodwill. But in each case the desire to cooperate with Washington, thereby proving China's merit as a partner and stabilizing China's relation with the United States, was a significant element of Beijing's reasoning.

Beijing slowly but steadily became a partner of the United States in upholding the global nuclear nonproliferation regime. In 1990 China attended, for the first time, a review conference of the Non-Proliferation Treaty (NPT), held every five years to review the treaty's performance. Two years later, China signed the NPT, which had first come into effect in 1970. In 1995, when the NPT review and extension conference met to consider the expiration of its twenty-five-year term, China participated actively.[29] It worked with Washington to renew and extend the NPT and to secure adherence of several major powers that remained outside the NPT (e.g., India, Pakistan, and Israel). At the United States' prompting, China issued in April 1995 a national statement on security assurances designed to persuade threshold nuclear weapons states to accede to the NPT.[30] Beijing then joined with the United States and other permanent UN Security Council members to issue resolution 984, extending a degree of UN protection to nonnuclear power states adhering to the NPT. As negotiation of a Comprehensive Test Ban Treaty (CTBT) gained momentum in 1996, China eventually came on board. Under U.S. pressure, Beijing dropped its initial insistence that nuclear weapons states (under the NPT) be allowed to continue "peaceful" tests under the proposed CTBT. China ceased nuclear testing and in September 1996 signed the treaty.[31] During 1997 and continuing into the aftermath of India's nuclear tests in May 1998, Beijing continued cooperating with Washington in dealing with South Asian proliferation issues. Even after Washington backed away from cooperation with China on South Asian issues for the sake of improved United States–Indian relations—a development many in China saw as a U.S. double-cross and a manifestation of U.S. containment—Beijing continued to work with Washington on nonproliferation issues.[32] In 2002 China finally published, and promised to begin enforcing, an export-control list for missiles and related technologies and materials. This was something Washington had long urged China to do. There were, however, significant differences between China's export-control guidelines and those of United States–sponsored missile technology control regulations.[33] Those loopholes *might* allow China to continue supporting its favored clients' missile-development programs.

Once again, the reasons for China's deepening adherence to the global nonproliferation regime cannot be reduced entirely to a desire to cooperate with Washington. But again that motivation was present and significant. Some Chinese analysts identified nuclear nonproliferation as an especially promising area for Sino-U.S. cooperation. Viewed differently, if Beijing had refused to cooperate with Washington on global nonproliferation issues, it could have seriously undermined the broadly cooperative Sino-American relation vital to China's development.

Of course, Beijing did not always cooperate with the United States. On many issues Beijing hewed to a line independent of, or even in conflict with, the United States. By the mid-1990s, for example, Beijing began siding with France and Russia against U.S. efforts at the UN to continue strict enforcement of the terms of the 1991 cease-fire with Iraq. Differences between Beijing and Washington also widened on the North Korean nuclear issue. And in South Asia, Beijing persistently refused U.S. demands to end its assistance to Pakistan's nuclear- and missile-development efforts—although it did accede to similar demands regarding Iran and other radical Muslim countries. But to a significant degree, Beijing actively sought cooperation with the United States in hopes of sustaining a friendly relation with the United States.

In mid-1996 Beijing embraced a U.S. proposal to place the Sino–United States relation in a "strategic perspective," which lead to a joint decision to "build toward a constructive strategic partnership," a determination announced during Jiang Zemin's October 1997 visit to the United States. It was an attempt to create a comprehensive framework for the elements of cooperation, as enumerated in the previous two paragraphs, and provide a surrogate for the lost stabilizing influence of the Cold War–era "quasi alliance" against the Soviet Union. When the concept of a Sino–United States strategic partnership became the target of sharp attack in the United States, China was dismayed at this apparent American unwillingness to accept China as a strategic and equal partner. In the simplified rhetoric of the U.S. debate from 1996 to 1998, a "China threat" was the counterpoise to "strategic partnership." If China were indeed a threat, it followed that the United States should not be so supportive of China's efforts to become more powerful. American unwillingness to view China as a strategic partner, in spite of China's considerable efforts to work with Washington, caused considerable frustration and resentment in China.[34]

Beijing's enthusiastic cooperation with the United States in the "war on international terrorism," following the al Qaeda attacks on the World Trade Center and the Pentagon in September 2001, was a recent episode of Beijing's desire to cooperate with the United States. Again, China rendered significant help to the United States. In the weeks after the September 11 attacks, while Washington was demanding that Pakistan's government in Islamabad decide whether it stood with the Taliban regime in Afghanistan or with the United States, China helped persuade Pakistan to side with the United States. Since a decision to align with the United States required abandoning the Afghanistan Taliban regime, which Pakistan had sponsored and supported over the previous six years, China's encouragement of Islamabad to break with the Taliban probably played an important role in Pakistan's tortured decision. China then supported U.S. efforts to mobilize the Asia–Pacific Economic Cooperation forum against terrorism. It approved Hong Hong's scrutiny of international financial flows for antiterrorist purposes, an approval that was critical since China's recovery of sovereignty over Hong Kong in 1997. Beijing exchanged antiterrorist intelligence with U.S. intelligence services. China did not oppose the U.S. war against the Afghan Taliban regime, and it played a positive role in consolidating the post-Taliban transitional government. One almost sensed in the swiftness and alacrity of China's support for the new U.S. war against terrorism relief that the Americans had finally found an enemy other than China. One thread of Chinese thinking in the 1990s was that the United States needed an enemy for imperial purposes—to keep defense budgets high, to mobilize domestic opinion for foreign interventions, and to keep allies in line. Many Chinese believed that this was the true reason for the emergence of the China threat theory in the United States. However, after September 11, the Americans had a genuine threat—moreover, one geographically and politically remote from China. Antiterrorism offered a new and perhaps solid basis on which to restabilize Sino–United States relations, as the anti-Soviet struggle had done prior to the end of the Cold War.[35]

Beijing's most important positive inducement to continued U.S. support for China's development was economic. Opening China's markets to U.S. goods and investment produced not only profits for American businesses but jobs for American workers. Such moves demonstrated that Sino-American economic cooperation was a win–win game. China's leaders made this point whenever meeting U.S. leaders or delegations, and their comments were reiterated by China's state-controlled media.

BEIJING'S NEGATIVE INSTRUMENTS OF LEVERAGE: CHINA'S "STICKS"

Regarding Beijing's "sticks," China had several negative instruments of leverage with which to use on Washington. First and perhaps most important of these was a willingness to call Washington's bluff when the United States threatened to roll back its economic support for China. On such occasions, Beijing would attempt to demonstrate that China was capable of accepting a reduction of bilateral economic interactions, if that was what Washington chose, but that China would not accede to American demands under threat. For example, during the confrontation over the linkage between China's human rights record and its enjoyment of most-favored-nation status during 1993 through 1994, Beijing signaled that, rather than capitulate to U.S. demands, China would tighten its belt and do without U.S. economic cooperation. It would be U.S. businesses who would lose most by being shut out of the large and rapidly growing China market, Beijing said. Hostile U.S. moves against China would mean that other Western non-U.S. businesses (German, French, Japanese, and Canadian) would benefit from participating in China's monumental development effort. Li Peng made this point when he told some visiting European dignitaries in early 1996, while relations with the United States were tense over Taiwan: "If the Europeans adopt more cooperation with China in all areas, not just in economic areas but also in political and other areas, I believe the Europeans can get more orders from China."[36]

Multiplying the leverage of the China market were efforts to mobilize the U.S. business community to lobby the U.S. government to do what was necessary to keep that market open to U.S. firms. During the 1993–1994 MFN-linkage confrontation, such Fortune 500 firms as Boeing, Motorola, and Caterpillar mounted a highly focused and effective effort to persuade Congress to reject the administration's linkage proposal.[37] Beijing did what it could to encourage these lobbying efforts. Ill-advised and naïve efforts to intensify pressure on U.S. politicians by making campaign contributions during the 1996 election cycle backfired.

Underpinning the strategy of Beijing's digging in its heels and refusing to back down before U.S. demands was a double asymmetry between the PRC and U.S. political systems. In a clash between governments in which both demand sacrifices by their citizens, a nonelected, authoritarian government arguably has a distinct advantage over an elected government ruling a free people. Authoritarian governments do not have to worry about being ousted by disgruntled voters. Authoritarian governments can suppress dissent while gearing up vociferous propaganda in support of official policies. Democratic governments confront a far more fickle public opinion, voiced by an independent media and protected by independent judicial organs. There is a second level of asymmetry as well having to do with the gravity of interests. The CCP was fighting for its survival, in a political and perhaps literal sense. For China's communist leaders the stakes were extremely high. Acceding to U.S. demands might, they believed, lead to the unraveling of their control over Chinese society and the CCP's demise à la the Soviet Communist Party in 1990 and 1991. U.S. leaders, however, were motivated either by a desire to better the lives of the Chinese people (as U.S. leaders insisted) or by a desire to create disorder that would weaken China (as China's leaders suspected was actually the case). Whichever U.S. goal was posited, it was considerably less immediate and weighty than the CCP's struggle for survival.

Another of Beijing's "sticks" was anti-unipolarity partnership with various countries. The earliest and most important of these was with Russia. During the last two years of the Soviet Union's existence, and in the aftermath of the Beijing massacre of June 1989, China aligned with the declining Soviet state in an effort to balance the United States. Deng Xiaoping imposed limits on this policy in line with his "don't assume leadership" policy, but the two sides stood symbolically together against Western triumphualism.[38] The Russian Federation (the successor state to the Soviet Union) opted to continue and deepen the partnership with China. The CCP, under Deng Xiaoping's guidance, overlooked profound displeasure with the anticommunism of Russia's new leadership and decided to continue the partnership with Moscow for the sake of countering the United States.

A major step in this direction came in December 1992, when a joint communiqué normalizing Russo–Chinese relations pledged the two countries not to join "any military or political alliance directed against the other party" or "allow its territory to be used by a third country to infringe on the sovereignty and security interests of the other party."[39] In effect, this pledge meant that neither country would cooperate with the United States against the other. The joint communiqué also declared common opposition "to hegemonism and power politics in any form," code words for U.S. domination of world affairs. The December 1992 communiqué was the first of an impressive series of bilateral declarations of partnership built up over the next decade. In 1994 came an agreement regarding the mutual non–first use and non–mutual targeting of nuclear weapons. In April 1996 the two sides formally proclaimed a "strategic partnership." In May 1997 the two sides issued a joint statement "on the multipolarization of the world and the establishment of a new international order."[40] In 1999 Beijing and Moscow undertook parallel diplomacy opposing NATO's intervention in Kosovo, Yugoslavia. They issued a joint statement calling for preservation of the antiballistic missile treaty of 1972—a treaty that the United States was considering abrogating (under the terms of the treaty) to clear the way for development of missile defense systems. Then, in July 2001, the two countries signed a Treaty of Good Neighborliness, Friendship, and Cooperation—a title reminiscent of the Sino-Soviet alliance of February 1950.

Strategic partnership with Russia served several Chinese purposes vis-à-vis the United States. In the first instance it ensured that newly democratic and postcommunist Russia would not become part of the Western bloc, thereby further strengthening Washington's global dominance. Concern with such a possibility was substantial in the immediate post–Soviet Union period, and it mounted once again after Vladimir Putin became Russian president in early 2000 and laid out a much more cooperative line toward the United States. Strategic partnership with Russia also strengthened China's position in the event of a confrontation with the United States over Taiwan—such as that which developed in January–February 1996, just before the formalization of the Sino-Russian strategic partnership. In the event of such a confrontation, strategic partnership with Russia would guarantee China secure rear areas and open lines of international transportation, considerably diminishing prospects that a U.S. naval blockade might force China into submission. More broadly, Sino-Russian cooperation diminished the United States' ability to orchestrate world events in ways antithetical to Chinese wishes, or so Beijing hoped.

Stated differently, a strong, cooperative relation with Russia and an assurance that Russo–Chinese cooperation would continue even in the face of possible U.S. hostility to China, demonstrated to Washington that efforts to coerce China would be costly and not likely to succeed. It would thus be wiser for Washington to abandon attempts to bully China and attempt instead to secure China's cooperation.[41] As a briefing on the Sino-Russian strategic partnership prepared for high-ranking cadre in early 1997 explained, U.S. global preeminence would continue for some time to come: "To realize its scheme of sole hegemony over the world, [the United States] will continue to implement its policies of hegemonism and power politics around the world, containing China's and Russia's development." China and Russia were both victims of "the 'containment' policies of the United States and other Western nations." This created "common interests and increasing mutual need" between them. As "relatively weak countries," China and Russia needed the support of each other. "China needs the support . . . of Russia to develop, . . . resist provocations, and achieve greater international maneuvering room."[42]

China's Russian card has to be played carefully. Too close an anti–United States partnership with Russia—a military alliance perhaps—might stimulate rather than deter U.S. hostility. Thus virtually every Sino-Russian joint declaration and virtually every Chinese analysis of the Sino-Russian strategic partnership contain a politically de rigueur disclaimer to the effect that the partnership "is not directed against any third country." The cadre briefing mentioned here explained the reason for this disclaimer: "The lesson of the Sino-Soviet alliance [of 1950] shows that regardless of its form, an alliance is by its nature directed against a third country and will bring about that third country's opposition, spoiling the international environment for economic construction and disadvantageous for concentration on economic development."[43]

Following the formation of the Sino-Russian "strategic partnership" in 1996, China formed "partnerships" of various sorts ("comprehensive," "cooperative," and "constructive" were common adjectives) with a number of other countries: France in May 1997; Canada, Mexico, Association of Southeast Asian Nations, and India in late 1997; the European Union, the United Kingdom, and Japan in 1998; and South Africa, Egypt, and Saudi Arabia in 1999. These partnerships strengthened Chinese leverage vis-à-vis the United States. They countered the China threat theory being used by some quarters in Washington to "contain China." They weakened and restrained hegemonism and power politics by insulating these relationships to some degree from the vicissitudes of Sino-U.S. conflict. They also helped create a new international order in which China was recognized as a major power, a development in accord with multipolarity and one in which many Chinese thought Washington sought to prevent.[44] They also signaled Washington that it should not count on carrying these countries, many of whom were U.S. allies, into an anti-China campaign. The message was clear: the United States should not count on being able to isolate China.

Preparation and demonstration of military strength has been Beijing's ultimate negative lever with the United States. Beijing's 2000 national defense white paper referred elliptically to the possibility of U.S. coercion. While "peace and development remain the two major themes in today's world," the white paper said, "relations among big powers are complicated, with many interwoven contradictions and frictions. . . . Hegemonism and power politics still exist. . . . Certain big powers [i.e., the United States] are pursuing 'neo-interventionism,' new 'gunboat policy' . . . threatening world peace and security."[45] China's leaders see substantial Chinese military power—military power adequate to impose severe causalities on, and deny victory to, the United States, if not actually defeat the United States—as essential for deterring U.S. military moves against China. PLA scenarios for United States' resort to force against the PRC run the gamut from possible U.S. intervention in support of Tibetan or Xinjiang separatists, to punitive military moves in the context in such crises as the airplane collision incident of April 2001, to a major preemptive strike against the CCP-led PRC to abort China's rise to global power status. But at the top of Chinese scenarios involving military conflict with the United States is war resulting from U.S. military intervention in a PLA effort to subordinate Taiwan.

During the post-1989 period, China's defense budgets grew steadily and substantially, unlike those during the 1980–1988 period, when military spending was low and stagnant (see table 8.7). Between 1992 and 2001, China's defense budget more than doubled, increasing by a whopping 222 percent, according to estimates by the Stockholm International Peace Research Institute. Some of that increased spending went for pay increases and to offset losses of PLA revenue as the military abandoned commercial enterprises in accordance with a 1998 directive. But a large portion of it went to augment the PLA's order of battle.

The dismantling of any viable technology control system for the Western nations in the early 1990s meant that a wide range of extremely advanced militarily relevant technology from those countries was available to China for the first time. Part of China's increased defense spending went to purchase those technologies. But the overwhelming bulk of China's imported military hardware and technology came from Russia. During the 1997–2001 period, China was the second-largest importer of weapons, purchasing over US$7.1 billion in weapons during that five-year period.[46] (Taiwan was the top-ranking weapons importer.) Most of that amount came from Russia. From Russia the PLA purchased a dazzling array of weaponry, including seventy-eight Sukoi-27 and seventy-six Sukoi-30 air-supremacy fighters; air-to-air, antiship, surface-to-air, and antiradar missiles; combat radars; and two extremely capable Sovremenny-class destroyers, specifically designed by the Soviet Union to destroy U.S. aircraft carriers.[47] Many of these Russian-supplied weapons were appropriate to air–naval battles around Taiwan.

PLA modernization was driven by scenarios of a conflict over Taiwan, including deterring or, if deterrence failed, actually defeating U.S. military forces. PLA strategists closely followed not only developments in warfare during the 1990s in which U.S. high-tech methods prevailed at low costs against powerful opponents, but also the doctrinal debate in U.S. strategic circles regarding information warfare. Indeed, U.S. military circles concluded that China was one of only a few countries that followed these debates on the revolution in military affairs. Based on its analysis of modern warfare, the PLA plan targeted a number of advanced capabilities necessary for China to fight successfully a war against a country such as the United States: long-range precision-strike capabilities; highly capable air defense; and technologies targeting the enemy's

230   *John W. Garver*

Table 8.7.   China's Growing Defense Spending

	1992	1993	1994	1995	1996	1997	1998	1999	2000	2001
Billions RMB	69.2	73.1	87.2	105	124	139	157	172	189	223
% Increase Over Previous Year	5.6	19.3	20.4	18.1	12.1	13	9.6	9.9	18	

Source: Stockholm International Peace Research Institute, *SIPRI Yearbook 2002: Armaments, Disarmament, and International Security* (Oxford: Oxford University Press, 2002), 273.

command, control, communications, computers, remote sensors, laser weapons, and intelligence systems. A large military research-and-development apparatus headed by the powerful State Commission on Science, Technology, and Industry for National Defense was involved in researching and developing weapons that would allow the PLA to decisively exploit such U.S. vulnerabilities as U.S. dependence on satellites, computers, big and vulnerable aircraft carriers, and a very few large forward-deployment bases in the western Pacific Ocean.[48] PLA strategists devoted considerable attention to how China could exploit U.S. vulnerabilities to defeat the United States.[49] A select committee of the U.S. Congress concluded that China conducted sweeping covert operations in the United States to acquire carefully targeted technologies useful to China's military-development programs.[50]

Growing PLA capabilities are periodically put on display, especially in the vicinity of Taiwan. The exercises were often conspicuously configured to devastate or conquer Taiwan, defeating in the process a U.S. intervention to thwart that effort. One key political objective of these exercises was to demonstrate to Washington that military conflict with China would not be easy or low cost. Less the U.S. obtain intelligence that might lead it to conclude otherwise, or obtain intelligence that would diminish China's advantages vis-à-vis the United States, Beijing strictly limited China's military exchanges with the United States. Visiting U.S. military personnel were allowed to see only a few model units, a practice which became a source of considerable discontent within the U.S. military.

China also maintains a credible nuclear deterrent against the United States. In 2002 China had twenty single nuclear-warhead intercontinental ballistic missiles (ICBMs) capable of hitting anywhere in the United States and about twenty-four shorter-range nuclear missiles that could reach the western part of the United States. The CIA estimates that most of China's ICBMs are targeted at the United States.[51] Many of the PLA's nuclear-armed medium-range ballistic missiles could hit U.S. forward-deployed forces in the western Pacific. China's defense planners worry deeply that U.S. development of missile defenses could nullify China's nuclear-deterrent capability against the United States.

Demonstrations of the PLA's nuclear capabilities were part of Beijing's demonstration of China's punitive capabilities. During the burgeoning confrontation over Taiwan in late 1995, PLA general Xiong Guangkai told a visiting United States ex-official that he was confident the United States would not intervene to protect Taiwan because Americans cared more about Los Angeles than about Shanghai. This message was taken quite seriously by the U.S. government as a threat to use nuclear weapons if the United States intervened in a cross-strait conflict. Subtler but equally effective are publicly announced exercises by the PLA's Second Artillery Division—the unit that handles China's nuclear weapons—as components of exercises against Taiwan. Occasionally these announcements specify that the purpose of these exercises is to counter putative foreign intervention in a cross-strait conflict. On still other occasions, China fires missiles unannounced to mark visits to China by high-level U.S. personnel. The point of these nuclear demonstrations is to dissuade U.S. leaders from concluding that they can coerce or bully China. They are intended to demonstrate, as Zhou Enlai once said regarding the possibility of a Soviet attack, that China is a tough piece of meat to chew.

China's military power plays several roles regarding the United States. First, a militarily powerful China will dissuade Washington from military moves contrary to China's interests—perhaps a U.S. campaign to unilaterally impose a unification plan on the Korean Peninsula, intervene militarily on behalf of a major uprising in Tibet, or rescue U.S. personnel being held in China. Regarding the last point, as the detention of twenty-three U.S. Air Force personnel detained on Hainan Island after the April 2001 airplane collision dragged on to well over a week, there was discussion in the United States of the possible use of military force to free the American hostages. Weighing against such ideas was the military effectiveness of the PLA, whose prowess signaled to Washington that the United States simply could not defeat China and that any attempt to do so would be extremely and ultimately unbearably costly for the United States. A militarily potent China keeps U.S. policy makers sober and cognizant of the need to secure China's cooperation rather than attempting to coerce it. A militarily potent China also lessens the likelihood that Taiwanese "splittists" will "declare Taiwan independence" or, if they do, that the United States would intervene on their behalf. Finally, China's leaders view military power as an essential component of what Chinese analysts call *comprehensive national power*. If China is to be treated with respect and as an equal by the United States, it must be militarily powerful. If China is militarily weak, it will be bullied and disdained. At least this is a core belief dominating China's contemporary thinking.

It is also possible that PLA capabilities are intended not only to deter the United States but to actually defeat the United States in a war over Taiwan.

Some PLA war planners apparently believe that China could actually achieve victory in such a war. Not a few PLA officers writing in PLA journals assert this point of view, whereas apparently none warns of the opposite possibility of China's defeat.[52] Some Chinese analysts also believe that a Sino–United States war over Taiwan would not necessarily disrupt the economic relationship between China and America, or at least that any disruption would be temporary with the economic relation reviving swiftly once the fighting stopped.[53] These hard-line views probably surface during Chinese debates over policy toward the United States. The mainstream position, however, is that military conflict with the United States would profoundly threaten China's post-1978 development drive.

CHINESE DEBATES OVER U.S. POLICY

Throughout the 1989–2003 period, China's leaders have debated the nature of U.S. intentions and the proper mix of carrots and sticks in dealing with the United States. Initially, in the immediate aftermath of the Beijing massacre, debate was confined to the top circles of the CCP. Then, as the political atmosphere relaxed and marketization advanced in the 1990s, other sectors of society were drawn into the debate. Indeed, in some ways the emergence of popular strains of anti-American nationalism was one of the most significant intellectual trends of post-1989 China.[54] By the end of the 1990s, debate over policy toward the United States had spilled into the academic community and even into public opinion. Broadly speaking, the red thread of this debate was whether China should seek cooperation and avoid confrontation with the United States, or whether close cooperation with the United States was dangerous and would in fact weaken China. If the latter was the case, then a more confrontational approach toward the United States was required.

There was a near consensus regarding the sinister hegemonist motives and nature of the United States. A few academic specialists argued that the United States held essentially benign intentions and pursued interests broadly convergent with those of China, but these views represented something of a radical fringe of Chinese opinion. Most parties to the debates of the 1990s agreed that the United States was a hegemonist power that sought to limit China's emergence and change its domestic political system to accord with U.S. values and interests. They disagreed, however, on the proper policy response to the United States.

Some top Chinese leaders—represented by foreign minister and vice premier Qian Qichen, premier Zhu Rongji, and eventually by Jiang Zemin himself—maintained that confrontation with the United States would severely undermine, and possibly even abort, China's extremely successful post-1978 development drive. The comprehensive national power of the United States was simply so great and so far superior to China's that confrontation with the United States would be a disaster for China.[55] China should avoid confrontation with the United States, if that could be done without sacrificing China's core values, especially China's claim to Taiwan and the CCP's absolute control over China's domestic affairs. Some analysts used a review of history to demonstrate that earlier rising powers that had come into direct confrontation with the reigning hegemonic power had invariably failed in their drive for international preeminence—for example, France against Britain in the eighteenth and nineteenth centuries; Germany against Britain and the Soviet Union, Germany, and Japan against the United States in the twentieth century. But those rising powers that had succeeded in avoiding confrontation with the incumbent paramount power and that had been able to cooperate with the resident hegemon had succeeded in their rise to preeminent status—England with the Netherlands in the seventeenth century, the United States with Britain in the twentieth century.[56]

Advocates of avoiding confrontation with the United States also argued that China would in fact be able to resist U.S. pressures and threats, unlike smaller victims of U.S. hegemonism. U.S. hegemonism might be able to work its will against Yugoslavia or Iraq—which Chinese analysts of all camps agreed were the major victims of U.S. hegemonist aggression in the post–Cold War period. China, however, was simply much stronger than Yugoslavia or Iraq. China's strength would enable it to fend off U.S. pressures and threats. Unlike Yugoslavia or Iraq, China had nuclear weapons. It had a large and battle-ready army that could not be easily defeated. China was a vast country with strong air defenses that simply could not be overwhelmed by a U.S. air blitz. U.S. leaders knew that China was a "tough piece of meat to chew" and understood very well the difficulties that an attempt to defeat China would encounter. Thus, while the United States did indeed engage in bullying, gun-boat diplomacy, and intervention in service of a U.S. desire for global domination, China should be confident of its ability to fend off such threats. Moreover, according to the advocates of U.S. engagement, the United States and China did have certain common interests—for example, maintaining peace and stability on the Korean Peninsula, the nonproliferation of nuclear weapons, and economic cooperation. China should stress these areas of cooperation while seeking to avoid confrontation. It should not respond irrationally or rashly to various U.S. moves; rather, it should seek by all means to maintain a cooperative relation with the United States as a crucial underpinning to China's development drive.

Advocates of a more forceful, confrontational policy toward the United States found much cause for concern. The United States, they believed, was following a secret, long-term strategy intended to overthrow the CCP, restrict the development of Chinese power, and perhaps even split Tibet, Xinjiang, or Taiwan from China. Since the collapse of the Soviet Union had created an "unbalanced international situation" and lifted fears of Soviet intervention from American minds, the United States had adopted a policy of unbridled military intervention in the internal affairs of sovereign states, especially the former socialist state of Yugoslavia. The United States was seizing on ethnic divisions within Yugoslavia to break up that socialist country just as it had done with the Soviet Union itself, or so many hard-liners believed. If the United States dared to intervene in those places, might it not intervene in Tibet if conditions were right? Regarding Taiwan, unrestrained and arrogant U.S. hegemonism was encouraging traitorous "splittists" to move ever further toward "Taiwan independence." The maintenance of NATO after the collapse of the Soviet Union indicated a continued U.S. desire for global domination. The expansion of NATO into Eastern Europe indicated the expanded lust for power of the United States. In Asia the United States was encouraging Japan to play a greater military role by drawing it into possible military conflicts in the Taiwan area. Furthermore, the United States was expanding military ties with countries all around China—with Japan, the Philippines, Vietnam, India, Mongolia, Kyrgzia, Uzbekistan, and Kazakhstan. The United States was also pushing forward with missile defense. Ostensibly, missile defense was directed against North Korea, but the actual secret purpose, China's hard-liners believed, was to negate China's nuclear deterrent. The United States wanted to be able to threaten to wage nuclear war against China—perhaps even to actually wage such war—without worry of Chinese retaliation.

New strands of anti-American nationalism emerged during the 1990s to color and contextualize élite CCP debates over U.S. policy. The United States was enthralled by a spirit of cultural superiority, imaging it could impose its values and institutions on the rest of the world. The immense power of the United States and the unbalanced world situation after the collapse of the Soviet Union combined with U.S. cultural arrogance to induce the United States to resort to power politics and subversive interference to remake other countries on the basis of U.S. values and interests. The United States was afraid of China's rapidly growing power. It regarded a powerful China as an obstacle to U.S. global domination. There were also racial and anticommunist ideological roots to this U.S. hostility to China. China was a nonwhite, non-Western, socialist country, whereas the United States was essentially white, Western, and capitalist. Anti-China forces in the United States were demonizing China before U.S. public opinion. The U.S. media constantly stressed the negative aspects of Chinese society or even invented slanderous stories about China, overlooking the immense progress China had made since 1978. Invented, fictitious stories about Chinese spying in the United States, about the euthanasia of orphans, about PLA plans to take over the Panama Canal, or about Chinese sale of weapons of mass destruction and their components to various countries—stories that Chinese public opinion believed were patently false—were being peddled by the U.S. government and media to whip up anti-China hysteria. Many Chinese wondered: did this not presage a hostile, coercive campaign against China?[57]

Some elements of the debate went even further. The United States was preparing genocide against the Chinese people, they asserted. The United States was racist to the core and hated China because it was a nonwhite power challenging America's white global domination. The United States was developing race-specific biological weapons and could use them to kill off the Chinese people as well as other nonwhite peoples. Had not the Americans enslaved Africans and conducted genocide against Native Americans?[58] It is doubtful if these extreme and nonsensical views reflected the beliefs of China's top leaders. They do, however, reflect the superheated anti-Americanism that emerged during the 1990s and framed élite policy debates.

As suggested earlier, the specter of the collapse of European communism haunted the Chinese debates of the 1990s. Advocates of different policies toward the United States drew different lessons from the Soviet collapse and used those lessons to argue for their preferred U.S. policies. One lesson the hard-liners drew from that collapse was the need for increased vigilance, internally and internationally. The People's Republic of China had to be ever prepared to defeat and smash the plots of hostile U.S. hegemonists and their minions within Chinese society. Moderates did not necessarily oppose vigilance, unless it was used as an excuse for opposing marketization and opening. But they did argue that confrontation with the United States, too heavy defense spending, and an overly militant Chinese foreign policy were the clearest ways for the CCP to repeat the Soviet Union's harsh experience. This difference was epitomized by a story told about a meeting of top CCP leaders in Beijing in December 1989 just following the execution by the Romanian military of the dictator Nicolae Ceausescu and his wife, communist tyrants who had been especially close to Beijing. China's leaders had assembled to watch a videotape of those events. As the film portraying the gruesome events played, someone in the audience broke the silence with the comment: "We'll be like this if we don't strengthen our proletarian dictatorship and repress the reactionaries." Deng Xiaoping replied: "Yes, we'll be like this if we don't carry out reforms and bring about benefits to the people."[59]

Two issues especially roused Chinese ire and stimulated calls for more forceful policies toward the United States: Taiwan and U.S. pressures regarding China's internal arrangements.

Taiwan is an issue of deep concern to the PLA, which views itself as protector of China's core values and interests. Ranking high among those is Taiwan. Stress on Taiwan also matches the PLA's interests in higher budgets, ambitious modernization, and a greater role in CCP élite politics. From the PLA perspective, Taiwan is the last major piece of territory lost by China during its century of national humiliation and remaining to return to the motherland. Ideally, Taiwan should move toward integration into the state system of the PRC under the generous "one country, two systems" doctrine promulgated by Deng Xiaoping for Hong Kong in 1984. At a minimum, the status quo of Taiwan must be maintained and Taiwan be prevented from drifting toward de jure independence and sovereignty. The splittist plots of traitors on Taiwan to establish "Taiwan independence" (the two words are always put in quotation marks in PRC media) must be confronted and defeated. So too must the United States if it dares to support those moves toward "Taiwan independence." If coercive pressure against Washington, or against Taibei with Washington standing behind it, leads to tension or even conflict with the United States, so be it. Acceptance of the negative costs may be the necessary costs of protecting the territorial unity and integrity of China. Just as foreign minister Chen Yi once said that China would go without pants to build atomic bombs, so China must now be willing to bear any sacrifice to prevent injury to China's claim to Taiwan.

The PLA viewed a number of post-1998 changes in United States–Taiwan relations as unacceptable infringements on China's "sovereignty" over Taiwan, therefore requiring forceful responses. The decision of president George H. W. Bush to sell 150 F-16 fighters to Taiwan during the 1992 presidential campaign was the first U.S. move to mobilize the PLA over the Taiwan issue. Paramount leader Deng Xiaoping ordered a relatively low-key response to Bush's F-16 sale decision. Many PLA leaders were dismayed by this and made their views known through a variety of means. Jiang Zemin, struggling to consolidate his succession to Deng as paramount leader, greatly needed PLA support and could not afford to oppose the PLA's strong patriotic views on Taiwan.[60]

As Taiwan democratized during the 1990s, it began moving away from the old verities of "one China" upheld under the authoritarian rule of Chiang Kai-shek and his son Chiang Ch'ing-kuo. Newly freed Taiwanese public opinion yearned for greater international respect, and Taiwan's new democratic politicians sought votes by catering to that yearning. In the United States there was great sympathy for the emerging democratic Taiwan. By 1994 there was strong congressional pressure on President Clinton to upgrade U.S. relations with Taiwan. At the explicit direction of Congress, the executive undertook a "Taiwan policy review," with the results being announced in September 1994. Changes in Taiwan policy included more direct contact between U.S. and Taiwanese officials, U.S. support for Taiwan's entry into the WTO, and allowing the geographic reference "Taipei" to appear in a new name for Taiwan's "unofficial" offices in the United States.[61] Then in May 1995 the United States allowed Taiwanese president Lee Teng-hui to visit the United States for a "private" visit. The reasoning behind these congressional moves was complex. One factor was the U.S. belief that China's profound economic dependency on the United States would more or less compel it to acquiesce to moves upgrading United States–Taiwan relations.

In response to the United States' elevating its relations with Taiwan, the PLA demanded and got a forceful punitive response, which took the form of the PLA's missile firings in July and August 1995 into the seas north of Taiwan and between Taiwan and Japan. Further military exercises began in March 1996, constituting the largest PLA mobilization since the 1979 war against Vietnam and the largest-ever PLA exercises in the Taiwan Strait. Some 150,000 troops simulated an invasion of Taiwan. The exercises included missile firings into zones only twenty-some miles off Taiwan's major harbors of Keelung and Kaohsiung, bracketing Taiwan and temporarily closing those harbors. During the exercises, the PLA for the first time conducted large-scale maneuvers involving land, sea, air, and nuclear forces under the command of a newly established war zone. Three hundred aircraft participated in the exercise.[62]

In response to PLA threats, the United States deployed first one, then two aircraft-carrier battle groups to Taiwan while delivering unprecedentedly direct and blunt warnings to Beijing that the United States was prepared to defend Taiwan.[63] The strength and directness of the U.S. response took many of China's leaders by surprise. The belief had developed over the previous several years that the United States was a soft pleasure-seeking individualistic society unwilling to bear sacrifice; thus, it would not respond effectively or forcefully to Chinese military moves to coerce Taiwan, or so Chinese leaders seem to have concluded. The swift and forceful response of the United States punctured those comfortable Chinese assumptions about the United States and made clear to China's leaders the dangers of a possible military clash with the United States. Most of China's leaders, and certainly the moderates represented by Qian Qichen and Zhu Rongji, understood that in all probability any significant military clash between the PRC and the United States would lead to the collapse of the Sino-American economic relationship.

The second major area of U.S. pressure that rouses great anger, suspicion, and resistance from China is U.S. pressure on China to modify its internal political or economic policies to comport more fully with U.S. values. The United States' linkage of MFN and human rights issues as well as its insistence that China open its domestic markets as part of entry into the WTO were the major instances of this phenomenon. In both cases Chinese hard-liners, led by Li Peng, argued that the purpose of U.S. demands was to weaken China and that they had to be adamantly rejected. Acceptance of U.S. demands regarding human rights would undermine CCP control, lead to social instability, and risk carrying socialism in China down the road taken by Eastern Europe and the Soviet Union. Acceding to U.S. demands to open wide China's markets would lead to destruction of China's state-owned enterprises, state control over the economy, and even to a foreign take-over of China's economy. Moderates such as Zhu Rongji, on the other hand, saw entry into WTO, even at the cost of acceptance of U.S. demands, as a way of further expanding and protecting the Sino-American economic relation.

A recent round of the ongoing Chinese debate over policy toward the United States came in 1999 and brought together U.S. economic and political pressures on China.[64] At that juncture NATO's intervention in the Kosovo region of Yugoslavia overlapped with a bold package of market-opening reforms offered by Zhu Rongji as a solution to the decade-long Sino–United States stalemate over China's entry into the WTO. NATO's intervention in Kosovo had begun in March 1999 and roused great concern in China. The UN Security Council, where China held a veto as a permanent member, was circumvented because of Russian obstruction. The NATO intervention in Kosovo seemed to China to establish a dangerous precedent for a United States–led NATO intervention in the purely internal affairs of a sovereign country. Many Chinese wondered whether it might not be followed by a similar intervention in Tibet, Taiwan, Xinjiang, or Inner Mongolia. When the PRC embassy in Belgrade was bombed by U.S. warplanes in early May, China's hard-liners and military concluded it was a deliberate attack. The United States was testing Chinese resolve, they asserted. Were China to prove irresolute, U.S. and NATO forces might move next against Tibet.

While the Kosovo war was underway, but shortly before the embassy bombing, Zhu Rongji traveled to the United States to lay before the United States a sweeping package of concessions regarding China's entry into the WTO. Li Peng and his allies seized on Zhu's proposed compromise package. They said that implementation of Zhu's plan would further Washington's plan to weaken, dominate, and control China. Now—that is, while the United States was attacking China's overseas embassies and probing China's resolve—was not the time to capitulate to U.S. pressure and bullying. China should stand firm, reject American demands, and prepare to rebuff further U.S. provocations. The debate between these two perspectives continued until November 1999. Jiang Zemin then decided in favor of Zhu. The Americans embraced Zhu's package, and agreement was quickly reached. On November 15, 1999, China and the United States announced agreement on the terms of China's WTO entry.

CONCLUSION

China's policies toward the United States are an ongoing two-level bargaining process. At one level, China's leaders bargain with the United States using a combination of positive inducements as well as threats and punishments to influence Washington's behavior. At another level China's leaders bargain among themselves over policy toward the United States. Those leaders disagree over the nature of China's interests vis-à-vis the United States, over U.S. capabilities (though not necessarily over U.S. intentions), and over the proper mix of positive and negative inducements to pursue China's interests. The outcome of debates among divergent perspectives among the Chinese leadership is greatly influenced by the moves and policies of the United States.

China's broad objective is to raise the standard of living of the Chinese people to a comfortable level and to establish China as a leading international power by the middle of the twenty-first century. Achieving this requires maintaining a stable and cooperative relation with the United States, thereby permitting China to continue drawing on the resources of the United States in China's development drive. But this must be done without sacrificing core Chinese interests. By the late 1990s, Beijing's application of carrots and sticks against Washington had essentially defeated U.S. efforts to compel the CCP to ease its tight political control over Chinese society. On the issue of opening China's markets to U.S. businesses, Beijing essentially acceded to Washington's demands, at least in principle. Taiwan, however, remains the major issue.

NOTES

1. Peter Schweizer, *Reagan's War: The Epic Story of His Forty-year Struggle and Final Triumph over Communism* (New York: Doubleday, 2002).

2. Richard Baum, *Burying Mao, Chinese Politics in the Age of Deng Xiaoping* (Princeton, N.J.: Princeton University Press, 1994), 304–5, 314. Ma Licheng and Ling Zhijun, *Jiaofeng, dangdai zhongguo sanci sixiang jiefang shilu* [Battle: Record of Three Episodes of Liberation of Thought in Contemporary China) (Beijing: Jinri zhongguo chubanshe, 1998), 165.

3. Joseph Pelzman, "PRC Textile Trade and Investment: Impact of the U.S.–PRC Bilateral Textile Agreements," *China's Economy Looks toward the Year 2000*, vol. 2, *Economic Openness in Modernizing China*, select papers submitted to the Joint Economic Commission, Congress of the United States, 94th Cong., 1st sess., May 21, 1986, 400, 412–13.

4. Report of the Trade Statistics Subgroup, Trade and Investment Working Group, Sino-U.S. Joint Commission on Commerce and Trade, October 17, 1995, Foreign Trade Division, U.S. Bureau of the Census, Washington, D.C.

5. *On Sino-U.S. Trade Balance*, Information Office of the State Council of People's Republic of China, March 1997, available at http://english.peopledaily.com.cn/whitepaper/16.html.

6. The U.S. data come from the Institute of International Education, a private group based in New York City. The group's website, opendoors.iienetwork.org, offers data for 1994 through 2002. Data for the earlier years were provided by the institute at special request. It is derived from a survey mailed annually to a set of twenty-seven hundred U.S. universities and colleges.

7. *On Sino-U.S. Trade Balance,* Information Office of the State Council of People's Republic of China.

8. Paul H. B. Godwin, "Changing Concepts of Doctrine, Strategy, and Operations in the Chinese People's Liberation Army, 1978–87," *China Quarterly*, no. 112 (December 1987): 572–90.

9. Jim Mann, *About Face: A History of America's Curious Relationship with China, from Nixon to Clinton* (New York: Alfred A. Knopf, 1999), 276.

10. Chalmers Johnson, "Breaking the Great Wall," *American Prospect* (January–February 1997): 24–29.

11. This is the central theme of Mann, *About Face*.

12. Mann, *About Face*, 120–24, 276.

13. Jonathan D. Pollack, "The United States, North Korea, and the End of the Agreed Framework," *Naval War College Review* 56, no. 3 (Summer 2003).

14. "China's Reluctance Irks U.S.," *Washington Post*, February 4, 2003.

15. Presentation by Professor Ren Xiao, Shanghai Institute of International Affairs, workshop on Sino-U.S. relations held at Georgia Institute of Technology, January 18, 2003.

16. "China's Reluctance Irks U.S.," *Washington Post*, February 4, 2003.

17. "China Breaks with Its Wartime Past," *Far Eastern Economic Review*, August 7, 2003, 24–25.

18. "U.S. Seeks Support to Press North Korea," *New York Times*, October 19, 2002, A6.

19. "Bush and Jiang Vow to Cooperate on North Korea Issue," *New York Times*, October 26, 2002, A8.

20. "China Urged to Put Pressure on N Korea over Nuclear Policy," *Financial Times*, February 9, 2003, 2.

21. "China's Reluctance Irks U.S.," *Washington Post*, February 4, 2003.

22. "China Breaks with Its Wartime Past," 25.

23. "From Beijing, Stern Words for an Uneasy Ally," *Sun* (Baltimore), March 28, 2003. "China Said to Have Cut Oil to North Korea," *Far Eastern Economic Review*, April 10, 2003, 26.

24. Mike Lampton, "China: Fed Up with North Korea?" *Washington Post*, June 4, 2003, A27.

25. "China Asserts It Has Worked to End Nuclear Crisis," *New York Times*, February 13, 2003.

26. Brent Scowcroft and Arnold Kanter, "A Surprising Success on North Korea," *New York Times*, May 1, 2003, A33.

27. See, *People's Daily* online, June 29, 1999, and June 30, 1999, at www.people daily.com. See also, John W. Garver, "The Restoration of China–Indian Comity Following India's Nuclear Tests," *China Quarterly*, no. 168 (December 2001): 879–85. Swaran Singh, "The Kargil Conflict: Why and How of China's Neutrality," *Strategic Analysis* 23, no. 7 (October 1999), at www.idsa-india.org.

28. "Kargil Special: U.S., China in Touch to Ensure Kargil Conflict Does Not Escalate," *Express India,* June 29, 1999, available at www.expressindia.com/news/18011399.htr.

29. *Agreement for Nuclear Cooperation between the United States and China: Communication from the President of the United States*, February 3, 1998. Report relating to approval and implementation of the agreement for nuclear cooperation between the United States and the PRC pursuant to 42 S.S.C. 2153 cd, 9–10.

30. See *Beijing Review,* April 24–30, 1995, 20.

31. Regarding China's role in the CTBT negotiations see, John W. Garver, *Protracted Contest: Sino-Indian Rivalry in the Twentieth Century* (Seattle: University of Washington Press, 2001), 354–64.

32. See "The China–India–U.S. Triangle: Strategic Relations in the Post–Cold War Era," *NBR Analysis* 13, no. 5 (October 2002): 5–56.

33. Phillip C. Saunders, "Preliminary Analysis of Chinese Missile Technology Export Control List," Center for Nonproliferation Studies, Monterey Institute of International Studies, September 6, 2002.

34. Qingguo Jia, "Frustration and Hopes: Chinese Perceptions of the Engagement Policy Debate in the United States," *Journal of Contemporary China* 10, no. 2 (2001): 321–30.

35. I explore China's response to September 11 in "Sino-American Relations in 2001: The Difficult Accommodation of Two Great Powers," *International Journal* (Spring 2002): 301–7.

36. Quoted in David M. Lampton, *Same Bed, Different Dreams: Managing U.S.–China Relations, 1989–2000* (Berkeley: University of California Press, 2001), 406.

37. Robert Dreyfus, "The New China Lobby," *American Prospect* (January–February 1997): 30–37.

38. John W. Garver, "The Chinese Communist Party and the Collapse of Soviet Communism," *China Quarterly*, no. 133 (March 1993): 1–26.

39. Foreign Broadcast Information Service–China (hereafter FBIS-CHI), December 18, 1992, 7–9.

40. "Joint Statement by the People's Republic of China and the Russian Federation on the Multipolarization of the World and the Establishment of a New International Order," *Beijing Review*, May 12–18, 1997, 7–8.

41. Sources on the Sino-Russian strategic partnership include John W. Garver, "Sino-Russian Relations," in *China and the World: Chinese Foreign Policy Faces the New Millennium*, ed. Samuel S. Kim (Boulder, Colo.: Westview Press, 1998), 114–23; Hung Nguyen, "Russia and China: Genesis of an Eastern Rapallo," *Asian Survey* 33, no. 3 (March 1993): 285–99; Raja Menon, "The Strategic Convergence between Russia and China," *Survival* 39, no. 2 (Summer 1997): 101–25.

42. Li Jiyu, "Zhong e fazhan mianxiang 21 shijie de zhanlue xiezuo huoban guanxi" [Development of Sino-Russian strategic cooperative partnership for the 21st century], *Heping yu fazhan* [Peace and Development], no. 1 (1997): 1–7.

43. Li Jiyu, "Zhong e fazhan mianxiang 21 shijie de zhanlue xiezuo huoban guanxi" [Development of Sino-Russian strategic cooperative partnership for the 21st century], 3.

44. Joseph Y. S. Cheng and Zhang Wankun, "Patterns and Dynamics of China's International Strategic Behavior," *Journal of Contemporary China* 11, no. 31 (May 2002): 235–60.

45. "China's National Defense in 2000," Information Office of State Council, FBIS-CHI-2000-1016.

46. *SIPRI Yearbook, 2002*, Stockholm International Peace Research Institute, 2002, 379.

47. *SIPRI Yearbook, 2002*, 420. Bates Gill and Taeho Kim, *China's Arms Acquisitions from Abroad: A Quest for "Superb and Secret Weapons,"* SIPRI Research Report 11 (Oxford: Oxford University Press, 1995).

48. Mark A. Stokes, *China's Strategic Modernization: Implications for the United States* (Carlisle, Pa.: Strategic Studies Institute, U.S. Army War College, 1999).

49. Michael Pillsbury, ed., *Chinese Views of Future Warfare* (Washington, D.C.: National Defense University Press, 1997).

50. U.S. National Security and Military. Commercial Concerns with the People's Republic of China. Select committee, U.S. House of Representatives, January 3, 1999, 105th Cong., 2nd sess., report 105-851 ("The Cox Report").

51. *SIPRI Yearbook, 2002*, 554.

52. Michael Pillsbury, *Dangerous Illusions*, n.d. This conclusion is based on Pillsbury's extensive survey of PLA publications, the first volume of which is cited in note 35.

53. For publications offering such a perspective see John Garver, "More from the 'Say No' Club," *China Journal*, no. 45 (January 2001): 151–58; also, "The (Former) Coming War with America," *Journal of Contemporary China* 12 (August 2003).

54. Zhao Suisheng, "Chinese Intellectuals' Quest for National Greatness and Nationalistic Writing in the 1990s," *China Quarterly*, no. 153 (December 1997): 725–45. Craig Smith, "Chinese Youths Darkening View of U.S.," *New York Times*, April 22, 2001, A8. Hongshan Li, "China Talks Back: Anti-Americanism or Nationalism? A Review of Recent 'Anti-American' Books in China," *Journal of Contemporary China* 6, no. 14 (1997): 153–60.

55. For an academic analysis arguing along these lines, see Chu Shulong, *Zhanlue yu guanli* [Strategy and Management], October 26, 1999, 13–18, FBIS: FTS19991026000196.

56. Examples of this argument in an influential journal are Shi Yinhong, "Guoji zhengzhi de shijixing guilu ji qi dui zhongguo de hushi" [The century laws of international politics and their warning for China], *Zhanlue yu guanli*, no. 5 (1995); and "Xifang dui fei xifang: Dangjin meiguo dui hua taidu de gengben yuanyin" [The West faces the non-West; contemporary America's attitude toward China and its basic reason], *Zhanlue yu guanli*, no. 3 (1996).

57. Wang Jisi, "The Role of the United States as a Global and Pacific Power: A View from China," *Pacific Review* 10, no. 1 (1997): 1–18. Yong Deng, "Hegemon on the Offensive: Chinese Perspectives on U.S. Global Strategy," *Political Science Quarterly* 116, no. 3 (Fall 2001): 343–65. Ming Zhang, "Public Images of the United States," in *In the Eyes of the Dragon: China Views the World* (Lanham, Md.: Rowman & Littlefield, 1999), 111–57. Wang Jisi, "Beauty—and Beast," *Wilson Quarterly* (Spring 2001): 61–65. Chen Jian, *The China Challenge in the Twenty-first Century: Implications for U.S. Foreign Policy*, U.S. Institute of Peace, Peaceworks, June 1998.

58. "More from the 'Say No' Club," 151–58.

59. Benjamin Yang, *Deng: A Political Biography* (Armonk, N.Y.: M. E. Sharpe, 1998), 257.

60. See John Garver, *Face Off: China, the United States, and Taiwan's Democratization* (Seattle: University of Washington Press, 1997), 47–66. Jianhai Bi, "The Role of the Military in the PRC Taiwan Policymaking: A Case Study of the Taiwan Strait Crisis of 1995–96," *Journal of Contemporary China* 11, no. 32 (August 2002): 539–72. You Ji, "Making Sense of the War Games in the Taiwan Strait," *Journal of Contemporary China* 6, no. 15 (1997): 287–305.

61. The policy review is discussed in *New York Times*, September 8, 1994, A5.

62. For an overview of the PLA exercises, see *Chinese Exercise Strait 961: March 8–25, 1996*, Office of Naval Intelligence, 1996.

63. For a description of a meeting between U.S. secretary of defense William Perry and director of the State Council's Office of Foreign Affairs Liu Huaqiu in early March, see Yoichi Funabashi, *Alliance Adrift* (New York: Council on Foreign Relations Press, 1999), 357–65.

64. See David M. Finkelstein, *China Reconsiders Its National Security: "The Great Peace and Development Debate of 1999,"* Project Asia, regional assessment, Center for Naval Analysis Corporation, Alexandria, Va., December 2000. See also David Lampton, *Same Bed, Different Dreams*, 331.

9

The Evolution of Beijing's Policy toward Taiwan during the Reform Era

Yun-han Chu

The making of Beijing's policy toward Taiwan during the reform era carries two seemingly contradictory characteristics. On the one hand, it has tremendous weight as a symbolic mark of leadership within the Chinese Communist Party (CCP). On the other hand, it has become increasingly subordinated to pragmatic consideration of domestic and external structural dimensions.

Symbolically, Taiwan remains one of the most exclusive and prominent policy domains reserved for the paramount leadership of the CCP. The top leader of each generation has evidently been motivated to carry the torch of the reunification campaign by himself and only by himself. Much in the way that the CCP élite of the past wanted to leave their personal mark on the party's evolving ideology, members of the recent leadership seem motivated to promulgate and pass down their signature guiding documents on the Taiwan issue, such as Deng Xiaoping's "one country, two systems" formula and Jiang Zemin's eight-point proposal of 1995.[1] The interest of these leaders in the stewardship of Beijing's policy toward Taiwan has symbolic and strategic significance. At the level of symbolic politics, reunifying Taiwan with the motherland is a "task of the century" that defines a leader's place in Chinese history. At the strategic level, managing the Taiwan issue is a daunting political task of pivotal importance. A mishandling of this potentially explosive issue could conceivably upset the strategic agenda by creating a series of crises, ranging from a major rupture in the external environment of the People's Republic of China (PRC; especially its relationship with the United States) to a cataclysmic outburst of nationalistic fury from below. Under a worst-case scenario, an escalating crisis in the Taiwan Strait could potentially set off a direct military clash with the United States; derail China's ongoing economic

reform; and, if one stretches the logic to an extreme, be the very issue that effects an end to the CCP regime. The significance of cross-strait relations
means that the generational turnover from Jiang Zemin to Hu Jintao cannot
be considered complete until Hu takes full command over Beijing's policy toward Taiwan. However, in the short run it also means that, for an inexperi-
enced and not-so-well-entrenched leader, the risk of taking charge of the Taiwan affairs might offset its slow-coming symbolic reward.

Ever since the dawn of the post-Deng era, the structural conditions and institutional arrangements surrounding the making of Taiwan policy have carried more significance than the leadership factor. In stark contrast with the
Taiwan policy domain of the 1980s, best characterized by a "Deng-in-
command" model, Beijing's policy toward Taiwan in the post-Deng era has
become more comprehensible and predictable as it increasingly falls into a
strong pragmatic, bureaucratic, and consensus-oriented pattern.[2] First, the
decision-making mechanism, while still bearing a fragment of the top leader's
personal mark, has on the whole become more institutionalized. Since 1993,
the structure of the Central Leading Group for Taiwan Affairs (CLGTA) has
consistently involved four systems that carry out essential political, military,
and intelligence functions in the Taiwan policy domain—namely, the foreign
affairs system, the united-front work system (which includes an extensive array of Taiwan Affairs offices installed at all levels of government), the People's Liberation Army (PLA) system, and the intelligence and counterespionage system.

Next, unlike their party elders—whose revolutionary credentials had empowered them to make decisions simply on the basis of raw intelligence, personal experiences, and individual political instinct—Jiang Zemin and indeed all
top Chinese leaders of his generation or younger come from technocratic or
professional military backgrounds and have been trained to rely more on policy analyses and recommendations provided by a range of research institutes
and departments. Although the decision-making process under Jiang Zemin involves only a small subset of senior party and military leaders, they all surround
themselves with an extensive array of think tanks and private advisors.[3]

More fundamental, during the reform era, a shared commitment among the
CCP leaders to certain higher-level national strategic priorities—most important, the nation's fundamental interests in maintaining a peaceful and stable
surrounding environment for the sake of economic modernization—has facilitated the development of intraparty consensus over the basic policy guidelines dealing with the Taiwan issue, despite the occasional quibble over operational guidelines and tactics. The forging of this consensus has been
expedited by a shared assessment, through a largely nonideological lens, of
the constraints and opportunities presented by the international environment,

by the Washington–Beijing–Taipei triangle, and by Taiwan's changing political and economic conditions. It has been widely shared among the CCP leaders that, so long as the prospect of peaceful reunification is effectively preserved, there is neither the urgency nor the strategic imperative to force a final resolution of Taiwan issues before China accomplishes its modernization task. Ultimately, reunification is a mission for the long haul. The only urgency that has become increasingly intense since 1994 is the near-term task to defuse the ticking bomb of Taiwan independence without critically straining China's relationship with the United States, without inadvertently prompting Japan to seek rearmament, without seriously disrupting the ongoing cross-strait economic exchanges, and without diverting too many national resources. Not an easy task. This means that in the making of Beijing's policy toward Taiwan, room for personal policy predilection is quite limited, and these limitations will only increase as China becomes more deeply enmeshed in the global economic system with each passing day.[4]

THE EVOLUTION OF POLICY-MAKING
APPARATUS IN THE POST-DENG ERA

During the Maoist era, the power of setting the guiding principle on the Taiwan issue rested firmly in the hands of Mao Zedong. Not even premier Zhou Enlai was in a position to make any final decision on important matters. During the reform era, Deng Xiaoping decided all important issues regarding Taiwan and Hong Kong; even Hu Yaobang and Zhao Ziyang had no chance to weigh in. However, as China entered the post-Deng era, the trend of replacing the more ideological, personalistic, and top-down pattern of decision making (typical of the Maoist era) with a more pragmatic, bureaucratic, and consensus-oriented pattern of the reform era has proliferated into the domain of Taiwan policy.[5] In stark contrast with the Deng-in-command model, the top leaders of the so-called third and the fourth generations found themselves operating in a more circumscribed policy environment.

Around the Fourth Plenary Session of the CCP's Fourteenth Central Committee in the fall of 1994—with the passing of influential elders, such as Li Xiannian, Wang Zhen, and Chen Yun, and with the rapid deterioration of Deng's health—the collective leadership of the third generation was finally in charge, and the transition to the post-Deng and postelder era was for all practical purpose complete. Not long before that, Jiang Zemin, the CCP secretary-general and the first among equals in the six-member Standing Committee of the Politburo, had already well positioned himself for a smooth power succession. After the Fourteenth Party Congress, he took over another important post, the president of the People's Republic of China, and forced his rivals Yang Shangkun and Yang Baibing out of the Central Military Commission (CMC). Parallel to the leadership turnover at the CCP's highest echelon, the policy apparatus responsible for Taiwan affairs had also undergone a major reorganization. In April 1993, Jiang Zemin replaced Yang Shangkun as the leader of the CLGTA. The memberships in the CLGTA were also thoroughly restructured. To begin with, the structure of the CLGTA was streamlined. The size of the membership was reduced from twelve to six, and only two of the previous members, Wang Zhaoguo and Jia Chunwang, remained in the reorganized CLGTA. The reappointed CLGTA consisted of the following official members:[6]

Jiang Zemin: leader of the CLGTA
Qian Qichen: deputy leader of the CLGTA and serving concurrently as the deputy leader of the Foreign Affairs Leading Small Group (FALSG)
Wang Zhaoguo: head of the CCP United-Front Work Department and the head of the CCP State Council Taiwan Affairs Office (CTAO)
Jia Chunwang: head of the Ministry of State Security
Xiong Guangkai: head of Second Department (military intelligence) of the General Staff Department of the CMC[7]
Wang Daohan: chairman of the Association for Relations across the Taiwan Strait (ARATS) and Jiang's political mentor as well as his most trustworthy policy advisor

The new structure suggested that four parametric changes had taken place in the Taiwan affairs policy apparatus during the transition to the post-Deng and postelder era. First, the decision-making process became more regularized and formalized. With Jiang's personal involvement, the CLGTA became the real inner circle where all important matters dealing with Taiwan were discussed and where policy proposals were formulated. In the past, the CLGTA had been merely a policy-coordinating mechanism among responsible party organs and state agencies; all previous leaders of the CLGTA, who were typically not senior cadres of the highest caliber,[8] did not take up active leadership role. Ever since early 1980s, the ultimate power in the area of Taiwan affairs had stayed in Deng's hands, not by any statue or formal position, but simply by his prestige and connections in the system. After the 1994 Fourth Plenary Session, the process became more formalized in the sense that, on the one hand, there were no more elders wielding power behind the curtain and, on the other hand, Jiang had to come forward and take over the helm of the CLGTA himself to exercise active leadership in the Taiwan policy domain.

Second, the decision-making function of the CLGTA became better delineated and more focused.[9] The scope of membership no longer covered all of the branch "systems" (*xitongs*) that were involved in the implementation of the Taiwan policy (see figure 9.1). With the downsizing of the inner circle, only key members representing systems that carried out "essential" political, military, and intelligence functions in the Taiwan policy domain were officially present (see shaded boxes).[10]

Included were the foreign affairs system, represented by Qian Qichen; the party united-front work system,[11] represented by Wang Zhaoguo and responsible for directly dealing with the authority and the people of Taiwan; the PLA system, represented by Xiong Guangkai; and the intelligence and counterespionage system, represented by Jia Chunwang. Wang Daohan's role was unique. He served as Jiang's personal representative and top advisor. Wang's membership in the CLGTA enabled him to handle—on behalf of Jiang Zemin, aboveboard and behind closed doors—the most sensitive high-level contact with Taiwan and with important third-party countries such as the United States and Japan. His membership also enabled him to organize an array of think tanks outside the normal bureaucratic system and to look after Jiang's personal political interests in the formulation and implementation of Taiwan policy. Ostensibly missing were the propaganda system and the finance and economic system. The propaganda system was not officially present, possibly because it only performed a supportive role. The finance and economic system was not directly involved in this high-level decision-making mechanism because, first, issues dealing with cross-strait economic ties were mostly of a technical, rather than political, nature; and second, the task of accelerating the cross-strait trade-and-investment flows had been delegated largely to the local governments, which out of their provincial interests had been very aggressive in attracting Taiwanese investment. During much of the 1990s, as the CLGTA concentrated itself on political decisions, the technical task of coordinating policy among economic ministries and between central and local authorities in dealing with cross-strait economic issues was transferred to a specialized coordinating mechanism under the State Council: the Economic and Trade Policy toward Taiwan Coordination Small Group,[12] headed by vice premier Li Langqing.

Third, this new leadership structure suggested that the domain of Taiwan policy revealed a more pragmatic, bureaucratic, and consensus-oriented pattern typical of the reform era. In the post-Deng era, the top leaders all came from a technocratic background; few of them claimed much practical experience in dealing with the Taiwan affairs. Unlike the elders, whose revolutionary credentials empowered them to make decisions simply on the basis of raw intelligence, personal experiences, and individual political instinct,

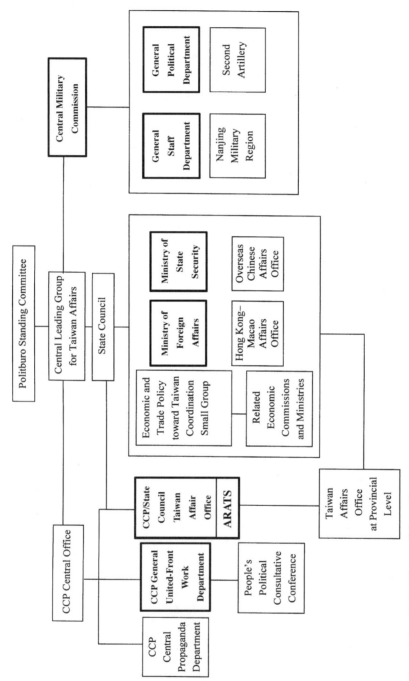

Figure 9.1. PRC's Taiwan affairs policy apparatus

Jiang and his colleagues had to rely more on the policy analyses and recommendations provided by a range of research institutes and departments (see figure 9.2).[13] It was quite possible that different systems would always try to advance their own policy priorities and protect their own organizational interests, but to be effective they had to back up their policy recommendation with quality information, robust scenario analysis, and well-articulated strategic reasoning. This meant that although the decision-making process was relatively closed—that is, only a small subset of senior party and military leaders at national level were involved—members of the CLGTA collectively operated in a more circumscribed policy environment. There was less room for personal policy predilection, as effective leadership had to be built on effective policies. Effective policies in the Taiwan policy domain essentially meant that they had to be concordant with the higher-level national strategic priorities on the one hand and with the changing situations and environments on the other.

Fourth, in the absence of a paramount leader, Jiang ultimately had to play a game of coalition politics in advancing his own policy agenda. However, the subset of senior party and military leaders that were represented in the CLGTA was more congenial than the third-generation collective leadership itself—namely, the Standing Committee of the Politburo. Besides Jiang and Wang, there were only two weighty members in the CLGTA, Qian Qichen and Xiong Guangkai, who reported directly to the two most influential members in the Standing Committee of the Politburo, respectively.[14] This meant that as long as Jiang was able to align Li Peng, the immediate boss of Qian Qichen in the State Council and the FALSG; Liu Huaqing, Xiong's superior; and Zhang Zhen, Liu's partner in the CMC, Jiang could push CLGTA's policy proposal through the Standing Committee of the Politburo as well as the politburo under most circumstances. While the outlook, intentions, and organizational interests of the foreign affairs system and that of the PLA system did not necessarily converge with Jiang's own, most Beijing watchers agreed that Li Peng and Liu Huaqing were Jiang's political allies at the highest reach of policy process and that their political interests were more compatible with his than Qiao Shi or Li Ruihuang. It was reasonable to assume that these few top civilian and military leaders generally interacted and consulted with one another collaboratively. Therefore, unlike the domestic policy domain that has been infested with wide-ranging, cross-level, complex, and fragile bargaining,[15] the problem of fragmentation of authority was not serious in the Taiwan policy domain. It went without saying that the structure of the CLGTA under Jiang Zeming was itself a product of coalitional politics engineered by Jiang himself, and it evidently helped strengthen his steering power and simplify the task of consensus building.

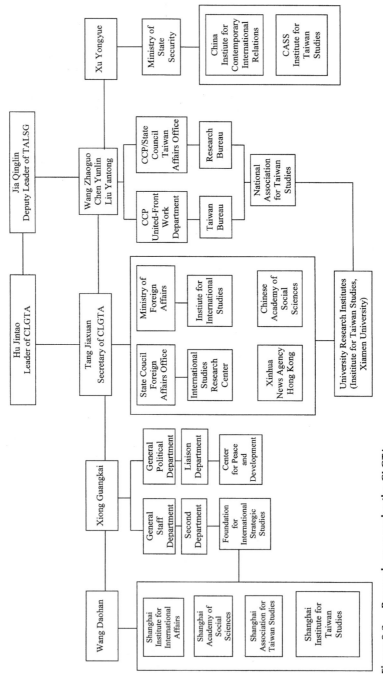

Figure 9.2. Research arms under the CLGTA

After the Fifteenth Party Congress and the Ninth National People's Congress, Jiang Zemin enjoyed an even firmer grip on the Taiwan policy. Qiao Shi, Jiang's only potential rival on the Standing Committee of the Politburo, stepped down. Also, with the retirement of Liu Huaqing, the PLA was no longer represented in the standing committee, symbolizing the resurgence of the party's supremacy over the military. Furthermore, the partial reorganization of the CLGTA in April 1998 attested to Jiang's unequivocal leadership in the Taiwan policy domain. The reappointment of the CLGTA members carried a strong element of continuity. All the previous members of the CLGTA stayed on except for Jia Chunwang, who left the Minister of State Security post and became the head of Public Security Ministry after Zhu Rongji reshuffled the State Council in March 1998. Three new members were admitted to the CLGTA: Chen Yunlin, who succeeded Wang Zhaoguo as the director of the CCP State Council Taiwan Affairs Office around early 1997; Zeng Qinghong, Jiang's general chief of staff and most trustworthy troubleshooter; and Xu Yongyue, who replaced Jia Chunwang as the head of the Ministry of State Security.[16] The appointment of Chen Yunlin and Xu Yongyao to the CLGTA was clearly on the basis of their official portfolio. The appointment of Zeng Qinghong suggested that Jiang wanted to put the operation of the CLGTA under the close supervision of the Central Office. It also suggested that Jiang Zemin wanted to buttress the political credentials of his most trustworthy protégé in this highly sensitive as well as prominent policy domain.

The leadership, structure, and process in the Taiwan policy domain during Jiang's tenure suggested two important developments. First, in the post-Deng era, Jiang succeeded in carving out Taiwan affairs as one of his exclusive domains of responsibility. While the ultimate decision-making power still rested at the politburo, as the leader of the CLGTA, Jiang nevertheless enjoyed effective control over agenda setting in this highly salient policy domain. He was more than "the first among equals" over Taiwan affairs. Most of the new policy proposals came out of his personal initiatives. Second, under Jiang's leadership, the PRC's policy toward Taiwan became more comprehensible as well as predictable. On the one hand, the policy process was relatively free of the problem of lengthy deadlocks and messy compromise, a problem typically associated with a diffuse and fragmented pattern of authority at the top. On the other hand, policy proposals coming out of the CLGTA tended to carry a strong element of pragmatism and realism, in part due to the growing significance of "think tanks" in the policy formulation process.[17] The consensus over Taiwan affairs was fostered by a common commitment to some higher-level national strategic priorities: first, and most important, the fundamental interest in maintaining a peaceful and stable surrounding environment for the sake of economic modernization; second, a shared assessment of the constraints and opportunities present in the international environment, in the United States–People's Republic of China–Taiwan triangular relations, and in Taiwan's changing political and economic conditions.

Soon after Hu Jintao was elected president of the People's Republic of China at the Tenth National People's Congress, the CLGTA was once again reorganized. As the new secretary-general of the CPP and the new head of the state, Hu took over the formal responsibility of managing the cross-strait relations. The membership of the current small leading group consists of the following nine members:[18]

Hu Jintao: CCP secretary-general and the head of the CLGTA, replacing Jiang Zemin

Jia Qinglin: chairman of the National People's Political Consultative Conference and new deputy head of the GLGTA, formally replacing Qian Qichen

Tang Jiaxuan: state councilor in charge of the foreign affairs and the secretary of the CLGTA, functionally replacing Qian Qichen's role in foreign affairs

Wang Gang: chief of the staff of the CCP Central Office and an alternate member of the politburo

Wang Zhaoguo: vice chairman of the National People's Political Consultative Conference

Liu Yantong: head of the CCP United-Front Work Department, replacing Wang Zhaoguo

Wang Daohan: chairman of the Association for Relations across the Taiwan Strait (ARATS)

Chen Yunlin: head of the CCP State Council Taiwan Affairs Office

Xu Yongyue: head of the Ministry of State Security

Xiong Guangkai: deputy chief of the General Staff Department of the CMC

The structure of the new membership reveals two interesting characteristics. First, the profile of the functional representation is largely kept intact. The scope of the new membership covers the same four systems as before. Four former regular members—Wang Daohan, Chen Yun-lin, Xu Yongyue, and Xiong Guangai—stayed on because their official portfolios remain unchanged. The three new regular members—Wang Gang, Tang Jiaxuan, and Liu Yantong—evidently owe their membership in the CLGTA to their new official portfolio in the PLA, foreign affairs, and united-front work system, respectively. Wang Gang, who replaced Zeng Qinghong in March 1999 as the chief of staff of the CCP Central Office, also took over Zeng's formal membership in the newly reorganized CLGTA.

Second, it reveals Jiang's remaining influence over Taiwan affairs and an incomplete power transition. As soon as the Sixteenth Party Congress was over, Hu Jintao found himself in a situation similar to that of Jiang in his early years, holding the seat of the CCP party chief. Like Jiang, who had to consult Deng on all important matters until his mentor's health deteriorated between late 1993 and early 1994, Hu is obligated to accord Jiang the status of a quasi-paramount leader before his time comes. Actually, Hu might find himself in a more precarious situation than Jiang faced in the early 1990s. Jiang was handpicked and backed up by Deng as the pivot of the third-generation leadership, whereas Hu is not Jiang's handpicked successor. Instead, Hu owes his taking over the helm of the CCP to Deng's implicit design a decade ago. For this reason, Hu Jintao is expected to adhere with great caution to Jiang's policy guidelines on Taiwan affairs.

More important, the Taiwan affairs, much like Jiang's chairmanship of the CMC, can be expected to be one of the last few remaining responsibilities that Jiang will relinquish, for dealing with the "treacherous Taiwan situation" has up to this point provided the major justification for the still-ambitious Jiang to cling to his last official post.[19] Furthermore, in his post of CLGTA leader, Hu's authority in managing the cross-strait relations will be circumscribed not only by the necessity to operate within the policy parameters laid down by his predecessor but also because he must share the stage with Zeng Qinghong, reputedly the second-most influential member of the newly elected nine-member Standing Committee of the Politburo; and Jia Qinglin, the new deputy head of the CLGTA. Zeng's credentials in this highly sensitive and salient policy area date back to the turbulent years between 1994 and 1996, when he served as Jiang's personal envoy in conducting negotiations with Lee Teng-hui's chief of staff, Su Chi-cheng, throughout a stream of secret meetings held in Hong Kong and Macao.[20] Zeng became an official member of the CLGTA in April 1998, shortly after the Fifteenth Party Congress. Jia Qinglin, whose credentials in the Taiwan affairs was limited to his tenure as the party chief of Fujian Province, becomes the Standing Committee of Politburo member in charge of the CCP's united-front work. Since Jia's controversial promotion to the standing committee is entirely due to Jiang's patronage, it appears that Jia will faithfully serve as a surrogate of Jiang and Zeng in the CLGTA. Jia's appointment to, as well as Xiong Guangkai and Wang Daohan's renewed membership in, the CLGTA clearly indicates that Jiang is keen in exerting his remaining influence over Taiwan affairs. In contrast to Zeng, Hu has had little exposure to the Taiwan issues during his entire political career. Hu's official debut on the stage of Taiwan affairs was his appearance at a ceremony on January 24, 2002, commemorating the seventh anniversary of the launch of Jiang's eight-point proposal.[21] At this bellwether event, sharing the stage with Zeng as moderator, Hu delivered the ceremonial opening remarks preceding Qian's much more elaborate policy speech. The joint appearance of Hu and Zeng at this highly publicized event in a way foreshadowed the delicate power-sharing scheme that emerged a year later.

While this power-sharing scheme may not be Hu's own choice, he should nevertheless be grudgingly content with holding less-than-full responsibility in the making of policy toward Taiwan during this early stage of his tenure. For his untested leadership, the portfolio of Taiwan affairs carries excessive political risk and minimal prospects for quick political reward. A mishandling of this potentially explosive issue could conceivably break his leadership. At the same time, operating within the existing guiding principles, the window of opportunity for Hu to engineer a major breakthrough in advancing the goal of peaceful reunification is not yet on the horizon. In this sense, Hu will not mind accommodating Jiang's determination to avoid ending his political career with a sour note on cross-strait relations; by way of fighting for his place in history, Jiang will be inadvertently holding this hot issue for Hu for a few extra years. More specifically, Jiang's retention of the chairman of CMC may help Hu control the strong military personalities in the CMC over the issue of Taiwan.[22] In the same token, it may be a blessing in disguise for Hu to have Jiang's protégés Zeng and Jia share responsibility as well as the potential liability with him in the active management of cross-strait relations. Thus, regardless of the shade of his personal predilections, for the next few years Hu shall have little incentive to contest Jiang's supreme authority on the Taiwan issue or deviate too far from Jiang's policy framework. It will be much more rewarding for him to invest his limited political capital in other priorities, in particular addressing the issue of growing social and regional disparity by steering a more balanced economic development strategy.[23]

THE EVOLUTION OF TAIWAN POLICY UNDER JIANG ZEMIN

Since the dawn of the reform era, the two fundamental principles have constituted Beijing's overarching guideline for the resolution of Taiwan issue— namely, "one country, two systems" and "peaceful reunification," as laid down by Deng Xiaoping in the beginning of the reform era[24] Beijing unveiled its first political overture for a "peaceful reunification" as early as the New Year holiday of 1979.[25] Over the years, Beijing has sweetened its peace overture with many specific proposals that allegedly guarantee Taiwan's high degree of political autonomy under the one-country, two-system formula. Specifically, Beijing has persistently induced Taipei to sit at the negotiation table and establish high-level political contact. PRC leaders repeatedly emphasize that everything, including the issue of Taipei's status in international community, is negotiable under the one-China principle, by which they mean Taiwan is an inalienable part of China.

This approach was based on the assumption that political negotiation is the only route to peaceful reunification. During much of the 1980s and early 1990s, all the united-front work, diplomatic, military, and economic measures targeted at Taiwan were designed for a two-sided strategic objective: to preserve the prospect for peaceful reunification and to cajole Taipei to the negotiation table.

Also throughout the 1990s, Beijing leaders put a lot of emphasis on accelerating bilateral economic exchange. In particular, Beijing was keen in pressuring Taipei to abandon its longtime ban on three links: direct trade, air, and sea. In Li Peng's words, achieving the three links would be a breakthrough in China's unification under the one-country, two-systems formula.[26] Interestingly, Beijing has been quite open about the political objectives of its trade and investment policy toward Taiwan. In its official documents, it called "to peddle the [domestic] politics through business; to influence the [Taiwanese] government through the people" (*yishangweizheng, yiminbiguan*). Specifically, Beijing tried to undermine Taiwan leadership's bargaining position by promoting the view that Taipei's persistence on continuing the ban on direct trade and direct air and sea links is politically futile and economically counterproductive.

However, as Taiwan's democratization unfolded, Beijing leaders became increasingly alarmed by the meaning and implications of the steady rise of Taiwanese nationalism claiming a new nationhood and separate identity. Since the 1995–1996 missile crisis in the Taiwan Strait, the more urgent task was redefined as "waging the battle against the 'separatist forces' on the island." The evolution of Beijing's policy toward Taiwan during the 1990s was in a large part about how Jiang Zemin and the members of CLGTA climbed up a stiff learning curve in figuring out how to arrest the rising tide of Taiwanese nationalism as well as live with Taiwan's chaotic pluralism and intractable democracy. The major lesson they learned was that without U.S. cooperation the PRC alone cannot defuse the ticking bomb of Taiwan's independence through political means. So Beijing's policy toward Taiwan became fully integrated with its effort in building up the leverage in the triangular strategic interaction among Beijing, Washington, and Taipei.

The Making of Jiang's Eight-Point Proposal

Although Jiang Zemin did not formally take over the full responsibility of managing the cross-strait relations until the spring of 1993, he had been actively involved in the policy-making process in his capacity of CCP party chief. His most trustworthy senior advisor, Wang Daohan, was directly involved in the secret negotiations with Lee Teng-hui's private envoy as early as 1990. A series of behind-the-scene negotiations between 1990 and 1992 paved the way for the holding of the first high-level semiofficial meeting, in Singapore April 2003. In it, Wang Daohan (chair of the ARATS) met his counterpart C. F. Goo (chair of the Strait Exchange Foundation, Taiwan's semiofficial agency in charge of cross-strait negotiations) and signed a series of agreements dealing with technical issues. Jiang was evidently so encouraged by this initial success of his engagement with Lee Teng-hui that he became confident enough that he wanted to put his personal mark on Beijing's Taiwan policy. Jiang decided to act on Wang Daohan's recommendation on drafting a new policy document on Taiwan issue after the first Goo-Wang talk.[27]

Formulating a new policy guideline on the Taiwan issue was a strong political statement about the coming of Jiang's era. An even more compelling reason for Jiang to take new policy initiatives toward Taiwan was perhaps the looming challenge of the cross-strait relation itself. Profound changes had taken place in the PRC's surrounding environment following the Tiananmen crackdown. First, in the international system, the frosty clarity of the Cold War was replaced by the confusion of the so-called new world order. The emerging structural configuration of the Asia–Pacific security order had made more room for Taiwan's diplomatic maneuvering. After the collapse of Soviet Union, the PRC was increasingly viewed by its neighbor countries as the major power aspirant, whose long-term strategic interests would be potentially in conflict with that of a defending hegemony (the United States) and a regional rivalry (Japan). Furthermore, the transformative potential of the new world order had for a while made it inviting for the people of Taiwan to explore an alternative path of nation building. At the same time, Taiwan's fast-paced democratization has brought about a realignment of state–society relations and a thorough indigenization of the Kuomintang (KMT) power structure. These concurrent developments had jointly precipitated a fundamental shift in Taiwan's overall orientation toward cross-strait relations as well as its international status.

During Taiwan's democratic transition, two trends seemed particularly disturbing for Beijing. The first was the rising support for Taiwan's independence and the corresponding decline of Chinese identity among the Taiwanese populace. Parallel to this trend was the phenomenal growth of the electoral strength of the Democratic Progressive Party (DPP) since the late 1980s. The second disturbing trend was the narrowing ideological distance between the incumbent KMT mainstream faction and the DPP. From the viewpoint of Beijing leadership, the two power blocs had not only formed a tacit alliance in ousting the KMT's nonmainstream faction but also gradually converged over a range of policy domain, from constitutional reform to cross-strait relations foreign policy. For instance, both favored the introduction of popular election for the president. Both emphasized the need to slow down the trend of cross-strait economic integration and to continue the ban on the direct trade, sea, and air links with mainland China. Against this backdrop, Beijing was increasingly alarmed by a series of bold foreign policy initiatives undertaken by Taipei, starting with the pursuit of "dual recognition"[28] in 1989 and culminating in launching an all-out drive for UN membership in early 1993. These moves amounted to a concerted effort for Taiwan's seeking a separate international identity and marked a clear departure from Taipei's long-standing one-China principle.[29]

These trends had serious consequences for Beijing's Taiwan policy. They dampened the prospect for a peaceful reunification over the long term and created a series of diplomatic crisis over the short run. Especially in the early part of 1990s, Taipei had effectively used its ascending economic and political status in the Asia–Pacific region to drive home the point that Beijing was unable to impose international isolation on Taiwan or block the gradual improvement in the island's external relations. Taipei effectively exploited the boycott of the West against Beijing in the aftermath of the Tiananmen crackdown and the eagerness of the French and American governments to salvage their distressed defense industries. Taipei won approval for the purchase of Mirage fighter-jets from France and F-16 fighter-jets from the United States in 1992. Taipei was admitted concurrently with Beijing and Hong Kong to the first minister-level regional economic consultation body—the Asian–Pacific Economic Cooperation (APEC) in 1991.[30] Also, in the winter of 1993–1994, Lee Teng-hui successfully conducted a so-called vacation diplomacy, paying unofficial visits to the Philippines, Indonesia, and Thailand. All these developments pointed to one possibility: the Taiwan issue was going to pose a major challenge to Jiang Zemin's untried leadership.

Around the time when Jiang took over the helm of the CLGTA, the cross-strait relations had shown ample signs of strain, in spite of the upward trend of cross-strait economic interdependence. The holding of the first Wang–Goo talk in Singapore in April 1993 did not bring about a political thaw across the straits as Beijing had hoped. The low-level negotiation over functional issues between the Strait Exchange Foundation (SEF) and ARATS stagnated. Throughout 1994, Taipei had persistently rejected Beijing's proposal to hold the second Wang–Goo talk. The cross-strait stalemate made Beijing increasingly anxious, as Taiwan continued to push for its international recognition and consolidate its democratic transition. At the same time, the diplomatic contest between Taipei and Beijing intensified following Taipei's launch of its UN membership drive in early 1993. Beijing perceived this move as a stepping stone for formal independence and responded first with the issuing of *White Paper on the Taiwan Problem and China's Unification*[31] in mid-1993, by which Beijing made a clear rejection on all the proposals raised by Taipei to participate in the international community, including "one China, two seats." Also, the PRC mobilized all diplomatic resources at its disposal to block Taiwan's attempt to reopen debate on Chinese representation in the General Assembly; at the same time, it pressured all major powers to reiterate their observance of the one-China principle. To send a strong warning signal, the PLA conducted its most extensive military exercises in forty years in autumn 1994. Furthermore, two unrelated incidents made the situation even worse. First, President Lee became critical of mainland Chinese leadership over the tragic criminal accident killing two dozen Taiwanese tourists in the Thousand-Island Lake in late March 1994. At the same time, Beijing leadership became deeply upset by the stunning statements that Lee Teng-hui made in his interview by a Japanese author, Ryotaro Shiba, in April 1994.[32] A crisis over the strait was clearly in the making.

From Jiang's point of view, the precarious situation required a new policy initiative. The old strategy, which placed much hope on the reopening of a CCP–KMT negotiation, was overtaken by the events. Also, Deng Xiaoping's "one country, two systems" formula provided little guidance on how to deal with the rising tide of Taiwan nationalism. It was imperative that Jiang find ways to prevent cross-strait relations from developing into a major crisis. Jiang's policy advisors figured out that to jump-start the peace process and lure the new KMT leadership back to the negotiation table, Beijing must offer some new policy incentives through the promulgation of a major policy proposal. However, a policy proposal of this nature required the collective endorsement of the politburo. Jiang could take the initiative but could not bear the full responsibility. Thus, a process of formulating a policy document got started as early as in the second half of 1993. The writing group consisted of leading Taiwan experts from all the major research institutes, including various PLA institutes. The draft document was circulated among members of the CLGTA and then among members of the politburo for comment. It was reported that Wang Daohan and Wang Zhaoguo were intimately involved in the revision process before its final approval, around the fall of 1994.

Jiang's eight-point proposal for peaceful reunification was significant in a number of ways. First, with the official approval of the politburo, the policy document enjoyed a solid political backing among the collective leadership of the third generation and became unequivocally *the* policy guideline on Taiwan affairs for the post-Deng era. Second, the document revealed an important strategic adjustment in Beijing's approach toward Taiwan. While upholding the "one country, two systems" formula, the new guideline placed more emphases on concrete proposals—for example, holding a cross-strait summit and signing an agreement to end the state of hostility, for stepwise rapprochement between Taiwan and mainland China during the pre-reunification stage. This suggested that the third-generation leadership discounted the possibility of speedy reunification. Instead, these leaders gave priority to reaching a bilateral accord under a transitional framework, which ideally would uphold the long-term prospect of peaceful reunification, facilitate bilateral economic exchange, stabilize the status quo, and preempt the independence option. In this way, Jiang could pass the hot issue of "Hong Kong first, Taiwan next" to the next generation while preserving a stable and peaceful surrounding environment for China's economic reform. Third, the proposal suggested that Jiang was ready for a political bargain. The document revealed that as long as Taipei is willing to come to the negotiation table under the principle of one China, Beijing stands ready to address Taipei's three preconditions for lifting the ban on "three links"—namely, that the PRC must renounce the use of force against Taiwan, recognize Taiwan as a political entity on equal footing, and allow Taiwan to have reasonable space for international participation. To sweeten the offer, the document implied that "one China" did not necessarily mean "the PRC," because throughout the proposal the name PRC never appeared. Fourth, the document reflected Beijing's new reading of Taiwan's internal politics. It acknowledged Taiwan's democratization and the resultant Taiwanization of the power structure; it recognized Taiwan's emerging political pluralism and tried to reach out to all political parties and social forces; and moreover, it suggested that despite a growing suspicion of Taipei's hidden agenda among Beijing leadership, Jiang still placed a high hope on Lee Teng-hui, who continued to enjoy a firm grip on Taiwan's mainland policy.

Little did Jiang and his top advisors know that this policy initiative actually reconfirmed Taipei long-held assumptions about the predicament of the CCP leadership. Lee Teng-hui continued to push his two-pronged strategy, meaning that any significant improvement on Taiwan–mainland relations had to be accompanied by a parallel measure to strengthen Taiwan's sovereign status in the international community.[33] First, Lee Teng-hui offered a lukewarm but largely positive six-point response to Jiang's peace overture in April 1995. Next, Taipei gave the cross-strait relations a boost by making a series of goodwill measures: agreeing to hold the second Wang–Goo talk in Beijing, to hold the talk annually, and to expand the agenda to include political issues. But at the same time, Taipei doubled its lobbying effort on Capitol Hill to pressure the White House to grant president Lee Teng-hui a visitor visa for his summer trip to Cornell University, his alma mater. Taipei's reading of Jiang's political predicament was probably right on the mark, but its calculation that Jiang would be lured to accept Taipei's favored rule-of-game turned to be quite off the mark.

The 1995–1996 Strait Crisis and the Aftermath

The White House's decision in May 1995 on Lee's visa took Beijing by surprise. The decision touched off Beijing's worst fear—that is, that the United States was pursuing an undeclared policy agenda of containing China and playing up the Taiwan card. To ward off the possible domino effect following Lee's visit to the United States, Jiang Zemin had little choice but allow the hard-liners to set the policy tone for the moment. Beijing immediately suspended the proposed second Wang–Goo talk. It then launched a week of missile tests off Taiwan's northern coast in late July to remind the United States, Japan, and Taipei of the dire consequences of sponsoring (or pursuing) the Taiwan independence cause. On the eve of the KMT congress for presidential nomination in late August, the PLA launched the second round of missile tests near a Taiwan-controlled off-shore island. With a clear aim of disrupting President Lee's reelection bid, Beijing's decided to extend the military threats well in to election day.

Rounds of live-ammunition exercise, however, did little to stop Lee's campaign momentum. The crisis in the strait might have actually helped Lee Teng-hui's reelection, as many traditional DPP supporters shifted their support based on the worry that Taiwan might lose ground to the PRC if the majority could not speak with one voice.[34] Besides, much of the potential damage that the PLA's military threats might have done to Lee's reelection bid was partially neutralized by the U.S. decision to send two battle groups to the international water near the Taiwan Strait. In the end, Lee walked away with a convincing victory, winning 54 percent of the popular vote in a four-way race.

Jiang Zemin apparently emerged out of the strait crisis unscathed. During the crisis, he had gone along with the PLA and allowed the hawkish option to run the full course. He also accommodated a more assertive PLA in managing cross-strait relations. From Jiang's point of view, the saber-rattling strategy was justified on the ground that the prospect for peaceful reunification had been threatened by what the PRC had perceived as Taipei's "creeping independence" strategy. This warning shot helped Taiwan as well as the United States and Japan have a better grasp of Beijing's bottom-line position and update their assessment about the risk associated with any attempt to change the status-quo unilaterally. However, in the aftermath of the crisis, it also became quite clear that the saber-rattling strategy had its limits and many undesirable side effects. It might have dampened the momentum of Taiwan independence movement for the short run, but at the same time it triggered an emotional backlash from many Taiwanese people. It also pushed the United States and Japan into a stronger military alliance and forced them to take a clearer position on extending security commitment to Taiwan.

One of the lessons that Jiang had drawn from the ill-fated attempt to cajole Taipei to the negotiation table in 1995 was that, unless the United States was interested in playing a more active role in status-quo management, Taipei could reject Beijing's peace overture at virtually no cost. To regain the control over the tempo of cross-strait relations, Jiang had to play up the U.S. card. Clinton's decision to rebuild the political foundation of United States–China relations, based on the concept of a forward-looking strategic partnership, gave Jiang Zemin a golden opportunity to revive the political momentum of peace overture toward Taiwan.

Beijing had been quite successful in persuading the Clinton administration to view Taipei's diplomatic venture through a separatist lens and perceive the need to restrain the independence aspiration. In exchange for the PRC's cooperation in other issue baskets, the U.S. government came out forcefully to urge the two sides to resume the dialogue, emphasizing that Taipei should take the initiative. Next, Jiang personally pressured Clinton to take an unambiguous stand on the issue of Taiwan's international status. During his first state visit to the United States, in October 1997, Jiang secured the pledge from the Clinton administration to the "three no's"—no support of Taiwan independence, no support for two Chinas (or "one China, one Taiwan"), and no support for Taiwan's membership in international organizations that require statehood. Furthermore, during Clinton's China trip in summer 1998, to reciprocate Jiang's bold move to broadcast live their joint press conference in Beijing, Clinton decided to publicly announce the three no's at a seminar held in Shanghai.

Beijing was also encouraged by the growing rift between the KMT's central leadership and Taiwan's business community over the issue of three links. The big businesses were eager to reactivate their mainland China projects as soon as strait crisis dissipated. Lee Teng-hui's "don't rush, be patient" (*jieji yongren*) policy of August 1996 had only a short-term effect on dampening the Taiwanese big businesses' "mainland fever."[35] The business community strongly advocated that the existing restriction on cross-strait exchange carried an increasingly higher economic price tag for Taiwan than it did for mainland China.

Entering the second half of 1997, the overall policy environment—from Beijing's perspective—seemed ripe for a revival of the peace process as all the strategic chips gradually fell into places: Beijing had regained the upperhand position in the diplomatic contest with Taipei; the July 1997 Hong Kong handover went smoothly; the difficult issue of personnel reshuffling at the highest echelon was largely settled on the eve of the Fifteenth Party Congress; and Jiang's first state visit to the United States was well underway. All these developments supposedly would strengthen Beijing's leverage at the negotiation table.

In perfect synchronization with Beijing's diplomatic move, Qian Qichen issued a statement less than three weeks before Jiang launched his first state visit to the United States to call on Taipei to hold preparatory talks to lay the groundwork for the opening of political talks.[36] On Jiang's return from the United States, Beijing offered the clearest gesture ever since the breakup of the semiofficial channel in June 1995 for its readiness to resume the cross-strait talks between the ARATS and the SEF.[37] Beijing's latest olive branch was followed by a major policy speech by Qian Qichen on the eve of the Lunar New Year in 1998 at a seminar in the Great Hall of the People to commemorate the third anniversary of Jiang Zemin's eight-point proposal. Qian called on Taiwan to respond to Jiang's offer to end cross-strait hostility and open discussions under the one-China principle. This time Qian sent a strong signal that Beijing had lowered the threshold for the opening of political talks with Taipei. Qian dropped hints that although negotiations must take place under the one-China principle, "one China" did not necessarily mean the People's Republic of China. Said Qian, "As far as cross-strait relations are concerned, one-China principle means there is only one China, Taiwan is a part of China, and the sovereignty and the territorial integrity of China cannot be divided." That was the most conciliatory note coming from Beijing's senior cadres on the sensitive issue of the one-China principle to date.[38] All these wooing efforts suggested that Jiang Zemin was undeterred by previous failed attempts to induce Taipei back to the one-China framework. He was motivated to give his eight-point proposal a new boost.

Under intensified U.S. pressure, Taipei responded to Beijing's latest peace overture by sending a high-level delegation led by C. F. Goo to visit Shanghai and Beijing in October 1998. Although Beijing was annoyed by the fact that Goo was instructed by Taipei to use this highly visible event to underscore its differences with Beijing over the issue of sovereignty, it was encouraged by the prospect of a reciprocal visit by Wang Daohan to Taiwan next year. To maximize the political impact of this historic visit, Beijing was ready to offer Taipei membership in certain specialized UN agencies, such as the World Health Organization, as long as Taipei was willing to negotiate its international status under the one-China principle.[39] To ward off Beijing's relentless efforts to put the genie of Taiwanese nationalism back into the one-China bottle, Lee Teng-hui dropped a political bombshell by announcing his "special state-to-state" formula in July 1999. A week later, Beijing fired the first warning shot by sending fighter jets crossing the "mid-strait line," an utterly menacing operation unseen in forty years. While mobilizing its troops along the coast, Beijing vehemently demanded that Taipei retract this policy announcement. It took U.S. brinkmanship to prevent the incident from escalating into a major crisis in the strait.[40] A devastating earthquake struck Taiwan on September 21 and inadvertently defused an imminent military crisis. Also gone was Jiang Zemin's second attempt to jump-start the cross-strait relations.

Coping with Taiwan's Political Earthquake

Toward the end of his official tenure as the CCP secretary-general, Jiang's position was so well entrenched and he had so many sufficient strings to pull that he did not have to worry about his immediate successor closely scrutinizing his record on the Taiwan issues. However, Jiang must have harbored lingering concerns that history might not treat him as kindly. Indeed, as he reflected over his own record, his handling of recurring political crises in the strait constituted a frustrating chapter of his leadership. On his watch, Beijing's peaceful reunification campaign suffered a series of major setbacks. His administration failed to stop Taipei from breaking away from the so-called one-China principle. Also, he learned the hard way how to live with, and work around, Taiwan's budding democracy. Repeatedly, Beijing's united-front strategies (intended to prop up pro-reunification forces in Taiwan) and its intimidating measures (intended to arrest the rising tide of Taiwanese nationalism) turned out to be futile or even counterproductive. The strategy to exert heavier military pressures on Taiwan might have persuaded Taipei from pursuing outright de jure independence, but it was not very effective in keeping Taipei's "creeping independence" strategy in check. Additionally, the intended psychological impact of this double-edged strategy was largely nullified by Taiwan's steady acquisition of higher-grade defensive weapon systems from the United States and a stepwise upgrading of United States–Taiwan military cooperation under the Bush administration. The Bush administration also firmed up the United States' security commitment to Taiwan; "strategic ambiguity," the policy under which Washington for two decades declined to say how it would respond to a PRC attack on Taiwan, was replaced by "strategic clarity." The "three communiqués," the legal pillars that oblige the United States to adhere to its one-China policy, have increasingly come to look like empty shells, their substance either worn out by the changing circumstances and countervailing precedents, or nullified by the elevated guiding authority of the Taiwan Relations Act. All such developments make it more difficult for Beijing to hold up the prospect for a peaceful resolution of the issue. The only development that has moved in a direction favorable to Beijing is the intensification of cross-strait economic ties. But so far, Beijing has not been able to find dependable ways to reap its promised political payoffs.

The most devastating blow to Beijing's reunification campaign was dealt by the electoral victory of the pro-independence DPP in March 2000. This unexpected political earthquake virtually shattered Jiang's hope for wooing Taipei back to the negotiation table before the expiration of his official term. Jiang and his top advisors had to hide their frustration behind the empty rhetoric of "listening to [Chen Shui-bian's] words and watching his deeds," suggesting that they had little choice but to put the DPP government on an extended political probation.[41] Once again, the credibility of his handling the cross-strait relations was on the line.

Beijing's policy toward Taiwan sat in limbo for almost a year and a half as Jiang and his top advisors sized up the political situation in a post-KMT, post–Lee Teng-hui Taiwan. While waiting for the outcomes of Taiwan's December 2001 legislative Yuan election, they were scratching their heads for new policy thinking that could help them spot the silver linings in the situation, redefine their tasks, and reset their priorities. This convalescing process also entailed a rehashing of the consensus's obtaining among members of the politburo over what adjustments in strategies and tactics were necessary to reverse the losing battle against the "separatist forces" on the island and rejuvenate the moribund peaceful reunification campaign.

Toward the end of 2001, a reformulated operational guideline began to take shape out of this long-convalescing process. At the same time, a post–September 11 strengthening of a Sino–United States strategic cooperation, a deteriorating set of economic and political conditions in Taiwan, and a faith in the long-term viability of a peaceful reunification campaign appeared to help the CCP leaders restore much of their confidence in their ability to defuse the ticking bomb of Taiwan independence.

From these reformulated operational guidelines came a new round of peace initiatives targeted at the people of Taiwan in general and the pragmatic elements within the DPP camp in particular. Much like the scenario in January 1998, Beijing assembled its propaganda machinery around a major policy speech by Qian Qichen at a ceremony commemorating the seventh anniversary of Jiang's eight-point proposal. Most notable, Qian was joined on the stage by Hu Jintao and Zeng Qinghong, reputedly the two most powerful figures of the up-and-coming leadership. The launch of this new peace overture, definitely the last on Jiang's watch, signaled that Jiang was determined not to end his official tenure with a sour note on cross-strait relations. The unprecedented joint appearance of Hu and Zeng on a Taiwan-centered occasion was designed to send the message that Jiang's best and final offer enjoyed the full backing of the fourth generation. Jiang probably also wanted to use this well-orchestrated policy speech to project a favorable public image, reassuring the CCP rank and file that Jiang and his top advisors were again on top of the treacherous situation and were resetting the tone of the internal discussion over the Taiwan issues well before the complicated upcoming negotiations over leadership succession, due to begin in the next few months. To reinforce Qian's policy speech, some of its key elements were subsequently reiterated by top Chinese officials at domestic and international occasions, including Jiang Zemin's public speech at Texas A&M University during his October 2002 trip to the United States. The crescendo reached its final climax at the Sixteenth Communist Party Congress, as certain selling points of the new peace overture became codified and enshrined in Jiang's party work report to the CCP's Sixteenth Congress.

Jiang's report officially codified Beijing's new formulation of how it defined the one-China principle.[42] The rephrasing was meant to address Taiwan's sensitivity over the issue of pro forma parity. He also tried to sweeten the "one country, two systems" formula by elaborating of what might conceivably be a set of value-added elements to the people of Taiwan.[43] For the first time, his report officially acknowledged that under the premise of the one-China principle, Beijing was willing to address Taipei's demand for an expanding international space.[44] Furthermore, Jiang's report reinserted a veiled threat that Beijing would not allow the Taiwan issues to drag on indefinitely.[45]

Chinese top leaders' carefully crafted policy initiatives reveal that they have undertaken some meaningful adjustments and adaptations to take into account the new developments across the strait and the windows of opportunity opened in the post–September 11 world. A number of significant policy signals came out of Beijing's most recent peace overture. First, Beijing's recent effort to repackage its old messages is significant in its own right. It suggests that members of the CLGTA have finally climbed up a stiff learning curve in figuring out how to live with Taiwan's chaotic pluralism and intractable democracy. They have paid more attention to the social pulse of the Taiwanese general public, and they have exhibited more concern with how Beijing's peace overtures might be received by the great majority of Taiwan's electorate.

Next the recent signals suggest that Beijing has reset its short-term priorities. It no longer lays its expectations on wooing Taipei back to the negotiation table under the premise of the one-China principle anytime soon. They have probably conceded to the idea that there is little chance that the DPP government is going to embrace the so-called 1992 consensus or acknowledge the one-China principle in any form acceptable to them. Furthermore, they have recognized that it is unrealistic to expect any democratically elected Taiwanese government to relinquish Taiwan's sovereign status under the rubric of the

Republic of China. Not even the so-called Pan-Blue camp (comprising the KMT and its offshoot parties) would go that far—its pro-unification orientation, support for the deepening of cross-strait economic integration, and willingness to embrace the 1992 consensus notwithstanding.

With dimming hopes for cutting political deals, Jiang and his top advisors concentrated all their efforts on promoting the three links in their last-ditch fight to improve the batting record before Jiang's full retirement. To this end, Beijing considerably lowered the political threshold for establishing the three links. Qian approved the negotiation module that helped renew the civil aviation agreement between Taiwan and Hong Kong after 1997 to cross-strait shipping and air links.[46] This manifest a marked shift in Beijing's priorities: during much of the 1990s, Beijing's top priority had always been tying down Taiwan with the one-China principle and wooing Taipei into political talks; this time it chose to make the three links priority over any political negotiation.

Furthermore, Beijing has demonstrated new flexibility in applying its united-front strategy. It has been trying to reach out to virtually all significant groups across the political spectrum of the island. As Taiwanese politics enters the post-KMT era, Beijing has placed more emphasis on cultivating goodwill with the pragmatic elements within the DDP camp. It welcomes virtually all DPP politicians to visit the mainland in their private capacity, regardless of their standing on the independence issue. Ostensibly, however, it tried to drive a wedge between the fundamentalist and the moderate within the DPP. In Qian's words, Beijing recognizes "the distinction between the great majority DPP members and the very tiny number of inscrutable separatists." It even proposed that once the DPP takes the "Taiwan independence provision" off its party charter, it will be possible for the CCP to engage the DPP on a party-to-party basis.

Pragmatic thinking also permeated Beijing's approach to the Washington–Beijing–Taipei triangular relations. More than ever, Beijing is keen to build up leverage within this triangular strategic relationship. For instance, in the weeks leading up to the 2002 summit meeting at Bush's ranch in Crawford, Texas, China moved to establish additional rules controlling the export of missile technology and dual-use biological and chemical agents, and it has tightened military export regulations, seeking to remove long-standing irritants in relations with Washington.[47] This represents a marked shift in Beijing's bargaining strategy; it used to link cooperation on proliferation issues with U.S. moves to limit arms sales to Taiwan. In contrast to this, Jiang Zemin suggested, during his meeting with President Bush in October 2002, that China could reduce its short-range missiles deployment facing Taiwan in exchange for a cutback in U.S. arms sales to the Taiwanese military.[48] China's recent move to turn its missile deployment into a strategic lever represents not only a sophisticated integration of its military strategy with its political strategy but also its earnest subscription to quintessential pragmatism. Previously China had demanded that the United States cut its arms sales to Taiwan unilaterally and offered no quid pro quo, always insisting that any issue involving its missile deployments was an "internal matter" and could not be discussed. China's latest strategic gesture is also symbolically significant in the way that it suggests that Beijing leadership has come close to acknowledging the United States as the de facto custodian over Taiwan, an attitudinal adjustment inconceivable only a few years ago.

All of the aforementioned suggest a shift that may be of deeper importance, a possible shift in Chinese top leaders' long-term vision and underlying assumptions. As they update their assessment about the challenges and opportunities brought about by the changing political and economic conditions in Taiwan and by the new developments taking place in the larger international context, a new confidence and a new perception of China's rising standing in the region can be posited as what accounts for the programmatic adaptability, new flexibility, and professed pragmatism identified here. This marked shift has manifested itself not just through the Chinese leaders' approach toward the issue of Taiwan but also in a score of other foreign policy issues, from South China Sea, the ASEAN–China Free Trade Agreement, nuclear proliferation, terrorism, drug trafficking, environmental issues, and the World Trade Organization. In the context of cross-strait relations, Chinese leaders increasingly appear to be approaching the Taiwan issue with a newly acquired confidence in the country's overall capacity to keep Taiwan within its political and economic orbit and with the implicit underlying assumption that "time is on the PRC's side." Therefore they can afford to be more flexible and patient, more reticent about Taipei's diplomatic venture, and more tolerant of stalemate or even short-term setbacks.

Their new confidence first came from an updated reading of the United States' strategic intentions, especially those of the Bush administration. While still harboring some lingering suspicions, they have become increasingly convinced that Washington is not disingenuous about its pledge of "not supporting Taiwan independence," through witnessing Washington's preventive diplomacy as well as its crisis management at work. For instance, Beijing leadership recognizes that the United States played an important behind-the-scenes role in installing the "five no's" pledge[49] into Chen Shui-bian's inaugural speech in May 2000.[50] Beijing also acknowledged the prompt actions taken by Bush's national security team to control the damage caused by Chen's remark on "two states on each side of the strait."

Their new confidence also stems from vast improvements over the past few years in the PLA's capacity to wage high-tech warfare and in a new recognition that the cross-strait military balance has moved steadily in Beijing's favor, given Taiwan's rapidly deteriorating fiscal capacity. Increasingly, its military capacity is becoming more than just a threatening gesture. Sustained increases in defense spending and new, high-tech weaponry now give Beijing leaders "an increasing number of credible options to intimidate or actually attack Taiwan" in the event that Taipei crosses the red lines. Beijing leadership also believes that maintaining a credible military deterrence is an indispensable element in reinforcing Washington's motivation and seriousness in harnessing the Taiwanese independence horse.

A further source of Beijing's new confidence stems from their rereading of the meaning and implications of Taiwan's transition into the post–Lee Teng-hui era. They have spotted quite a few silver linings in the DPP-reigning sky. There has been a marked shift in the popular opinion in favor of further economic integration with Chinese mainland, especially among the young generation. Grim long-term prospects have prompted a large number of small-business owners and young professionals, believing that Taiwan's economy has passed its prime, to look seriously for career opportunities in the mainland. Many of them began to resettle their families in Shanghai and other metropolitan areas.

Most important, Beijing leaders' new confidence is fueled by the staggering trend of cross-strait economic integration and its political implications. Mainland China has rapidly evolved into Taiwan's largest export market, an indispensable manufacturing platform for its export-oriented sector, its most important source of trade surplus, and the top recipient of the island's outbound capital flows. Taiwanese companies have a total investment of at least US$70 billion in China, with more than sixty thousand projects in operation and with more than three-quarter-million Taiwanese expatriates minding the business on the mainland. More than half of Taiwan's listed companies and virtually all of the island's top conglomerates have set up subsidiaries or joint ventures in China.[51] Many of them will soon generate bigger revenues in the Chinese mainland market than in Taiwanese and thus become more susceptible to Beijing's regulatory authority and goodwill. None of these developments has escaped Beijing's policy makers' observation.

Finally, Chinese leaders have also learned how to use their newly gained strategic leverage in strengthening their hand in forming a diplomatic united-front among virtually all significant players in the region for containing Taiwan's push for formal independence. China has rapidly become an indispensable part of the global economy. While China becomes intensively enmeshed with the outside world, its trading partners are equally vulnerable to this syndrome of complex interdependence. China is now the biggest export market for Japan, South Korea, and virtually all neighboring economies. For all China's major trading partners, their stake in the regional peace has grown to such extent that a military showdown in the strait has become something almost unthinkable and utterly unacceptable. An outbreak of military conflict between China and the United States would surely trigger a rupture in the global supply chains, send the world economy into a deep recession, and create a major havoc in the international financial market. An updated assessment of China's changing strategic environment has reinforced Beijing's confidence in China's overall capacity to keep Taiwan within its political and economic orbit.

CONCLUSION: THE PROSPECT OF
CROSS-STRAIT RELATIONS UNDER HU JINTAO

No Chinese leaders can afford to be seen as being soft on the Taiwan issue, especially at a time of power succession. For China's leaders, the Taiwan issue is inextricably related to national self-respect and regime survival. The Chinese leadership would thus almost certainly fight to avoid the loss of Taiwan if it concluded that no other alternative existed. However, as long as the Chinese leaders remain confident about China's overall capacity to keep Taiwan within its political and economic orbit and that "time is on the PRC's side," they can afford to be more patient, more reticent about Taipei's political provocation, and more tolerant of stalemate or even short-term setbacks.

Hu Jintao assumed the formal responsibility of managing the cross-strait relations soon after being elected the president of the People's Republic of China at the Tenth National People's Congress. Navigating in the shadow of still-ambitious Jiang, Hu has neither the incentive nor the desire to alter his predecessor's basic policy framework, which was first laid out in Jiang's eight-point proposal and then enshrined in his farewell party work report to the CCP Sixteenth Party Congress.[52] More fundamental, even as Jiang Zemin steadily withdraws himself from the active management of cross-strait relations, Hu will find himself operating under a similar set of external and internal constraints. The delicate power-sharing arrangement construed at the Sixteenth Party Congress left Hu with even less latitude for personal predilections over this sensitive issue than Jiang had held at a similar stage of power succession in the early 1990s.

However, Hu also found out quickly after taking over the helm that he probably will not have the luxury of passing the hot issue to the next generation. He would be compelled to wrestle with the Taiwan issue on his watch. Less than a year in his capacity of the leader of CLGTA, Hu Jintao and his trouble-shooting premier, Wen Jiabao, were confronted with another one of Chen Shui-bian's startling political ventures—his pledge to hold Taiwan's first referendum on cross-strait relations during Taiwan's March 2004 election. This time Hu and Wen have dealt with the boiling situation with a level of calm and confidence not seen before. They avoided employing a saber-rattling strategy altogether and relied almost exclusively on exerting diplomatic pressure to make Taipei backpaddle.

Beijing exerted tremendous pressure on the Bush administration, asking Washington to rein in Chen Shui-bian under a veiled threat of military showdown. The crescendo of the United States' open objection to Chen Shui-bian's referendum plan reached its climax on December 9, 2003, when Bush, in front of the visiting Wen Jiabao, made a sternly worded remark criticizing the Taiwan leader for his intention to "unilaterally change the status quo." In addition, with the help of the White House, Beijing has successfully nullified an initiative by some members of the Taiwan caucus of the U.S. Congress to pass a joint resolution supporting Taiwan's controversial referendum. This is the first incident in recent memory where Beijing prevailed in a behind-the-scene political wrangling between China and Taiwan in swaying the senior leadership of the U.S. Congress. Also, at the urge of Chinese leaders, the governments of Japan, Germany, France, South Korea, and the ASEAN countries have all lined up behind the Bush administration, registering their disapproval in loud and clear languages—something inconceivable only a few years ago. This latest round of Beijing-orchestrated diplomatic strangling culminated in French president Jacques Chirac's remark calling the March 2004 referendum "a grave mistake" that would destabilize Asia. In the end the DPP government was pressured to back off from its earlier pledge to use the referendum to affirm Chen Shui-bian's "two states on each side of the strait" formulation or to demand that China withdraw ballistic missiles targeting the island. Instead, the DPP government put a watered-down version of the two propositions on the ballot to make the unprecedented referendum seemingly less provocative. Although Beijing was disappointed by the outcomes of Taiwan's recent presidential election, it could still see a ray of hope in the fact that the two referenda on relations with the mainland were nullified by Taiwan's electorate, as they failed to pass the legal threshold of 50 percent turnout.

The reelection of Chen Shui-bian will no doubt severely strain the cross-strait relations over the next few years. The election result dashed the hope that Beijing can "count on the people of Taiwan" in reversing the rising tide of Taiwanese nationalism. Furthermore, Beijing believes that Chen's plan for another referendum in late 2006—to rewrite the constitution, which preserves Taiwan's few formal ties to China—would move Taiwan much closer to permanent separation from the mainland China. The fourth-generation leadership will thus feel compelled to devise a contingency plan and take a cool-headed review of China's national priorities. It will also be doubly motivated to accelerate

China's military and diplomatic preparations. These leaders still believe that their main task is to convince Washington that, to avoid the loss of Taiwan, the Chinese leadership would almost certainly have to resort to coercive strategy, even if it entails sacrificing good relations with the West and the economic benefits that accrue from those relations. They are still pinning their hope that under an intensive U.S. intervention, Chen might not be able to deliver a new constitution, as a 2006 referendum may be voted down by many worrisome Taiwanese voters, much as it was the case for the 2004 referendum. As long as the Chinese leadership still believes that the United States also wants to avoid a military clash over Taiwan, it would allow Washington's preventive diplomacy to run its full course before it concludes that no other alternatives exist.

NOTES

1. Jiang Zemin unveiled his historic proposal, entitled "Continue to Promote the Reunification of China," on January 30, 1995, the eve of the Chinese Lunar New Year. For a text of his proposal, see the website of the Taiwan Affairs Office of the State Council at www.gwytb.gov.cn:8088/index.asp.

2. For an elaborative analysis of this point, see Yun-han Chu, "Jiang Zemin and the Evolution of Beijing's Policy toward Taiwan," in *China Under Jiang Zemin*, ed. Hung-mao Tien and Yun-han Chu (Boulder, Colo.: Lynne Rienner, 2000).

3. For an analysis of the policy research apparatus supporting the CLGTA during the Jiang's era, see Yun-han Chu, "Jiang Zemin and the Evolution of Beijing's Policy toward Taiwan," and Michael Swaine, "Chinese Decision-Making regarding Taiwan," in *The Making of Chinese Foreign and Security Policy in the Era of Reform*, ed. David M. Lampton (Stanford, Calif.: Stanford University Press, 2002).

4. This view is also shared by other analysts. See, for example, Lampton, *The Making of Chinese Foreign and Security Policy in the Era of Reform*.

5. For this general trend, see Carol Lee Hamrin and Suisheng Zhao, eds., *Decision-Making in Deng's China* (Armonk, N.Y.: M. E. Sharpe, 1995).

6. Please refer to Yang Kai-huang, "Zhonggong duitai zhengce jieshi yu pinggu" [An explanation and evaluation of PRC's taiwan policy], *Dongwu zhengzhi xuebao* [Soochow Review of Political Science] 7 (1997): 66–103; and Tsai Wei, "Zhonggong duitai zhengce de juece zuzhi yu guocheng" [The decision-making apparatus and process of the PRC's taiwan policy], *Zhongguo dalu yanjiu* [Journal of Mainland China Studies] 40, no. 5 (May 1997).

7. Xiong was later on promoted to the deputy chief of general staff.

8. Before Jiang, Liao Chenzhi (the former head of the CCP United Front Department and the State Council Overseas Chinese Affairs Office), Deng Yingchao (the widow of Zhou Enlai), and Yang Shangkun (the nominal head-of-state) had by turn served that post. See Yang Kai-huang, "Zhonggong duitai zhengce jieshi yu pinggu" [An explanation and evaluation of PRC's taiwan policy].

9. Also, before this reorganization, to reduce redundancy and simplify the task of policy coordination, the CCP Taiwan Affairs Office and the State Council Taiwan Affairs Office were merged into one in March 1991.

10. Of course, it is quite possible that some systems were not entitled to an official membership but were invited to sit in the regular meetings of the CLGTA.

11. The CCP/State Council Taiwan Affairs Office is supervised by the Central Committee General Office and the State Council. Its primary function is to carry out united-front work toward Taiwan. At the same time, it is responsible for the coordination among State Council agencies.

12. In Chinese, it is called *duitai jingmao gongzuo xietiao xiaozu.*

13. For an analysis of the role of various research institutes and departments in the overall Taiwan affairs policy apparatus, see Tsai Wei, "Zhonggong duitai zhengce de juece zuzhi yu guocheng" [The decision-making apparatus and process of the PRC's taiwan policy].

14. Li Ruihuan is Wang Zhaoguo's superior in the united-front work system. However, as far as Taiwan policy is concerned, Wang reports to Jiang rather than to Li Ruihuan.

15. For the model of fragmentation of authority, see Kenneth Lieberthal and David M. Lampton, eds., *Bureaucracy, Politics and Decision Making in Post-Mao China* (Berkeley: University of California Press, 1992).

16. Based on the report of the *United Daily News*, April 20, 1998.

17. One can always question how the quality of the policy analysis conducted by these Taiwan-affairs think tanks. My personal observation is that they are on the whole getting better over time as far as monitoring Taiwan's internal political dynamics. The reasons are quite simple. First, most of the leading analysts have taken field trips to Taiwan. Second, most of them conduct frequent contacts with scholars and specialists from Taiwan. Third, they get easy access to Taiwan's leading newspaper and political commentaries, which provide a rich source of information. Some PLA-related research institutes even regularly browse through Taiwan-based websites.

18. See the report and analysis by Hong Kong–based *Wenhui Daily*, October 25, 2003. This is worth noting that this authoritative report refuted some earlier reports about the membership of Kuo Boxiong, the vice chairman of the Central Military Commission, in the CLGTA.

19. It was reported that Jiang's political allies in the politburo cited the "treacherous Taiwan situation" in asking president Jiang Zemin to remain in his post of CMC chair. According to CNN, this orchestrated decision was made by the twenty-five-member politburo shortly after its members had been elected into office at the first plenary session of new Central Committee. See the report by Willy Wo-Lap Lam, CNN senior China analyst, "Taiwan Issues Keep Jiang in Army Role," November 22, 2002, CNN, Hong Kong, China.

20. *China Times* carried a series of revealing reports about the secret meeting across the Taiwan Strait through "private envoys" in mid-July 2000. About the secret meetings between Zeng and Su, see *China Times*, July 20, 2000, 3.

21. See a report by Zhu Jianlin, *China Times*, January 25, 2002, 13.

22. According to media reports, sources close to the Jiang camp said that Jiang had expressed doubts in private about Hu's ability to control the powerful personalities on the new CMC. They included CMC vice chairmen–general Guo Boxiong and Cao Gangchuan and the newly promoted chief of staff General Liang Guanglie. The trio had in closed-door meetings given vent to hawkish views about the need to "expedite military preparation" to reabsorb Taiwan.

23. It was reported that in his first two months as Communist Party chief, Hu Jintao has moved swiftly to create an image for himself as a champion of China's forgotten poor, see Erik Echholm, "China's New Leader Works to Set Himself Apart," *New York Times*, January 12, 2003.

24. Deng laid down the basic guideline of peaceful reunification at a CCP high-level meeting held December 8–22, 1978. The "one country, two systems" formula was first unveiled during his interview by Chinese American scholar Yang Liyu in 1983.

25. Ye Jianyin, the chairman of the National People's Congress Standing Committee, unveiled this historic speech, entitled "Message to Compatriots in Taiwan," which is also known as Ye's nine points, as it contains nine bullet points. For a full text, see *Beijing Review*, February 3, 1986.

26. Government report to the Sixth Plenary Meeting of the Seventh National People's Congress, April 1993.

27. On this point, also refer to Sheng Lijun, "China Eyes Taiwan: Why Is a Breakthrough So Difficult?" *Journal of Strategic Studies* 21, no. 1 (March 1998): 65–78.

28. *Dual recognition* means that a foreign government simultaneously extends diplomatic recognition to the PRC and the ROC (Republic of China) governments. Taipei made its first attempt on July 20, 1989, when the ROC government established formal diplomatic ties with Grenada, in spite of the fact that St. George had maintained formal ties with Beijing since 1985 and officially recognized the government of the PRC as the "sole legal government of China." See Chu Yun-han, *The Security Challenge for Taiwan in the Cold War Era*, East Asian Institute report, Columbia University, February 1995.

29. Around the early 1990s, it became a widely held view among the incumbent native élite that adherence to the one-China principle endangered the ROC's sovereign status in the international community. This principle has entrapped Taiwan in diplomatic isolation since early 1970s. Also, this principle provides Taiwan with little multilateral guarantee against PRC's forced retrocession, while giving the PRC all the pretexts it needs to refuse foreign intervention in the case of military confrontation.

30. Following the Asian Development Bank precedent, Taiwan was admitted with Taipei's de facto acceptance of the designation "Taipei, China." That formula honors the principle of one China while acknowledging the reality of two Chinese regimes and, consequently, two governments.

31. Jiang Zemin did not inject much personal input into this sternly phrased document, which had taken shape during Yang Shangkun's tenure.

32. On the impact of the interview on the perception of Beijing leadership, see Sheng Lijun, "China Eyes Taiwan."

33. This is deemed politically prudent because it can dispel the suspicion of the DPP and alleviate the fear of a substantial portion of the population that favors the

preservation of status quo. It is also deemed strategically necessary because only with a stronger multilateral backing for Taiwan's political autonomy will Taiwan have the confidence to engage mainland China into closer economic cooperation and possibly direct political negotiation. It also helped clear away any false impression that the international community might have about the possibility that the two sides were moving fast toward a political rapprochement.

34. Most opinion polls show that the traditional DPP votes accounted for at least a fifth to a quarter of the 54 percent popular vote that went to Lee Teng-hui. This is evidented by the aggregate election statistics as well. For instance, there is a gap of 9 percent popular vote between the overall electoral support received by the DPP presidential candidates and that of the National Assembly candidates.

35. For a background of the so-called *don't rush, be patient* policy, see *China Times*, August 15, 1996, 1.

36. Xinhua News Agency, September 30, 1997.

37. The ARATS issued an invitation to Chiao Jen-ho, SEF secretary-general, for his prospective participation in a seminar to be held in Xiamen around late November, with the implicit understanding that Chiao will be able to meet with his counterpart, Tang Shubei, Beijing's top negotiator and executive vice chairman of ARATS.

38. In a private meeting with some visitors from Taiwan, Wang Daohan reportedly offered an even more flexible intepretation of the one-China principle. It was quoted that he characterized the one-China principle as a commitment to an ongoing process of constructing a new and unified China. However, *Wenghui Bao* of Hong Kong later on ran report to correct such characterization.

39. The story about a World Health Organization offer was based on Professor Chiu Hung-tai's account published in *United Daily*, May 25, 2003.

40. The Clinton administration immediately dispatched a high-level mission led by assistant secretary Stan Roth to Beijing to put out the political flame by reassuring PRC leadership that the United States abides by its one-China policy, does not endorse Lee's formula, and will stop Taipei from going any further. At the same time, Richard Bush, the U.S. envoy, rushed to Taipei to stop several pending constitutional amendments that were designed to institutionalize the "special state-to-state" formula from going into their second reading in the National Assembly. Without a full confidence in Lee's political credibility, Richard Bush actually reached out to the DPP, asking the opposition to back off from this highly provocative and irreversible political move.

41. This wait-and-see approach was best illustrated by the fact that Beijing's official propaganda organs had refrained themselves from attacking Chen Shui-bian personally for more than two years after his inauguration. This self-restraining measure was lifted only after Chen Shui-bian assumed the DPP chairmanship in July 2002 and later issued controversial statements about "one country on each side of the strait," on August 3. See the analysis by Wang Zhouchong, *China Times*, July 26, 2002, 11; and the report by Kang Zhangrong quoting ranking PRC official's remark about why Beijing gave up its hope on Chen Shui-bian after the two-year probation, *Commercial Times*, October 1, 2002, 11.

42. The old formula in defining its one-China principle—that is, "There is only one China in the world, Taiwan is a part of China, and the sovereignty and the territorial

integrity of China cannot be divided"—has been replaced with a slightly different version: "There is only one China in the world. The Chinese mainland and Taiwan are part of China, and China's sovereignty and territorial integrity can not be divided."

43. Again, in Jiang's own languages, "[Taiwan compatriots] will enjoy a lasting peace. Taiwan may then truly rely on the mainland as its hinterland for economic growth and thus get broad space for development. Our Taiwan compatriots may join the people on the mainland in exercising the right to administer the country and sharing the dignity and honor of the great motherland in the international community."

44. The original texts in Jiang's report read as follow: "[We] can discuss issues of formally ending hostility between the two sides, Taiwan's space of international activities suitable for its position in the economic, cultural and social fields, and the political position of the Taiwan authorities."

45. In a 2000 white paper, "The One-China Principle and the Taiwan Issue," the PRC authority cited, "Taiwan indefinitely refuses to conduct political negotiation"; as such, it would constitute one of the three conditions that might justify the use of military forces to recover Taiwan.

46. Under that module, the difficult issue—namely, who has the jurisdiction over what—was avoided by giving private business associations authority to conduct negotiation and sign accords on behalf of their respective civil aviation authorities.

47. John Pomfret, "China Embraces More Moderate Foreign Policy," *Washington Post* Foreign Service, October 24, 2002.

48. John Pomfret, "China Suggests Missile Buildup Linked to Arms Sales to Taiwan," *Washington Post* Foreign Service, December 10, 2002.

49. The five no's are as follows: no declaration of independence, no alteration of the "Republic of China" name, no referendum on independence, no insertion of "special state-to-state relations" concept into the constitution, and no need for a renunciation of the national unification guidelines.

50. It became widely known later on that Raymond Burghart, the American Institute in Taiwan (AIT) director, had several intensive consultations with president-elect Chen Shui-bian during the drafting stage of his inauguration speech. Also it was alleged that Beijing had obtained the transcript of Chen's speech in advance through the U.S. channel.

51. According to the official statistics of the Taiwan Security Commission, at the end of the third quarter of 2002, around 60 percent of the companies listed on the Taiwan Stock Exchange have invested in the mainland, and around 55 percent of the listed companies in the OTC market have done so. See *China Times*, January 19, 2003.

52. As a Beijing's overseas propaganda organ, *Ta Kung Pao* of Hong Kong put it, "Jiang Report [to the Sixteenth Party Congress] to have 'guiding significance' for work on Taiwan." See *Ta Kung Pao*, November 12, 2002, editorial, "A Guiding Document for the Work of the Communist Party of China toward Taiwan."

10

Democracy and Human Rights in Chinese Foreign Policy: Motivation and Behavior

Ming Wan

China's human rights diplomacy since the 1989 Tiananmen crackdown is well understood.[1] What is less understood is the motivation driving Beijing's human rights policy, which is the focus of this chapter. Human rights in foreign policy may be seen either as a motivator or as an issue where other motives drive the policy. In China's case, Beijing has engaged in human rights diplomacy not because it believes in democracy and human rights per se but because the United States and the West have confronted China over the issue. Chinese human rights diplomacy, which is motivated by regime survival, thus fundamentally differs from American human rights diplomacy, which is motivated by a strong conviction of rights and democracy as central values, although actual conduct of U.S. foreign policy is influenced by traditionally defined national interests in security and commerce. At the same time, while China's conduct of human rights diplomacy has shown little change, its underlying motivations—aspirations, fears, and pride—are more nuanced and have evolved over time. China's evolving motivation has so far affected mainly the non–human rights dimensions of its foreign policy, but it still matters for China's rights diplomacy because it influences the parameters for Chinese foreign relations. Chinese motivational changes also offer clues for how Chinese human rights diplomacy may change in the future.

MOTIVES IN FOREIGN POLICY

Motives have long been recognized as important goals for state actions. As Thucydides said millenniums ago, "honor, fear, and interest" are three strong motives for states.[2] To demonstrate how motives affect behavior, we should study motives as well as the beliefs regarding how best to accomplish them. Combinations of motives, beliefs, and styles create foreign policy orientations.[3] Motives and foreign policy beliefs are not easy to identify. Hidden in decision makers' heads, they are not directly observable; we observe them indirectly, by actors' words and actions. But the motives and beliefs expressed in words may be manipulated to disguise what has truly driven actions, and the motives and beliefs inferred from actions may lead to a circular thinking about the cause and effect. To minimize the problem of circular thinking, I decipher motives and beliefs from important Chinese texts. To reduce the danger of post hoc rationalization, I discuss broad motives and beliefs beyond specific acts. These motives discussed are then matched with Chinese foreign policy behavior.

Political psychologists have developed sophisticated methods of content analysis for studying motives and belief systems.[4] This chapter adopts a simple content analysis. It does not test the typologies created by early political psychologists; rather, it focuses on what motivates Chinese foreign policy related to human rights. I anchor my analysis of the continuity and change in primary Chinese motives by reading the political reports delivered to national party congresses.[5] Meticulously debated and prepared as one of the key issues on the agenda of party congresses, these reports reflect the collective or dominant thinking by the party-state at a given moment and therefore open a window into Chinese motives. I supplement these political reports with other Chinese texts and scholarly works. My analysis has been informed by frequent conversations with Chinese officials and analysts and by my observations, although space limit does not allow detailed citations.

CHINESE FOREIGN POLICY MOTIVES BEFORE 1989

The Socialist Agenda

The Chinese Communist Party (CCP) held six national congresses from the founding of the People's Republic of China in 1949 to the June 4 Tiananmen incident in 1989. The first four emphasized a strong socialist agenda whereas the next two set a reform agenda.

State president Liu Shaoqi delivered the political report to the Eighth Party Congress on September 15, 1956.[6] The report revealed strong aspirations for building a "great socialist country." Based on its assessment that revolutionary goals had been largely accomplished, Liu called, first, for the establishment of a strong legal system to maintain social order and repress the remnants of "counterrevolutionaries"; and, second, for a shift from direct actions by masses, a dominant approach employed in the revolutionary stage. The report exhibited strong confidence in China's domestic situation and international environment. In foreign policy, it called for a strong alliance with Moscow, good-neighbor relations with the countries around China, and an expressed interest in peaceful coexistence with the United States.

While Liu's report reflected the dominant thinking in the party and the government, Mao Zedong and his supporters had a different agenda of continuous revolution and confrontational foreign policy. Mao launched the Cultural Revolution in 1965 to remove Liu, Deng Xiaoping, and other "revisionists" through direct actions by mobilized masses and through the backing of a loyal military. The political report delivered by vice party chairman Lin Biao to the Ninth Party Congress on April 1, 1969, exhibited a high revolutionary zeal and a strong fear of enemies inside and outside China.

By the time premier Zhou Enlai presented the political report to the Tenth Party Congress on August 24, 1973, Lin Biao had died trying to escape to the Soviet Union after a failed coup against Mao. Zhou's report echoed Mao's revolutionary rhetoric although it was known at the time that Zhou preferred to restrain the excesses of the Cultural Revolution and to shift the focus of the party to production. Having recently received President Nixon to China, Zhou alluded to the evolving Sino-American rapprochement by distinguishing "necessary compromises between revolutionary countries and imperialist countries" from "collusion and compromise between Soviet revisionism and U.S. imperialism."

Mao died in September 1976. At the Eleventh Party Congress in August 1977, Hua Guofeng promised to continue Mao's agenda, even though he had arrested Mao's wife and her radical allies and declared the end of the Cultural Revolution. His report resonated with people when it declared the country's objective as building "a great, powerful and modern socialist country before the end of this century." But Hua's approach was to rebuild a planned economy with imported technologies and plants—and he still stressed class struggle. He listed promotion of democracy as the seventh of the eight tasks facing the party and the nation, which meant restoring democratic centralism and allowing democracy within the party and within the people.

The four reports discussed here sent a strong socialist message, differing only in how radical the party-state should be. With the party-state's emphasis on either "people's democratic dictatorship" or "continuous revolution," human rights were systematically and massively violated in this period, an important source of grievances for many human rights activists in later years.[7] Moreover, massive abuses of party and government cadres, as well as the usual suspects on the list of class enemies during the Cultural Revolution, would be a crucial reason for China's legal reform in 1978.[8]

Ironically, China's huge human rights problem did not prevent Beijing from taking a moral high ground in its foreign policy, evoking self-determination, anticolonialism or antiracism in its support for Third World countries against the West.[9] Beijing did not frame its approach as human rights diplomacy at this time and merely used the moral reasons as weapons against its enemies. In fact, there was little consciousness of human rights and still less willingness to talk about rights in Chinese discourse.[10] Equally important, Beijing did not have to engage in human rights diplomacy during this period when the West did not take the rights issue to China. In fact, the United States did not have a human rights policy until 1974.

The Reform Agenda

Under Deng Xiaoping's leadership, the Third Plenum of the Eleventh CCP Central Committee, held in December 1978, shifted the party's central task from class struggle to economic construction. The conference communiqué emphasized promotion of democratic centralism, seeing too much centralism and too little democracy in recent years. It urged institutionalization and legalization of democracy and equality before law. Since 1978 the Chinese government has pushed for economic and legal reform, and it is widely accepted that Chinese legal reform is principally meant to facilitate economic reform.[11]

Thanks to both types of reform, Chinese human rights improved, but ironically the Chinese human rights problem caught international attention after reform started. Foreign journalists and rights activists suddenly had better access to China and came to see the country's human rights problems, past and present. Equally important, China's initial opening enhanced Chinese citizens' ability to network with fellow Chinese as well as with foreign journalists and activists. The Democracy Wall Movement between 1978 and 1979 and democracy movements in later years provided a strong basis for the West to express concerns over human rights in China; foreign pressure cannot be seen as interference in China's domestic affairs if Chinese themselves are fighting for freedom. Moreover, the Chinese government's repression of dissidents provides rally points for international rights activists who lobby their governments to take stronger actions against Beijing.

Secretary-general Hu Yaobang presented the political report to the Twelfth Party Congress on September 1, 1982. Hu's report strongly endorsed the 1978 Third Plenum's decision to shift focus to economic development. Nevertheless, the 1982 report reveals a fear of challenging the party from those who wanted more political freedom from the party. At the same time, the report emphasized legal reform and suggested that the party should abide by the laws it has created. Regarding foreign policy, the report called for an independent foreign policy. Significantly, Hu cited patriotism as a foundation of Chinese foreign policy.

Secretary-general Zhao Ziyang delivered the political report to the Thirteenth Party Congress on October 25, 1987. The 1987 report has been the most forward-looking in regards to political reform since the founding of the People's Republic of China. About one-quarter of the report was devoted to political reform, which loosely includes administrative reform, electoral reform, socialist democracy, and rule of law, genuine implementation of which would contribute to better civil and political rights for Chinese citizens. Zhao declared boldly, "Without reform of the political structure, reform of the economic structure cannot succeed in the end."[12] Rather than fear of any enemies, the 1987 report revealed a strong fear that China would fall further behind in global competition and that "China will not be able to take its rightful place in the world." At the same time, the report demonstrated growing confidence in the correctness of economic reform. It pointed out that "in the last nine years the national economic strength has increased more rapidly and the people have obtained greater material benefits than in any other period since the founding of the People's Republic," which was rightly attributed to economic reform and opening to the outside world.

Zhao's vision of political reform did not materialize. The social forces unleashed after 1978 came to clash with the conservative core within the party. Zhao lost his position in the 1989 Tiananmen crackdown. While China had been seen as moving along a trajectory of economic reform to political reform before 1989, it went on a different path of economic reform without political reform—understood as electoral democracy, multiparty system, and independence of judiciary, which remains the case to this day.

China's human rights diplomacy in the 1980s shifted from that of a revolutionary state to that of a participant in the international human rights regime, consistent with its basic line of reform and opening. Beijing toned down its moral judgment on the West. After all, Beijing was less confident than before. Reform implies flaws in the existing Chinese system and a need to learn from developed countries—that is, the West. The fear of falling behind implies that China does not want to be with those who have fallen behind. All these implications of China's strategic choice for reform were not consciously debated at the time but have become salient in the past few years.

Deng's policy of opening up to the outside world meant participation in the existing international system, which includes a crucial human rights component. In the 1980s, China gradually joined the international human rights regime.[13] Although China joined the United Nations in October 1971, it did not join any human rights treaties until reform started. Some Chinese diplomats attribute this delay to the fact that the Chinese government needed to study the complex human rights treaties, most of which had been adopted before China's entry into the UN.[14] But more important, China's domestic politics was so radical in the early 1970s that it would be virtually impossible for any leader to touch the sensitive subject of human rights. By contrast, China joined the following international human rights treaties in the 1980s. China also recognized thirteen International Labor Organization conventions in July 1984.[15]

Convention on the Elimination of All Forms of Discrimination against Women—signed July 17, 1980; ratified November 4, 1980

International Convention on the Elimination of All Forms of Racial Discrimination—accession December 29, 1981; effective February 28, 1982

Convention Relating to the Status of Refugees—accession September 24, 1982; effective December 23, 1982

Protocol Relating to the Status of Refugees—accession September 24, 1982; effective September 24, 1982

International Convention on the Suppression and Punishment of the Crime of Apartheid—accession April 18, 1983; effective May 18, 1983

International Convention against Apartheid in Sports—signed October 21, 1987; effective April 3, 1988

Convention against Torture and Other Cruel, Inhuman or Degrading Treatment or Punishment—signed December 12, 1986; effective November 3, 1988.

Convention on the Prevention and Punishment of the Crime of Genocide—ratified April 18, 1983; effective July 17, 1983

China desired to be part of the international community, although it selected less-sensitive treaties to begin with, and Beijing did not see itself as a principal target of international human rights pressure. China experienced only diplomatic skirmishes in the 1980s, when the U.S. Congress expressed concerns over Tibet and China's family planning, to which China responded indignantly. Until the mid-1980s the United States and other Western nations largely exempted China from human rights pressure due to a strategic need to meet the Soviet challenge, support for Deng's bold economic reform, and concern about their past misbehavior in China.[16]

CHINESE FOREIGN POLICY MOTIVES IN THE EARLY 1990s

Secretary-general Jiang Zemin presented the political report to the Fourteenth Party Congress on October 12, 1992. What stands out in the 1992 report is a lengthy discussion of China's human rights diplomacy. In fact, Jiang devotes about one-third of the section on the international situation and Chinese foreign policy to human rights issues, explicitly and implicitly. The report asserts explicitly that

> the founding of the People's Republic of China put an end to the Chinese people's tragic history of suffering from long aggression, oppression and humiliation, and it fundamentally changed the situation of human rights in China. The people have become the masters of the country and have steadily built their own new life. The Constitution of our republic has given basic protection to all the people's rights. China has acceded to a series of international conventions on human rights and agrees to the conduct of international dialogues on human rights on an equal footing. In the final analysis, the question of human rights is a matter within each country's sovereignty; China is resolutely opposed to the use of human rights to interfere in other countries' internal affairs.

Implicitly, the report mentions the "five principles of peaceful coexistence" three times, which includes noninterference in one another's internal affairs. In that spirit, the report states that "the peoples of all countries are entitled to choose the social systems and paths of development that suit their specific conditions"; that "China will never try to impose its social system or ideology on other countries, nor will China allow other countries to impose their social systems and ideologies on it"; and that "whenever, on any pretext, any country encroaches upon the independence and sovereignty of others and interferes in their internal affairs . . . it will be internationally condemned."

The report's highlighting of human rights as a foreign policy issue reflects the reality of intense Western rights pressure on China after 1989. The United States, Western Europe, Japan and others imposed diplomatic, economic, and military sanctions on Beijing, bilaterally and multilaterally. China reacted strongly against Western pressure while making some symbolic concessions.[17] Beijing could accommodate Western criticism only if it reversed its verdict on the crackdown and began a genuine political reform, which it adamantly refused to do. The 1992 report makes that position clear. "In late spring and early summer of 1989, a political disturbance broke out, and the Party and the government, relying on the people, took a clear-cut stand against unrest. They quelled the counter-revolutionary violence in Beijing, defending the power of the socialist state and the fundamental interests of the people and ensuring the continued progress of reform, the opening up and modernization."

Three motives drove China's tough response to Western rights pressure. First, as discussed at the beginning of the section, the Chinese government expressed a strong historical sense of humiliation and victimization. National pride, sharpened by this historical awareness, dictated a strong response to the West. The second motive was fear of instability and regime collapse, which would result from yielding to Western pressure. The third motive was confidence in the Chinese Communist Party's proven ability to withstand foreign pressure and sanctions. The last two motives are not obvious in the 1992 report. By October 1992 China had already weathered the worst of Western sanctions. All three principal motives are revealed in Deng's twenty-six talks recorded from February 26, 1989, to February 21, 1992.[18] Deng's motives were not hidden in coded messages; rather, they were passionately expressed mantras. Deng's mind-set mattered because he remained dominant in China's policy making in the early 1990s, even though Jiang was the party secretary-general. Furthermore, Deng's strategic vision was thoroughly integrated into the 1992 political report.

At the same time, we should place China's human rights diplomacy in the context of its broad post-1989 foreign policy approach. The clash with the West made it necessary to reach out to the Third World countries. There was a sense in Beijing that the old friends might have been neglected when China was rushing toward modernization in the 1980s. But China did not turn its back on the West. China did not retaliate against major powers such as the United States and France over rights disputes. Beijing practiced its own engagement policy, seeking to improve relations with the West while refusing to make substantive concessions over human rights.

The main motivation for this approach is that the Chinese leadership remained committed to economic modernization, despite being challenged by the leftists.[19] The Chinese aspiration to become a great nation and the Chinese belief that economic development was the key to achieving that objective did not change after the Tiananmen incident. Further economic reform necessitated greater economic cooperation with the West, not less. The 1992 report made this clear. Immediately after discussion of the 1989 Tiananmen incident, Jiang emphasized that "the Central Committee explicitly proclaimed that the Party's basic line and the policy decisions made by the Thirteenth National Congress were correct." Jiang assessed the past fourteen years (since 1978) as a positive period where "we have made major progress in developing the economy, improving the people's living standards and increasing the overall strength of the country," thanks to reform and opening as "the dominant feature of the new period." Accordingly, Jiang concluded, "We must, first and foremost, persevere in economic development as our central task. . . . We must never waiver in it, except in case of a large-scale foreign invasion." Deng talked about adhering to economic reform and opening before and after the June 4 crackdown, and he reasoned that the party could win people back by continuing reform, which demonstrators did not oppose.[20] In fact, worried about losing momentum for reform, Deng had made a highly publicized tour to several southern provinces early in the year to promote faster economic reform. The 1992 report highlighted the "important talks given by Comrade Deng Xiaoping" during his southern tour.

China's measured response to Western pressure reflected Beijing's calculations of the degree to which the West "threatened" its political regime. Obviously, Western human rights pressure fell far short of "a large-scale foreign invasion," which would place China on a war footing. Deng repeatedly expressed the view that foreign criticism could not bring down the Chinese government as long as the party leadership stood united and "focused on accomplishing a few tasks that satisfy people." The collapse of the Soviet Union and East European communist governments increased Deng's suspicion of the Western motives but did not weaken his confidence in the correctness of his approach, which the 1992 report endorsed. In accordance with the central party task for reform and opening, the 1992 report saw the questions of peace and development as the two top priorities. This basic assessment of the international situation began in the 1987 report and continued in the 1997 and 2002 reports.[21] This assessment was necessary for the Chinese government to feel secure enough to concentrate on economic development. Moreover, the report shows that Beijing did not feel that vulnerable. China's relations with neighboring countries had improved tremendously.

CHINESE FOREIGN POLICY MOTIVES IN THE MID-1990s

Jiang Zemin delivered his second political report to the Fifteen Party Congress on September 12, 1997. Compared with the 1992 report, the 1997 report does not spend nearly as much space on human rights diplomacy. It states explicitly, "It is still serious that human rights and other issues are used to interfere in the internal affairs of other countries." Implicitly, the report says, "We do not impose our social system and ideology upon others, nor will we allow other countries to force theirs upon us." The report repeats this message against interference in internal affairs on two other occasions. In particular, the report says that states "should persist in dialogue, not confrontation, in properly handling their differences by proceeding from their long-term interests and the overall task of promoting world peace and development. We are opposed to imposing or threatening to impose sanctions without good reason."

The 1997 report's more relaxed discussion of human rights disputes with the West reflects gradually eased Western rights pressure on China between 1992 and 1997. The Japanese government resumed yen loans to China after merely one year and sent to China its prime minister in August 1991 as well as the emperor in October 1992. European nations followed suit shortly afterward. President Clinton delinked human rights and most-favored-nation trade status in May 1994. In the United Nations Human Rights Commission, Beijing prevented passage of a resolution on China. Although Western criticism of China's human rights remained, it gradually became ritualized and marginalized on Western diplomatic agenda in China.[22]

The party's basic policy line, which sets the parameters for China's human rights diplomacy, did not change, as seen in the 1997 report. Held shortly after Deng's death, the theme of the Fifteenth Party Congress was to continue his policy line of reform and opening. Jiang declared, "Firmly adhering to the line formulated since the Third Plenary Session of the 11th Central Committee means firmly upholding the banner of Deng Xiaoping Theory." At the same time, Jiang began experimenting with his own theoretical contributions. The third section of the report, which talks about the historical status and significance of Deng's theory, leads to the next section, focused on "the primary stage of socialism." Jiang's key point is that "during the primary stage, it is all the more necessary to give first priority to concentrating on their development. . . . The principal contradiction in society is the one between the growing material and cultural needs of the people and the backward production." Jiang announced, "Development is the absolute principle. The key to solution of all China's problems lies in our own development." Development as the absolute principle would become the party's mantra.

The reification of economic development in the party-state's thinking had a conflicting impact on the party's basic policy concerns. On the one hand, to achieve development, Beijing needed to ensure international cooperation and avoid an unstable environment around China. This policy reality offered the outside world the opportunity to influence Chinese behavior, including its human rights behavior, which is why China continued to engage in human rights dialogues with the West and sought broad cooperation with the West despite its criticism of China's rights records.

The party also knew that it was essential to further reform to achieve economic development. The 1997 report recognizes the nonpublic sector as "an important component part of China's socialist market economy" and that "it is necessary to improve the legal system concerning property and protect the legitimate rights and interests of, and fair competition among, all types of enterprises and at the same time exercise supervision and control over them according to law." In the sixth section, on reform of political structure and legal system, Jiang recognizes that "developing democracy must go hand in hand with the efforts to improve the legal system so that the country is ruled by law."[23] The limitation in his vision was also obvious. "Building socialist democracy is a gradual historical process, so it should be advanced under the leadership of the Party, in light of China's conditions, step by step, and in an orderly way." Legal reform and village elections were not adopted for foreign policy reasons, but they came to serve as China's selling points in human rights dialogues with the West. Beijing regularly cited them as proof of improvements in China's human rights record.[24]

However, Beijing's focus on development has elevated "political stability" to "a principle of overriding importance." The following paragraph from the 1997 report clearly represents a developmentalist, authoritarian agenda.[25]

> In the primary stage of socialism, it is of the utmost importance to balance reform, development and stability and to maintain a stable political environment and public order. Without stability, nothing could be achieved. We must uphold the leadership by the Party and the people's democratic dictatorship. We should promote material progress and cultural and ethical progress, attaching equal importance to both. We must eliminate all factors jeopardizing stability, oppose bourgeois liberalization and guard against the infiltrating, subversive and splittist activities of international and domestic hostile forces. We must balance the intensity of reform, the speed of development and people's ability to sustain them, promoting reform and development amid social and political stability and securing social and political stability through reform and development.

This paragraph interweaves several themes—namely, that the party leadership is central to stability, that stability is the condition for development, and that any challenge to stability would be dealt with harshly. In fact, the 1997 report talks about "one central task and two basic points" (*yige zhongxin, liangge jibendian*), where the central task is economic development and the two basic points are adherence to the "four cardinal principles"—keeping to the socialist road, upholding the people's democratic dictatorship, leadership by the Communist Party, and Marxism–Leninism and Mao Zedong thought—and the policy of reform and opening up. The four cardinal principles gradually became only about party leadership. Resulting from its determination to maintain political dominance, the party-state continued to repress organized dissent, which threatened its political dominance and, by its own twisted logic, China's social and political stability. Beijing's continuous repression makes it impossible for the West to discontinue rights pressure, given lobbying pressure of rights activists and intense media attention.

Fear of political instability was part of a complex mixture of fear and confidence revealed in the 1997 report. On the one hand, the report strikes a tone of optimism. The report asserts, "As the new century is approaching . . . we are confronted with unprecedented favorable conditions and excellent opportunities" because "peace and development have become the main themes of the present era," because "considerable overall national strength has been built up in China . . . especially over the past 20 years," and because "our Party has established the basic theory and basic line of building socialism with Chinese characteristics which have proved to be correct in practice." China's confidence was also boosted by the return of Hong Kong on July 1, 1997.

On the other hand, the report warns people that while the party seized some historical opportunities, it "lost some as well." China began to fear that the United States, Japan, and some other countries viewed a rising China as a potential or actual threat. In an implicit recognition of growing China threat sentiments abroad, the 1997 report declares that "China's development will not pose a threat to any other country" and that "China will never seek hegemony even when it becomes developed in future." Beijing understood full well that actions taken by the United States and others out of fear of China would make China's modernization more difficult to achieve. But Chinese strategic thinkers and leaders were not yet ready to acknowledge how Chinese territorial claims, particularly the People's Liberation Army's large military exercises to intimidate Taiwan in 1995 and 1996, had alarmed the United States and neighbors of China. Many believed that the China threat view was motivated by a conspiracy to prevent China from becoming powerful.[26] Human rights disputes were thus seen as the outcome to, rather than a source of, a perceived American attempt to contain and weaken China.[27]

Chinese bureaucrats and the public had largely lined up behind the party by the mid-1990s due to domestic and international developments. Domestically, Deng's emphasis on continuous economic reform yielded tangible results for everyone to see. Many came to buy the party line that political stability is important for achieving quick economic development and that the party rule might be necessary for China's historic transformations. Unlike diplomas in the 1980s, when highly educated Chinese often had far lower incomes than private entrepreneurs, diplomas in the 1990s became tickets for wealth and prestige. Government officials now enjoyed higher salaries and major perks such as housing. An ongoing civil service reform promised to further improve the situation for civil servants. By the mid-1990s, government officials had come to expect higher salaries down the line. Improvement in personal situations and in the nation gave Chinese officials greater job satisfaction and a sense that the party might have been right after all. Officials' personal aspirations thus converged with the nation's aspirations. Chinese diplomats saw U.S. criticism of China's human rights as really about ending its one-party system and, thus, as inconsistent with China's political reality and aspirations.[28]

On the international front, Chinese nationalism—with the government's encouragement—grew among officials and the general public due to a number of incidents after 1993, such as the U.S. Navy's search of the Chinese freighter

Yinhe and the failed bid for the 2000 Olympics, which the Chinese public blamed on U.S. political interference. In discussions with Chinese diplomats and officials in this period, I sensed a strong indignation toward the United States and an equally strong conviction that the U.S. human rights pressure was simply an excuse for keeping China weakened and subordinated, a humiliating situation that Chinese patriots should not allow to happen.

Personally motivated officials made a difference in Beijing's performance in human rights diplomacy, by now routinized for the Chinese government. At this time, there was little need for new instructions from the top leadership. As a senior Chinese human rights diplomat said affirmatively, the buck stopped in the Human Rights Division in the ministry.[29] Chinese diplomats conducted energized human rights diplomacy. As an example, careful organization and preparation, driven by career aspirations and a fear of diplomatic setbacks on one's watch, are institutional keys to China's success in blocking resolutions on China at the UN Human Rights Commission.

CHINESE FOREIGN POLICY MOTIVES SINCE 2001

Jiang delivered his third political report to the Sixteenth Party Congress on November 8, 2002. The 2002 report mentions human rights only once, in the fifth section, which is on political development and restructuring, saying that it is essential to ensure that "human rights are respected and guaranteed." It is striking that the 2002 report does not use the phrase *human rights* at all in the foreign policy section although it alludes to the issue when it voices strong objection to interference in internal affairs. More so than the 1997 political report, the 2002 report reflects the political reality that United States' human rights policy toward China had become ritualized and marginalized. The terrorist attacks on the United States on September 11, 2001, dramatically reoriented the Bush administration's foreign policy to war on terrorism, which elevated the importance of strategic cooperation with China and further marginalized the human rights issue on the bilateral diplomatic agenda.[30]

The 2002 report builds on the 1997 report. Economic development remains the party's central task. The 2002 report calls economic development "the fundamental principle." At the same time, the report continues to regard stability as "a principle of overriding importance." If anything, Jiang saw the experiences of the past five years (since the 1997 party congress) and the past thirteen years (since he became party secretary-general) as reinforcing the wisdom of this basic approach. Taking great pride in the nation's achievements—and, by extension, his own—Jiang called the past thirteen years (1989–2002) a period "in which China's overall national strength has risen by a big margin, the people have received more tangible benefits than ever before, and China has enjoyed long social stability and solidarity and had a good government and a united people." He added that "China's influence in the world has grown notably, and the cohesion of the nation has increased remarkably." The report makes it clear that China's national aspiration to become powerful through economic development has become even stronger and that the recent success has given the party leadership confidence to continue down this path.

What distinguishes the 2002 report from the 1997 report—and as it had been expected—is the prominent status given to Jiang's "important thought of three represents." Developed from spring of 2000, the three represents refer to the Chinese Communist Party's representing "the development trend of China's advanced productive forces, the orientation of China's advanced culture and the fundamental interests of the overwhelming majority of the Chinese people."[31] The theory represents Jiang's effort to redefine the nature of the party and to provide the party with a new basis of legitimacy to ensure its continuous rule in a rapidly changing global and domestic environment.[32] The three represents have been driven by fear that the party may lose its historic relevance and even lose its power due to its serious internal problems, such as corruption. In April 1999, Jiang raised the issue of a "confidence crisis" for the CCP when he came to realize the magnitude of the Falun Gong movement.[33] The party leadership had good reason to be worried. An extensive investigation project in 2000—organized by the CCP Organization Department, in collaboration with the organization departments of six provincial and autonomous region party committees—revealed the extent of mass dissatisfaction with the party and with party officials, particularly over corruption, which threatens the survival of the CCP.[34] As warned by Li Junru, a vice president of the Central Party School and one of the party's leading theorists, one cannot overstate the danger facing the party. Young cadres are not the same as the old revolutionaries who won the country. Masses will have little tolerance of them if they detach themselves from people, fail to discipline themselves, or fail their responsibilities. If masses see a systemic problem of corruption in the party, they will question whether the party should rule China. He warns that, just like a backward nation that will be abused, a backward political party will lose power if it does not keep up with the development needs of advanced productive forces and if it fails to meet the fundamental needs of the masses.[35]

The three represents are also driven by fear that with rapid economic globalization China might miss the boat and fall further behind, which would put the country in a situation where it would be roughed up by stronger powers. As a typical example of such sentiment, Yu Yunyao, executive vice president of the Central Party School, warned that "the speed and impact of modern science and technology centered on information technology and life sciences in the contemporary world is simply beyond imagination. . . . We are developing but others are as well. If we do not try to catch up, the gap [with advanced nations] may widen further. History tells us that a country, particularly a large one like China, would be in a dangerous situation if it keeps being left behind in science and technology by developed nations."[36]

At the same time, Chinese thinking now focuses on whether China itself can make the effort to develop rather than focus on what the West might do to prevent China from growing. While recognizing the structural and institutional advantages enjoyed by the West, the Chinese government sees a clear opportunity to catch up. Deng Xiaoping first discussed the notion of China's opportunity after Tiananmen, which has become prevalent in Chinese discourse in recent years. As a recent example, Hu Jintao reiterated in a November 2003 politburo study meeting that China should seize the first twenty years of this century as a crucial strategic opportunity for economic construction.[37]

The three represents have practical implications for China's foreign policy. It is based on a significant reassessment of China's relations with the United States and the West. The 2002 report urges the nation to fulfill three historic tasks: "to propel the modernization drive, to achieve national unification, to safeguard world peace and promote common development." The term "common development" (*gongtong fazhan*), which could be more accurately translated as "development together," would be a basis for cooperation with the international community.[38] The reason Jiang cites for this assessment is the need to "keep pace with the times" (*yushi jujin*). The essence of the changed time is globalization and pluralization of the Chinese economy and society, which virtually all the Chinese commentaries on the three represents cite as the background for Jiang's theoretical innovation. As had some other key new ideas in the report, the notion of common development had been discussed before the Sixteenth Party Congress. Hu Jintao, for example, talked about the three historic tasks in March 2001.[39]

The party now treats the realization of communism as a distant ideal rather than as an immediate policy objective. The 2002 CCP constitution made the following statement about communism: "The highest ideal of communism pursued by the Chinese Communists can be realized only when the socialist society is fully developed and very advanced. The development and improvement of the socialist system is a long historical process." As a result, the idea of common development justifies cooperation with the developed nations and the borrowing of any civilizational creations from the West, including political and cultural institutions and ideas. That interpretation is not present in the 2002 political report, but it is widely shared among the policy élite, who have engaged in lively internal discussion of various sensitive topics for the past three years. Wang Changjiang, for example, sees all excellent cultural traditions and all excellent cultural products as incorporated into the content of advanced culture. It follows then that China, to develop healthily, should learn from foreign cultures. He notes that the West has accumulated rich experience in political cultures, such as with election, political participation, competitive public service, and citizens' self-rule based on centuries of practice. As a result, the CCP should learn from these experiences, albeit critically.[40] Moreover, the party's fear of regime collapse and falling behind developed nations is now mainly about its own weakness than foreign subversion and encirclement, a significant shift from its previous fear of a Western conspiracy. While difficult to quantify, this trend is obvious if one reads the Chinese texts cited in the chapter and talks to Chinese officials and scholars.

China's economic reform, which began in 1978, was ultimately meant to make China part of the developed world. It is a plan that should create for China a new national identity, one that is more compatible with the West. Such a long-term implication was not seriously debated in the early days, since people did not know what to expect of China's effort to develop from a low economic base and since most Chinese citizens were used to thinking of the Chinese nation as a victim of Western imperialism. For the past few years, however, the Chinese have seen dramatic improvement in the material conditions of the nation, and many have seen their lives dramatically improve. It has thus begun to occur to people that what China has really been doing is becoming more like the modern nations. Therefore, China should abandon a victimization complex and act as a responsible major power.[41]

Moreover, many Chinese have found their social values and lifestyles more like those of citizens in the developed countries than they had originally thought. This Chinese development is to be expected. As Ronald Inglehart has argued, economic development leads to a shift from survival values to self-expression values—tolerance, trust, political activism, well-being, and freedom of speech, which he suggests form a strong predictor of stable democracy. Basing his findings on a world values survey and an international rating of democracy, Inglehart found that China has a much lower level of democracy than its public's values would predict. In fact, China ranks higher in self-expression values than Taiwan, which has already developed into a democracy.[42] The CCP's own internal survey has also indicated the extent of the Chinese public's exposure to Western ideas. Conducting a 2000 survey with over five thousand respondents, the Organization Department of the Zhejiang Provincial CCP Committee found that 34.5 percent of those surveyed had some knowledge of "some Western schools of thought"; 51.2 percent had some knowledge of Christianity; 28.5 percent partially accepted Western culture and its political system; and 85.8 percent wanted to learn Western science and technology.[43] The survey confirms casual observation of the developmental stage of China's more developed coastal areas. No systematic data on Chinese policy élite views and beliefs exist, but conversations with them offer anecdotal evidence of an even more drastic shift toward Western values and lifestyles, even in cases where they oppose specific Western policies. Since September 11, 2001, a majority of Chinese analysts have opposed an alleged unilateralist approach by the Bush administration; however, the Chinese élite are forced to acknowledge that they want to be part of the modern and civilized world and have no interest in associating with cave-dwelling terrorists.

China's economic, political, and social developments explain the evolving view of human rights in China. In fact, Xu Xianming, president of the China Politics and Law University, claims that the third generation of leadership, under Jiang Zemin, came to formally recognize the universality of human rights and see them as a collective product of the civilization of humankind. By contrast, the first generation of leadership, under Mao, saw human rights as belonging to capitalism. The second generation, under Deng, differentiated a Chinese version of human rights from the Western version, although it was interested in building China's own human rights system.[44]

The new Chinese thinking discussed here has already had a visible impact on China's foreign policy behavior since 2001, which explains its more constructive participation in international affairs. Hu's participation in the North–South dialogue at the G-8 summit in France in June 2003 is a case in point.[45] China's new thinking also explains a conciliatory approach to the United States, and Chinese officials and theorists want the United States to know what Beijing has been doing.[46] Since September 11, we see the Chinese government cooperating with the Bush administration on the war on terrorism and in the North Korean nuclear crisis; adopting a more restrained stance on Taiwan, despite what it considers to be provocations from the island's leaders; and avoiding active opposition to war in Iraq. Beijing has also been more accommodating over human rights, releasing some prominent rights activists on the American lists given to Beijing; resuming human rights dialogues with Washington and allowing the U.S. human rights delegation to visit Xinjiang; and agreeing to let UN investigators examine China's prisons. Nevertheless, China remains unwilling to accept Western criticism of its human rights record, now more for national pride than out of fear. Furthermore, four months after the United States agreed not to sponsor a resolution on China at the UN Human Rights Commission in April 2003, the U.S. government complained publicly that Beijing had not met its specific pledges.[47]

LOOKING INTO THE FUTURE

If we look into the future, we see that China's new thinking, if fully implemented, should make China converge more with the United States, thus soft-
ening the fundamental conflict of political systems between the two nations,
which underlies recent bilateral tensions. For one thing, China's vision of its
own development and America's vision of China overlap more now than previously. The "peaceful evolution" that Americans want to see in China can
now be easily rephrased in the Chinese terminology as "peacefully keeping
pace with the times."[48] China's national pride is not seen as compromised,
since Chinese analysts see everyone else evolving as well, including the
United States. As an example of China's evolving interest to alleviate foreign
concern of its rising power, the Central Party School has been conducting a
large project called "Peaceful Rise" (*Heping Jueqi*) since early 2003.[49] There
are also signs that China's integration into the world economy and its accepting an information revolution that the government can no longer fully control
may finally be forcing the Chinese government to change its behavior. A case
in point is Beijing's decision to acknowledge a serious cover-up regarding the
country's SARS (severe acute respiratory syndrome) crisis, which resulted in
its firing not only its minister of health but its own mayor in April 2003. In
short, a weakened ideological clash with the United States would obviously
change the parameters of China's human rights diplomacy and take the sharp
edge off Sino-U.S. rights disputes.

At the same time, China's new thinking reveals a severe limitation as far
as democracy and human rights are concerned. While it is an improvement
for the party to hope to keep up with the times, party leaders and theorists
mainly talk about economic globalization centered on advanced technologies as the principal feature of the times while failing to recognize that democracy and human rights define our times and help to explain the expansion of economic globalization itself. A more powerful but nondemocratic
China will generate more fear and concern than it will respect in the world.
While it is an improvement for the party to acknowledge the need to be
more accountable to the Chinese citizenry, the reform the party now envi-
sions still follows a top-down approach and relies on self-policing to make
the government more efficient. Ordinary citizens will continue to have limited capacity to prevent abuses by officials, let alone hold the party-state accountable. While it is an improvement for party theorists to ponder what it
means to be a ruling party, their basic logic is that since the Chinese Communist Party *is* ruling, it *should* be ruling. It is also a wishful thinking that
the party can control and co-opt all the new social forces unleashed by economic reform.

The limitation in Chinese new thinking means that the party-state will continue to repress those who dare to envision a China in their own ways. As the 2002 report warns, "We must strengthen state security, keeping vigilance against infiltrative, subversive and separatist activities by hostile forces at home and abroad." Likewise, the Chinese commentaries reveal a stern stance on "the hostile forces" threatening the party dominance. In a major publication by the Central Party School to promote new strategic thinking consistent with the three represents, Hou Shaowen equates hostile forces with organizations such as Falun Gong. He sees four new developments in the activities of the hostile forces. First, they are trying to organize "legal parties" as opposition parties to the CCP. Second, they are attempting "force entry" into China to undermine the Chinese political system by setting up firms, establishing foundations, and creating social organizations. Third, they use high-tech tools to create democracy on the Internet and infiltrate China with overseas journals. Fourth, they try to create religious incidents and split China with national self-determination.[50] In fact, the Chinese government may become even more repressive against the disadvantaged and the disgruntled, such as unemployed workers and poor peasants, whose interests the party-state no longer serves.[51] The Chinese government's continuous repression of dissent will keep alive the cause for international concerns, although what the United States and the West will choose to do depends on their strategic calculations and domestic politics.

CONCLUSION

This chapter has committed much space to broad themes of Chinese foreign policy. It would be desirable to be more focused on human rights and democracy, but Beijing's motivations for human rights diplomacy have been subordinated to its broad foreign policy motivations. This chapter shows that aspirations for national power and prestige, fears of regime collapse and falling behind in the world, and pride in past glory and recent modernization progress have been the main motivators for Chinese foreign policy since 1978. While Beijing's conduct in human rights diplomacy has demonstrated little change in recent years, significant change has taken place beneath the surface in the substance of the three motivators and in their relative importance. Aspirations for power have become all-important, but how power is achieved is increasingly seen as contingent on economic reform and a friendly relationship with the West. Human rights and democracy have not become national aspirations, but they have become legitimate topics for legal and policy debates. With continuing economic growth and relatively stable politics, pride in reform achievements has increased. Ironically, fears for regime collapse have also increased in the past few years, but threat is increasingly seen as originating from within the Communist Party itself than from foreign subversion. These changes in motivations are being reflected more in non–human rights dimensions of Chinese foreign policy at this point. At the same time, Chinese motives remain out of step with the developed world that the Chinese nation now aspires to join.

NOTES

1. See Ann Kent, *China, the United Nations, and Human Rights: The Limits of Compliance* (Philadelphia: University of Pennsylvania Press, 1999); Rosemary Foot, *Rights beyond Borders: The Global Community and the Struggle over Human Rights in China* (Oxford: Oxford University Press, 2000); and Ming Wan, *Human Rights in Chinese Foreign Relations: Defining and Defending National Interests* (Philadelphia: University of Pennsylvania Press, 2001).

2. Thucydides, *The Peloponnesian War*, trans. Richard Crawley, revised. T. E. Wick (New York: Modern Library, 1982), book 1, chap. 76.

3. David G. Winter, Margaret G. Hermann, Walter Weintraub, and Stephen G. Walker, "The Personalities of Bush and Gorbachev Measured at a Distance: Procedures, Portraits and Policy," in *American Foreign Policy: Theoretical Essays*, 4th ed., ed. G. John Ikenberry (New York: Longman, 2002), 516–44.

4. David C. McClelland, *The Achieving Society* (Princeton, N.J.: Van Nostrand, 1961); Alexander L. George, "The 'Operational Code': A Neglected Approach to the Study of Political Leaders and Decision-Making," *International Studies Quarterly* 13, no. 2 (June 1969): 190–222; Stephen G. Walker, "The Motivational Foundations of Political Belief System: A Re-analysis of the Operational Code Construct," *International Studies Quarterly* 27, no. 2 (June 1983): 179–202; Robert Axelrod, ed., *Structure of Decision: The Cognitive Maps of Political Elites* (Princeton, N.J.: Princeton University Press, 1976); Margaret G. Hermann, "Examining Foreign Policy Behavior Using the Personal Characteristics of Political Leaders," *International Studies Quarterly* 24, no. 1 (March 1980): 7–46.

5. The Chinese versions of these reports can be found in the website of the *People's Daily* (www.people.com.cn). The official English versions can be found in *Beijing Review*. The English translations of set phrases and direct quotes from these political reports are from the Chinese official versions. This author has translated into English direct quotes from other Chinese texts.

6. The Central Party School recently published an article praising its two "commanding heights," namely, "abundant criticism" and a democratic election for the central committee. China News Agency, July 2, 2003 (www.chinanews.com.cn/n/2003-07-02/26/319848.html), accessed on July 1, 2003. The interest in the Eighth Party Congress relates to recent discussions on improving democracy within the party as a key to political reform.

7. R. Randle Edwards, Louis Henkin, and Andrew J. Nathan, *Human Rights in China* (New York: Columbia University Press, 1986); Yuan-li Wu et al., *Human Rights in the People's Republic of China* (Boulder, Colo.: Westview Press, 1988); Hongda Harry Wu, *Laogai: The Chinese Gulag*, trans. Ted Slingerland (Boulder, Colo.: Westview Press, 1992).

8. Ming Wan, "Legalization in China: International Human Rights Law and Domestic Politics," paper delivered at the workshop "Legalization and Politics in East Asia," Aoyama Gakuin University, Tokyo, December 6, 2003.

9. Andrew J. Nathan, "Human Rights in Chinese Foreign Policy," *China Quarterly*, no. 139 (September 1994): 623–27.

10. There was virtually no scholarly discussion of human rights from 1949 to 1978. According to the studies by a Wuhan University research team, only one essay was written on rights in China in this period (on Chinese citizens' right to work, published in April 1959). Han Depei, ed., *Requan de lilun yu shijian* [Theories and Practice of Human Rights] (Wuhan, China: Wuhan daxue chubanshe, 1995), 1127.

11. For an example of Chinese explanations, see a study manual prepared by the Central Party School, *Yifazhiguo yu yidezhiguo xuexi wenda* [Questions and Answers for Studying "Ruling the Country by Law" and "Ruling the Country by Virtue"] (Beijing: Zhonggong zhongyang dangxiao chubanshe, 2001), 12–14. For select literature in English, see Stanley B. Lubman, ed., *China's Legal Reform* (Oxford: Oxford University Press, 1996); Stanley B. Lubman, *Bird in a Cage: Legal Reform in China after Mao* (Stanford, Calif.: Stanford University Press, 1999); and Randall Peerenboom, *China's Long March toward Rule of Law* (New York: Cambridge University Press, 2002).

12. For a manual to guide studies of political reform, see Chen Yizi and Chen Fujin, eds., *Zhengzhi tizhi gaige jianghua* [Speeches on Political System Reform] (Beijing: Renmin chubanshe, 1987). The editors and contributors had participated in the research on political reform for the report. Chen and some contributors fled China after Tiananmen.

13. See Kent, *China, the United Nations, and Human Rights*.

14. Tian Jin et al., *Zhongguo zai lianheguo* [China in the UN] (Beijing: Shijie zhishi chubanshe, 1999), 200. Beijing did become a party to several Geneva Conventions in the 1950s and 1960s. China joined the two 1978 protocols in 1983.

15. Office of the High Commissioner for Human Rights, "Status of Ratifications of the Principal International Human Rights Treaties," www.unhchr.ch/pdf/report.pdf, and www.unhchr.ch/html/intlinst.htm (accessed July 13, 2003); Chinese Foreign Ministry, www.fmprc.gov.cn/chn/premade/45115/duobian.htm (accessed July 14, 2003); and International Labor Organization, www.ilo.org (accessed January 29, 2003).

16. Harry Harding, *A Fragile Relationship: The United States and China since 1972* (Washington, D.C.: Brookings, 1992), 198–206; and Roberta Cohen, "People's Republic of China: The Human Rights Exception," *Human Rights Quarterly* 9, no. 4 (November 1987): 447–549.

17. Foot, *Rights beyond Borders*; and Wan, *Human Rights in Chinese Foreign Relations*.

18. Deng Xiaoping, *Dengxiaoping wenxuan* [Selected Works of Deng Xiaoping] 3 (Beijing: Renmin chubanshe, 1993).

19. For the debate after Tiananmen, over whether China should follow a socialist or a capitalist path, see Ma Licheng and Ling Zhijun, *Jiaofeng dangdai zhongguo sanci sixiang jiefang shilu* [Clash: Records of the Three Thought Liberations in Modern China] (Beijing: Jinri zhongguo chubanshe, 1998), 155–93.

20. Deng, *Dengxiaoping wenxuan* [Selected Works of Deng Xiaoping], 296–327.

21. By contrast, the 1956 report discussed peaceful competition and peaceful coexistence with the West. The 1969 report saw the danger of American imperialists and Soviet revisionists waging major and early wars. The 1973 report predicted a pending greater disorder despite a temporary relaxation. The 1977 report saw the prospect of war increasing. The 1982 report changed the tone and suggested that world peace might be maintained if the people of the world unite against hegemonism and expansionism.

22. China's analysts recognized and welcomed such a development. See, for example, Li Yunlong, *Zhongmei guanxi zhong de renquan wenti* [The Human Rights Issue in Sino-American Relations] (Beijing: Xinhua chubanshe, 1998). Note however, human rights set limit on China's relations with the West and Japan. Wan, *Human Rights in Chinese Foreign Relations*.

23. See Jiang Zemin, *Lun youzhongguo tese shehuizhuyi zhuanti zhaibian* [On Socialism with Chinese Characteristics: Excerpts by Subjects] (Beijing: Zhongyang wenxian chubanshe, 2002), 326–37.

24. Wan, *Human Rights in Chinese Foreign Relations*, 17–19. As a recent example, Hu Jintao told the French parliament on January 27, 2004, that the Chinese government was studying the issues regarding the International Covenant on Civil and Political Rights and would submit it to the National People's Congress for ratification when it is ready. This qualified pledge was clearly designed to improve China's image in France and to advance Beijing's diplomatic objective to build a strong relationship with Europe.

25. See Jiang, *Lun youzhongguo tese shehuizhuyi* [On Socialism with Chinese Characteristics: Excerpts by Subjects], 210–18.

26. Not everyone shared this view in Beijing. A former CCP department chief viewed the rise of the China threat theory as partially due to the fact that "our leaders are not always rational in their behavior" (conversation, Beijing, May 29, 1996). But coming from a liberal who had been purged with Hu Yaobang, his view was not the dominant one in Beijing. A former vice foreign minister also acknowledged that the PLA exercises went too far. They made the United States and Japan move closer to each other; it made ASEAN suspicious of China; and it indirectly helped Lee Teng-hui's electoral success. He criticized this policy as inconsistent with Deng's strategy of keeping a low profile in foreign relations (conversation, Beijing, May 22, 1996).

27. See Institute of Legal Studies of the Chinese Academy of Social Sciences, ed., *Dangdai renquan* [Contemporary Human Rights] (Beijing: Zhongguo shehui kexue chubanshe, 1992); Song Huichang, *Xiandai renquanlun* [Contemporary Theory of Human Rights] (Beijing: Renmin chubanshe, 1993); Zhu Feng, *Renquan yu guojiguanxi* [Human Rights and International Relations] (Beijing: Beijing daxue chubanshe, 2000).

28. A former vice foreign minister noted that American human rights diplomacy is really about China's one-party system. While he wanted to avoid confrontation with the United States and attributed some of the bilateral problems to the Chinese leadership, he emphasized that "China cannot learn everything from America" and that "we have our own tradition and situation" (conversation, Beijing, May 22, 1996).

29. In an hour-long interview, he exhibited conviction in the justice of a firm Chinese response to Western rights pressure and confidence in fending off Western pressure (interview, Beijing, May 23, 1996).

30. But human rights remain a constraining factor on America's relations with China. Wan Ming, "Renquan wenti benzhishang de bianyuanhua he xingshihua" [Human rights issue: Marginalization and ritualization], in *Xianzhixing jiechu bushi zhengfu duihua zhengce zouxiang* [Constrained Engagement: Possible Trend of Bush's China Policy], ed. Hao Yufan and Zhang Yandong (Beijing: Xinhua chubanshe, 2001), 393–419. In fact, Rosemary Foot argues that the U.S. human rights policy toward China "has arguably become stiffer in rhetorical terms." Rosemary Foot, "Bush, China and Human Rights," *Survival* 45, no. 2 (Summer 2003): 169. For one U.S. official's view on the importance of human rights, as well as other issues for forging a genuinely cooperative relationship between the U.S. and China, see Richard N. Haass, "China and the Future of U.S.–China Relations," speech at the National Committee on U.S.–China Relations, December 5, 2002, at www.ncuscr.org/articles andspeeches/haass_speech.htm (accessed on September 1, 2003).

31. The definition is from *The Constitution of the Communist Party of China*, adopted at the Sixteenth Party Congress on November 14, 2002.

32. See Jiang Zemin, *Lun sange daibiao* [On Three Represents] (Beijing: Zhongyang wenxian chubanshe, 2001); Research Department of the Central Party School, ed., *Sange daibiao yu mianxiang ershiyi shiji de zhongguo gongchandang* [Three Represents and the Chinese Communist Party Facing the Twenty-first Century] (Beijing: Zhonggong zhongyang dangxiao chubanshe, 2001); Shi Taifeng and Zhang Hengshan, "Lun zhongguogongchandang yifazhizheng" [On the Chinese Communist Party governing by law], *Zhongguo shehui kexue* [China Social Sciences], no. 1 (January 2003): 13–24; Gang Lin, "Ideology and Political Institutions for a New Era," in *China after Deng*, ed. Gang Lin and Xiaobo Hu (Stanford, Calif.: Stanford University Press, 2003), 39–68.

33. Yu Yunyao, "Anzhao sangedaibiao de yaoqiu quanmian jiaqiang xinshiqi dang de jianshe" [Strengthen the party's development comprehensively according to the requests of the Three Represents], in *2000–2001 zhongguo diaocha baogao xinxingshixia renmin neibu maodun yanjiu* [2000–2001 China Investigation Report: Studies of the Internal Contradictions among People in the New Environment] (internal publication), ed. CCP Organization Department project team (Beijing: Zhongyang bianyi chubanshe, 2001), 16.

34. *2000–2001 zhongguo diaocha baogao xinxingshixia renmin neibu maodun yanjiu* [2000–2001 China Investigation Report: Studies of the Internal Contradictions among People in the New Environment]. The six local collaborators are from Hunan, Sichuan, Zhejiang, Liaoning, Anhui, and Xinjiang. The investigation was also conducted by the CCP Organization Department in Hunan, Ningxia, Shandong, Guangxi, and Hainan.

35. Li Junru, "Sange daibiao yu mianxiang ershiyi shiji de dang de jianshe" [Three Represents and the party's development in the twenty-first century], in *Sange daibiao yu mianxiang ershiyi shiji de zhongguo gongchandang* [Three Represents and the Chinese Communist Party Facing the Twenty-first Century], 68–72.

36. Yu, "Anzhao sangedaibiao de yaoqiu quanmian jiaqiang xinshiqi dang de jianshe" [Strengthen the party's development comprehensively according to the requests of the Three Represents], 3.

37. China News Agency, November 25, 2003, at www.chinanews.com.cn/n/2003-11-25/26/373411.html (accessed on November 25, 2003).

38. For the notion of common development and to a shift of communism to a distant ideal in the new party constitution, see Lin Gang, "Zhonggong de liron chuangxin he yishixingtai zhuanxing" [The Chinese Communist Party's theoretical innovations and ideological transformations], in *Weilai zhongguo tuihua de jiquanzhuyi* [China's Future: Totalitarianism on Retreat], ed. Lin Jialong (Taipei: Taiwan zhuku, 2004), 105–28.

39. Hu's essay was first published in a newspaper on March 19, 2001. It was then included as the preface to a study material for Three Represents. Hu Jintao, "Anzhao sange daibiao yaoqiu jiaqiang he gaijin dang de jianshe" [Strengthen and improve party's development according to the Three Represents], in *Sange daibiao yu mianxiang ershiyi shiji de zhongguo gongchandang* [Three Represents and the Chinese Communist Party Facing the Twenty-first Century], 1.

40. Wang Changjiang, "Luoshi sange daibiao xuyao chulihao wuge guanxi" [The five relationships need to be better handled to implement the Three Represents], in *Sange daibiao yu mianxiang ershiyi shiji de zhongguo gongchandang* [Three Represents and the Chinese Communist Party Facing the Twenty-first Century], 210–12.

41. For example, see Ye Zicheng,"Zhongguo shixing daguo waijiaozhanlue shizai bixing" [China must exercise major power diplomacy], *Shijie jingji yu zhengzhi* [World Economics and International Politics], no. 1 (2000): 5–10; and Jin Xide, "Zhongguo xuyao daguo xintai [China needs the mind-set of a major power], *Huanqiu shibao* [Globe Times], September 12, 2002.

42. Ronald Inglehart, "How Solid Is Mass Support for Democracy—and How Can We Measure It?" *PS: Political Science and Politics* 36, no. 1 (January 2003): 51–57.

43. *2000–2001 zhongguo diaocha baogao xinxingshixia renmin neibu maodun yanjiu* [2000–2001 China Investigation Report: Studies of the Internal Contradictions among People in the New Environment], 146–47.

44. Xu Xianming, preface to *Renquan yanjiu* [Human Rights Research], ed. Xu Xianming (Jinan: Shandong remin chubanshe, 2001), 3–4.

45. Chinese commentators largely portrayed Hu's visit from a positive global perspective. See, for example, *Guoji xianqu daobao* [International Herald Tribute], June 1, 2003, at http://news.sina.com.cn/c/2003-06-01/14111123020.shtml (accessed on June 1, 2003); *Beijing wenbao* [Beijing Evening News], June 2, 2003, at http://news.sina.com/cn/c/2003-06-02/17331127500.shtml (accessed on June 2, 2003); China News Agency, June 5, 2003, at www.chinanews.com.cn/n/2003-06-05/26/310971.html (accessed on June 5, 2003).

46. Based on my conversations with Chinese officials and scholars for the past two years, including two recent research trips to Beijing and Shanghai in 2002. As a most

recent example, a researcher at the Shanghai Institute for International Studies explained to me that Beijing has become more cooperative with the United States over the North Korean crisis partly because of its new national identity arising out of a greater integration into the global economy (correspondence, May 11, 2003). His view is consistent with those of other influential foreign policy analysts in China.

47. Philip Pan, "China Ignoring Rights Pledges, U.S. Charges," *Washington Post*, August 21, 2003.

48. The Chinese government was extremely critical of the notion of peaceful evolution previously. As an example, a commentary in *Beijing Review* declared shortly after the June 4 incident that peaceful evolution "is just a coup d'etat by other means" by capitalist countries. Shu Yu, "The West's Peaceful Evolution Examined," *Beijing Review*, October 23–29, 1989, 13.

49. Zheng Bijian, a former executive vice president of the school and now the head of the China Reform Forum, led a delegation to the United States in December 2002 and believes that efforts have to be made by the Chinese to seek cooperation with the West and to alleviate foreign concerns for China's rise. He proposed this large project when he returned to China. Hu Jintao promptly approved the project and decided to let the school to take the lead (conversation with a scholar familiar with the project, Washington, D.C., April 29, 2003). As an indication of the importance of the project, Zheng's team, which included scholars from outside the party school, received over two million yuan, an unheard of sum for Chinese social science research. (conversation with the scholar, February 2004). The peaceful rise theme was prominent in Premier Wen Jiabao's speech at Harvard University on December 11, 2003. Chinese embassy in the United States, "China's Peaceful Rise Relies on Own Efforts for Development: Premier," at www.china-embassy.org/eng/zt/first%20beginning/t56059 .htm (accessed on January 7, 2004).

50. Hou Shaowen, "Baochi shehui zhengzhi wending wenti" [Maintaining social and political stability], in *Zhongguo mianxiang ershiyishiji de ruogan zhanlue wenti* [Several Strategic Issues Facing China in the Twenty-first Century], ed. Zheng Bijian and Yang Chungui (Beijing: Zhonggong zhongyang dangxiao chubanshe, 2000), 248–69.

51. As a recent example, the Chinese government sentenced two labor leaders to seven years and four years, respectively. The two led thousands of unemployed workers in massive protests in an industrial city in China's northeast. Philip Pan, "Two Chinese Labor Leaders Get Prison Terms," *Washington Post*, May 10, 2003.

3 LEVELS OF CHINESE NATIONAL SECURITY:

- INTERNAL
- NEIGHBORHOOD SECURITY
- GLOBAL

IMPORTANT POINTS:

- JEIGE MENTALITY
- PEACEFUL EVOLUTION
- "GO WEST" CAMPAIGN
- CONTAINER SECURITY INITIATIVE
- DISCUSSION OF TIBET + UIGHERS

- "NEW FOUNDATION" OF SINO-US RELATIONSHIP?

  - SUSTAINABLE?

- SEE LAST PARA P. 319

11

Terrorism and Chinese Foreign Policy

Andrew Scobell

NATIONAL SECURITY WITH CHINESE CHARACTERISTICS

Terrorism as a major concern for the People's Republic of China (PRC) is a relatively recent phenomenon. It became a topic worthy of domestic concern in the 1980s, a topic of significant concern in China's Asian neighborhood in the 1990s, and the subject of grave concern at the global level during the first decade of the twenty-first century.

Civilian and military élite in the PRC tend to take a comprehensive, multi-layered view of their country's national security. These leaders measure their country's security in terms of comprehensive national power (*zonghe guoli*) including not just strictly military criteria but also economic and political aspects such as "political stability."[1] China's leaders also view national security as encompassing at least three levels: internal security, security in China's own Asian neighborhood, and global challenges to China's security. Of special concern to Chinese leaders are interactions, or linkages, between these levels. Moreover, China's leaders, like those of other communist party-states, tend to possess a siege mentality, viewing the world beyond their borders as a dangerous and hostile environment and seeing their own homeland as filled with threats and perils.[2]

Terrorism has caused considerable alarm in China in the first decade of the twenty-first century precisely because it is seen as attacking all aspects of national power, having linkages across the three levels of security, and entailing secret conspiratorial activities that by their very nature are difficult to detect. These features tend only to increase the degree of siege mentality in Beijing. While Beijing has a heightened awareness of ethnic separatism and terrorism in border regions as well as a new appreciation of terrorism as a

SEIGE MENT-ALITY

global problem, China's leaders view their principal terrorist threat as coming from alienated Han workers in the urban heartland. Publicly this is classified as criminal activity—a public security issue for local authorities—and is not officially considered terrorism.[3] Whatever the preferred terminology, the violent and nonviolent acts of angry and desperate unemployed or unpaid Chinese workers strike terror into the hearts of Beijing's leaders (see the section entitled Terrorism and Internal Security).

Chinese analysts tend to assess that China is at low risk for "becoming the target of a global terrorism offensive." According to Wu Yungui, director of the Institute of World Religions at the Chinese Academy of Social Sciences, Osama bin Laden has "never openly criticized China or identified it as a potential target."[4] Moreover, Beijing's perception of global security trends has not altered as a result of the high-profile terrorist incidents of recent years. According to then–foreign minister Tang Jiaxuan, speaking in March 2002,

> The September 11th incident has made it more evident that in the international situation uncertain factors are on the rise and threats posed by non-traditional security problems loom larger, thus making the international security situation grim and complicated. However . . . [the] world balance of power has not fundamentally changed and the Incident has not altered the basic world patterns and . . . peace and development remain the themes of the present times.[5]

For Beijing, terrorism is primarily seen as a domestic concern of long standing and, while real, is considered manageable. Certainly there are actual links between internal and external actors, but these appear to be relatively modest in nature and scope. It is in China's interests, however, to play up the threat and hype the transnational linkages as an integral part of Beijing's foreign policy agenda in the early twenty-first century. In foreign policy, Beijing has attempted to make the most of the opportunity presented by September 11, 2001, to promote China's national interests, specifically to justify its domestic crackdown on ethnic activists, to enhance its reputation as a responsible global citizen, and to improve its relationships with specific countries, notably the United States. In the past, China's siege mentality and extreme caution have resulted in minimal initiative in Beijing's foreign policy. In recent years, however, particularly since September 11, Beijing has pursued a more activist diplomacy in areas such as Central Asia and the Korean Peninsula.[6] Driven by the fear of emerging threats or looming crises, China's leaders have recognized that they have much to gain by stepping out of their traditional comfort zone on occasion to take the initiative and embrace selective multilateralism.[7]

This chapter considers how terrorism fits into China's foreign policy and national security concerns. First, I assess how terrorism is perceived in the context of China's national security calculus. Next I examine how Beijing views the threat of terrorism within China, on China's borders, and at the global level. Finally, I draw some preliminary conclusions and consider some implications of my analysis.

TERRORISM AND NATIONAL SECURITY

Terrorism (*kongbuzhuyi*) comes from the Chinese word *kongbu,* which is composed of the characters *kong,* which translates as "terror," "fear," or "dread"; and the character *bu,* which translates as "fear" or "be afraid of." But what specific actions constitute terrorism in the Chinese view is rarely artic- ulated, and terrorism tends to be broadly conceived and often undefined—this is even true in amendments to China's criminal code made in December 2001 establishing terrorist offenses and their penalties.[8]

Generally speaking, the Chinese Communist Party (CCP) believes that while its enemies engage in terrorism, communists themselves do not. As an insurgent and guerilla movement, the CCP and the hapless peasants it cham- pioned were the victims of the "white terror" (*baise kongbu*) perpetrated by the "local tyrants and evil gentry." However, according to Mao Zedong, it was justifiable for Chinese communists or their supporters to engage in "just a lit- tle terror" in the cause of furthering the revolution.[9]

In the 1980s, Beijing confronted terrorism from disaffected Han and some ethnic minority extremists who were indigenous to China, but the problem was seen as manageable and essentially domestic. That terrorism was not viewed as a serious problem is evident from the fact that terrorism was not even listed as a criminal offense in China's criminal code promulgated in 1979; indeed, the word did not even appear anywhere in the code. However, certain crimes generally associated with terrorism, such as hijacking and sabotage, were con- sidered serious enough to be designated as capital offenses.

In the 1990s, terrorism became closely associated with Uighur extremists, whom the Chinese believed were receiving training and support from Muslim extremists based in other states neighboring China. Although there was no dis- cussion of terrorism in the 1998 defense white paper, the 2000 defense white paper does mention the topic in passing. The provocative book published by two People's Liberation Army (PLA) colonels in 1999 titled *Chaoxian zhan* (Unrestricted Warfare) contains some pointed discussion of terrorism, includ- ing several mentions of Osama bin Laden.[10] Also mentioning terrorism are the "Dushanbe Statement" of 2000, issued by the "Shanghai Five" states (China, Russia, Kazakhstan, Kyrgyzstan, and Tajikistan); and the "Shanghai Conven- tion," issued in June 2001 by these same countries plus Uzbekistan.

By the first decade of the twenty-first century Beijing's understanding of
terrorism had broadened. Since September 11, Chinese leaders began to recognize terrorism as having a global dimension with terrorist groups maintaining extensive transnational linkages. The defense white paper issued in
December 2002 places terrorism as a key threat confronting China, and the
word is mentioned fifty times in the document. The white paper states:

> In recent years, terrorist activities have notably increased, and constitute a real
> threat to world peace and development. The "September 11" terrorist attack,
> which caused a great loss of lives and property, has aroused the universal con-
> cern of the international community. China, too, is a victim of terrorism. The
> "East Turkistan" terrorist forces are a serious threat to the security of the lives
> and property of the people of all China's ethnic groups, as well as the country's
> social stability.[11]

TERRORISM AND INTERNAL SECURITY

Chinese leaders view internal security as the most crucial aspect of national
security. They view internal security not merely as a matter of maintaining
law and order within China's borders but also as a parallel with maintaining
Chinese Communist Party (CCP) rule of the country. Any threat or potential
threat to continued CCP rule is viewed as a serious danger to internal security. In recent decades, the greater threat to continued party rule has been so-
called peaceful evolution. This refers to the gradual erosion of CCP power via
subversive foreign bourgeois influences promoting dangerous ideas such as
capitalist democracy; of course, the United States is perceived as the major
source of this threat.

However, China's leaders have also become increasingly concerned
about more immediate threats to national unity and social stability. In particular, Beijing has become alarmed at the breakdown of basic law and order that has accompanied economic reforms and the loosening of central
controls in the post-Mao era. The result has been periodic crackdowns on
crime and lawlessness—the "strike hard" campaigns. The dislocations and
hardships endured by Chinese workers and peasants as a result of the increasing role of market forces since the late 1980s have triggered waves of
unrest and protest, although, with the exceptions of the student-led protest
movement of 1989 and Falun Gong sect a decade later, these have tended
to remain localized and contained by the authorities.

Nevertheless, these manifestations of social disruption are of major concern to Chinese authorities—especially the wave of bombings in the wake of
September 11, 2001. During a three-week period between late November and

mid-December 2001, twenty-eight explosions reportedly occurred in various Chinese cities prompting a series of emergency high-level meetings in Beijing to consider countermeasures.[12] In fact, while Chinese authorities have played up the ethnic separatist–terrorist threat and its transnational connections, they appear far more alarmed about terrorism committed by Han Chinese. Probably "the worst terrorist act in the history of the People's Republic" occurred in the city of Shijiazhuang, in central China, on March 16, 2001, when four bombs detonated within the space of one hour at separate locations killing more than one hundred persons and seriously injuring at least thirty-eight others.[13] The authorities claimed that the destruction was the work a lone forty-one-year-old unemployed male who was quickly identified and arrested after a brief manhunt. Reportedly his motivation was a bitter feud with relatives and former neighbors.[14]

The aforementioned incidents and growing concerns about terrorism generally prompted authorities to expedite a whole series of measures, including, in December 2001, making commission of a terrorist act, consorting with terrorists, and financing terrorism all criminal acts; and in early 2002 creating an antiterrorism bureau in the Ministry of Public Security.[15]

Of the six causal factors for bombings in China listed by premier Zhu Rongji at a December 2001 meeting, only one was identified as "ethnic separatism."[16] Why is this so? Because acts of terror brought on by the Han Chinese strike at the heart of the China proper and underscore the party-state's greatest nightmare: coordinated urban worker unrest in the heartland. Factory layoffs and social dislocation have prompted isolated but numerous instances of terrorism by disgruntled workers and other alienated citizens.[17] These acts are usually bombings because explosives are widely used in industry and agriculture and because they are easily obtained.[18] In early 2002 a suicide bomber detonated explosives outside a department store in Urumqi, killing himself and a high-ranking policeman and injuring several other law enforcement personnel. According to the official China news service, the bomber was a disturbed Han Chinese afflicted with the AIDS virus, not a member of an ethnic minority favoring separatism.[19]

Also starting in the 1980s, ethnic minorities in China have increasingly engaged in collective action against the party-state or against Han Chinese interlopers, perpetrating certain acts of violence. While actual terrorist attacks remain sporadic, Uighur radicals appear to be getting better armed, organized, and more capable. Serious violent incidents occurred in Xinjiang between Uighurs and Chinese security forces in 1981 and 1990. The former incident occurred in Kashgar after a raid by Uighur radicals on a PLA armory, and the latter occurred in Baren (a town outside of Kashgar) when armed police tried to disperse a large anti-Chinese rally.[20] In March 1997 a bomb exploded in a crowded Beijing bus during rush hour, injuring thirty people. It came on the heels of a series of bus bombings in Xinjiang, and a Uighur group based in Turkey claimed responsibility for the blast.[21] Chinese security forces have tried to crack down on such groups, with mixed success. In August 2001, for example, Chinese paramilitary police raided a reported terrorist hideout near the Xinjiang city of Kuqa. Although the raid netted firearms, explosives, and the bodies of three dead suspected extremists, several more managed to escape and the local police chief was shot dead in the operation.[22]

The defense white paper of December 2002 states that a top domestic security priority for China is to "stop armed subversion and safeguard social stability." The Chinese tend to conflate "terrorism with separatism and extremism" or at least see them as "closely connected." According to Liu Yaohua, deputy director of public security in Xinjiang, for Uighurs who advocate independence, "ethnic separatism is their goal, religious extremism is their garb, and terrorist acts are their means."[23]

Beijing claims that between 1990 and 2001 Uighur terrorists launched two hundred attacks resulting in 162 deaths and 440 injuries. The incidents reportedly included bombings, assassinations, attacks on government buildings, arson, poisonings, riots, acquisition of firearms, ammunition, and military training.[24] The statistics in the official report, issued in January 2002 by the Information Office of the State Council, are probably exaggerated. Significantly, however, the most serious "separatist incident" in Xinjiang in recent years is not included in the report. This event occurred in early February 1997 in the city of Yining. Hundreds of Uighurs were peacefully protesting a Chinese crackdown on religious and cultural activities. When security forces attempted to break up the crowd, instead of dampening their ardor and dispersing the assemblage, the teargas and water cannon enraged the demonstrators and attracted more people onto the streets. The police reportedly fired into the crowd: at least dozens of people were killed and injured, including security personnel, and thousands were detained. Most of the fatalities were probably inflicted by Chinese security forces.[25]

In spring 2000 Beijing launched the "Go West" campaign, the focus of which was to develop the economy of China's western autonomous regions and provinces, especially their infrastructure. A significant driver behind the campaign was to strengthen Beijing's hold on China's strategic border areas. Chinese leaders reportedly viewed the campaign as the "fundamental guarantee for us to foster national unity, to maintain social stability, and to consolidate the borders." General Chi Haotian, on an inspection tour of the far west, asserted that the campaign was essential to "consolidating national defense and realizing the country's long-term security and stability."[26] According to Xinjiang party secretary Wang Lequan, speaking in mid-2001, "We [China] need to always keep our economic development pace faster than that of surrounding countries and our living standards higher . . . [because] those are the only ways to keep the firm support of the people of all ethnic groups . . . and to conscientiously resist and oppose all subversive acts of ethnic separatism."[27] Local officials in Xinjiang, interviewed in mid-2002, told a foreign reporter that they believed Uighurs became radicalized and turned to terrorism because of the conditions of poverty around them. They expressed the belief that the "Go West" development campaign would weaken separatist impulses in the autonomous region.[28]

TERRORISM AND GOOD NEIGHBORLINESS

In recent years, Beijing has increasingly concentrated on improving its relations with other Asian capitals, especially those of countries bordering China. China endeavors to be on good terms with all its neighbors to ensure a peaceful and less-threatening environment. As Beijing's December 2002 defense white paper states, the country is "striving for . . . a favorable climate on China's periphery."[29]

Central Asia (and Xinjiang)

With the dismemberment of the multinational Soviet empire in the early 1990s, China suddenly gained three new neighbors: the Central Asian states of Kazakhstan, Kyrgyzstan, and Tajikistan. China became increasingly worried about the spillover effect of ethnoseparatism. Fundamentally, for Beijing, Central Asia had become "an unpredictable zone from which Turkic nationalism and Islamic ideologies could radiate into Xinjiang."[30] China began to develop closer relations with the new states of Central Asia with these and other priorities in mind.

First, China wanted to secure its own borders by building security relationships with each of these countries and Russia. This meant resolving territorial disputes and developing confidence-building measures to demilitarize the region and improve cooperation between the three countries' armed forces, which were objectives largely accomplished by the mid-1990s.[31] Second, China wanted to increase economic ties to Central Asia. In particular Beijing has sought to enhance its energy security with a particular focus on Kazakhstan's oil and gas resources. Third—and of greatest relevance to this chapter—China wanted to cooperate with these countries to counter "terrorism, separatism, and extremism." China feared that there were growing links between radical Islamic movements based in other states—particularly Central Asian countries, including Afghanistan—and Uighur separatist movements in Xinjiang. Implicit was the thinking that the terrorists were transnational, that the separatists were ethnic, and that the extremism was religious.[32]

One "well-placed Chinese official" told the *Far Eastern Economic Review* in October 2001 that he estimated Taliban-ruled Afghanistan to be host to "between 2,000 and 3,000 Uighur militants from Xinjiang."[33] As of January 2002, Chinese police had reportedly "arrested over 100 terrorists who had sneaked into Xinjiang after being trained in terrorist bases in Afghanistan and other countries."[34] According to Xinjiang party secretary Wang Lequan, approximately one thousand Xinjiang militants were trained by al Qaeda in camps in Kandahar and Mazzar-I-Sharif.[35] Moreover there were reportedly coordination and cooperation between Xinjiang groups and Osama bin Laden's organization. An East Turkistan Islamic movement leader apparently met with bin Laden in early 1999.[36]

The threat to the security of Xinjiang was the "main element" in China's Afghanistan policy, according to one Chinese analyst. Initially, this fueled Beijing's efforts to engage the Taliban. The high point was in December 2000, when the PRC's ambassador to Islamabad Lu Shunlin met with Mullah Omar. The Chinese diplomat sought assurances that the Taliban would not train Xinjiang Uighurs, whereas the Afghan leader wanted China to block United Nations sanctions against Afghanistan. Reportedly, neither man was able to achieve his goal.[37] China has also attempted to develop good ties with post-Taliban Afghanistan. Beijing promised US$150 million in aid to president Hamid Karzai during his visit to China in January 2002.[38] China also moved promptly to reopen its embassy in Kabul, and foreign minister Tang Jiaxuan paid a visit to the Afghan capital in 2002.[39]

Countering terrorism, separatism, and extremism is given as a primary goal of the Shanghai Cooperation Organization (SCO). Indeed, according to Tang Jiaxuan, the SCO "was the first international organization that set counterterrorism as its target."[40] The SCO was formally established in mid-2001, but the organization has its roots in the an informal gathering in 1996 attended by Russia, Kazakhstan, Tajikistan, Kyrgyzstan, and China, forming a group that became known as the Shanghai Five. In 1999 these five states agreed to establish an antiterror center in Bishkek, Kyrgyzstan.

The urgency for such antiterror cooperation was brought home to Beijing in June 2002, when first-secretary Wang Jianping of the Chinese Embassy in Bishkek was shot dead in his car. Four months later, in October 2002, China and Kyrgyzstan conducted what was described as a small "joint antiterrorism military exercise."[41] The exercise lasted two days and involved some three hundred troops as well as tanks and helicopters.[42] It is extremely unusual for the PLA to conduct military exercises of any kind with the armed forces of another country. Significantly, this was the first multinational military exercise conducted by the PLA on foreign soil and the first war game conducted with a foreign military using live fire.[43] Such unprecedented activities prompted the December 2002 defense white paper to declare: "The Shanghai Cooperation Organization has made outstanding progress in building mutual trust and developing state-to-state relationship[s] based on partnership rather than alliance and on anti-terror cooperation."[44]

Additional pathbreaking SCO activities occurred in 2003. First of all, the heads of state of member countries held their third summit in Moscow in May. They agreed on the establishment of an SCO secretariat in Beijing and selected the first secretary-general of the organization, ambassador Zhang Deguang of China.[45] Second, in early August 2003, China's armed forces conducted a two-phase antiterrorism exercise with the militaries of four other SCO countries (Uzbekistan did not participate). The first phase was held in Kazakhstan and the second was held in Xinjiang. The initial phase included soldiers from Kazakhstan, Kyrgyzstan, and Russia, with China and Tajikistan sending observers. The second phase involved Chinese and Kyrgyz forces, with Russia, Kazakhstan, and Tajikistan providing observers. More than one thousand troops participated in the exercise, which was presided over by PRC minister of national defense General Cao Gangchuan and senior defense officials from the other SCO states. This multilateral exercise was the first held under the auspices of the SCO, and it marked the first time that foreign forces have participated in an exercise inside the PRC.[46]

South Asia: Controlling Islamic Extremism and Tibetan Separatism

Two South Asian states loom large for China as it addresses the problems of terrorism, separatism, and extremism: India and Pakistan. Islamabad is the centerpiece of Beijing's efforts to manage its relations with the Muslim world. Two core issues are China's treatment of its own Muslim population and persuading Muslim states not to support terrorism and separatism or encourage extremism. Meanwhile, New Delhi is the key capital for Beijing as it addresses the challenge of Tibet. China would like to manage—if not resolve—the Tibetan problem, and doing so requires India's cooperation.

Beijing appears to have reached a key realization in recent years that Muslim/Uighur groups were more dangerous and problematic than Tibetans. The active, high-profile Dalai Lama, who won the Nobel Prize for peace in 1989, was initially considered the priority; however, Chinese thinking has changed.[47] The Uighur groups have become increasingly radicalized as part of an internationalist Islamic movement. Some Uighurs have gone abroad and fought as foot soldiers for Muslim causes around the world while the Uighur

cause itself has received greater foreign support and attention. The Islamic ji-
hadi groups' possessing global networks and transnational ethnic groups that
abound in Central Asia have made the Uighurs a far more daunting group
with which the Chinese party-state has to deal.

In contrast to the Muslims of Xinjiang, Tibetan activists—although they are
motivated, mobilized, spread all over the world, and are a cause célèbre in the
West—have tended to be less inclined to resort to violence. While Tibet exiles
were armed and trained by the U.S. Central Intelligence Agency at the height
of the Cold War, Tibetans have in recent years tended to eschew violent struggle. Moreover, Beijing seems to believe that the Tibetan question can and
should be resolved or at least managed through peaceful, diplomatic means.
Beijing has conducted an on-again, off-again dialogue with the Dalai Lama's
Tibetan government-in-exile, based in Daramsala, India, over the years and
these continued in 2002 and 2003.[48]

The Tibet issue is a significant part of China's differences with India, and
major strides appear to have been made between Beijing and New Delhi.
Prime minister Atal B. Vajpayee paid a landmark six-day visit to China in
June 2003. China traded de facto recognition of Indian control of the Hi-
malayan kingdom of Sikkim (seized by New Delhi in 1975 but never accepted by Beijing) in exchange for Indian official acknowledgment that Tibet
is part of China. Moreover, in a joint statement issued by the two governments, India agreed not to allow Tibetans "to engage in anti-Chinese political
activities."[49]

TERRORISM AND GLOBAL SECURITY

Beyond strictly neighborhood issues, Beijing has global security concerns regarding terrorism. Of foremost concern are China's relations with the United
States and, since September 11, the United States–led war on terrorism. The
Islamic/Arab world is also of significant concern to the Beijing goverment, especially in its work to ensure China's continual supply of oil from the region
and to dissuade the region's countries from supporting Uighur separatism.

United States (and the Global War on Terrorism)

A top priority for Beijing has been for it to maintain a cordial relationship
with Washington. China's highest national priority is to ensure that its economy continues to enjoy robust growth (and hence maintain domestic stability), which is dependent on peace and development in Asia and the world. For
this to continue China desires a vibrant economic relationship and cordial

strategic cooperation with the United States. Beijing has nothing to gain in the foreseeable future from a deterioration in Sino–United States relations.

Before September 11, China's relations with the United States were rocky at best. While relations had improved since the resolution of the Hainan Island incident of April 2001, the administration of president George W. Bush continued to regard China with considerable suspicion and perceive the country as a looming strategic competitor.[50]

Following the coordinated terrorist incidents of September 11 and the resulting death and destruction in New York City (the World Trade Center), northern Virginia (the Pentagon), and Shanksville, Pennsylvania (United flight 93), Bush announced the launching of a global war on terrorism. Chinese president Jiang Zemin was quick to reach out to Bush. In a message sent on September 11, Jiang condemned the attacks and expressed his condolences. Jiang then telephoned Bush on September 12 promptly offering China's cooperation in the worldwide counterterrorism struggle. Also on September 12, China voted for UN Security Council resolution 1368, condemning the terrorist threat.

The Chinese were also the victims of global terrorism. Although not widely publicized, as many as eighteen Chinese citizens lost their lives in the September 11 terrorist attacks.[51] What is interesting is that the Chinese authorities have made scant mention of these losses. The same is true of how Beijing handled the deaths of two Chinese contract workers, kidnapped by terrorists in the southern Philippines, who were killed in August 2001 in a shootout between Filipino security forces and the kidnappers.[52] Perhaps one reason Beijing does not widely publicize these tragedies is to avoid drawing attention to the Chinese government's inability to protect its citizens working and traveling overseas.

Yet China's support for the United States–led global struggle against terrorism has been qualified.[53] Beijing has been prepared to share intelligence on terrorist groups and follow terrorist financial flows. China has also been supportive of Pakistan's decision to cooperate with the United States in the global war on terrorism (discussed shortly). There are notable indications of the growing security and law enforcement links between China and the United States. The two governments signed an agreement to open a Federal Bureau of Investigation liaison office in Beijing during attorney general John Ashcroft's three-day visit to China in October 2002.[54] And in July 2003, U.S. and Chinese customs officials signed an agreement in Beijing to cooperate in the Container Security Initiative. Under the agreement, U.S. officials will be stationed at ports in the cities of Shanghai and Shenzhen. The task of the personnel will be to certify that containers bound for U.S. destinations are free of weapons or dangerous materials that could be used by terrorists.[55]

Beijing, however, has been far less keen on U.S. military operations against countries deemed havens for terrorists, countries suspected of being ready to provide weapons of mass destruction to terrorists, or countries how have used or might use weapons of mass destruction to terrorize their neighbors. Beijing stressed that the way to eradicate terrorism was to address the "root causes" under UN auspices than through exclusively unilateral military means. "The fight against terrorism requires conclusive evidence, clear targets and conformity with the purpose and principle of the UN Charter. . . . The leading role of the UN and its Security Council should be brought into full play."[56]

In January 2002 Bush identified Iraq, Iran, and North Korea as comprising an "axis of evil" because of their record of supporting terrorism and their efforts to develop and proliferate weapons of mass destruction or their delivery systems. Beijing condemned the moralistic rhetoric and became concerned that Washington's war against terrorism was morphing into a campaign to justify the overthrow of regimes around the world that were unfriendly to the United States.[57]

As the United States geared up for a conflict with Iraq, China wondered which regime would be targeted next: would it be Iran or North Korea? By mid-January 2003, Beijing had become increasingly alarmed that Washington's next target might turn out to be its truculent neighbor in Pyongyang.[58] North Korea had long been a mercurial socialist regime, and bilateral relations had been strained for most of the 1990s, with the collapse of the Eastern European communist regimes and the then disintegration of the Soviet Union. Beijing did not seek to fill the void left by Moscow, and indeed Beijing moved closer to Seoul, establishing diplomatic relations with South Korea in 1992. But by 2002 Pyongyang had become a major headache for Beijing with its endless demands for Chinese aid and assistance; influx of hundreds of thousands of refugees fleeing famine, starting in the mid-1990s; and its embarrassing high-profile asylum seekers seeking refuge in foreign diplomatic missions in 2001 and 2002.[59]

While Beijing could tolerate these irritants in its close but uncomfortable relationship with Pyongyang, the emergence of a creeping nuclear crisis in late 2002 set off Chinese alarm bells. China feared that North Korea's admission to U.S. assistant secretary for East Asia and Pacific affairs James Kelly during his visit to Pyongyang in October 2002 would turn out to be just the justification the United States would need to take military action against North Korea. As a result China leaped into action arranging a meeting in April 2003 between Pyongyang and Washington, hosting it in Beijing. Then, when this meeting failed to produce results or subsequent rounds of talks three months later, China again went on the diplomatic offensive with a special envoy, deputy foreign minister Dai Bingguo, visiting first Pyongyang and then

Washington. The outcome was six-party talks—involving China, Japan, North Korea, South Korea, Russia, and the United States—held in Beijing in late August 2003. China sought to arrange a new round of talks, although the earlier sense of urgency was gone by September 2003, as Beijing had concluded that U.S. military action against Pyongyang was no longer imminent.[60]

China was circumspect about U.S. and coalition operations in Afghanistan in late 2001 and early 2002 but did not actively oppose the effort via the United Nations or elsewhere. Chinese forces did not intervene in Afghanistan, but China did seal its common border. Meanwhile, on Iraq, while China was not supportive of the military action, it did not take the lead in opposing Operation Iraqi Freedom. Of course the attention and irritation of Washington was not focused on Beijing in this instance but on two capitals that were perceived by some Americans as "fair weather friends": Paris and Berlin.

Some Chinese analysts have claimed that the war on terrorism is the "new foundation" of China's strategic relations with the United States.[61] This claim seems exaggerated, although the cooperation has noticeably improved the climate of relations between Washington and Beijing. Both sides are genuinely satisfied with the modest but real cooperation. China was pleased when, in late 2002, the UN Security Council and the United States classified the East Turkistan Islamic movement (ETIM) as a terrorist group. The United States was pleased by what assistant secretary of state for East Asia and Pacific affairs James Kelly called the "unprecedented extent of counterterrorism information sharing." Still, some Chinese are uncertain about how to view the fact that despite Washington's rhetoric, the ETIM has not been added to the State Department's "list of designated foreign terrorist organizations."[62] Currently ETIM is designated as a terrorist group by a presidential executive order, which does not demand the same heavy burden of proof and judicial process required for an organization to be added to the State Department's high-profile list. As a practical matter, the fact that ETIM is not on the State Department's list makes no difference as to how Washington treats the group.[63]

As one astute U.S. security analyst has observed, "It appears that China's support of the war against terrorism does not and will not fundamentally alter the Sino-U.S. relationship."[64] A leading Chinese security analyst concurs, opining that "the substance of Sino-U.S. relations has not changed since . . . September 11, 2001, despite improved atmospherics. The underlying strategic view of each state remains deeply suspicious of the other's intentions, limiting the scope of cooperation."[65] Moreover, according to another prominent U.S. analyst, whether Sino–United States cooperation in the antiterror struggle "is sustainable is a key question."[66]

China has made considerable efforts to maintain good relations with the Islamic world. Chinese interests include securing oil and denying its support for

Muslim extremist groups in China.[67] Beijing's closest friend in the Muslim world is Islamabad: for China, Pakistan has served as its bridge to other Islamic states. For Islamabad, Beijing has been its most reliable friend and patron bar none: China has provided Pakistan with weaponry and key military technical assistance, and it has served as a counterweight to its massive South Asian nemesis India. Coordination between Beijing and Islamabad has also been helpful to both governments as each grapples with the threat of terrorism domestically and the turbulence associated with the ongoing U.S. military coalition operations in Afghanistan and Iraq.[68]

In October 2001, foreign minister Tang Jiaxuan told foreign minister Sheikh Hamad of Qatar, concurrently chair of the Organization of the Islamic Conference, just before an urgent meeting of the conference, that China desired to improve "consultation and cooperation with Islamic countries in fighting terrorism." He explained that China recognized "Islamic countries are also the victims of terrorism" and stressed that China "opposed . . . associating terrorism with any religion, nationality, or religion."[69]

CONCLUSION

One of Beijing's most respected elder statesmen, the late Li Shenzhi, writing in August 2002, opined that "it cannot be said that China has made any major new change in foreign policy" in the aftermath of September 11, 2001.[70] Nevertheless, China has become increasingly concerned with terrorism. This concern was initially an exclusively manageable domestic security issue, but by the late 1990s it had taken on a more serious open-ended foreign policy dimension as well. Beijing was specifically concerned with Han Chinese worker unrest and ethnic groups within China becoming radicalized because of direct support or indirect encouragement from transnational terrorists. The attacks of September 11 only heightened this concern.

China has sought further cooperation with states on its periphery to counter terrorism, starting with Russia and the countries of Central Asia. Perhaps the most important goal behind the formal establishment of SCO in June 2001 was cooperation against terrorism.

The global war on terrorism led by the United States has had positive and negative outcomes. On the positive side, counterterrorism is yet another issue on which China and other countries, including major powers such as the United States, can find common ground and cooperate against. On the negative side, Beijing worries that this global antiterrorism struggle is providing Washington with an excuse to exert its power and increase its influence in Asia and around the world. China is concerned about the U.S. military presence in Central Asia and Iraq; the improved U.S. security ties with India; and enhanced defense cooperation with Japan and the Philippines. Some elite wonder whether these steps might also be aimed at containing China.[71]

Terrorism is now a major topic of concern for China, and it is an issue that will figure prominently in Beijing's foreign policy for the foreseeable future. For the time being the U.S. global offensive against terrorism offers China a useful opportunity to enhance its international status and improve relationships with the United States and other states while providing additional justification for cracking down on domestic ethnic militants and dissidents.

NOTES

This chapter represents solely the views of the author and not those of the United States government, Department of Defense, or U.S. Army.

1. See, for example, the discussion in Michael Pillsbury, *China Debates the Future Security Environment* (Washington, D.C.: National Defense University Press, 2000), chap. 5; for mention of "political stability," see 224.

2. Indeed, it is probably no exaggeration to label Chinese leaders as paranoid. See Andrew Scobell, *China's Use of Military Force: Beyond the Great Wall and the Long March* (New York: Cambridge University Press, 2003), 33–34; Fei-Ling Wang, "Self-Image and Strategic Intentions: National Confidence and Political Insecurity," in *In the Eyes of the Dragon: China Views the World,* ed. Yong Deng and Fei-Ling Wang (Lanham, Md.: Rowman & Littlefield, 1999), 21–45.

3. Author's interviews with Chinese analysts in September 2003.

4. Nailene Chou Wiest, "PRC to Strengthen Economic Ties with Islamic Nations," *South China Morning Post,* November 30, 2002 (Internet edition), appearing in Foreign Broadcast Information Service–China (hereafter FBIS-CHI).

5. "People's Republic of China Foreign Minister Tang Jiaxuan News Conference at National People's Congress," Ministry of Foreign Affairs of the People's Republic of China Internet website (Beijing) in English, March 6, 2002, carried by FBIS-CHI.

6. Other scholars have noted this but tend to argue that this is a manifestation of a newfound Chinese confidence and maturity rather than a motive driven by Beijing's insecurities. See, for example, Taylor Fravel and Evan Medeiros, "China's New Diplomacy," *Foreign Affairs* 82 (November/December 2003). For a pre–September 11, 2001, assessment that stresses China's insecurities as a key driver, see Fei-Ling Wang, "To Incorporate China—a New China Policy for a New Era," *Washington Quarterly* 21, no. 1 (Winter 1998): 67–81.

7. For more on China's growing interest in multilateralism, see Jing-dong Yuan, *Asia-Pacific Security: China's Conditional Multilateralism and Great Power Entente* (Carlisle Barracks, Pa.: U.S. Army War College Strategic Studies Institute, January 2000); and Jianwei Wang, "Managing Conflict: Chinese Perspectives on

Multilateral Diplomacy and Collective Security," in Deng and Wang, *In the Eyes of the Dragon*, 73–96.

8. Amnesty International reports on "the lack of definition of 'terrorism,' 'terrorist organization,' and 'terrorist crime.'" The standing committee of the National People's Congress adopted these amendments on December 29, 2001, and they entered into force the same day. See *China's Anti-terrorism Legislation and Repression in the Xinjiang Uighur Autonomous Region*, March 22, 2002, Amnesty International index ASA 17/010/2002, accessed at http://web.amnesty.org/library/index/ENGASA 170102002.

9. The quotes are taken from "Report on an Investigation of the Peasant Movement in Hunan (March 1927)" in *Selected Works of Mao Tse-tung*, vol. 1 (Peking: Foreign Languages Press, 1967), 39.

10. Qiao Liang and Wang Xiangsu, *Chaoxian zhan* [Unrestricted Wafare] (Beijing: Jiefangjun Wenyi Chubanshe, 1999), chap. 2.

11. *China's National Defense in 2002* (Beijing: Information Office of the State Council of the People's Republic of China, December 2002), 70.

12. Li Tzu-ching, "Zhu Rongji's Instructions on Handling Explosive Cases," *Cheng Ming* (Hong Kong), January 1, 2002, in FBIS-CHI.

13. The quote is from Gordon G. Chang, *The Coming Collapse of China* (New York: Random House, 2001), 283.

14. Wang Leming and Zhai Wei, "Demon Rounded Up in Net of Heaven—True Account of Cracking Vicious '16 March' Explosion Case in Shijiazhuang," Xinhua Domestic Service (Beijing), March 25, 2001, in FBIS-CHI.

15. Xiong Guangkai, "Dangqian quanqiu fankongxing shi jiqi qiying zhanwang" [The global counter terrorism campaign: Current situation and future prospects], *Guoji zhanlue yanjiu*, no. 2 (2003): 4.

16. Li Tzu-ching, "Zhu Rongji's Instructions on Handling Explosive Cases."

17. Chien She, "Ministry of Public Security to Set Up Anti-terrorist Department," *Kuang Chiao Ching* (Hong Kong), January 16, 2002, in FBIS-CHI; Li Tzu-ching, "Zhu Rongji's Instructions on Handling Explosive Cases."

18. Chien She, "Ministry of Public Security to Set Up Anti-terrorist Department."

19. Agence France-Presse, February 1, 2002, in FBIS-CHI.

20. Richard Baum, *Burying Mao: Chinese Politics in the Age of Deng Xiaoping* (Princeton, N.J.: Princeton University Press, 1994), 324.

21. "A Bomb in Beijing," *Economist*, March 15, 1997, 37–38.

22. Philip Pan, "In China's West, Ethnic Strife Becomes 'Terrorism,'" *Washington Post*, July 15, 2002.

23. Pan, "In China's West, Ethnic Strife Becomes 'Terrorism.'"

24. *East Turkistan Terrorist Forces Cannot Get Away with Impunity* (Beijing: State Council Information Office, January 2002) in Xinhua Domestic Service (Beijing), January 21, 2002, in FBIS-CHI.

25. "People's Republic of China: No Justice for Victims of the 1997 Crackdown in Guljin (Yining)," Amnesty International press release, February 4, 2003, accessed at http://web.amnesty.org/library/Index/ENGASA1701112003?open&of=ENG-CHN.

26. Both quotations appear in Elizabeth Economy, "China's Go West Campaign: Ecological Construction or Ecological Exploitation?" *China Environment Series* (Washington, D.C.: Woodrow Wilson Center), no. 5 (2002): 4.

27. Wang was speaking on June 29, 2001, at a ceremony commemorating the eightieth anniversary of the founding of the CCP. The text of the speech was carried in the July 30, 2001, issue of *Xinjiang Ribao* and appears in FBIS-CHI.

28. Pan, "In China's West, Ethnic Strife Becomes 'Terrorism.'"

29. *China's National Defense in 2002*, 11.

30. Lena Jonson, "Russia and Central Asia," in *Central Asian Security: The New International Context*, ed. Roy Allison and Lena Jonson (Washington, D.C.: Brookings Institution; and London: Royal Institute of International Affairs, 2001), 117.

31. For a concise overview of these security developments, see Guangcheng Xing, "China and Central Asia," in Allison and Jonson, *Central Asian Security*, 159–61.

32. For an explicit elaboration, see Ba Zhongtan et al., *Zhongguo guojia anquan zhanlue wenti yanjiu* [Research on Chinese National Security Strategy Issues] (Beijing: Zhongguo Junshi Kexue Chubanshe, 2003), 239–41.

33. David Murphy and Susan V. Lawrence, "Beijing Hopes to Gain from U.S. Raids on Afghanistan," *Far Eastern Economic Review*, October 4, 2001, 18.

34. *East Turkistan Terrorist Forces Cannot Get Away with Impunity.*

35. "Over a Thousand Xinjiang Separatists Trained in Afghanistan," *Sing Tao Jih Pao* (Internet edition), March 5, 2002, in FBIS-CHI.

36. Tian Yi, "Exclusive Report: East Turkistan Terrorist Organizations' Source of Funding," *Shiji Jingji Baodao*, Guangzhou, February 20, 2003, in FBIS-CHI.

37. Murphy and Lawrence, "Beijing Hopes to Gain from U.S. Raids on Afghanistan," 19.

38. Henry Chu, "Response to Terror; China Pledges More Afghan Aid," *Los Angeles Times*, January 25, 2002.

39. "China," in *Asia Pacific Security Outlook 2003*, ed. Charles E. Morrison (New York: Japan Center for International Exchange, 2003), 51.

40. "Foreign Minister Tang Jiaxuan News Conference at National People's Congress," Ministry of Foreign Affairs of the People's Republic of China Internet website (Beijing) in English, March 6, 2002, carried by FBIS-CHI.

41. *China's National Defense in 2002*, 71.

42. "China," in Morrison, *Asia Pacific Security Outlook 2003*, 51.

43. "China," in Morrison, *Asia Pacific Security Outlook 2003*, 51.

44. *China's National Defense in 2002*, 6.

45. Xu Tao, "SCO: Example for the World," and Anonymous, "Returning in Triumph," both in *Beijing Review*, June 12, 2003, 26, and 3, respectively.

46. Robert Sae-Liu, "China Looks Outward with Exercise Programme," *Jane's Defence Weekly*, September 24, 2003; and Xu Zhuangzhi and Fan Qing, "Armed Forces of the Shanghai Cooperation Organization Member States Successfully Conclude Joint Anti-terrorism Exercise 'Joint 2003,'" Xinhua Domestic Service (Beijing), August 12, 2003, translated in FBIS-CHI.

47. Jen Hui-wen, "China Modifies Strategy to Strike against East Turkistan," *Hsin Pao* (Hong Kong), November 30, 2001, in FBIS-CHI.

48. James Kynge, "China and India Aim for Tibet Deal," *Financial Times*, June 24, 2003, 1

49. James Kynge, "China and India Agree on Border Concessions," *Financial Times*, June 25, 2003, 7.

50. Andrew Scobell, "Crouching Korea, Hidden China: Bush Administration Policy toward Pyongyang and Beijing," *Asian Survey* 42, no. 2 (March/April 2002): 343–68.

51. According to New York City Department of Health statistics, eighteen of the victims were identified as being born in China. See www.nytimes.com/library/national/met_VICTIMS-020419_ol.html. The number of fatalities among PRC citizens is probably fewer because a good number of these eighteen were likely to have been naturalized U.S. citizens.

52. A third Chinese citizen was freed by the authorities. Xinhua Domestic Service (Beijing), in English, October 20, 2001, in FBIS-CHI.

53. Denny Roy, "China and the War on Terrorism," *Orbis* 46, no. 3 (Summer 2002): 511–21.

54. Elizabeth Rosenthal, "Ashcroft Says U.S. Will Place Agents in China," *New York Times*, October 25, 2002.

55. "China, U.S. Strengthen Anti-terrorism Cooperation in Container Security," Xinhua Domestic Service (Beijing), in English, July 29, 2003, carried in FBIS-CHI.

56. *China's National Defense in 2002*, 70.

57. "China Is Not in Favor of Use of the Term 'Axis of Evil' in International Relations," Xinhua Domestic Service (Beijing), February 2002, in FBIS-CHI.

58. Andrew Scobell, "China and North Korea: The Limits of Influence," *Current History*, 102, no. 665 (September 2003): 274–78.

59. Andrew Scobell, "China and North Korea: The Close but Uncomfortable Relationship," *Current History* 101, no. 656 (September 2002): 280–81.

60. Author's interviews with Chinese analysts in September 2003.

61. Author's interviews with Chinese analysts in May and June 2002.

62. For the quotes, see James A. Kelly, assistant secretary of state for East Asia and Pacific Affairs, "U.S.–East Asia Policy: Three Aspects," remarks at the Woodrow Wilson Center, Washington, D.C., December 11, 2002, accessed on www.state.gove/p/eap/rls/rm/2002/15875.htm. For the list, see "Fact Sheet, Office of Counter Terrorism, May 23, 2003: Designated Foreign Terrorist Organization," accessed at www.state.gov/s/ct/rls/fs/2003/12389.htm. For Chinese puzzlement as to what this omission means, see Chia Yen, "Why the U.S. Lists 'East Turkistan' as a Terrorist Organization?" *Ching Pao* (Hong Kong), October 1, 2002, in FBIS-CHI.

63. Information provided to the author by a State Department official.

64. Roy, "China and the War on Terrorism," 518.

65. "China," in Morrison, *Asia Pacific Security Outlook 2003*, 51. The author of these words is Qinghua University professor Chu Shulong.

66. Thomas J. Christensen, "China," in *Strategic Asia 2002–2003: Asian Aftershocks*, ed. Richard J. Ellings and Aaron L. Friedberg (Seattle, Wash.: National Bureau of Asian Research, 2002), 81.

67. On oil, see Ed Blanche, "China's Mideast Oil Diplomacy," *Middle East* (London), January 2003, 48–51.

68. Anthony Kuhn, "Response to Terror: Pakistan Reaffirms Its Close Relations with China," *Los Angeles Times*, December 21, 2001; Devin T. Hagerty, "China and Pakistan: China and Pakistan: Strains in the Relationship," *Current History* 101, no. 656 (September 2002): 284–89.

69. "PRC Foreign Minister Tang Jiaxuan Calls Russia, Other Counterparts over Terrorism," Xinhua Domestic Service (Beijing), in English, October 9, 2001, in FBIS-CHI.

70. Li Shenzhi, "A Talk on the Diplomacy of the People's Republic of China," *Zhanlue yu Guanli*, August 1, 2002, in FBIS-CHI, August 30, 2002.

71. Author's interviews with Chinese analysts in May 2002.

Selected Bibliography

CHINESE-LANGUAGE SOURCES

Ba Zhongtan et al. *Zhongguo guojia anquan zhanlue wenti yanjiu* [Research on Chinese National Security Strategy Issues]. Beijing: Zhongguo junshi kexue chubanshe, 2003.

Cai Xianwei. *Zhongguo da zhanlue: lingdao shijie de lantu* [China's Grand Strategy: a Blueprint for Leading the World]. Haikou: Hainan Press, 1996.

Central Party School. *Yifazhiguo yu yidezhiguo xuexi wenda* [Questions and Answers for Studying "Ruling the Country by Law" and "Ruling the Country by Virtue"]. Beijing: Zhonggong zhongyang dangxiao chubanshe, 2001.

Chen Weixiong. *My Experience in the UN Security Council*. Beijing: Economic Daily Press, 2001.

Chen Yizi and Chen Fujin. eds. *Zhengzhi tizhi gaige jianghua* [Speeches on Political System Reform]. Beijing: Renmin chubanshe, 1987.

Chen Yue. *Zhongguo guoji diwei fenxi* [Analysis of China's International Status]. Beijing: Contemporary World Press.

Cheng Yehui. "Nanwang shimao tanpan de zuihou guankou" [Can't Forget the Last Hurdle of WTO Negotiations]. *Zhongguo jingji shibao* [Chinese Economic Times], September 19, 2003.

Chu Shulong. "Quanmian jianshe xiaokang shehui shiqi de zhongguo waijiao zhanlue" [China's diplomatic strategy during the period of comprehensively building a well-off society]. *Shijie Jingji yu Zhengzhi* [World Economics and Politics], no. 8 (August 2003).

Deng Xiaoping. *Deng Xiaoping Wenxuan* [Selected Works of Deng Xiaoping]. Vol. 3. Beijing: Renmin chubanshe, 1993.

———. *Deng Xiaoping Wenxuan* (1975–1982) [Selected Works of Deng Xiaoping]. Beijing: Renmin chubanshe, 1986.

325

Gao Lianfu. "East Asia regional cooperation entered the stage of institutionalization." *Taipingyang Xuebao* [Pacific Journal], no. 2 (2001).

Han Depei, ed. *Requan de lilun yu shijian* [Theories and Practice of Human Rights]. Wuhan: Wuhan daxue chubanshe, 1995.

He Dalong. "9.11 hou guoji xingshi de zhongda bianhua" [Major changes in international situations after 9/11]. *Shishi ziliao shouce*, no. 4 (October 2002).

Hou Shaowen. "Baochi shehui zhengzhi wending wenti" [Maintaining social and political stability]. In *Zhongguo mianxiang ershiyishiji de ruogan zhanlue wenti* [Several Strategic Issues Facing China in the Twenty-First Century], edited by Zheng Bijian and Yang Chungui. Beijing: Zhonggong zhongyang dangxiao chubanshe, 2000.

Hu Angang. "Xiaokan shehui" [Little comfort society]. In *2003 nian zhongguo shehui xingshi fenxi yu yuche* [Analysis and Forecast of China's Social Conditions in 2003], edited by Ru Xin et al. Beijing: Shehui Kexue Wenxian Press, 2003S.

———. *Zhongguo xiayibu* [The Next Step of China]. Chengdu: Sichuan Renmin Press, 1996.

Hu Angang and Meng Honghua. "Zhongmeirieying youxing zhanlue ziyuan bijiao" [A comparison of tangible strategic resources among China, the US, Japan, Russia, and India]. *Zhanlue yu guanli* [Strategy and Management], no. 2 (2002): 26–41.

Hu Zhaoming. "The present and future of East Asian cooperation." *Study of International Issues*, no. 1, 2001.

Huan Xiang. *Zhongheng shijie* [Overview of the World]. Beijing: World Affairs Press, 1985.

Information Office of the State Council. "2002 nian zhongguo de guofang" [China's national defense, 2002]. *Renmin Ribao* (overseas edition), December 10, 2002.

Institute of Legal Studies, the Chinese Academy of Social Sciences, ed. *Dangdai renquan* [Contemporary Human Rights]. Beijing: Zhongguo shehui kexue chubanshe, 1992.

Institute of Strategic Studies, CCP Central Party School. *Zhongguo heping jueqi xindaolu* [The New Route of China's Peaceful Rise]. Beijing: Zhonggong zhongyang dangxiao chubanshe, 2004.

Jiang Zemin. *Lun sange daibiao* [On the Three Represents]. Beijing: Zhongyang wenxian chubanshe, 2001.

———. *Lun youzhongguo tese shehuizhuyi zhuanti zhaibian* [On Socialism with Chinese Characteristics: Excerpts by Subjects]. Beijing: Zhongyang wenxian chubanshe, 2002.

———. "Quanmian jianshe xiaokang shehui, kaichuang zhonggguo teshe shehuihuizhuyi shiye xinjubian" [Building a well-off society in an all-out effort, creating a new situation for the cause of Chinese-style socialism—Report at the Sixteenth Chinese Communist Party Congress, November 8, 2002]. *Renmin Ribao* (overseas edition), November 18, 2002: 1–3.

Kang Xiaoguang. "Weilai 3–5 nian zhongguo dalu zhengzhi wendingxing fengxi" [Analysis of the political stability issue in Chinese mainland in the next 3–5 years]. *Zhanlue yu guanli* [Strategy and Management], no. 5 (2002).

Li Junru. "Zhengque lijie he jianchi dang de jiajixing" [Correctly understand and uphold the party's class nature]. In *Xinshiji de sikao* [Thinking in the New Century], edited by Lin Rong. Vol.1. Beijing: Central Party School Press, 2002: 163–72.

Li Shengming and Wang Yizhou, eds. *2003 Nian quanqiu zhengzhi yu anquan baogao* [2003 Yellow Book of International Politics and Security]. Beijiing: Shehui Kexue wenxian Press, 2003.

Li Xiguang and Liu Kang. *Yaomohua Zhongguo de beiho* [The Plot to Demonize China]. Beijing: Zhongguo shehui kexue chubanshe, 1996.

Li Yunlong. *Zhongmei guanxi zhong de renquan wenti* [The Human Rights Issue in Sino-American Relations]. Beijing: Xinhua chubanshe, 1998.

Li, Jingyu, and Wang Jun. "The prospect of East Asian economic development under the cooperative framework of 10 + 3." *Peace and Development Quarterly*, no. 2 (2001).

Lin Rong, ed. *Xinshiji de sikao* [Thinking in the New Century]. Vol.1. Beijing, Central Party School Press, 2002.

Liu Jianfei. *Meiguo yu fangong zhuyi: lun meiguo dui shehui zhuyi guojia d yishixingtai waijiao* [The U.S. and Anti-communism: On the American Ideological Diplomacy against Socialist Countries]. Beijing: Chinese Social Science Press, 2001.

———. "Renqing fankong yu fanba de guanxi" [Understanding the relationship between anti-terrorism and anti-hegemonism]. *Liaowang zhoukan* [Outlook Weekly], Beijing, no. 8 (February 24, 2003): 54–56.

———. "Zhongguo Minzhu zhengzhi jianshe yu zhongmei guanxi" [The construction of democratic politics in China and Sino-US relations]. *Zhanlue Yu Guanli* [Strategy and Management], no. 2 (2003): 76–82.

Liu Xiaoxue. "Summary of the international seminar on East Asian cooperation." *Dangdai Yatai* [Contemporary Asia-Pacific], no. 10 (2002).

Lou Yaoliang. *Diyuan zhengzhi yu zhongguo guofang zhanlue* [Geopolitics and China's National Defense Strategy]. Tianjin: Tianjin Remin Press, 2002.

Lu Gang and Guo Xuetang. *Zhongguo weixie shui: jiedu "zhong weixie lun"* [Whom Does China Threaten? Interpreting "The China Threat Theory"]. Shanghai: Xueling chubanshe, 2004.

Luo Weilong. "Zhongguoren yao shuo bu" [Chinese ant to say no]. *Taipingyang Xuebao* [Pacific Journal], Beijing, no. 2 (1995).

Ma Licheng and Ling Zhijun. *Jiaofeng: dangdai zhongguo sanci sixiang jiefang shilu* [Clash: Records of the Three Thought Liberations in Modern China]. Beijing: Jinri zhongguo chubanshe, 1998.

Ma Licheng. "Duiri guanxi xinsiwei" [New thinking on relations with Japan]. *Zhanlue yu guanli* [Strategy and Management], no. 6 (2002).

Pang Guang. "An analysis of the prospect of 'Shanghai Five.'" In *Thinking of the New Century*, edited by Ling Rong. Beijing: Chinese Central Party School Press, 2002.

———. "The development of Sino-Russian relations and the SCO under the new situation." *Chinese Diplomacy*, no. 4 (2003).

———. "SCO under new circumstances: challenge, opportunity and prospect for development." *Journal of International Studies*, no. 5 (2002).

Pang Zhongying. "China's Asian strategy: Flexible multilateralism." *World Economy and Politics*, no. 10 (2001).

——, ed. *Quanqiuhua, fanquanqiuhua yu zhongguo: lijie quanqiuhua de fuzhaxin yu duoyangxin* [Globalization, Anti-globalization, and China: Understanding the Complexity and Diversity of Globalization]. Shanghai: Renmin Press, 2002.

Project Group of the Chinese Academy of Sciences. *Zhongguo ke chixu fazhan zhanlue baogao* [Report on China's Sustainable Development Strategy, 2003]. Beijing: Kexue Press, 2003.

Qin Yaqing. "Guojia shengfen, zhanlue wenhua he anquan liyi" [State identity, strategic culture, and security Interests]. *World Economics and Politics*, no.1 (2003).

Qing Wenhui and Sun Hui. "Hou lengzhan shidai de zhongguo guojia anquan" [China's national security in the post–Cold War era]. *Zhanlue yu guanli* [Strategy and Management], no. 1 (2001): 3–9.

Qiu Yuanping. "Mianxiang shijie de xuanyan" [Declaration to the world]. *Qiushi*, no. 3, 2003.

Research Department of the Central Party School, ed. *Sange daibiao yu mianxiang ershiyi shiji de zhongguo gongchandang* [Three Represents and the Chinese Communist Party Facing the Twenty-First Century]. Beijing: Zhonggong zhongyang dangxiao chubanshe, 2001.

Ruan Zongze. "Dui 21 shiji zhongmeio xin sanjiao guanxi de jidian kanfa" [Several thoughts on the new Sino-American-Russian triangular relationship in the twenty-first century]. *Guoji wenti yanjiu* [Studies of International Affairs], no. 5 (2001).

Shen Jianing. "APEC Shanghai huiyi yu zhongguo de guoji xingxiang" [APEC meeting in Shanghai and China's international image]. *Guoji Zhengzhi Yanjiu*, no. 1 (2002): 115–18.

Shen Jiru. "On the mutual adaptation between China and APEC." *World Economics and Politics*, no. 5 (2002).

——. *Zhongguo budang 'bu xiansheng'—dangdai Zhongguo de guoji zhanlue wenti* [China Should Not Play 'Mr. No': The Problem of China's Contemporary International Strategy]. Beijing: Jinri Zhongguo chubanshe, 1998.

Shi Taifeng and Zhang Hengshan. "Lun zhongguogongchandang yifazhizheng" [On the Chinese Communist Party governing by law]. *Zhongguo shehui kexue* [China Social Sciences], no. 1 (2003): 13–24.

Shi Yinhong. "Guanyu Zhonguo de daguo diwei jiqi xingxiang sikao" [Thoughts on China's great power status and its image]. *Guoji Jingji Pinglun*, September/October 1999: 43–44.

——. "ZhongRi jiejin yu 'waijiao geming'" [Sino-Japanese *rapprochement* and the "diplomatic revolution"]. *Zhanlue yu guanli* [Strategy and Management], no. 2 (2003).

Shi Yinhong and Song Deji. "21 shiji qianqi zhongguo guoji taidu, waijiao zhixue he genben zhanlue sikao" [China's international attitude, diplomatic philosophy, and basic strategic thinking in the first part of the twenty-first century]. *Zhanlue yu guanli* [Strategy and Management], Beijing, no. 1 (2001).

Song Huichang. *Xiandai renquanlun* [Contemporary theory of human rights]. Beijing: Renmin chubanshe, 1993.

Song Qiang, Zhang Zangzang, and Qiao Bian. *Zhongguo keyi shuobu* [China Can Say No]. Beijing: Zhonghua gongshang lianhe chubanshe, 1996.

Song Xinning. *Guoki zhengzhi jingji yu zhongguo duiwai guanxi* [International Political Economy and Chinese Foreign Relations]. Hong Kong: Social Sciences Press, 1997.

Su Ge. "Lun zhongmeie guanxi" [On the Sino-US-Russian relationship]. *Guoji wenti yanjiu* [International Affairs], Beijing, no. 4 (2002).

Tang Shiping. "2010–2015 nian de zhongguo zhoubian angquan huangjin" [Security environment along China's periphery in 2010–2015]. *Zhanlue yu guanli* [Strategy and Management], Beijing, no. 5 (2002).

——. "Zailun zhongguo de da zhanlue" [Another treatise on China's grand strategy]. *Zhanlue yu guanli* [Strategy and Management], Beijing, no. 4 (2001): 29–37.

Tang Shiping, and Zhang Yunling. "Zhongguo de diqu zhanlue" [China's regional strategy]. *Shijie jingji yu zhengzhi* [World Economics and Politics], no. 6 (2004): 8–13.

Tang Yongsheng. "China and the UN peacekeeping operations." *Shijie jingji yu zhengzhi* [World Economics and Politics], no. 9 (2002).

——. "Zonghe anquan yu zongti zhanlue" [Comprehensive security and grand strategy]. *Shijie Zhishi* [World Affairs], no. 20 (October 16, 1996).

Tian Jin et al. *Zhongguo zai lianheguo* [China in the UN]. Beijing: Shijie zhishi chubanshe, 1999.

Tiang Zhongqing. "East Asia cooperation and China's strategic interest." *Dangdai Yatai* [Contemporary Asia-Pacific], no. 5 (2003).

Tsai Wei. "Zhonggong duitai zhengce de juece zuzhi yu guocheng" [The decision-making apparatus and process of the PRC's Taiwan policy]. *Zhongguo Dalu Yanjiu* [Journal of Mainland China Studies] 40, no. 5 (1997).

Wan Ming. "Renquan wenti benzhishang de bianyuanhua he xingshihua" [Human rights issue: Marginalization and ritualization]. In *Xianzhixing jiechu bushi zhengfu duihua zhengce zouxiang* [Constrained Engagement: Possible Trend of Bush's China Policy], edited by Hao Yufan and Zhang Yandong. Beijing: Xinhua chubanshe, 2001.

Wang Hui. "Diguo de haiyang shiye jiqi zai haiyang shidai de zhuanbian" [Imperial world views and its changes in the sea era]. *Zhongguo shehui kexue pinglun* [Chinese Social Science Review] 1, no. 2 (2002): 402–35.

Wang Jianguo. "Zhongguo zhaunxing shiqi zhengzhi minzhuhua yu zhengzhi wending de guanxi" [The relationship between political democratization and political stability in China's transitional period]. *Shehui zhuyi yanjiu* [Studies of Socialism], no. 3 (2002).

Wang Jincun. "An advance of historical significance—from "Shanghai Five' to 'Shanghai Cooperation Organization,'" *Shijie jingji yu zhengzhi* [World Economics and Politics], no. 9 (2001).

Wang Jisi. "Gailun zhongmeiri sanbian guanxi" [On the triangular relationship among China, the U.S. and Japan]. In *Xinshiji de sikao* [Thinking in the New Century], edited by Lin Rong. Vol. 1. Beijing, Central Party School Press, 2002.

Wang Xiaolong. "The Asia-Pacific economic cooperation and the regional political and security issues." *Dangdai Yatai* [Contemparary Asia-Pacific], no. 4 (2003).

Wang Yizhou. *Quanqiu zhengzhi he zhongguo waijiao* [Global Politics and China's Foreign Policy]. Beijing: Shijie zhishi chubanshe, 2004.

Wen Jieming et al., eds. *Yu zongshuji tanxin* [Chat with the General Secretary]. Beijing: Zhongguo shehui kexue chubanshe, 1997.

Wu Kechang. "Zhengzhi fazhan yu zhengzhi wending" [Political Development and Political Stability]. *Qiusuo* [Explore], no. 2 (2002).

Xiong Guangkai. *"Dangqian quanqiu fankongxing shi jiqi qiying zhanwang"* [The global counter terrorism campaign: current situation and future prospects]. *Guoji zhanlue yanjiu* [Study of International Strategy], no. 2 (2003).

Xiong Guangkai. "The new security concept advocated by China, a speech at the London Institute of International Strategic Studies." *Guoji zhanlue yanjiu* [Study of International Strategy], no. 3 (2002).

Xu Xianglin. "Yi zhengzhi wending wei jichu de zhongguo jianjin zhengzhi gaige" [China's gradual political reform based on political stability]. *Zhanlue yu guanli* [Strategy and Management], Beijing, no. 5 (2000).

Xu Xianming. "Preface." In *Renquan yanjiu* [Human Rights Research], edited by Xu Xianming. Jinan: Shandong remin chubanshe, 2001.

Yan Xuetong. *Zhongguo guojia liyi fenxi* [An Analysis of China's National Interest]. 2nd ed. Tianjin: Tianjin Renmin Chubanshe, 1997.

Yan Xuetong, et al. *Zhongguo jueqi—Guoji huanjin pinggu* [International Environment for China's Rise]. Tianjin: People's Press, 1998.

Yang Kai-huang. *"Zhonggong duitai zhengce jieshi yu pinggu"* [An explanation and evaluation of PRC's Taiwan policy]. *Dongwu zhengzhi xuebao* [Soochow Review of Political Science], no. 7 (1997): 66–103.

Ye Zicheng. "Zhongguo shixing daguo waijiaozhanlue shizai bixing" [China must exercise major power diplomacy]. *Shijie jingji yu zhengzhi* [World Economics and Politics], no. 1 (2000): 5–10.

Yu Jianhua. "The development of SCO and the exploration of new interstate relations." *Chinese Diplomacy*, no. 7 (2003).

Yu Yunyao. "Anzhao sangedaibiao de yaoqiu quanmian jiaqiang xinshiqi dang de jianshe" [Strengthen the party's development comprehensively according to the requests of the Three Represents]. In *2000–2001 zhongguo diaocha baogao xinxingshixia renmin neibu maodun yanjiu* [2000–2001 China Investigation Report: Studies of the Internal Contradictions among People in the New Environment], edited by the CCP Organization Department Project Team. Beijing: Zhongyang bianyi chubanshe, 2001.

Zhang Tuosheng. ed. *Huanqio tongci liangre: Yidai lingxoumen de guoji zhanlue sixiang* [Same to the Whole Globe: The International Strategic Thoughts of a Generation of Leaders]. Beijing: Zhongyang Wenxian Press, 1993.

Zhang Wenmu. "Quanqiuhua jincheng zhong de zhongguo guojia liye" [China's national interest in the process of globalization]. *Zhanlue yu guanli* [Strategy and Management], no. 1 (2002): 52–64.

Zhang Yunling. "East Asian cooperation and the construction of China-ASEAN free trade area." Dangdai Yatai [Contemporary Asia-Pacific], no. 1 (2002).

———, ed. *Weilai 10–15 nian zhongguo zai yatai diqu mianlin de guoji huanjing* [The International Environment Confronting China in the Next 10–15 Years]. Beijing: Zhongguo shehui kexue chubanshe, 2003.

Zhu Feng. *Renquan yu guojiguanxi* [Human Rights and International Relations]. Beijing: Beijing daxue chubanshe, 2000.

Zhu Tingchang, et al., eds. *Zhongguo zhoubian anquan huanjin yu anquan zhanlue* [China's Security Environment and Strategy in the Neighboring Areas]. Beijing: Shishi chubanshe, 2002.

ENGLISH-LANGUAGE SOURCES

Abramowitz, Morton, Funabashi Yoichi, and Wang Jisi. *China-Japan-U.S.: Managing the Trilateral Relations*. Tokyo and New York: Japan Center for International Exchange, 1998.

Achary, Amitav. *Regionalism and Multilateralism*. Singapore: Times Academic Press, 2002.

Alagappa, Muthiah, ed. *Asian Security Order, Instrumental and Normative Features*. Stanford, Calif.: Stanford University Press, 2003.

Axelrod, Robert, ed. *Structure of Decision: The Cognitive Maps of Political Elites*. Princeton, N.J.: Princeton University Press, 1976.

Barbalet, J. M. *Emotion, Social Theory, and Social Structure: A Macrosociological Approach*. New York: Cambridge University Press, 1998.

Baum, Richard. *Burying Mao: Chinese Politics in the Age of Deng Xiaoping*. Princeton, N.J.: Princeton University Press, 1994.

Berger, Joseph, and Morris Zelditch Jr. *Status, Power, and Legitimacy: Strategies and Theories*. New Brunswick, N.J.: Transaction Publishers, 1998.

Bi, Jianhai. "The Role of the Military in the PRC Taiwan Policymaking: A Case Study of the Taiwan Strait Crisis of 1995–96." *Journal of Contemporary China* 11, no. 32 (2002): 539–72.

Branscombe, Nyla R., and Daniel L. Wann. "Collective Self-esteem Consequences of Outgroup Derogation When a Valued Social Identity Is on Trial." *European Journal of Social Psychology* 24, no. 6 (Nov.–Dec. 1994): 641–57.

Brooks, Stephen G., and William C. Wohlforth. "American Primacy in Perspective." *Foreign Affairs* 81, no. 4 (July/August 2002).

———. "Power, Globalization, the End of the Cold War." *International Security* 25, no. 3 (Winter 2000/01): 5–53.

Brown, Harold, Joseph W. Prueher, and Adam Segal, eds. *Chinese Military Power*. Independent Task Force Report. New York: Council for Foreign Relations, 2003.

Brown, Michael E., Sean Lynn-Jones, and Steven Miller, eds. *Debating the Democratic Peace*. Cambridge, Mass.: MIT Press, 1996.

———. *East Asian Security*. Cambridge, Mass.: MIT Press, 1996.

Brown, Michael et al., eds. *The Rise of China*. Cambridge, Mass.: MIT Press, 2000.

Brown, Roger. *Social Psychology*. 2nd ed. New York: The Free Press, 1986.

Bruner, Jerome and Leo Postman. "On the Perceptions of Incongruity: A Paradigm." In *Perception and Personality*, edited by Jerome Bruner and David Krech. Durham, N.C.: Duke University Press, 1950.

Chang, Gordon. *Coming Collapse of China*. New York: Random House, 2001.

Chen, Jian. *Mao's China and the Cold War*. Chapel Hill: University of North Carolina Press, 2001.

Cheng, Joseph Y. S., and Zhang Wankun. "Patterns and Dynamics of China's International Strategic Behavior." *Journal of Contemporary China* 11, no. 31 (May 2002): 235–60.

Christensen, Thomas J. "China." In *Strategic Asia: Power and Purpose 2001–02*, edited by Richard J. Ellings and Aaron L. Friedberg. Seattle, Wash.: National Bureau of Asian Research, 2001.

———. "Posing Problems without Catching Up: China's Rise and Challenges for U.S. Security Policy." *International Security* 25, no. 4 (Winter/Spring, 2000/01): 5–40.

———. *Useful Adversaries: Grand Strategy, Domestic Mobilization, and Sino-American Conflict, 1947–1958*. Princeton, N.J.: Princeton University Press, 1996.

Chu, Yun-han. *The Security Challenge for Taiwan in the Cold War Era*. New York: East Asian Institute Report, Columbia University, February 1995.

Cohen, Roberta. "People's Republic of China: The Human Rights Exception." *Human Rights Quarterly* 9, no. 4 (November 1987): 447–549.

Cohen, Warren. *East Asia at the Center: Four Thousand Years of Engagement with the World*. New York: Columbia University Press, 2000.

Copeland, Dale. "Economic Interdependence and the Future of U.S.-Chinese Relations." In *International Relations Theory and the Asia-Pacific*, edited by G. John Ikenberry and Michael Mastanduno. New York: Columbia University Press, 2003.

———. *The Origins of Major Power*. Ithaca, N.Y.: Cornell University Press, 2000.

Crane, George T. "Imagining the Economic Nation: Globalization in China." *New Political Economy* 4, no. 2 (July 1999): 215–32.

Deng, Yong. "Globalization and Multipolarization in Chinese Foreign Policy." *Harvard China Review* 4, no. 1 (Fall 2003): 18–21.

———. "Hegemon on the Offensive: Chinese Perspectives on US Global Strategy." *Political Science Quarterly* 116, no. 3 (Fall 2001): 343–65.

Deng, Yong, and Fei-ling Wang, eds. *In the Eyes of the Dragon: China Views the World*. Boulder, Colo.: Rowman & Littlefield Publishers, 1999.

Deng, Yong, and Thomas G. Moore. "China Views Globalization: Towards a New Great Power Politics?" *Washington Quarterly* 27, no. 3 (Summer 2004): 117–36.

Dittmer, Lowell, and Samuel S. Kim, eds. *China's Quest for National Identity*. Ithaca, N.Y.: Cornell University Press, 1993.

Economy, Elizabeth. "China's Go West Campaign: Ecological Construction or Ecological Exploitation?" *China Environment Series*, Issue 5, 2002, Washington, D.C.: Woodrow Wilson Center.

Economy, Elizabeth, and Michel Oksenberg, eds. *China Joins the World: Progress and Prospects*. New York: Council on Foreign Relations Press, 1999.

Edwards, R. Randle, Louis Henkin, and Andrew J. Nathan. *Human Rights in China.* New York: Columbia University Press, 1986.

Evans, Peter B., Harold Jacobson, and Robert Putnam, eds. *Double-Edged Diplomacy: International Bargaining and Domestic Politics.* Berkeley and Los Angeles: University of California Press, 1993.

Fairbank, John K., ed. *The Chinese World Order: Traditional Chinese Foreign Relations.* Cambridge, Mass.: Harvard University Press, 1968.

Fewsmith, Joseph. "Historical Echoes and Chinese Politics: Can China Leave the Twentieth Century Behind?" In *China Briefing 2000: The Continuing Transformation*, edited by Tyrene White. Armonk, N.Y.: M. E. Sharpe, 2000.

Fewsmith, Joseph, and Stanley Rosen. "The Domestic Context of Chinese Foreign Policy: Does 'Public Opinion' Matter?" In *The Making of Chinese Foreign and Security Policy in the Era of Reform*, edited by David Lampton. Stanford, Calif.: Stanford University Press, 2001.

Finkelstein, David M. *China Reconsiders Its National Security, "The Great Peace and Development Debate of 1999."* Project Asia, Regional Assessment, The Center for Naval Analysis Corporation, Alexandria, Virginia, December 2000.

Foot, Rosemary. "Bush, China and Human Rights." *Survival* 45, no. 2 (Summer 2003).

———. *Rights beyond Borders: The Global Community and the Struggle over Human Rights in China.* Oxford: Oxford University Press, 2000.

Fravel, Taylor, and Evan Medeiros. "China's New Diplomacy." *Foreign Affairs* 82 (November/December 2003).

Friedman, Edward, and Barrett L. McCormick, eds. *What If China Doesn't Democratize? Implications for War and Peace.* Armonk, New York: M. E. Sharpe, 2000.

Fu, Ying. "China and Asia in a New Era." *China: An International Journal* 1, no. 2 (September 2003): 304–12.

Funabashi, Yoichi. *Alliance Adrift*, New York: Council on Foreign Relations Press, 1999.

Garrett, Banning. "China Faces, Debates, the Contradictions of Globalization." *Asian Survey* 41:3 (May/June 2001): 409–27.

Garver, John W. "The China-India-US Triangle: Strategic Relations in the Post-Cold War Era." *NBR Analysis* 13, no. 5 (October 2002).

———. *Face Off: China, the United States and Taiwan's Democratization.* Seattle: University of Washington Press, 1997.

———. "More from the 'Say No' Club." *The China Journal*, no. 45 (January 2001): 151–58.

———. *Protracted Contest, Sino–Indian Rivalry in the Twentieth Century.* Seattle: University of Washington Press, 2001.

———. "The Restoration of China-Indian Comity Following India's Nuclear Tests." *The China Quarterly*, no. 168 (December 2001): 879–85.

———. "Sino-Russian Relations." In *China and the World, Chinese Foreign Policy Faces the New Millennium*, edited by Samuel S. Kim. Boulder, Colo.: Westview Press, 1998.

———. "Sino-American relations in 2001, the difficult accommodation of two great powers." *International Journal*, Spring 2002.

George, Alexander. "The 'Operational Code': A Neglected Approach to the Study of Political Leaders and Decision-Making." *International Studies Quarterly* 13, no. 2 (June 1969): 190–222.

Gill, Bates, and Evan Medeiros. "Foreign and Domestic Influences in China's Arms Control and Nonproliferation Policies." *The China Quarterly*, no. 161 (March 2000): 66–94.

Gill, Bates, and Taeho Kim. *China's Arms Acquisitions from Abroad: A Quest for "Superb and Secret Weapons."* SIPRI Research Report 11. Oxford: Oxford University Press, 1995.

Gilpin, Robert. *War and Change in World Politics.* Cambridge: Cambridge University Press, 1981.

Godwin, Paul H. B. "Changing Concepts of Doctrine, Strategy, and Operations in the Chinese People's Liberation Army, 1978–87." *China Quarterly*, no. 112 (December 1987): 572–90.

Goldstein, Avery. "The Diplomatic Face of China's Grand Strategy: A Rising Power's Emerging Choice." *China Quarterly*, no. 168 (December 2001): 935–64.

Gowa, Joanne. "Democratic States and International Disputes." *International Organization* 49, no. 3 (Summer 1995): 511–22.

Gries, Peter H. *China's New Nationalism: Pride, Politics, and Diplomacy.* Berkeley: University of California Press, 2004.

———. "Tears of Rage: Chinese Nationalism and the Belgrade Embassy Bombing." *China Journal*, no. 45 (July 2001): 25–43.

Gries, Peter H., and Peng Kaiping. "Culture Clash? Apologies East and West." *The Journal of Contemporary China* 11, no. 30 (February 2002): 173–78.

Gurtov, Melvin. *China and Southeast Asia—The Politics of Survival; A Study of Foreign Policy Interaction.* Baltimore: Johns Hopkins University Press, 1975.

Hamrin, Carol Lee, and Suisheng Zhao, eds. *Decision-making in Deng's China.* Armonk, N.Y.: M. E. Sharpe, 1995.

Harding, Harry. *A Fragile Relationship: The United States and China since 1972.* Washington, D.C.: The Brookings Institution, 1992.

Harris, Stuart. "China and the Pursuit of State Interests in a Globalizing World." *Pacific Review* 13:1 (February 2001): 15–29.

Held, David, Anthony McGrew, David Goldblatt, and Jonathan Perraton. *Global Transformations.* Stanford, Calif.: Stanford University Press, 1999.

Hermann, Margaret G. "Examining Foreign Policy Behavior Using the Personal Characteristics of Political Leaders." *International Studies Quarterly* 24, no. 1 (March 1980): 7–46.

Hogg, Michael A., and Dominic Abrams. *Social Identifications: A Social Psychology of Intergroup Relations and Group Process.* New York: Routledge, 1988.

Hu, Weixing, Gerald Chan, and Daojiong Zha, eds. *China's International Relations in the 21st Century.* Lanham, Md.: University Press of America, 2000.

Hu, Hsien-chin. "The Chinese Concepts of 'Face.'" *American Anthropologist* 46 (1944).

Huang, Yasheng *FDI in China.* Case Study Series. Cambridge, Mass.: Harvard Business School, 2003.

Hughes, Christopher. "Globalization and Nationalism: Squaring the Circle in Chinese International Relations Theory." *Millennium* 26:1 (1997): 103–24.

Ikenberry, G. John, ed. *America Unrivaled: The Future of the Balance of Power.* Ithaca, N.Y.: Cornell University Press, 2002.

Jervis, Robert. *The Logic of Images in International Relations.* Princeton, N.J.: Princeton University Press, 1970.

———. *Perception and Misperception in International Politics.* Princeton, N.J.: Princeton University Press, 1976.

———. "Theories of War in an Era of Leading-Power Peace." *American Political Science Review* 96, no. 1 (March 2002): 1–14.

———. "Understanding the Bush Doctrine." *Political Science Quarterly* 118, no. 3 (Fall 2003): 365–88.

Ji, You. "Making Sense of the War Games in the Taiwan Strait." *Journal of Contemporary China* 6, no. 15 (1997): 287–305.

Jia, Qingguo. "Frustration and Hopes: Chinese Perceptions of the Engagement Policy Debate in the United States." *Journal of Contemporary China* 10, no. 2 (2001): 321–30.

Johnson, Chalmers. *Peasant Nationalism and Communist Power: The Emergence of Revolutionary China.* Stanford, Calif.: Stanford University Press, 1962.

Johnston, Alastair Iain. "China's Militarized Interstate Dispute Behavior, 1949–1992." *China Quarterly*, no. 153 (March 1998): 1–30.

———. *Cultural Realism: Strategic Culture and Grand Strategy in Chinese History* . Princeton, N.J.: Princeton University Press, 1995.

———. "Is China a Status Quo Power?" *International Security* 27, no. 4 (Spring 2003): 5–56.

———. "Prospects for Chinese Nuclear Force Modernization: Limited Deterrence Versus Multilateral Arms Control." *The China Quarterly*, no. 146 (June 1996): 548–76.

Johnston, Alastair Iain, and Robert Ross, eds. *Engaging China: The Management of an Emerging Power.* New York: Routledge, 1999.

Jonson, Lena. "Russia and Central Asia." In *Central Asian Security: The New International Context*, edited by Roy Allison and Lena Jonson. Washington, D.C. and London: Brookings Institution and the Royal Institute of International Affairs, 2001.

Kang, David. "Hierarchy and Stability in Asian International Relations." In *International Relations Theory and the Asia-Pacific*, edited by G. John Ikenberry and Michael Mastanduno. New York: Columbia University Press, 2003.

Katzenstein, Peter, ed. *The Culture of National Security: Norms and Identities in World Politics.* New York: Columbia University Press, 1996.

Katzenstein, Peter, and Takashi Shiraishi, eds. *Network Power: Japan and Asia.* Ithaca, N.Y.: Cornell University Press, 1997.

Kent, Ann. *China, the United Nations, and Human Rights: The Limits of Compliance.* Philadelphia: University of Pennsylvania Press, 1999.

Kim, Samuel S. "China and the United Nations." In *China Joins the World: Progress and Prospects*, edited by Elizabeth Economy and Michel Oksenberg. New York: Council on Foreign Relations, 1999.

———. *China, the United Nations, and World Order.* Princeton, N.J.: Princeton University Press, 1979.

———, ed. *China and the World: Chinese Foreign Policy Faces the New Millennium.* Boulder, Colo.: Westview Press, 1998.

———, ed. *The International Relations of Northeast Asia.* Lanham, Md.: Rowman & Littlefield, 2004.

Kugler, Jucek, and Douglas Lemke. "The Power Transition Research Program: Assessing Theoretical and Empirical Advances." In *Handbook of War Studies II*, edited by Manus I. Midlarsky. Ann Arbor: University of Michigan Press, 2000.

Kunczik, Michael. *Images of Nations and International Pubic Relations.* Mahwah, N.J.: Lawrence Erlbaum Associates Publishers, 1997.

Lampton, David M., ed. *The Making of Chinese Security and Foreign Policy.* Stanford, Calif.: Stanford University Press, 2001.

———. *Same Bed, Different Dreams, Managing U.S.-China Relations, 1989–2000.* Berkeley: University of California Press, 2001.

Lardy, Nicholas R. *Integrating China into the Global Economy.* Washington, D.C.: Brookings Institution, 2002.

Lieberthal, Kenneth, and David M. Lampton, eds. *Bureaucracy, Politics and Decision Making in Post-Mao China.* Berkeley: University of California Press, 1992.

Lin, Gang, and Xiaobo Hu, eds. *China after Deng.* Stanford, Calif.: Stanford University Press, 2003.

Lu, Ning. *The Dynamics of Foreign-Policy Decisionmaking in China.* 2nd ed. Boulder, Colo.: Westview Press, 2000.

Lubman, Stanley B. *Bird in a Cage: Legal Reform in China after Mao.* Stanford, Calif.: Stanford University Press, 1999.

———., ed. *China's Legal Reform.* Oxford: Oxford University Press, 1996.

Madsen, Robert A. "The Struggle for Sovereignty between China and Taiwan." In *Problematic Sovereignty: Contested Rules and Political Possibilities*, edited by Stephen D. Krasner. New York: Columbia University Press, 2001.

Mancall, Mark. *China at the Center: 300 Years of Foreign Relations.* New York: Free Press, 1984.

Mann, Jim. *About Face, A History of America's Curious Relationship with China, From Nixon to Clinton.* New York: Alfred A. Knopf, 1999.

Mansfield, Edward D., and Jack Snyder. "Democratization and the Danger of War." *International Security* 20, no. 1 (Summer 1995): 5–38.

McClelland, David C. *The Achieving Society.* Princeton, N.J.: Van Nostrand, 1961.

Mearsheimer, John. *The Tragedy of Great Power Politics.* New York: W.W. Norton & Company, 2001.

Menon, Raja. "The Strategic Convergence between Russia and China." *Survival* 39, no. 2 (Summer 1997): 101–25.

Mercer, Jonathan. *Reputation in International Relations.* Ithaca, N.Y.: Cornell University Press, 1996.

Moore, Thomas G. "China and Globalization." In *East Asia and Globalization*, edited by Samuel S. Kim. Lanham, Md.: Rowman & Littlefield, 2000.

———. *China in the World Market: Chinese Industry and International Sources of Reform in the Post-Mao Era.* New York: Cambridge University Press, 2002.

————. "China's International Relations: The Economic Dimension." In *The International Relations of Northeast Asia*, edited by Samuel S. Kim. Boulder, Colo.: Rowman & Littlefield Publishers, 2004.

Moore, Thomas G., and Dixia Yang. "Empowered and Restrained: Chinese Foreign Policy in the Age of Economic Interdependence." In *The Making of Chinese Foreign and Security Policy in the Era of Reform, 1978–2000*, edited by David M. Lampton. Stanford, Calif.: Stanford University Press, 2001.

Moravcsik, Andrew. "Taking Preferences Seriously: A Liberal Theory of International Politics." *International Organization* 51, no. 4 (Autumn 1997): 513–53.

Nathan, Andrew J. "Human Rights in Chinese Foreign Policy." *China Quarterly*, no. 139 (September 1994): 623–27.

Nathan, Andrew, and Robert Ross. *The Great Wall and the Empty Fortress: China's Search for Security*. New York: W.W. Norton, 1997.

Nau, Henry R. *At Home Abroad: Identity and Power in American Foreign Policy*. Ithaca, N.Y.: Cornell University Press, 2002.

Organski, A. F. K., and Jacek Kugler. *The War Ledger*. Chicago: University of Chicago Press, 1980.

Owen, John M., IV. "Transnational Liberalism and U.S. Primacy." *International Security* 26, no. 3 (Winter 2001–02): 117–52.

Pearson, Margaret M. "The Major Multilateral Economic Institutions Engage China." In *Engaging China: The Management of an Emerging Power*, edited by Alastair Iain Johnston and Robert S. Ross. London: Routledge, 1999.

Peerenboom, Randall. *China's Long March toward Rule of Law*. New York: Cambridge University Press, 2002.

Peng, Kaiping, Daniel Ames, and Eric Knowles. "Culture and Human Inference: Perspectives from Three Traditions." In *Handbook of Cross-cultural Psychology*. Oxford: Oxford University Press, 2001.

Pettigrew, Thomas. "The Ultimate Attribution Error: Extending Allport's Cognitive Analysis of Prejudice." *Personality and Social Psychology Bulletin* 5, no. 4 (1979): 461–76.

Pillsbury, Michael. *China Debates the Future Security Environment*. Washington, DC: National Defense University Press, 2000.

————, ed. *Chinese Views of Future Warfare*. Washington, D.C.: National Defense University Press, 1997.

Pollack, Jonathan D., ed., *Strategic Surprise: U.S.-China Relations in the Early Twenty-First Century*. New Port, R.I.: Naval War College Press, 2003.

————. "The United States, North Korea, and the End of the Agreed Framework." *Naval War College Review* 56, no. 3 (Summer 2003).

Przystup, James. "China, Japan, and the United States." In *The U.S.-Japan Alliance*, edited by Michael J. Green and Patrick Cronin. New York: Council on Foreign Relations Press, 1999.

Ross, Robert S., and Jiang Changbin, eds. *Re-Examining the Cold War: U.S.-China Diplomacy, 1954–1973*. Cambridge, Mass.: Harvard University Press, 2001.

Roy, Denny. "China and the War on Terrorism." *Orbis*, 46:3 (Summer 2002): 511–21.

Ruggie, John Gerard. "Multilateralism: The anatomy of an institution." *International Organization* 46, no. 3 (Summer 1992): 561–98.

Saunders, Philip C. "China's American Watchers: Changing Attitudes Towards the United States." *China Quarterly*, no. 161 (March 2001): 41–65.

———. "Supping with a Long Spoon: Dependence and Interdependence in Sino-American Relations." *China Journal*, no. 43 (2000): 55–81.

Schweller, Randall L. "Realism and the Present Great Power System: Growth and Positional Conflict over Scarce Resources." In *Unipolar Politics: Realism and State Strategies after the Cold War*, edited by Ethan K. Kapstein and Michael Mastanduno. New York: Columbia University Press, 1999.

———. *Deadly Imbalances: Tripolarity and Hitler's Strategy of World Conquest*. New York: Columbia University Press, 1997.

Scobell, Andrew. *China's Use of Military Force: Beyond the Great Wall and the Long March*. New York: Cambridge University Press, 2003.

———. "The Chinese Cult of Defense." *Issues and Studies* 37, no. 5 (2001): 100–27.

Shambaugh, David. *Beautiful Imperialist: China Perceives America, 1972–1990*. Princeton: Princeton University Press, 1991.

———. *European and American Approaches to China: Different Beds, Same Dreams*. Washington D.C.: Sigur Center for Asian Studies, George Washington University, March 2002.

———. *Modernizing China's Military: Progress, Problems, and Prospects*. Berkeley: University of California Press, 2003.

Sheng, Lijun. "China Eyes Taiwan: Why Is a Breakthrough so Difficult?" *Journal of Strategic Studies* 21, no. 1 (March 1998): 65–78.

Snyder, Jack. "Anarchy and Culture: Insights from the Anthropology of War." *International Organization* 56, no. 1 (Winter 2002): 7–45.

Stokes, Mark A. *China's Strategic Modernization: Implications for the United States*. Carlisle, Pa.: Strategic Studies Institute, US Army War College, 1999.

Sutter, Robert. "Why Does China Matter?" *Washington Quarterly* 27, no. 1 (Winter 2003/04): 75–89.

Swaine, Michael. "Chinese Decision-Making Regarding Taiwan." In *The Making of Chinese Foreign and Security Policy in the Era of Reform*, edited by David M. Lampton. Stanford, Calif.: Stanford University Press, 2001.

Swaine, Michael D., and Ashley J. Tellis. *Interpreting China's Grand Strategy: Past, Present, and Future*. Santa Monica, Calif.: Rand, 2000.

Tajfel, Henri. *Human Groups and Social Categories: Studies in Social Psychology*. Cambridge: Cambridge University Press, 1981.

Taylor, Donald, and Vaishna Jaggi. "Ethnocentrism and Causal Attribution in a South Indian Context." *Journal of Cross-Cultural Psychology* 5, no. 2 (1974): 162–71.

Taylor, Jay. *China and Southeast Asia: Peking's Relations with Revolutionary Movements*. New York: Praeger Publishers, 1976.

Tien, Hung-mao and Yun-han Chu, eds. *China Under Jiang Zemin*. Boulder, Colo.: Lynne Rienner, 2000.

Unger, Jonathan, ed. *Chinese Nationalism*. Armonk, N.Y.: M. E. Sharpe, 1996.

Van Ness, Peter. *Revolution and Chinese Foreign Policy: Peking's Support for Wars of National Liberation*. Berkeley: University of California Press, 1970.

Walker, Stephen G. "The Motivational Foundations of Political Belief System: A Reanalysis of the Operational Code Construct." *International Studies Quarterly* 27, no. 2 (June 1983): 179–202.

——, ed. *Role Theory and Foreign Policy Analysis*. Durham, N.C.: Duke University Press, 1987.

Waltz, Kenneth. "Structural Realism after the Cold War." *International Security* 25, no. 1 (Summer 2000): 5–41.

——. *Theory of International Politics*. New York: McGraw-Hill, 1979.

Wan, Ming. "Economic Interdependence and Economic Cooperation: Mitigating Conflict and Transforming Security Order in Asia." In *Asian Security Order: Instrumental and Normative Feature*, edited by Muthiah Alagappa. Stanford, Calif.: Stanford University Press, 2003.

——. *Human Rights in Chinese Foreign Relations: Defining and Defending National Interests*. Philadelphia: University of Pennsylvania Press, 2001.

Wang, Fei-Ling. *Organizing through Division and Exclusion: China's Hukou System*. Stanford, Calif.: Stanford University Press, forthcoming.

——, ed. Special Issue on SARS in China, Part I. Special issue. *Chinese Law and Government* 36, no 4 (July–August 2003).

——, ed. Special Issue on SARS in China, Part II. Special issue. *Chinese Law and Government* 36, no. 6 (November–December 2003).

——, ed. Special Issue on SARS in China, Part III. Special issue. *Chinese Law and Government* 37, no. 1 (January–February 2004).

——. "To Incorporate China—A New China Policy for a New Era." *Washington Quarterly* 21, no. 1 (Winter 1998): 67–81.

Wang, Hongying. "Chinese Culture and Multilateralism." In *The New Realism: Perspectives on Multilateralism and Word Order*, edited by Robert Cox. Tokyo: United Nations University Press, 1997.

——. "Crisis and Credibility: China's Exchange Rate Policy in the Aftermath of the Asian Financial Crisis." In *Monetary Order: Ambiguous Economics, Ubiquitous Politics*, edited by Jonathan Kirshner. Ithaca N.Y.: Cornell University Press, 2002.

Wang, Jianwei. "Coping with China as a Rising Power." In *Weaving the Net*, edited by James Shinn. New York: Council on Foreign Relations, 1996.

——. *Limited Adversaries: Post-Cold War Sino-American Mutual Images*. New York: Oxford University Press, 2000.

Wang, Jisi. "Beauty—and Beast." *Wilson Quarterly*, Spring 2001: 61–65.

——. "China's Changing Role in Asia." The Atlantic Council of the United States. January 2004, at www.acus.org/Publications/occasionalpapers/Asia/WangJisi_Jan_04.pdf (accessed August 16, 2004).

——. "The Role of the United States as a Global and Pacific Power: A View from China." *Pacific Review* 10, no. 1 (1997): 1–18.

Wendt, Alexander. "Collective Identity Formation and the International State." *American Political Science Review* 88, no. 2 (June 1994): 384–96.

Whiting, Allen S. *China Crosses the Yalu: The Decision to Enter the Korea War*. New York: McMillan Company, 1960.

———. *China Eyes Japan*. Berkeley: University of California Press, 1989.

———. "China's Use of Force, 1950–1996, and Taiwan." *International Security* 26, no. 2 (Fall 2001): 103–31.

———. *The Chinese Calculus of Deterrence: India and Indochina*. Ann Arbor: University of Michigan Press, 1975.

Wohlforth, William C. "The Stability of a Unipolar World." *International Security* 24:1 (Summer 1999): 5–41.

Wu, Hongda Harry. *Laogai: The Chinese Gulag*. Translated by Ted Slingerland. Boulder, Colo.: Westview Press, 1992.

Wu, Yuan-li et al. *Human Rights in the People's Republic of China*. Boulder, Colo.: Westview Press, 1988.

Yahuda, Michael. *The International Politics of Asia-Pacific, 1945–1995*. New York: Routledge, 1996.

Yan, Xuetong. "The Rise of China in Chinese Eyes." *Journal of Contemporary China* 10, no. 26 (February 2001).

Yu, Bin. "Historical Ironies, Dividing Ideologies and Accidental 'Alliance': Russian-Chinese Relations into the 21st Century." In *The Rise of China in Asia*, edited by Carolyn Pumphery. Carlisle, Pa.: Strategic Studies Institute, 2002.

Yuan, Jing-dong. *Asia-Pacific Security: China's Conditional Multilateralism and Great Power Entente*. Carlisle Barracks, Pa.: U.S. Army War College Strategic Studies Institute, January 2000.

———. "Culture Matters: Chinese Approaches to Arms Control and Disarmament." In *Culture and Security: Multilateralism, Arms Control and Security Building*, edited by Keith Krause. London: Frank Cass, 1999.

Zhang, Shuguang. *Economic Cold War: America's Embargo against China and the Sino-Soviet Alliance, 1949–1963*. Stanford, Calif.: Stanford University Press, 2001.

Zhang, Yongjin, and Greg Austin, eds. *Power and Responsibility in Chinese Foreign Policy*. Canberra, Australia: Asia Pacific Press, 2001.

Zhao, Suisheng, ed. *Across the Taiwan Strait: Mainland China, Taiwan, and the 1995–1996 Crisis*. New York: Routledge, 1999.

———. "Chinese Intellectuals' Quest for National Greatness and Nationalistic Writing in the 1990s." *China Quarterly*, no. 153 (December 1997): 725–45.

———. "Chinese Nationalism and its International Orientations." *Political Science Quarterly* 115, 1 (2000): 1–33.

Zheng, Yongnian. *Discovering Chinese Nationalism in China: Modernization, Identity, and International Relations*. New York: Cambridge University Press, 1999.

Zimbardo, Philip G., and Michael R. Leippe. *The Psychology of Attitude Change and Social Influence*. Philadelphia: Temple University Press, 1991.

Zweig, David. *Internationalizing China: Domestic Interests and Global Linkages*. Ithaca, N.Y.: Cornell University Press, 2002.

Index

Acheson, Dean, 109
AFC. *See* Asian financial crisis
Ancient Chinese world order, 22, 56.
  See also pax sinica, tributary system
APEC. *See* Asia-Pacific Economic
  Cooperation
apology diplomacy, 103–9
APT. *See* ASEAN plus Three
ARF. *See* ASEAN Regional Forum
ARF Security Policy Conference, 139
arms embargo, 58, 64
ASEAN. *See* Association for Southeast
  Asian Nations
ASEAN-China Free Trade Agreement,
  121, 139, 168–71
ASEAN plus One, 166–71
ASEAN plus Three, 121, 139, 167–69,
  176–77, 188–90
ASEAN Regional Forum, 136–37, 140,
  174–76, 188–90
ASEM. *See* Asia-Europe Meeting
Asia-Europe Meeting, 126, 135
Asian financial crisis, 11, 65, 92–93, 97,
  125, 127, 140, 141, 142, 149
Asia-Pacific Economic Cooperation, 59,
  60–62; and China's views on
  globalization, 125, 129–30, 135, 139,

147, 151; and China's views on
  regionalism, 167–77, 188–90
Association for Southeast Asian
  Nations, 63, 135; in China's
  regionalism, 167–77, 188–90; and
  Taiwan, 272

Barbalet, J. M., 107
Berger, Joseph, 58
Brooks Stephen, 10, 12
Bush administration. *See* George W.
  Bush
Bush, George W., 54, 61, 62, 63, 163,
  204, 268, 272

Central Leading Group for Taiwan
  Affairs (of CCP), 247–56, 259, 267,
  271
Century of humiliation. *See*
  victimization
Chaoxian Zhan (Unrestricted Warfare),
  307
Chen Shui-bian, 269–73
Cheung, Peter, 8
China Can Say No, 110–12
China threat theory, 13, 54, 62, 65, 148,
  224

About the Contributors

Yong Deng is associate professor of political science at the U.S. Naval Academy. His publications include two books: *Promoting Asia–Pacific Economic Cooperation: Perspectives from East Asia* and *In the Eyes of the Dragon: China Views the World* (coeditor with Fei-Ling Wang). He is also a guest editor of a special symposium on United States–China dialogue over China's international futures in *Journal of Contemporary China*. His papers have appeared in such academic journals as *China Quarterly*, *Asian Survey*, *Harvard China Review*, *Pacific Affairs*, *Journal of Strategic Studies*, *Political Science Quarterly*, and *Washington Quarterly*.

Fei-Ling Wang is an associate professor and the director of the China Summer Program at the Sam Nunn School of International Affairs, Georgia Institute of Technology, Atlanta. He is the author of three books, of which the most recent is *Organizing through Division and Exclusion: China's Hukou System* (forthcoming), and he is the coeditor of *In the Eyes of the Dragon: China Views the World* (with Yong Deng, 1999). He has published over forty articles as contributions to edited collections and to such journals as *Asian Weekly*, *China Quarterly*, *Journal of Contemporary China*, *Harvard International Review*, *Problems of Post-Communism*, *Pacific Affairs*, and *Washington Quarterly*.

Yun-han Chu is a professor of political science at the Taiwan National University in Taipei and president of the Chiang Ching-Kuo Foundation for International Scholarly Exchange.

John W. Garver is professor at the Sam Nunn School of International Affairs, Georgia Institute of Technology, Atlanta. He has authored seven books

347

on Sino-Soviet, Sino-American, and Sino-Indian relations and nearly a hundred articles on China's foreign relations. He is a member of the National Committee on United States–China relations; participates frequently in various Asia policy-related fora; and has lived for extended periods in China, Taiwan, India, and Pakistan. He speaks Chinese and German. He is the recipient of awards from the U.S. National Academy of Science's Committee on Scholarly Communications with the People's Republic of China, the Fulbright Foundation, the U.S. Department of Education, the Chiang Ching-Kuo foundation, the U.S. Institute for Pakistan Studies, the Pacific Cultural Foundation, and the Smith Richardson Foundation. He set up and directed for a number of years an exchange program between Georgia Tech and Fudan University in Shanghai. He currently serves on the editorial boards of *China Quarterly*, *Journal of Contemporary China*, *Asian Security*, and *Journal of America–East Asian Relations*.

Peter Hays Gries is assistant professor of political science at the University of Colorado at Boulder and codirector of the Sino-American Security Dialogue. He is interested in the political psychology of international relations in general and Sino-American and Sino-Japanese relations in particular, as well as state legitimation in China. He is author of *China's New Nationalism: Pride, Politics, and Diplomacy* (2004) and is coeditor (with Stanley Rosen) of *State and Society in 21st-Century China: Crisis, Contention, and Legitimation* (2004). He has recently published in *Political Psychology*, *Journal of Contemporary China*, *International Security*, and *China Journal*.

Thomas G. Moore is associate professor and director of undergraduate studies in the Department of Political Science at the University of Cincinnati, where he teaches courses on international political economy, U.S. foreign policy, and Asian politics. He is the author of *China in the World Market: Chinese Industry and International Sources of Reform in the Post-Mao Era* (2002). Moore has also written numerous scholarly articles on subjects such as China's participation in the world economy and U.S. policy toward Asia.

Andrew Scobell is associate research professor in the Strategic Studies Institute at the U.S. Army War College and adjunct professor of political science at Dickinson College. His research focuses on political and military affairs in the Asia–Pacific Region. He is the author of *China's Use of Military Force: Beyond the Great Wall and the Long March* (2003).

Ming Wan is associate professor in the Department of Public and International Affairs, George Mason University. He has held postdoctoral fellowships at Harvard from the Program on United States–Japan Relations, at the John M. Olin Institute for Strategic Studies, and at the Pacific Basin Research Center of Kennedy School of Government; and he was a visiting research scholar at Tsukuba University and a Luce fellow in Asian Policy Studies at the Sigur Center for Asian Studies of George Washington University and the Woodrow Wilson Center. He has published two books: *Human Rights in Chinese Foreign Relations: Defining and Defending National Interests* (2001) and *Japan between Asia and the West: Economic Power and Strategic Balance* (2001). He has also published in journals such as *Asian Survey*, *Orbis*, *Pacific Affairs*, and *International Studies Quarterly* and in various edited volumes. His current research interests include Sino-Japanese relations, human rights legalization in China, human rights and democracy in Chinese foreign policy, and international political economy of East Asia.

Hongying Wang is assistant professor of political science at the Maxwell School of Citizenship and Public Affairs, Syracuse University. She is the author of *Weak State, Strong Networks: The Institutional Dynamics of Foreign Direct Investment in China* (2001). She has also published a number of articles on Chinese political economy and foreign relations in academic journals and edited volumes.

Jianwei Wang is professor and chair of the Department of Political Science at the University of Wisconsin, Stevens Point. He is also a lecture professor of Political Science at the School of International and Public Affairs at Fudan University and a senior associate at the Shanghai Institute of American Studies. His research focuses on Sino-American relations, Chinese foreign policy, and East Asia security affairs. His most recent publications include *Limited Adversaries: Sino-American Mutual Images in the Post Cold War Era* (2000), *Power of the Moment, America and the World after 9/11* (coauthor).